Contents

To Jim Dyos

Preface

This book is the product of about a dozen years' research, some of which was not originally intended for the present purpose. My initial research was in the field of newspaper history and, though dimly aware of it at the time, I struck a vein of political consciousness which informed opinion across a wide range of issues. Later when I began my study of Leeds politics, I was able to explore the institutional framework of this intense urban political sensibility. Having completed a doctorate, I extended the chronological range of the Leeds material and ventured further afield to other cities in a search for evidence for a more general model of urban history in the nineteenth century. The present book is the fruit of that search and it has benefited much from the help of many whose aid I am delighted to acknowledge.

I am indebted to the School of History at Leeds which not only gave me my undergraduate training but also provided the opportunities to pursue two postgraduate research projects. I owe much to the early guidance of Asa Briggs and Donald Read, who were my initial mentors. At a later stage Arthur Taylor and Gordon Forster were sympathetic and helpful supervisors. Over the years many scholars have been generous in the provision of advice and guidance. I am pleased to record thanks to Michael Rose, Norman McCord, Maurice Beresford, Peter Hennock, Bob Morris, Vic Gatrell, and Reg Ward. Many others with whom I had less frequent contact, and countless librarians, also deserve thanks. Jack Reynolds, my colleague at Bradford, has provided much stimulating conversation and has been characteristically generous in sharing with me his unrivalled knowledge of Bradford history. Two of our research students, David Ashforth and Adrian Elliott, gave me interesting leads which flowed from their work and I thank them both. I have learned a great deal, especially about source material, from the many theses I have consulted and I am grateful to their authors for permission to cite their work. I am particularly indebted to Tom Nossiter, with whom I have had some healthy disagreements, but who also supplied valuable statistical data with the appropriate instruction. The dedication records my respectful thanks to one who has encouraged and supported my work over a number of years.

Nearer home Carol Baxendale made an excellent job of typing up a complex manuscript and Jim Morgan demonstrated his friendship by reading the book at both typescript and proof stage. I thank him for his many useful suggestions. At home my wife and family bore well the mounting piles of photocopies which littered every room. It has been a pleasure to deal with Leicester University Press, for whom Peter Boulton has been unfailingly courteous and helpful. I trust that those who, by their aid, have demonstrated the existence of a community of scholars will consider that I have used their counsel wisely. Responsibility for errors and shortcomings remains mine alone.

DEREK FRASER
University of Bradford
November 1975

Tables and maps

Introduction   The structure of politics in Victorian cities

'Politics are the vital element of all *elections – parliamentary, municipal, parochial or philanthropic.'* Porcupine, 8 November 1862

Politics involve the pursuit and exercise of power, and debate and conflict over policy. Urban politics in mid-nineteenth-century England concerned power and policy over a very broad field of local and national affairs. Politics for Victorians, unlike ourselves, began not at Westminster but at their own front gates. Whether the pavement was drained and swept, whether the poor should be incarcerated in workhouses, whether Dissenters should pay church rates depended upon the exercise of power and were issues of as much intrinsic political interest as great questions of national policy. Politics intruded into the whole urban experience and the limited political world of parliamentary elections, identified by many historians as the stuff of urban politics, was not a political boundary recognized by contemporaries. The mid-nineteenth-century political activist pitched his tent in whatever battlefield was open to him. Urban politics ran through many channels.

The diverse political experience of urban Victorians may perhaps be best understood by reference to the institutional structure of Victorian cities. This book argues the case for utilizing a mode of analysis which examines political activity in four areas of the urban experience. These are 1) parochial and township administration, 2) municipal government, 3) parliamentary elections, and 4) political agitation. This essentially archaeological model conceives of layers of political activity at different levels of urban life, with political issues taking on the character of boreholes penetrating each stratum. In the second and third quarters of the nineteenth century (loosely named here 'Victorian') this variegated political structure existed, particularly in those four provincial cities identified in the 1867 minority clause as distinctively metropolitan, Leeds, Manchester, Liverpool and Birmingham. It is these cities which figure most prominently in this book, with other towns (Leicester, Nottingham, Salford, Bradford, Gateshead, Sheffield, and Preston) in a supporting role. In this age of great cities urban politics were a touch-stone of urban society.

In all four areas of activity described in this book political passion was a persistent though not continuous feature. That passions were roused by parliamentary elections or in political agitation was hardly surprising and these two areas have been widely acknowledged as highly political by all historians. However the relationship between the two has not always been clarified, particularly in mechanistic psephological work which views the vote as merely the expression of a social context. The large cities were no doubt at one end of a spectrum of constituencies which stretched from the relatively independent political communities of the metropolitan cities to the totally deferential and dependent rural seats which were no more than appendages to the local ruling family. Issues were important in the large urban constituencies and so there was a very close connection between elections and pressure groups, each responding to the forces imparted by the other.

The area of municipal politics has received less attention from historians, some of whom perhaps view this level as essentially non-political. We shall find in fact how important a part was played by party politics from the 1830s onwards and will identify in the municipal council a key focus for a resolution of the contest between rival élites in urban society. Even where one-party rule reduced the impact of party conflict we shall notice how the power exercised by municipal authority was the subject of dissension which caused political disputes. Above all issues of improve-ment, superficially non-political, could in practice generate enormous political heat as urban society faced up to the problems of environmental control and the public provision of social utilities. Basic questions about the legitimate use of the power of the urban community were involved in the mundane subjects of water and drains.

That municipal affairs could be political, however, would not be totally unexpected to students of nineteenth-century English history, and perhaps the most surprising feature of this analysis is the amount of political involvement and interest to be found in parochial and township administration. It has often been presumed that in these petty affairs there was matter of interest only to the antiquarian. Yet to exclude these institutions from an analysis of urban society seriously distorts the realities of the contemporary political structure. The minor institutions were politicized in three main ways. First, they were real political in-stitutions in their own right and so were of local interest because of their intrinsic power and authority. Second, they could assume a political importance much beyond this intrinsic authority by being sucked into an overall local struggle for power in which these institutions became either alternative or additional battlegrounds in the party conflict. Third, they could be the local instruments for advancing a great political cause either by neutralizing the power involved or exercising that power in conformity with the wishes of urban groups active in the relevant movement. In the face of the evidence, only a small part of which is cited in this survey, historians can hardly ignore parochial and township politics in the future as they have done in the past.

All of the minor institutions related in some way to the vestry, which was the origin of all parochial bodies. The politicizing of the vestry was fundamental to the politicizing of all minor institutions. It is interesting to note that while Dr Foster portrays a very different picture of urban politics from that here, he nonetheless identifies the crucial role the vestry played in working-class politics.[1] Working-class radicals in Oldham based their whole strategy on control of the local political system and, significantly, they found that mastery of vestry institutions was more important in the achievement of their political objectives than electing their own M.P.s. Elsewhere, as in the case of Salford, the most petty issue (in this case church bell ringing at public expense – see p. 30) could assume major importance in local political affairs. The churchwardens embodied all three aspects of politics mentioned above. They had an important area of power over parochial expenditure; they were part of the local struggle for power; and they could advance the cause of Dissenters. To contemporaries, church affairs were naturally political for as the Manchester radical, Elijah Dixon, explained in 1840, 'I take it if there be one place more proper for politics than another it is the Church'.[2] Similarly, the Poor Law was intrinsically a political institution with the largest local expenditure at its disposal, together with a large slice of patronage. It too was drawn into the local political battle, most noticeably in the 1830s and 1840s and again in the 1870s. Poor Law policy was a matter of great controversy and reformers of all opinions hoped to use administration to advance their cause. In different ways in various towns the office of improvement commissioner and highway surveyor likewise assumed a political importance, especially in years of acute tension in urban politics. The minor institutions were always prey to petty jobbery, and as one critic pointedly asked, 'if men who devote time and attention to Local Boards cannot get their own private entrance lighted without being charged with jobbery or something worse, what's the use of their being members of the Board at all?'[3] While the Poor Law could mean that the chairman of the guardians had his garden dug by paupers, it also involved real power and authority. As one disappointed applicant for a Poor Law position in Manchester claimed, 'the Guardians can do as they please, they have complete despotic power'.[4] Could anything be more political than the exercise of despotic power?

It is hoped that the present survey will establish a case for the politicizing of minor institutions in the mid-nineteenth century. However, something more is involved in the analysis. It is argued not simply that parochial and township administration was political but that politics at this level were a part of an overall political structure, encompassing the whole of urban life. The fourfold institutional model involves an analysis of areas of political activity which had at once an independent political viability and an important relationship with the other areas of the urban political structure. Each strand in the political process is worthy of independent study but a full understanding of its significance can only be reached by identifying its relationship to the whole.

Contemporaries understood, as perhaps we have not, that they were operating within a comprehensive political system whose ramifications engrossed the total urban experience. Yet they were in very little doubt that they were fighting the same battle at different levels rather than fighting separate battles in discrete units. Dale's important instruction to his followers is very apposite here – 'he may serve Christ on the polling booth or on the platform, in Parliament, in the Town Council or on the Board of Guardians'.[5] Dale was not referring simply to a mission to do good works but pleading for participation within the urban political system. The significant thing was his implicit recognition that the political system was indeed variegated and composed of several seams. Politics at one level inevitably had an impact elsewhere in the political structure and so the reunion of middle- and working-class radicals in 1851–2 found its echo deep in the political system as Chartist highway surveyors in Leeds were supported by Liberals in a township poll. At about the same time a Sheffield politician complained that divisions within local Liberalism had 'appeared in their wardmotes, their elections and had been carried even into the sanitary affairs of the borough'.[6]

Developments within the minor institutions were assessed as much for their wider significance as for their intrinsic importance. A parochial poll on a church rate or a Poor Law election could be taken as an indication of opinion on the great issues of the day. When Birmingham Tories succeeded in gaining a Poor Law majority in 1840, the victory was hailed as showing that 'the people are growing tired of the reign of Radicalism . . . Birmingham has set an example to the nation by declaring for Conservatism'.[7] In such ways were the minor political offices cloaked with imperial significance, for as a Leeds Tory put it, delightfully encapsulating the idea of a total political system, 'the Whigs of North West ward were part and parcel of a mighty power which was at work in the British Dominions that was attempting the separation of Church and State and the ultimate destruction of the Protestant Religion'.[8] Great political issues thus played their part in an apparently non-political context. Joshua Hobson's attempts to remodel the Leeds Improvement Act of 1842 (see p. 94) and Isaac Ironside's manipulation of the Sheffield Highway Board a decade later (p. 108) were experiments in fundamental democracy.

Nor could municipal government ever be completely freed from a political milieu. When Leeds Liberalism split on education in 1847 voluntaryists took their first revenge on state education Liberals by replacing offending aldermen on the Leeds town council. Prominent Liberals who had not supported Sturge in 1847 'at the next annual meeting of our honourable Town Council . . . were dispossessed of their Aldermanic dignity', and because of this municipal insult, refused to support Eardley in the Riding in 1848.[9] Activists saw municipal elections as part of the wider political confrontation and so Liverpool Liberals in 1862 were engaged in a push to gain the aldermen and elect the mayor, by which 'we secure possession of the Town Hall and that done we return two members for Liverpool and dumbfound Lord Derby'.[10] The march against aristocratic rule began in the backstreets of Everton ward as observers realized that 'the condition of local affairs cannot but affect the higher interests of both parties in connection with the Parliamentary representation'.[11] Significantly, when one Liverpool party worker strongly urged the separation of municipal from parliamentary politics he was over-ruled. Charles Rawlins asked in 1846, 'is it well to accumulate all the personal and party bickerings from every year's local struggle and encumber great national questions with the heap of rubbish?'[12] His peers replied in effect that the annual 'heap of rubbish' was an integral part of the political game they were playing. It was thus no novelty in the age of the caucus when it was confirmed that 'the names of Liberal and Conservative are accepted by both sides as embodying a distinct policy in Municipal as in Parliamentary Government'.[13]

Parliamentary elections were themselves prey to the tensions created in the lower levels of the political system. If the turbulence in the foundations were severe enough the whole political structure shook. Elections and candidates could be subjected to pressures of little relevance to parliamentary business. The innocuous post of governor of Owen's College Manchester exposed the member for North Lancashire to pressure from Dissent (see p. 268). Similarly in Salford those in the humble office of police commissioner received an unpalatable jolt to their political security when a displaced radical issued an ominous warning, 'you have stood in need of us before and you will again – remember the next general election'.[14] With so much political activity existing at the different levels of the urban political structure, we can hardly accept the picture, sometimes purveyed, of the towns being politically inert between general elections.[15]

The political system described in this book is one inhabited primarily by middle-class activists. The evidence presented does not support the interpretation that the politics of city life in the middle decades of the nineteenth century were dominated by a class struggle between bourgeoisie and proletariat. Perhaps that conflict was more apparent in the smaller industrial towns such as Oldham than in the great cities which dominate this survey. In the larger towns the evidence appears to point overwhelmingly to a contest for power within the urban middle class itself and between that urban élite and the landed gentry. Those proscribed from political participation tended to attach themselves to one or other of the contending parties or sought to exercise power at levels in the urban political structure which were amenable to popular influence. In the most obvious expression of the popular demand for political rights, the suffrage reform movement, there was a sustained plea for admission to, rather than replacement of, the existing political system. The occasions, such as 1842, when a fundamental alienation threatened the whole social and political fabric were exceptional. It was much more normal for working-class radicals to advance their cause through the assumption of a role in the variegated institutional structure which characterized urban society. In the half-century or so from 1825 the great cities were only occasionally the battleground in the Marxian class struggle.

That same middle class which figured so prominently in urban political activity also dominated the world of Dissent, which acquired a distinctively middle-class image. As one speaker remarked to the congregational Union in 1848, 'preaching, buildings, ministers, manners, notions and practices – all have on them the air and impress of English middle-class life'. Another at the same conference made explicit the middle-class crusade: 'Our special mission is neither to the very rich nor the very poor. We have a work to do upon the thinking, active, influential classes – classes which inhabit neither courts nor cottages, but which gathered into cities, and consisting of several gradations there, are the modern movers and moulders of the world.'[16] Two years later a northern Baptist conference expressed almost identical views: 'It will be a woeful day for the churches of Christ, when they consist exclusively of the rich and extremely poor. Those to whom God has given neither poverty nor riches are the men, who, we hope, may ever constitute the large majority in Christian churches.'[17] The characteristic composition of Dissenting congregations in the mid-nineteenth century well reflects the essentially middle-class nature of urban politics in Victorian England.

On occasion, middle-class consciousness could express itself in a very exclusive way, reinforced by residential zoning closely related to wealth and status. The wealthy corn merchant and radical politician Joseph Sturge found himself assailed by aggrieved neighbours when he proposed, no doubt as an act of philanthropy, to open his fields in exclusive Edgbaston as a playground. His attention was drawn to

> the serious annoyance and disturbance such a course would bring into the neighbourhood as also to the great deterioration it would cause to our respective properties . . . nothing could prevent beershops being opened as near as possible to the grounds, and stalls and Booths being erected in the immediate vicinity leading to the congregating of characters of the worst description . . . we feel satisfied that you yourself would ultimately regret bringing so serious a disturbance into the neighbourhood.[18]

The urban aristocracy – the merchant princes of Liverpool, the cotton lords of Manchester, the textile kings of Leeds or the metal magnates of Birmingham – were a natural élite which was yet politically, socially and economically linked to classes of neither great riches nor great poverty which covered such a wide span of the variegated and complex urban social structure. Though the owner of the largest flax-spinning firm in Europe, the Marshall family of Leeds, was obviously capitalist and its factory operatives obviously proletarian, nevertheless a large proportion of the population of an industrial city like Leeds was obviously neither one nor the other. The many gradations between the embryonic proletariat and the large-scale capitalist exemplified the character of Victorian cities and their politics.

These middling ranks of urban society contained some elements of cohesion by virtue of the nexus of economics, and it was sometimes the links that bound apparently diverse groups together which struck contemporaries, rather than the gulf in wealth between them. When some wealthy Liverpool councillors adopted too aristocratic a manner in 1862 an acute local observer remarked revealingly, 'Between the representative who sells tea cotton or iron by the hundredweight and the constituent who vends it wrapped in blue paper parcels or made into shirts or shovels, we really cannot undertake to appreciate all the lines of distinction and demarcation.'[19] One of the dangers of too rigorous a class analysis which explains the impact of industrialization solely in terms of a society divided between capital and labour is the tendency to underestimate the diffusion of wealth among groups between the two extremes.

Details of personal wealth are hard to come by, but two examples of politically active men regarded in their own day as socially inferior may perhaps illustrate the fact that men of moderate means were to be found quite low in the social structure.

When Liverpool Liberals put their party on a more organized basis in the 1850s they appointed an ex-barber as their paid secretary and this illustrates how the political system found a role for humble men, essential footsoldiers in the political army. Yet this very ordinary man, William Brumfitt, had managed to become a property owner in a small way of business. He first bought two houses as a member of a small building society, to which he added 16 tenements which were mortgaged at £1,200. Later he built a further eight houses, one of which was a public house, which were mortgaged for a further £2,500. When questions were asked as to how he paid off his mortgages he pointed out that in addition to his salary he had received fees from M.P.s for assistance at elections. He added,

> I may say I was not without some means when I became secretary of the association. I had two places of business both of which were let for a good will and then there was my stock which together brought me something considerable . . . I have been as thrifty and as careful as I could in the hope that I might have some little provision to support me when the Reform Association no longer required my services. I know that political popularity is very unstable.[20]

By thrift and a keen business acumen William Brumfitt had thus established himself financially while his betters bemoaned how the political system necessitated aid from the low born.

Brumfitt was a close confidant of George Melly, a Liverpool merchant prince, and while the latter was nursing Preston he came into close touch with a local party worker, Edward Ambler, who had a modest printing and stationery shop. Ambler was very self-effacing and did not consider himself to be ranked in the same class as Melly or the leading Preston Liberals. Indeed with a certain obsequiousness he urged Melly not to address letters 'esquire' since 'I have a strong dislike to the fashionable title, which in many instances – as your own – is graceful and fitting, but not when applied to a tradesman such as I am'.[21] For all his modesty Ambler, like Brumfitt, had prospered and owned business or property interests in several parts of the county. He was in fact a voter in three separate constituencies, Preston, North Lancashire and South Lancashire, each requiring a separate property qualification. It was the Brumfitts and Amblers who were so crucial in the mid-century political system, exemplifying the early judgement that 'a plodding shopkeeper on a committee who sees that the Registration is attended to does more good than a dozen wealthy squires who reserve all their energy for the Election itself'.[22]

At every stage in the political process we shall find organization a vital factor in the amorphous and anonymous city. Organization was found to be one mode of compensation for the lack of all-embracing bonds such as characterized rural society. This emphasis upon organization was at once distinctively urban, bourgeois and Victorian. The grouping together for social, political and economic activities was as much a feature of the period as of the city. In 1867 it was recorded that 'ours is peculiarly an age of social organisations. Men are combining their powers and resources in order to secure one common end. . . . "Societies", "Unions", "Leagues" meet us on every hand.'[23] There was a certain paradox here, for while organization was distinctively urban and middle-class it ran counter to that individualism so dear to bourgeois hearts. Men were warned that in their passion for combination they should not forget that they were 'living conscious, personal beings each having his own heart to commune with, his own trials to endure, his obligations to discharge, his own work to do'.[24]

Party cohesion was the objective of organization whose main ally was patronage. The fruits of each level of political activity were gathered partly in a system of spoils which rewarded the party faithful. Men were bound to a party by family, religion or political conviction and each would be strengthened by a public recognition of service or loyalty. The rewards were conditioned as much by the social status of the aspirant as by the level of the political institution. By a process of almost natural adjustment the workings of patronage produced rewards whose political importance matched the social standing of the political activist. Noticeably it was when such a natural relationship was violated (by passing over an aspirant to the bench, for instance) that party rows occurred and tension accrued. When the veil that hides the intricate workings of the urban political system is removed the system of patronage can be seen in operation. At the humblest level this meant rendering a small service to advance the business interests of a loyal voter. Edward Ambler wrote to George Melly in 1863 on behalf of 'an old franchise voter for Trinity Ward who voted for the liberal candidate at the last election. He is desirous of obtaining a truck for the purpose of carrying fish for sale.'[25] A 30*s.* dole was deemed an appropriate reward for this scale of political involvement. The next stage might be general assistance in finding employment, perhaps for one who had moved from one town to another. Thus Arthur Megson, who had been a minor Liberal politician in Leeds, sitting as councillor for south ward from 1845–8, was sponsored by George Hadfield, Liberal M.P. for Sheffield, for a railway job in Manchester. George Wilson, party manager for the Manchester school, was urged to aid one who had been 'an active agent in all good work . . . in a political and commercial sense'.[26] Somewhat more prestigious were corporation posts, and municipal reform produced opportunities to reward political servants. Municipal office required proof of long service and such could be sustained for Robert Bunting, an applicant for the post of borough treasurer in Manchester, who had 'given his time money and talents to almost every liberal cause for the last 20 years and was always acknowledged one of the most arduous canvassers in Town'.[27] Beyond lay the honorific posts of mayor, alderman and above all magistrate, which were reserved for natural social leaders. Even here a proven record of political achievement was necessary and one Liverpool aspirant complained after not finding his name in the commission, 'I do wish to be a Borough magistrate and think that both in Politics . . . and in other respects I had some claim.'[28] A fish cart for a humble voter, a railway job for a minor municipal politician, a corporate post for the long-serving party worker, a seat on the bench for the urban élite: these were the rewards which kept the urban political system and the urban social structure in equilibrium.

The more honorific, unpaid posts were primarily status symbols which were sought as a means of legitimizing the role of social leader. As Manchester anti-incorporation radicals recognized, one of the objects of the charter of incorporation was to provide the means by which economic, social and political authority could be strengthened. Natural leadership could be reinforced by political office and the stability of urban society thus ensured. Public deference to such leadership could only be maintained if political leaders conformed to the code of respectability the Victorian gentleman held so dear. The Baptist minister J. E. Giles, an active and vitriolic political pastor, was forced to leave Leeds for some unspecified sexual licence, having in his peccadiloes 'gone rather too much in the way of all flesh'.[29] His great political reputation was not sufficient to silence the whispers of scandal. For offending a very different canon in the moral code, a Liverpool councillor was forced to resign by his own political colleagues. One of the merchant princes criticized the councillor's near-dishonesty and complained: 'really on this point of extravagant living while debts to small tradesmen are unpaid something must be done soon or we shall have some grounds for a revolution against those who call themselves gentlemen . . .'[30] Having the councillor 'Kicked out . . . on moral grounds' let in a radical who was not acceptable to the local Liberals, yet this political reverse was preferable to a situation which potentially threatened the essence of bourgeois political dominance.

It was in Liverpool that a junior member of the bourgeois élite reminded his peers that in their ward 'the perpetual complaint . . . is that the *gentlemen* in the ward hold aloof' and of the need to hold their party together 'that is not to be done without the sacrifice of time and thought on the part of the leaders'.[31] Politics made heavy demands upon the families, careers and businesses of urban activists who sacrificed much in the pursuit of political success. Often political engagements conflicted with business commitments. Baines asked himself why he put in such long hours as an urban M.P., 'why submit to this daily and nightly drudgery when it is a source of no profit . . . particularly when . . . doing all this business for others you must be neglecting your own',[32] and Cobden was but the most famous urban activist whose business suffered because of politics. Sometimes politics simply had to take second place to the needs of business. J. G. Marshall cited poor health as his reason for resigning as M.P. for Leeds in 1852 but really it was, as he explained to his brother, his 'seeing that our concern wanted my personal labour and attention'.[33] At a time when the presence of Mark Philips would have aided the cause of Gibson and Bright in Manchester he was unable to attend their Easter tea party: 'I have made my arrangements for Easter week which I must spend here with my secretary on very important private business which I cannot postpone. I cannot give up my time during our short Easter holiday to public matters.'[34] No doubt the excuse of business was welcome in view of the delicate political situation in Manchester in 1847.

Families as well as businesses sometimes suffered. Frequent absence from home was a cross that political wives had to bear, a cross borne more easily when belief in the political cause was shared between husband and wife. When George Wilson, feeling guilty about his prolonged stay in London in 1843 on behalf of the League, wrote to his wife asking whether he should return, she replied stoically, 'I consider it is a critical time with this great question and as long as we know that the carrying out and gaining this cause is expected to benefit all mankind I do think that Private Feeling should give way to Public Good.'[35] Others could not so easily accept the lonely vigil, and William Brown, Lancashire M.P. and Liverpool merchant prince, whose palatial home in Richmond Hill must have housed many servants and retainers, could not travel the short distance from Liverpool to Manchester for fear of leaving his wife overnight. He desired to attend a meeting to which he had been invited in 1854,

did Mrs Brown's health permit but she gets so nervous at night and never closes her eyes if I am absent that I feel it is my first duty not to leave her. If it was a day meeting that I could return in the evening I could run up, Mrs Brown is something better than she has been but I am afraid of anything that will throw her back . . . you must make the best excuse for me you can.[36]

Some years earlier Brown and his fellow county member Alexander Henry had to miss an important Manchester meeting because of a prior social engagement at a dinner organized by the mayor of Liverpool. Since press notices widely publicized the presence of county members at the Manchester meeting Brown requested to be released from his engagement. The mayor refused and so Brown begged for leave to depart from the dinner at nine to enable them to attend the Manchester meeting. His request received a frosty answer.

> The mayor says that he has taken great pains to form this party; that it is neither a mere festive nor a political one but that it is formed of all the leading men of the different mercantile bodies of Liverpool in order to bring them into direct communication and that he feels to let the county members leave his party early in the Evening would break it up and defeat his intentions . . . he is quite indisposed to listen to the proposal and he declines to consent. . . . The end of it is the Mayor holds you and the others positively to the engagement.[37]

Social priorities had to come before political commitment and so Brown reported to his Manchester friends that they could not attend 'without violating that etiquette amongst gentlemen which I am sure none of you would approve of'.[38] Again there was reference to an unwritten code of ethics by which bourgeois authority could be sustained.

It was not only gentlemen, so-called, whose time and energies were sapped by politics; at a much lower level the same personal sacrifices were required. The personal dominance achieved in the parochial affairs of Sheffield in the early 1850s by Isaac Ironside was only sustained by his indefatigable energies and almost full-time commitment to politics. When late on a Tuesday evening in November 1852 Ironside was called upon to reply to a toast at a ward dinner he mildly protested: 'it was hardly fair that he should be worked night and day in the cause of the public. After attending the Sheffield vestry meeting on Monday evening he finished up at the Brightside ward dinner where he was playing at municipals till one o'clock in the morning. He had attended four meetings that day besides a consultation in the afternoon and there he was now called upon to reply to a toast.'[39] Ironside's commitment was an exaggerated version of a general popular involvement in politics which generated interest and enthusiasm at all levels of urban political life. We should not underestimate the excitement injected into workaday lives by politics. Political activity could move dull inert spirits to the highest passions.

Indeed politics were to be found everywhere in the urban experience. Political advantage could be gained on the magistrates' bench in a simple question like early closing, and a Liverpool J.P. was alerted in 1872: 'at the Magistrates' meeting today you will have a glorious opportunity to promote the true interests of the liberal party and to win golden opinions by advocating the workman's wishes. Much Tory power is at present in the hands of the Publicans and we shall be able to break it, with the help of the working men.'[40] The same party struggle expressed itself in the question of appointments, for instance to honorary medical posts in voluntary hospitals. This also spread outside the public sector and could be found in the commercial world. A Preston Liberal canvassed support for a candidate for an agency with the Sun insurance company, writing that 'he is a *Radical*, his opponents every one of them are Tories . . . he is also a member of your persecuted Church'.[41] Fire insurance had a small part to play in the personal fulfilment of Liberal Unitarians. The prior organization for a political object characterized many facets of urban life, and when Cobden was criticized for canvassing in the Chamber of Commerce dispute of 1845 he replied vigorously, 'as for the plea that there was a previous canvass against Mr Birley, why the same thing takes place on every division in the House of Commons, at every railway contest, every parish vestry when any party wishes to carry a particular motion'.[42] A chamber of commerce, a railway board, a parish vestry, all were as political as the House of Commons. One is drawn back to our opening quotation – 'politics are the vital element of *all* elections – parliamentary, municipal, parochial or philanthropic'.[43]

Such attitudes point to an awareness of a comprehensive political system of variegated levels and no single document asserted such awareness in so unequivocal a way as Cobden's pamphlet *Incorporate Your Borough*. Cobden appears at every level in this analysis and he was perhaps the foremost urban political activist in Victorian England. It is therefore fitting that his words should be cited to summarize a complex concept. The young Cobden instinctively recognized that a political system existed in which the most local political achievement could conduce to the good of a wider political object. He wrote at the beginning of his pamphlet,

> The battle of our day is still against the aristocracy . . . The lords of Clumber, Belvoir and Woburn, although they can no longer storm your town, and ransack your stores and shops, at the head of their mailed vassals, are as effectually plundering your manufacturers and their artizans; for, by the aid of their parchment votes and tenants-at-will serfs, they are still enabled to levy their infamous bread tax upon your industry . . . imitate your forefathers by union and coopera-

tion; amalgamate all ranks in your town, by securing to all classes a share in its government and protection; give unity force and efficiency to the intelligent and wealthy community of Manchester, and qualify it by organisation, as it already is entitled by numbers to be the leader in the battle against monopoly and privilege. In a word, INCORPOR-ATE YOUR BOROUGH.[44]

For Cobden the great political issue of his day was the class struggle between bourgeoisie and aristocracy, between town and county, for the soul of England, and his cause would be served by asserting urban authority through incorporation. The Victorian town halls were fortresses in the battle against country estates. The municipal stream was but one tributary of the great political river, whose course is charted in the rest of this book.

Part One
Parochial and Township Administration

1 The vestry as a political institution

'The House of Commons is not the House of Commons of my time, and I have no wish to re-enter it. If I had a taste for business, I might be a member of the Marylebone vestry.'
'Mr Ormsby' in B. Disraeli, *Sybil* (1877 edn), 299

The precise origins of the parish vestry lie embedded deep in the historical process. Joshua Toulmin Smith, the arch-opponent of centralization in the mid-nineteenth century, saw vestries as part of that ancient Anglo-Saxon collection of ward-motes, folk-motes, borough-motes and shire-motes which were the pride of English local self-government. The right of assembly in the vestry was the heritage of all English freemen and it was upon the vestry that with the passage of time many administrative functions devolved. In many places there was a complex intermingling of parochial and manorial institutions but by the nineteenth century manorial authority had become effete while the vestry was still vital and politically alive. In London particularly, vestries had become by the seventeenth and eighteenth centuries the main organ of local government and had a wide variety of administrative and quasi-judicial functions.

Much of the authority of the vestry, as of Parliament, came from its power of taxation. Consent of the ratepayers in vestry was required for most of the parochial expenditure associated with the maintenance of the fabric of the church or the relief of the poor. The more secular expenditure involved in highways, improvement, scavenging, and watering also required at least nominal consent. Many parochial and local administrative offices were appointed by the vestry and while formal authority often lay with the magistrates it was common for the bench to defer to vestry authority by choosing from lists approved by parish meetings.

As the local community gradually required greater social organization, so functions were sometimes removed from the vestry, either by prescriptive right of large ratepayers resting on common law to establish local oligarchies or by private Acts which could equally establish oligarchies of improvement commissioners and the like. These were the so-called 'statutory authorities for special purposes' but even here there was often a residual authority in the vestry sometimes over election, more often over expenditure, which left the vestry with still considerable powers. Particularly in Poor Law affairs there were often disputes about where authority lay, whether in the constituted legal body or with the ratepayers in vestry. In Leeds in 1834 a short-lived but extremely bitter wrangle occurred over whether the appointment of a new master of the workhouse lay with the elected workhouse board or with the vestry itself. In Gateshead at the end of the 1840s an even more serious dispute arose over whether the appointment of an assistant overseer lay with the guardians or the ratepayers. This dispute so polarized the town as not only to embitter Poor Law elections but for a time to determine party conflicts in both municipal and parliamentary spheres as well. As the boroughreeve of Manchester reminded a newly appointed deputy constable: 'though the *power* of appointing you rests with ourselves for the present, and with our successors when they come into office, the Leypayers of the Town in vestry assembled have the power of fixing the salary as *they* may think right, as all our municipal expenditure must be sanctioned by them.'[1]

In short the vestry was an essential part in that ancient English system of local self-government which determined that there should be, in Toulmin Smith's words, 'fixed, frequent, regular and accessible meetings together of the Folk and People, in every part, for the common purposes of getting justice nigh at hand, and of dealing it, and also of understanding, discussing, and determining upon, all matters of common interest'.[2] The vestry was the organ of a species of natural historical democracy based upon the individualist freeborn Englishman. This ideal, if it ever existed, was subjected in the first half of the nineteenth century to two amending processes, each the result of fundamental social change consequent on industrialization, yet in a sense contradictory. These two processes were, first, what Redlich and Hirst called the destruction of the vestry by middle-class encroachment,[3] and second, the politicizing of vestries by men whose political ambitions were frustrated elsewhere.

The parish meeting of rational citizens calmly arriving at a consensus, described by Toulmin Smith, had little relationship with the noisy, often riotous assemblies familiar to men of the eighteenth and nineteenth centuries. Population growth and mobility had swelled vestries to unmanageable proportions and, where acclamation was the main mode of decision-making, rational argument was at a low premium. A

Manchester doggerel-monger has created an image familiar in the industrial revolution period:

> A bull ring, – Gibbs parlour – a French chamber sitting
> Are decorous all, when compared to the meeting
> Held in April to settle the Quarter's Accounts
> When outrageous disputes about trifling amounts
> As excuse was sufficient – the sum but a farthing –
> To turn God's Holy Temple into a Beer Garden.[4]

The beer garden atmosphere of the vestry of the early nineteenth century made sound policy and administration difficult and above all enraged the larger ratepayers, whose wishes and interests were often ignored in the clamorous rejection of their suggestions.

Though the vestry's power rested on taxation those who exercised it often paid none. Newcomers to the town, those exempt from rates because they lived in cheap accommodation, those many citizens who compounded with their landlords and paid no rates personally, those on permanent or temporary relief, lodgers, these and others might attend vestries in large numbers and sway its decisions, yet were legally not qualified to do so. Significant differences often emerged when decisions acclaimed in the vestry were put to a poll of ratepayers. In Leeds it was claimed that 'great numbers of them that attend vestry meetings border upon pauperism',[5] and one may notice that when the Leeds Chartists first attempted to participate in local government they were successful in the two contests that were carried by acclamation in the vestry (churchwardens and improvement commission) but failed in those that went to a poll (council and surveyors of highways). In Liverpool it was claimed that four-fifths of the inhabitants in 1851 would be legally debarred from voting in a vestry poll, though they might all attend the vestry.[6]

The social dislocation of industrial change had enabled the vestry to become a focus for a reversal of the norm, as population gained that influence which many felt ought to be exercised by property. One of the main aims of the Sturges Bourne Acts of 1818 and 1819 was to remedy this situation. By the latter of his two Acts, the Select Vestries Act of 1819, Sturges Bourne provided for the election of 'select vestries' which were in effect parish committees to run the Poor Law with the help of paid assistant overseers. These provisions were a response to the difficulties of running the Poor Law in the face of population growth and economic fluctuation. More controversial was his Parish Vestries Act of 1818 which introduced a scale of voting whereby a ratepayer would have between one and six votes depending on the size of his property. This was intended to redress the balance in favour of wealth as against mere

numbers and this principle of multiple voting was later enshrined in the
Poor Law Amendment Act. The clear intentions of the Sturges Bourne
Acts was to reduce the power of the masses, particularly in populous
parishes.

This emasculation of the vestry was widely resented and in Salford,
where a select vestry was adopted, there was no doubt that the Act had
been 'framed for the sole purpose of curbing the liberties of the people'.[7]
For Toulmin Smith it was symptomatic of the centralizing tendency of
the day that the ancient rights of the ordinary citizen should be thus
usurped:

> There is no ground on which this unrighteous Act can be supported.
> It is purely oligarchical in intention and result. It gives to those to
> whom their wealth of itself already gives a vantage ground the most
> unequal additional advantage of counting manyfold over the man of
> less wealth but equal brains . . . There is no greater blot upon our
> Statute Book than Sturges Bourne's Act.[8]

Much the same tendency may be observed in the attempt to alter the
financial basis of the Manchester Police Commissioners in 1828. Meetings
had become riotous, too many poorer citizens were participating, and the
propertied leaders were constantly being overruled. Hence the proposal,
eventually amended, to set the qualification to vote for a Manchester
Police Commissioner at £25 r.v. and the qualification to sit as one at £35
r.v. It was consonant with the motives of the prime movers of the new
bill that it should be voted on by the vestry in a Sturges Bourne poll.[9]

Alongside this deliberate attempt to reduce the impact of the humble
in the vestry may be placed the development which politicized the vestry
and made it even more important. The same sort of people who wished
thus to control the masses were themselves seeking for means to enshrine
their economic wealth in political leadership. The *nouveau riche* manufacturer or merchant, often a newcomer to the town, equally often a
Dissenter, sought that elusive status to sanctify his economic achievement. As the sociologists have it, they were seeking to legitimize their
role as social leaders. Yet the institutional structure was distinctly
unpromising from this point of view. Most of the new industrial towns
were unrepresented in Parliament, were governed by close corporations or
other oligarchies, and were supervised by borough and county benches
almost exclusively Tory-Anglican in composition. Since other avenues
to political advancement were closed, the Whig/Liberal or radical
Dissenter pitched his tent in the only political battleground available, the
vestry. This process was reinforced by Dissenters' grievances which also
focused attention on parochial affairs.

Hence in many places a Liberal or radical vestry emerged as a political counterweight to a Tory oligarchy as part of a battle between rival élites within the urban middle class. This was clearly seen by the Municipal Corporation Commission when it visited Leeds:

> In cases where the election is popular as in the choice of Commissioners under the local acts the persons selected are all of one political party professing the opposite opinions to those entertained by the majority of the corporation: which is accounted for by the necessity of balancing the influence of the corporation . . . being resorted to in self defence.[10]

The practicalities of Leeds politics determined that an assault upon an inviolate close corporation had to begin in the vestry. Though the free-men of Liverpool had some influence through the election of the mayor, in that city also the vestry had perforce to be the medium of political opposition. No less than eight vestry polls were demanded by Whig-radicals in 1832 alone and as the Webbs put it, 'they revenged themselves on the Tory party turning the half yearly meeting at the old Parish Church into pandemonium'.[11] The infamous electoral corruption of Leicester Corporation could not be reversed in any municipal contest and so the initial pre-reform battle had to be fought in the parish vestries particularly St Margaret's where 'a miniature reform struggle' was commenced.[12] Even in unincorporated towns, oligarchies of commissioners were often immune and so, as indicated by the Manchester verse already quoted, the vestry became the natural political focus.

The vestry institutions of parochial and township administration were attractive because alternatives were lacking. This no doubt enhanced their political importance beyond their intrinsic value, but there were real powers over church affairs, over the Poor Law, over improvement and over highways, the exercise of which could vitally affect the citizen. It was just because the London vestries exercised real powers that Mr Ormsby in *Sybil* found the Marylebone vestry an object worthy of his political ambition. Chadwick had no doubts as to their importance and he concluded that 'almost everywhere the practical influence of the vestry is very great; that it forms, in fact, the ruling authority of the parish, a sort of council of government'.[13] Since the vestry provided experience of what the Sheffield radical Isaac Ironside called 'the science of direct legislation' it was a valuable breeding ground for proscribed politicians whose careers flowered later. Large numbers of urban political activists first emerged politically in some humble parochial office in the early decades of the nineteenth century. As municipal authority became established so the vestry declined, receiving a mortal wound with the abolition of church rates in 1868. Yet as late as 1868 a vestry poll could have important subsidiary political consequences and a Liverpool politician reported: 'the vestry contest last month caused a large number of Catholics to pay their rates before the usual time – this will give us I fancy near 1,000 votes in the Borough contest as they will vote with us.'[14]

The politicizing of the minor institutions of local government was not the creation of the caucus politics of the 1870s but of the disequilibrium between the social and political structures half a century earlier. Men deprived of political opportunities elsewhere sought success and achievement in parochial and township administration. Before municipal reform, Liberal vestries counter-balanced Tory oligarchies and after it artisan and working-class vestries counterbalanced bourgeois-dominated councils. The term 'parochial' implies that the associated powers were unimportant: this is not so, for even when the issues were trivial their significance was weighty in local affairs, those which touched men most closely. Whether bells should be rung in Salford at the ratepayers' expense was a minor question yet in a pregnant context:

> this is a question of minor consequence in itself but is of the utmost importance in its results, as the future of the Local Affairs of the Town will greatly depend upon its decision; therefore if it be carried against us the authorities of the town will be enabled in future to carry any favourite measure they may think proper to bring forward by putting the same iniquitous act [Sturges Bourne's] into operation, in order to confirm their oppression and the leypayers will not be able to resist them.[15]

When the poll ended in what was deemed a defeat for the Sturges Bourne Act the vanquished too recognized that the cessation of bell ringing signified important changes:

> For such a change has taken place
> Twill bring this borough in disgrace
> And we must be dictated to
> By 'Lord Mayor' and his *Worthy Crew*
> Who think they have a claim to merit
> By encouraging a party spirit.[16]

The parochial became political and so vestry institutions became an integral part of the urban political system. The chapters that follow analyse the institutions based upon the vestry or growing out of it. These comprise the office of churchwarden, the Poor Law, the improvement commission and the boards of surveyors of highways.

2
The churchwardens

*'They say it is horrible to make the Church a political
arena, for my part I know no difference between true
politics and religion. I take it, if there be one place more
proper for politics than another it is the Church.'* Elijah
Dixon, Manchester radical, April 1840

The office of churchwarden was the first of the parochial institutions to
be politically contested, and by the early 1830s had in most towns
become the focus of fierce political rivalry. The churchwarden acted as a
sort of business manager to the parish, levying church rates for the
maintenance of the fabric of the church, the provision of its running
costs, the purchase of its equipment and sometimes the payment of
ancillary staff. Three characteristics made the office of churchwarden
worthy of political consideration. First, its intrinsic status was high,
especially in pre-incorporation days, and, for instance, was important
enough to attract the elder Robert Peel to the office in Manchester in
1812. Second, it involved the exercise of considerable power over parish
affairs including the maintenance of the poor. Third, the exercise of that
power was manifest mainly in the levy of a church rate whose legitimacy
came to be challenged by Dissenters.

In Leeds, as in many cities, the initial political interest stemmed from
a desire to control parish expenditure in the vestry. As early as 1819
Edward Baines, editor and proprietor of the *Leeds Mercury*, had begun a
three-year campaign to get accounts published.[1] Later in the 1820s it
was realized that the best way of limiting expenditure was to capture a
majority of the eight wardens elected for Leeds township each Easter. In
1827 Liberals and Tories elected four wardens each and in 1828 the
Tories lost the control of the churchwardens which they were not to
regain for 20 years. The senior churchwarden was John Armitage
Buttrey, an Anglican woolstapler, who had first been elected in 1826, and
he began a régime of strict economy.[2] Even Tory Anglicans were grateful

since the building of new parliamentary churches had put extra burdens on ratepayers. Liberals elected six wardens in 1828 and five in the four elections between 1829 and 1832.

In 1833 a fierce Tory counter-assault began, and before the vestry meeting the whole Tory organization was set in motion: 'circulars are written – canvassers are out – lists are distributed – aldermen, parsons, lawyers sit in close conclave.'[3] Baines led the Liberal attack with the claim that expenditure had been cut from £1,500 to £500, and amid the din of a disorderly meeting the Tory list was abandoned.[4] Buttrey's economies meant that the 1832 rate was sufficient for two years' expenditure and so a rate was not needed in 1833. Buttrey was congratulated for lessening 'the obnoxious tax of church rate' and Baines confidently predicted that church rates were finished in Leeds.[5]

In fact the battle was far from over, and the Tory attack was renewed in 1834 when 4,000 people attended the vestry meeting. A three-hour dispute arose over the first nomination when Baines, now M.P. for Leeds, proposed Buttrey for the east division. The Tory nomination was Robert Perring, editor of the *Intelligencer*, and his supporters demanded a poll when the show of hands went in favour of Buttrey. The vicar wished to adjourn for the poll, which the Liberals opposed, and amid a growing outcry several people were threatened for brawling in church. The vicar, exasperated by the dispute, eventually left the meeting: 'The plan was to bully, beat down, to tire out the Chairman, to intimidate the opponents of Orange monopoly – the meeting therefore acted upon their instructions and refused anything like fair play.'[6] 'Fair play' was needed to distinguish ratepayers from mere vestry crowds. With the meeting abandoned to Liberal control, the other wardens were elected and their names entered into the vestry minutes as though nothing untoward had happened. The demand for a poll was denounced as a move to 'gratify party spleen' by 'a few snarling poll brawling tories'.[7]

The Tories having been repulsed again, they now resorted to law. After failing to get a poll which had been legitimately requested they pleaded at King's Bench that the 1834 election was invalid and a *mandamus* was issued ordering new elections. There was jubilation at a decision which had proved that Baines and Buttrey were not above the law, and Tories claimed to be seeking merely 'a fair participation of power'.[8] The new elections were to be held only eight weeks before the term of office ended and to avoid further conflict two Tory solicitors pleaded for a 50–50 share of the wardens, a compromise which was flatly rejected. Thus only a few weeks after the general election of 1835 Leeds was once more plunged into a party political battle just as contentious as that for a parliamentary contest. Handbills and placards were issued and rival support drummed up which in the event was not used, for the

Tories decided to postpone their effort until the next annual election.[9]

The desire for a poll had been postponed and not abandoned. Tories had lost all faith in rowdy vestry meetings which displayed 'sans culotteism in one of its worst forms' and one of the Tory placards promised to 'pour on the heads of the lovers of incessant agitation the accumulated indignation of an insulted parish'.[10] The demand for a poll at the 1835 Easter vestry was predictable and was not on this occasion opposed at a quiet vestry meeting. The Tory case rested on Church versus Dissent, but the Liberals – in view of Buttrey's Anglicanism – fought the battle on parochial economy. In the previous year when a poll had been anticipated Baines had written from London to his son:

> The tories have often talked of turning out Mr. Buttrey but they have never yet succeeded, indeed the parishioners unless they prefer extravagance to economy will never allow it. Nor would a poll by plurality of votes save them for the tories around them would rather pay 300 £ a year than 1500 £ and many would vote for Mr. B. on that ground.[11]

This proved to be a judicious prophecy and Buttrey was elected by 4,551 to 1,625, while his colleagues returned similar results.

This unpalatable confirmation of Liberal control had an unpleasant sting in the tail for Perring and his friends. The vestry resolved that those who had demanded the poll should pay the expenses incurred, since the contest had been 'to the serious annoyance of the parishioners and (led to) the interruption of industry and tranquillity ... an insult to the Vestry and a factious annoyance to the Parish.'[12] Perring was furious with this decision, arguing that election expenses should be met out of church rates, which were not being levied. Buttrey was forced to ask for a $\frac{1}{2}d$. rate at the end of 1835 and this was opposed by the more radical Dissenters, led by the Unitarian wool merchant Darnton Lupton, who wished to abolish church rates entirely. Buttrey as an Anglican insisted that they must provide bread and wine for the sacrament and he took the legalistic line that legitimate expenses had to be met from church rates, the levy of which could not be legally refused. His supporters carried the day with the point that it would be unfair to leave the Liberal wardens to foot the bill themselves. For the last time a church rate was levied in Leeds, requested by Liberal wardens and granted by a Liberal vestry.[13]

A few months later the régime which had effectively abolished church rates in Leeds came to an end. A completely new Liberal list was elected in April 1836 with Edward Johnson replacing Buttrey as senior churchwarden. The opening up of the town council demoted the office somewhat, and five of those elected in 1835 entered the council in 1836.

Buttrey himself sat as a councillor from 1836 to 1841 and several of his colleagues had distinguished municipal careers after having served their apprenticeship as churchwardens. After his withdrawal, Dissenters monopolized most of the vacancies in place of the Liberal Anglicans of the earlier period. There was no change in party composition, with Liberals carrying seven wardens each year, but in terms of church rates economists like Buttrey, who believed that some legitimate expenses had to be incurred, were replaced by abolitionists who wanted outright voluntaryism in their attack upon the Church.

'Church in danger' would thus continue to motivate Tory Anglican parochial activity, which was further stimulated by the appointment to the parish of Leeds of the High Church clergyman, W. F. Hook. Hook's appointment enthused the right-wing Tories and produced in the 1837 Easter vestry one of the most turbulent vestry meetings ever held in the town. A near riot broke out when Edward Baines junior disputed the curate's right to nominate the vicar's churchwarden, pending Hook's arrival from Coventry. Liberal wardens were elected, but not before the curate had been subjected to two hours' verbal abuse for refusing to accept a motion condemning his own action in appointing John Garland as vicar's warden, a post he had occupied since 1832.[14]

As soon as Hook arrived he decided to prevent rowdy meetings in church and to stop 'profane outrages' such as sitting on the holy table. He reprimanded the wardens for failure to provide for the church and insisted that they summon a vestry for the levy of a rate. The situation was very different in the summer of 1837 from that 18 months earlier. Then a sympathetic vestry in effect guaranteed the expenses of Liberal wardens, but now a hostile crowd were bent on frustrating a reactionary churchman demanding his legal rights. Hook's son-in-law allowed his admiration for the great man to reverse the historical truth when he recorded, 'The day was gained. The rate was passed.'[15] In fact the rate was refused on the motion of Darnton Lupton and radical Baptist minister J. E. Giles.[16]

Hook certainly rallied support for the Anglicans in Leeds and planned to rebuild the parish church. It was fear that these alterations would be charged to church rates which led to a large attendance at the 1838 Easter vestry. Baines junior's sermon on the evils of church rates and the virtues of voluntaryism was superfluous in the absence of the expected Tory challenge.[17] Hook continued to identify himse l: with Tories, not least by his hurried return from Europe to canvass and vote in the 1841 general election, and therefore Leeds Dissenters felt that they must 'in pure and necessary self defence elect Dissenters to be Churchwardens'.[18] In 1839, 1840 and 1841 Liberal Dissenters were elected fairly easily, in the last year unopposed.

It was during 1841 that a situation arose in which some Dissenters were prepared to tolerate the renewal of church rates. The macabre discovery that gravediggers were having to move bodies from existing graves to accommodate new corpses led to a demand for a new cemetery to replace the 'pestilential parochial burial grounds'. In passing, the *Mercury* conceded that a rate might be the only solution to finance the new burial grounds.[19] Tories did not bother to contest the 1841 election on the grounds that a rate was inevitable, the assumption also held by Hook when he summoned a special vestry in December 1841.[20] Hook claimed that Baines and the *Mercury* supported a church rate and at a prior meeting a split occurred in the Liberal party between those who wished merely to refuse a rate and those like the two Baineses who wished to suggest a means of resolving the burial question. Baines junior was particularly incensed at what he deemed a garbled report of this private meeting which appeared in the *Leeds Times*, edited by Samuel Smiles. He resented the personal attack upon himself, since he had for eight years 'taken the most decided stand against the system and had (by the request of successive yearly meetings of the Liberals – *private* meetings they were and *never published*) for those eight years moved the Liberal churchwardens at the vestries'.[21]

The man who had thus led at previous vestries was now shouted down, since the combination of the pronouncements of Hook and Smiles made the younger Baines appear as a mere apologist for church rates. As he feared, the vestry enthusiastically rejected a church rate, yet at the same time refused to allow him to move an amendment suggesting a possible solution to the burial problem. Baines was left to argue his case in the *Mercury* and he continued to maintain that on this question Dissenters could tolerate a rate since they would benefit from the provision of new burial grounds.[22] In contrast to his stance on education in 1847 (see below, p. 271), Baines now took the pragmatic rather than the ideological line.

A solution was found in the Burial Grounds Act which Parliament passed in conjunction with the Leeds Improvement Act of 1842. The council was enabled to provide burial grounds and to separate consecrated from unconsecrated ground, satisfying both Anglicans and Dissenters and avoiding 'unpleasant collisions in Vestry Meetings on the subject of church rates'.[23] By the time of the 1842 Act Liberals had relinquished parochial control, handing over to a Chartist list elected against both Liberal and Tory opposition. It was a measure of the weakness of the church party that Hook conceded before the election that 'the contest was between the Chartists and the Radicals' and Samuel Smiles commented on the church, 'she is in the very jaws of Chartism'.[24]

Since grave doubts remained about the status of many who had carried the Chartist list, a Liberal demand for a poll could have been expected. In fact none was forthcoming once the Chartists guaranteed that no rate would be levied. It had been primarily to abolish church rates that Dissenters had continued to fight parochial contests and Liberals were happy to leave the humble tasks of the wardens to Chartists so long as rates were not revived. There was another three-cornered contest in 1843, but in 1844, 1845 and 1846 the Chartists were returned unopposed. By then Chartists were able to emulate their Liberal pre-decessors of two decades earlier and use parochial politics to compensate for inability to control superior offices. Hook pronounced them infinitely preferable to the Liberal Dissenters they had replaced.

The decline of Liberal interest in parochial affairs owed much to Hook's growing moderation. Neither the rebuilding of the church nor the provision of new burial grounds was financed by church rates, though from a legalistic point of view they could have been. By the mid-1840s Hook had embarked upon an Anglican appeal based upon equity and intrinsic truth rather than legality. In order to provide every poor man with a pastor, Hook proposed the division of the populous parish of Leeds into 21 smaller parishes. This would mean a loss of something like £400 p.a. for Hook personally, but he believed that 'unless the Church of England can be made in the manufacturing districts the Church of the poor which she certainly is not now, her days are numbered'.[25] By 1846 Hook was arguing that the Church had no greater claim to special treatment than any other body and concluded that 'the taxes are collected from persons of all religions and cannot be fairly expended for the exclusive maintenance of one'.[26] When this was the theology preached by the vicar of Leeds, Liberal Dissenters had no need to involve themselves in the affairs of the Anglican Church.

In 1847 the Tories regained their former empire when they defeated the Chartists, a success repeated in 1848, 1849 and 1850.[27] In vain the Chartists requested Liberal support for a poll but the fear of church rates was now so remote that it could not rekindle Liberal interest. The last flickers of interest concerning surplice fees at the new burial grounds were finally doused when the council settled the issue in 1850, the year of the last contested warden's election.[28] By mid-century the prevailing conditions which had politicized the office of churchwarden a quarter of a century earlier had disappeared. Municipal and Poor Law reform had debased the status of the churchwarden, whose power had by now become effete, and the issue of church rates, which had injected real controversy into parochial affairs, was now settled. Now that the church-wardens had been removed from Leeds politics, the election of a church-warden had become a two-minute Anglican ritual before a handful of people.

A similar description has been recorded on the mid-century situation in Manchester: 'From 1850 therefore the election of Churchwarden became merely a matter of ecclesiastical concern and the inextricable mingling of religious and civil government that had existed as far back as history relates came to an end.'[29] In Leeds the churchwarden had become political in three ways: because of the intrinsic status or power of the office; by being drawn into an overall local struggle for power; and as an agent in the Dissenting campaign against church rates. In Manchester it was only the latter two which were important and in discrete periods. From about 1820 until 1835 the radical campaign against church rates built up until they were abandoned by a despairing Anglican establishment. Then, after a short non-political hiatus, the office of churchwarden became the political focus of the party battle over incorporation, in the years from 1838 to 1841.

In Manchester as elsewhere the building of parliamentary churches put an intolerable strain upon the yield of church rates and so brought the financial position of the Church into contention well before there was a concerted Dissenting political attack. The Manchester vestry was predominantly concerned with financial control and it was natural that the economizing zeal which was centred on the constables' accounts should be extended to those of the churchwardens. In the 1820s Whig-Radical Dissenters had modest parochial goals, hoping merely to limit Anglican demands to what was strictly legal expenditure. It was a strategy of gnat-bites rather than body blows and it was annoying rather than weakening to local parochial authority.

In 1820 a church rate to equip the new parliamentary churches had been defeated by 720 votes to 418.[30] In 1823 the payment of choristers in the church had been disallowed and in 1825 an attempt was made to prevent the purchase of expensive silver plate. Before the vestry meeting handbills were circulated 'written with a bitter and inflammatory spirit which accused the Warden and fellows of "ostentatious extravagance or grasping selfishness, by the exaction of new and unheard of titles".'[31] At a four-hour meeting the attack was led by the unitarian Thomas Potter who denounced the attempt 'to increase the power and patronage of an already overgrown establishment'. The relatively moderate Dissenting position of the 1820s was best expressed by J. E. Taylor, editor of the *Guardian*, who told the predominantly Anglican assembly that it was not simply a question of money: 'those who conscientiously differed from the established Church but were compelled to contribute to its support did undoubtedly regard with jealousy any attempt to strain those contributions beyond the strict limits to which they were by law confined'.[32] On this occasion the Anglican party was victorious and both the purchase of silver plate and the collection of disputed gallery pew rents went ahead.

In the mid-1820s a Tory commentator could remark on the good humour with which Dissenters accepted their defeat,[33] but by the early 1830s a much sterner spirit had been introduced into the sectarian battle. The opposition of bishops in the House of Lords to the Reform Bill had its parochial consequences in fierce vestry contests in many places in 1832. By 1833 some Manchester radicals had decided that mere control of expenditure was insufficient and that the Leeds example of capturing the office of churchwarden itself must be emulated. As at Leeds there was one large parish but there were only three churchwardens, who were elected each Easter along with sidesmen, later confirmed as overseers.

Prime mover in this extension of the ecclesiastical battle was Archibald Prentice, the radical proprietor of the *Manchester Times*, and he put the amendment to the Anglican list at the 1833 Easter vestry meeting. The familiar discrepancy between vestry crowds and actual ratepayers deprived Prentice of his immediate success in getting his amendment carried. The popular vote in the vestry was reversed by a massive Sturges Bourne poll defeat for the radicals. The result was partly due to general distaste for the whole business of Sturges Bourne distortion and many of Prentice's supporters abstained. It also owed something to the nascent division in Manchester middle-class liberalism which meant that some moderates did not approve of Prentice's strategy. The poll sheets have survived and from these we find that the Potters, Wm Neild, J. E. Taylor and several other prominent Liberal leaders voted against Prentice.[34] In 1825 Taylor had in fact specifically excluded a Dissenting contest for the office of churchwarden and in 1833 the *Guardian* was doubtful of the wisdom of this frontal assault. Even on later church rates contests it was recorded that 'Mr Taylor caricatured us in the Guardian'.[35] The poll sheets also permit a rare analysis of the effects of a Sturges Bourne poll which may be tabulated.

Table 1. Churchwardens' poll, Manchester 1833

	Anglican list	Radical list
Votes	2059	28
Voters	804	26
Ratepayers with six votes	130	—

A Sturges Bourne poll could thus exaggerate a majority by more than $2\frac{1}{2}$ times where over 16 per cent of the ratepayers had six votes to cast.

The Liberals fared much better when the churchwardens attempted to levy the 1833 church rate, since they could for the most part agree with the traditional Dissenting policy of limiting the demands of the church. Thomas Potter was now supported by George Hadfield, a Congregationalist lawyer who was later to be radical M.P. for Sheffield, in a demand for a six-monthly adjournment. This went to a poll in which the Liberals gained a narrow victory, later reversed on a scrutiny.[36] However it was already clear by the summer of 1833 that Anglicans in Manchester would be opposed at every turn.

As the 1834 election approached Prentice complained that 'the town has too long submitted to the system of self nomination' and he warned that in the light of past experience an *adjourned* poll was useless, for a Liberal victory could only be secured by a poll of those present.[37] A riotous vestry meeting followed with the opposition led by the radical artisan James Wroe, who censured the chairman, the Rev. C. D. Wray, already unpopular because of his decision in the previous year to allow spurious votes to stand. Again the church party carried their list on a poll and again many of the opposition refused to vote because they disputed the poll's legality.[38] Both sides in any case recognized that the main battle would come in the summer on the levy of a rate.

When the churchwardens attempted to levy another halfpenny rate Hadfield and Potter moved an amendment against the rate. Apart from the contentious question of the morality of church rates there was in Manchester the practical injustice that these rates were collected from only one-third of the ratepayers.[39] The inevitable poll produced an excited contest in which both sides resorted to some doubtful tactics. The incursion of disputed Salford voters particularly incensed the Tories who complained that the Dissenters included 'the scum and refuse of the borough of Salford, not leaving even the brothels unvisited' and Hadfield recalled that 'the stir was greater than at any election for Members of Parliament'.[40] The Whig-Radical opposition was elated when the poll resulted in a victory 7,119 to 5,897 against the church rate.[41] Once more the *Guardian* took up an equivocal position, wanting to have the best of all worlds, and Prentice remarked of Taylor: 'He had his bread buttered on one side by the Whigs and on the other by the Tories. It would be cruel to prevent him holding it out to the Radicals for a covering of appetite-provoking anchovy paste.'[42]

The Liberal victory was again reversed on a scrutiny and the rate was levied but doubts on the scrutiny induced many to refuse to pay. The church was approaching an impasse. Both in 1833 and 1834 a rate had only been laid with extreme difficulty after disputed polls and scrutinies.

A further bitter confrontation could be anticipated in 1835, especially when an enthusiastic prior meeting was harangued by Prentice and others and had agreed to resist the imposition of another rate at the vestry. The usual defeat of the rate at the vestry meeting did not result in the wardens asking for a poll. Instead they took up Thomas Potter's offer of a voluntary subscription which he launched with a £50 donation.[43]

Manchester's church leaders found, as Hook discovered later in Leeds, that Dissenters voluntarily contributed towards an expense which they would not legally meet. From 1835 church rates were abandoned in a strategic withdrawal by the church. Paradoxically the Liberals had never legally prevented a rate, for they had never carried their own list of nominations and their poll victories against the rate had been reversed in 1833 and 1834 on a scrutiny. Yet the compromise of a voluntary subscription had its appeal in a situation of sectarian division, legal disputation, expensive elections and partial payment of rates. Without winning *de jure* the dissenters had won *de facto*.*

The end of church rates perhaps demoted the office of churchwarden and in 1836 two of the original Anglican nominees declined to serve. Prentic was as anxious as ever that these parochial spoils should be shared:

> He had hitherto found that the appointments to this office had been confined to one class of politicians and all others were carefully excluded. They had at length run the round of their party . . . they could not find any more efficient men among the tories, he therefore invited the churchwardens to retire and select three gentlemen of other political sentiments.[44]

Prentice put alternative nominations which were defeated by over 200 in yet another Sturges Bourne poll.[45] He was dissatisfied with the result but his only recourse was to go to King's Bench, which he declined.

Once Dissenters had been relieved of church rates their interest in the churchwardens' elections declined sharply so that the 1837 election passed off quietly and in that of 1838 the nominations of the outgoing wardens were accepted without incident by a very small vestry meeting.[46] The senior churchwarden thus quietly ushered in at the 1838 Easter vestry, George Clarke, a prominent Conservative cotton spinner, proved to be the most controversial warden in Manchester's parochial history. Half-way through his term of office Manchester was incorporated and overnight the post of churchwarden was re-politicized by being sucked into the fierce battle over incorporation. This is discussed later, but at this stage it may merely be noticed that the levy of a borough rate devolved upon the churchwardens, who were charged with its collection and delivery to the new council.†

Perhaps accepting, in the *Chronicle*'s words, 'the utter hopelessness of any attempt to procure officers favourable to their pretensions in open vestry', the incorporation party relied on the newly appointed Liberal

---

* A similar position resulted in Bradford in the early 1840s where rates were levied but not paid and eventually abandoned.

† It may clarify a complex story if this section is read in conjunction with the review of Manchester's incorporation battle in Chapter 6.

borough magistrates to reverse the re-election of Clarke in April 1839.[47] Clarke had been presented with a requisition to serve a second term and when he was confirmed in office by the county magistrates the *Guardian* predicted that 'all parochial and municipal business of the town will shortly be at a dead lock'.[48] Clarke soon fulfilled the prophecy by refusing to pay the borough rate over to the new council in view of its doubtful legality. Clarke's property was distrained, not without riotous opposition from his workpeople, and in August 1839 a vestry meeting packed with working-class anti-incorporators supported the wardens in their refusal to obey the council's precept. A further battle occurred at Clarke's mill in February 1840 when the sheriff, supported by large numbers of police, enforced a second distress warrant upon Clarke's property.[49] The Tory-Chartist alliance against the municipal charter was now firmly sealed.

The Liberal incorporation party led by Cobden now realized that their only way out, pending a decision on the *Rutter* v. *Chapman* case which would decide the legality of the charter, was to capture the office of churchwarden so that sympathetic wardens could then hand over the funds to their allies in the council. Hence the 1840 election for this minor parochial office came to be the most fiercely contested that Manchester had witnessed. The political interest derived not from parochial or church questions but from the accident which in 1840 made the office of churchwarden the lynch-pin of the whole local government system. The overall political battle for control of Manchester now politicized the office, where before it had been the question of church rates. Formerly a vote at a churchwarden's election had been a vote for or against a church rate, now it was to be for or against the charter. The financial implications of incorporation were a major plank in the Tory case and ratepayers were warned: 'elect their tools as churchwardens and they will fleece you to the very skin'.[50]

The importance which Tories attached to the 1840 contest may be gauged by the nomination of Thomas Hornby Birley, a member of one of the most prominent Tory Anglican families in Manchester. Clarke's list was opposed by Cobden's, which was seconded by his fellow Liberal Thomas Hopkins. Hopkins claimed that the key question was the tenacity of the Tory hold upon the office of churchwarden and 'their determination not to let persons of what are called liberal principles go into office'. It was not Cobden's party which had politicized parochial affairs, he claimed:

I lament that the appointment of churchwardens and sidesmen should assume a political complexion: but circumstances of an over-whelming and controlling nature have driven us into a line of conduct that we would rather avoid if we could. . . . I say those who commence making a subject political when it ought not to be so are the parties to blame; they compel us to follow their example.[51]

The main opposition to Cobden at the vestry meeting came not from Tories but from the two radicals James Wroe and Elijah Dixon. This was most significant, for both had previously been active at vestries in alliance with Liberal Dissenters against Tory Anglican nominations. Now the incorporation question had turned them against their former friends. Equally significantly, neither referred to church questions in opposing Cobden's list. Wroe reiterated his familiar theme that the charter was a back-door method of introducing the new Poor Law, while Dixon, veteran of Peterloo, saw this as part of a move to establish a Liberal middle-class oligarchy:

> They are in possession of place or rather they want to be in possession and the moment they secure it there will be no more liberality for the poor cottager at £1 a year. . . . How agreeable it is to have the thing nicely managed by forty or fifty individuals nominating one another. It will not do, Mr Cobden and you are at the bottom of it.[52]

In an expensive and fiercely contested four days' poll the Tory list was carried with a majority of over 4,000. Both sides resorted to extreme tactics but it seems that the Tories were better organized and had greater funds at their disposal. They took the 1840 churchwardens' election extremely seriously, 'contesting the matter as if it had been an election of members for the county'. Indeed the Tories felt that parliamentary issues were as much at stake as parochial ones, ascribing their victory to 'abhorrence of Whiggery and of Whig devices such as Whig corporations Whig Poor Laws and Whig Police' and deducing from a churchwardens' poll that the ratepayers of Manchester 'have no confidence in the present ministers'.[53] On the face of it their achievement was minor, merely holding on to a parochial office which they had always monopolized. Yet the symbolic significance was great and explains Tory reactions to the victory, 'chairing Mr George Clarke and parading the town with banners and bands of music and ringing of bells as if the salvation of the state had been achieved by their success in the election of churchwardens'.[54]

The *Guardian* might thus mock the minimal success, unaware that to a Manchester Tory-Anglican the 1840 victory was tantamount to the salvation of the state for it said something about how local power should be exercised and by whom. This can only be appreciated by recalling the Tory position under Thomas Fleming in 1820. Fleming had led an oligarchy which monopolized total local power. Tory Anglicans dominated the police commissioners, shared among themselves the manorial offices of boroughreeve and constable, and monopolized the parochial posts of churchwardens and overseers. In the next two decades their control of the police commissioners was removed, the manorial offices became effete and their overseers' nominations were legally challenged. Only the office of churchwarden remained to salve the Tory pride. This prize did not fall into Liberal hands in 1840 and that fact was taken by Tories to signal a victory over the charter.

In the event it proved no such thing, for the legality of the charter was confirmed and the only Tory tactic was removed. So soon after this hard-fought victory the Tories discovered that it mattered nought who held the office since the churchwardens were legally bound to lay the rate. Once more the churchwardens' elections lapsed into political insignificance and in 1842 only 30 people attended the Easter vestry.[55] What little influence over borough affairs the churchwardens retained was removed by a legal ruling in 1850 that the overseers were the only legal rating authority. By that date Dissenters had long ceased to take any interest in vestry contests but Anglicans themselves caused a flurry of excitement at the end of the 1840s in the celebrated Manchester church question. This involved a dispute over the division of the large parish of Manchester and the proper role and function of the wealthy collegiate chapter of Manchester parish church. Chartist intervention, aimed mainly at the pernicious effects of Sturges Bourne, complicated what was in reality an internecine struggle between evangelicals and the chapter.[56] The office of Manchester churchwarden briefly became again a tactical strong-point before falling into oblivion in the 1850s.

In Birmingham the same pattern of events had occurred in the early 1840s after a decade of bitter conflict. Dissenters were first moved to action by Joseph Parkes, later the great Whig party manager, who discovered that the town's free grammar school charter prohibited Nonconformists from the board of governors. The political drive thus generated was focused on the vestry and much confusion attended the levy of a church rate in 1830.[57] The 1831 church rate proved to be the last levied in the parish of Birmingham, although the contiguous parish of Aston within the borough boundary managed to levy a rate in 1836 and 1842–3.[58] There were seven churches within the parish which each elected its own churchwardens, with the main attention focused on the central church of St Martin's from which parochial affairs were organized.

A major turning point occurred in 1832 when the Birmingham Political Union entered the fray and nominated T. C. Salt, later one of Birmingham's Chartist delegates, as the churchwarden for St Martin's. It is a measure of the importance that vestry affairs could assume that an agitational body such as the Political Union, whose main aim was the

passing of the Reform Bill, should concern itself with the election of a
minor parish office. In fact the successful battle against church rates was
seen by one local observer as an example of Political Union organization
enabling Dissenters to unite for opposition.[59]

What was called 'indecent contention and disgraceful clamour' enabled
Salt to be elected in April 1832.[60] Four months later Salt surprised his
nominees in the Union by demanding a church rate, warning that he
would levy one even without vestry consent. Even more surprising, he
was supported in this move by the radical George Edmonds, son of a
Baptist preacher, and by the Whig Parkes, who had sparked off the
Dissenting movement in the first place.[61] Salt, almost certainly an
Anglican, took the line, obviously supported at this stage by some
Dissenters, that church rates could not legally be refused and that
wardens were under both a legal and a moral obligation to maintain the
fabric of the church and its services. There was some support for a
moderate Anglican standpoint which would willingly have relieved
Dissenters of this burden:

> We do *now* accept their pecuniary aid is a *coercive* tax, and a voluntary
> payment is surely less obnoxious, less disgraceful . . . the Church
> Establishment is not dependent on the pockets of dissenters and if it
> were, justice and reason demand that we should not be so degraded
> . . . inordinate revenues unequally distributed – close vestries packed
> with men covetously seeking the 'goods' of the Church – excessive
> rates beyond the necessities of their objects – the pluralists – the
> *politicians* of the hierarchy – these corruptions have brought us to this
> pass.[62]

Notwithstanding such rare Anglican enlightenment the battle over
church rates polarized the religious and political forces and swamped this
species of moderation. This was no doubt what Parkes had in mind in
unsuccessfully appealing for a rate in 1832 when he called for an end to
vestry contests with their 'scenes of local division and agitation so
adverse to good feeling and the real interests of society'.[63]

In 1833 the Birmingham Political Union again invaded the vestry to
support the nomination of R. W. Winfield, a Dissenter who announced
immediately that he would not levy a rate. He was re-elected in 1834
along with others whose main claim to public notice was their so-called
'political notoriety'.[64] So many of the churches within the parish were
now deprived of necessary income that Anglican leaders decided to take
a town poll as an attempt to restore the church rates which had been
refused largely through 'the influence of the leaders of the late Political
Union'.[65] The town poll was clearly a move to reduce the role of vestry
crowds and tilt the balance back in favour of ratepayers. This was the

occasion for Anglicans to assert the central role of the Church: 'Whatever should weaken it, would in the same degree weaken the common weal; whatever should overthrow it would in sure and immediate consequence bring down the goodly fabric of that constitution, whereof it is a constituent and necessary part.'[66] Clearly greater issues were at stake than the apparently minor question of whether Birmingham parish should levy a 4*d.* rate.

With all but the staunch Anglican and the wavering Methodist against the Church, the rate was defeated by 6,699 to 1,723, with the main attack led by William Pare, Benjamin Hadley and the Catholic Rev. M'Donnell, all prominent Political Union figures.[67] The connection between such minor parochial incidents and the great affairs of state was manifest in the candidature of Richard Spooner at the 1835 election. He was invited to stand immediately after the defeat in the town poll, fighting mainly on a church and state platform. Previously an important figure in the urban challenge to landed dominance and a former ally of Attwood, Spooner was regarded by local Tories as a vigorous defender of the Church, the existence of which was threatened by such developments as the attack upon church rates.[68] The emergence of Spooner was a Tory-Anglican riposte to a town poll, whose decision had 'virtually settled the question of church rates in Birmingham parish for ever'.[69]

At the time it did not seem so, for the Church party was not yet willing to admit defeat and in 1836 mounted their most serious challenge for the churchwarden's election since 1831. The contest between Brown, a churchman, and Winfield, a Dissenter, symbolized in Birmingham the whole struggle between the church and its enemies. Though Winfield, with radical support, was successful in the initial vote the rector, amid a near riot, declared Brown the churchwarden after a scrutiny.[70] As ever the key question was the church rate and the mouthpiece of Birmingham dissent warned of perpetual discord: 'Religion demands the extinction of church rates! Morality demands the extinction of church rates! Justice demands the extinction of church rates! There can be no peace between Dissent and the Church . . . no quiet can be had in England until church rates are abolished.'[71] As if to prove the point a large town meeting on church rates in February 1837 broke up in confusion with the Dissenters, 'the Philistines of Idolatory Puritanism and atheism', adjourning to a meeting house leaving the Anglicans, the defenders of 'political injustice spiritual tyranny and irreligious bigotry', in possession of the public office.[72]

The battle was rejoined at the 1837 Easter vestry when R. K. Douglas, editor of the *Birmingham Journal* and author of the Chartist National Petition, led what he specifically termed a political rather than a religious attack upon church rates.[73] Winfield was again elected against

Brown and the noisy meeting was characterized by frequent censures from the rector for the unruly leaders of Dissent. So bad was the conduct that the two worst offenders – William Pare, secretary of the Reform Registration Society, and G. F. Muntz, soon to be the town's M.P. – were prosecuted for rioting in church.[74] Muntz, renowned for his violent temper, having once assaulted a journalist who had attacked him in print, was proud of his Anglicanism but opposed church rates. At the first hearing both Muntz and Pare were found guilty and only later achieved an implied acquittal when the case was allowed to lapse at the retrial.[75]

A case at Warwick Assizes no doubt had a sobering effect and the 1838 vestry was a much quieter affair despite the intervention of the revived Birmingham Political Union on behalf of P. H. Muntz, chairman of the Reform Association, who was to serve two terms as mayor from 1839.[76] By the end of the 1830s Douglas was arguing in his editorials that church rates had become a very subordinate grievance,[77] and the feeling that rates had effectively been destroyed in Birmingham probably led to a fall in interest which led to the defeat in 1840 of Benjamin Hadley, late a delegate to the National Convention. This was regarded in Tory circles as a straightforward political victory for the local Conservatives.[78] Again in the context of a local Whig or Liberal dominance, Tory victories in churchwardens' elections were hailed as a party triumph.

R. K. Douglas was now forced to reconsider his position in the light of an expected counter-assault from the church, and he once more led the attack at St Martin's. So great was the conflict in 1841 that a week's adjournment was required to take a poll on who should occupy the chair at the vestry meeting.[79] The decisive battle was now at hand, for it appeared that the archdeacon at Coventry was prepared to insist upon the laying of a rate. It was always open to the Church to get a writ of *mandamus* to enforce the churchwardens' duty of levying a rate, in the absence of which the wardens could find themselves personally liable for the legitimate expenditure of the parish.

When the news broke that a special vestry meeting was to be held in the town hall in September 1841 there was a double outcry. First, according to George Edmonds, there had been a compact between the parties that church nominations would be allowed in return for the voluntary abolition of church rates. This compact was clearly being repudiated. Second, there was a familiar Sturges Bourne ploy to restrict participation to those entitled, but with an unfamiliar twist. Actual admission to the meeting was to be granted solely to those possessing specially issued certificates of payment of rates.[80] A committee was formed by the Liberals as much to organize the attendance of their supporters as to oppose the rate. As before, the initial dispute arose over who should take the chair and in the ensuing chaos of taking a poll on this the large numbers of police present had difficulty in maintaining order. When the poll on the actual rate was declared the Church had been resoundingly defeated by 7,281 to 628. In fact this was the number of voters and the precise number of votes cast was never calculated although multiple voting under Sturges Bourne was utilized.[81] The automatic Tory reaction was to ask for a scrutiny but the overwhelming nature of the defeat made this a hopeless tactic and the demand was soon dropped.[82] Perhaps as a substitute one last attempt was made to levy a rate in February 1842, and yet again R. K. Douglas led the anti-rate party at the vestry meeting. The poll ended even more ignominiously for the Church, with only 74 votes in favour of the rate and 300 against.[83] These were now the dying convulsions of a defeated party, and when T. C. Salt was once more elected warden in April 1842 church rates, which had been dead in Birmingham since 1831, were finally buried.[84]

It was also by the early 1840s that church rates in Nottingham were finally laid low. In this strong centre of Dissent, where Nonconformists provided 25 of the town's 30 places of worship in 1832, the campaign was directed against the three parish churches of St Peter, St Nicholas and St Mary. The parish of St Peter appears to have been quiet and the initial assault came in St Nicholas, where rates were refused at two stormy vestries in 1833 and again in 1834 and 1835.[85] Here the leaders were Benjamin Boothby and George Gill, two prominent local radicals who nominated a radical at the 1834 election and supported Sturge in the election of 1842.

It was assumed that the other parishes would follow the lead from St Nicholas and the most controversial dispute arose in the parish of St Mary where the church rates issue was finally fought out. There was a noticeable increase in intensity of feeling on the church rates question at the beginning of 1834 and the radical editor Richard Sutton reminded his readers that Parliament would redress grievances only when the people had shown themselves determined to be rid of them: 'Shall we any longer bear the enormous church rates? Shall we submit to the burdens imposed upon us by the clergy any longer when it is in our power to resist them? No, no, let every dissenter do his duty and the shackles fall off us for ever.'[86] This clarion call infected extra enthusiasm into an anti-church rate meeting in January 1834, addressed mainly by Nonconformist ministers.[87]

The effects were soon seen in St Mary's vestry where the Dissenter Samuel Bennett, a bookseller and printer of the local Whig *Mercury*, was elected churchwarden. As Sutton explained, it was only opposition to church rates which induce Dissenters to 'elect one from their own body to an office connected with another denomination'.[88] That church rates

were the cause of Bennett's nomination was confirmed when the Quaker
Samuel Fox proposed the motion to refuse a rate in June 1834 at a
vestry under Bennett's chairmanship.[89] The refusal of a rate at St Mary's
in both 1834 and 1835 appeared to have settled the issue, but the unpopular Whig proposals of 1837 which attempted to solve the problem
nationally revived Tory interest and the contested warden's election of
1837 was partly a Tory gesture against the government.

That election was preceded by a town meeting on church rates at which
the Church party were defeated.[90] The meeting led to much press comment, with the Tory *Journal* warning that the fall of the Church would
overturn the throne and urging church supporters 'to condense themselves into a wall of fire around the sacred institution which has long
proved the glory and safeguard of the land'.[91] In this atmosphere of
heightened emotion the St Mary's churchwarden's election of 1837 took
on the extra significance of a symbolic test case. The Tory nomination
was John Hicklin, proprietor and editor of the *Journal*, who had for
several months been championing the Anglican cause in his paper.
Dissenters viewed the election as a vote for or against church rates but
Hicklin argued otherwise. Given that his opponent John Rogers was a
radical dissenter the question was

> whether a Churchman shall be allowed to administer the internal
> government of the Church or whether a Dissenter is to be forced into
> a situation which compels him to do what savours very strongly of
> perjury – namely make a solemn declaration to fulfil the duties of an
> office which he never intends faithfully to discharge.[92]

Hicklin had certainly exposed a key issue. Political activists often wished
to capture an office in order to exercise the power which that office controlled. In the case of churchwardens, Dissenters wished to capture the
office in order to prevent the power being exercised at all.

It is clear that Tories expended a great deal of money and effort in the
churchwarden's poll of 1837 and Hicklin was elected by 1,864 to 1,497,
much to the surprise of Richard Sutton who could not believe that
radical Nottingham would elect a Tory warden.[93] Once more the minor
success assumed mammoth proportions and, as in Manchester and
Birmingham in 1840, local Tories in Nottingham welcomed the 1837
victory as a significant reversal of Whig-Radical fortunes. Indeed
Hicklin was confident that the political future of the town as a whole had
been determined by a churchwarden's election and he prophesied that
Nottingham would 'recover her ancient character for loyalty and patriotism'.[94] The more sober Whig view that 'Mr Hicklin is welcome to his
triumph but he may rely upon it he will *take nothing* by his motion'[95]
proved correct. Despite Hicklin's presence as churchwarden in the chair,

St Mary's vestry again refused a rate in July 1838, demonstrating the hollowness of the 1837 victory.[96]

There the matter remained for five years, revived only because St Mary's, the most beautiful church in Nottingham, was in urgent need of repair to prevent its partial collapse. Archdeacon George Wilkins insisted on the levy of a church rate for repairs, since the maintenance of the fabric of the church was the most legitimate of charges to be borne by the rates. Even for so necessary a task the Dissenters would not compromise and once more Sutton rallied his followers, 'we call upon every ratepayer who values liberty of conscience, or Christian principle to record his vote immediately against the iniquitous demand'.[97] The rate was easily defeated by 719 to 111 and Sutton rightly concluded: 'the result of the poll has rung the knell of church rates in Nottingham'.[98] The archdeacon appealed to the mayor as Tories bemoaned the collapse of St Mary's without a church rate, which elicited the predictable reply that Anglicans should, like Dissenters, voluntarily maintain their churches by subscriptions.[99] By the time St Mary's had become too dangerous to hold services there the *Journal* conceded that alternative ways of maintaining parish churches had to be found and that 'all provocations of animosity and bitter feeling should be removed'.[100] Nottingham churchmen in 1843 had arrived at that moderate Dissenting position expounded by Joseph Parkes in Birmingham in 1832. Of necessity St Mary's was saved by a voluntary subscription launched in 1844, to which Dissenters contributed.[101] Yet another parish had been pressed into enforced voluntaryism.

It was Nottingham's sectarian activity which induced an observer in nearby Leicester to call the town 'a focus for the most outrageous frenzy of radicalism in Church and State'.[102] Yet it has often been Leicester which has been cited as the centre of the most rabid anti-State Church activity. It was from Leicester that Edward Miall launched a lifetime's career of Nonconformist politics directed mainly at the church establishment and he confirmed that in the later 1830s the State Church 'was the town's burning issue'.[103] It was Leicester which produced a church rates martyr in the person of William Baines, imprisoned in 1840; and the local Dissenting journal claimed that the town had played a greater part than any other in the struggle against church rates, a view confirmed by Leicester's modern historian.[104] This exultation in Leicester's leading role as a centre of radical Dissent obscures the fact of persistent Tory Anglicanism in the town which a brief comparison indicates. Birmingham's last church rate was levied in 1831 and Leeds, Manchester and Nottingham terminated the levy of rates in the mid-1830s. Church rates in Leicester did not disappear until 1849. Clearly the Church was in a stronger position than the pre-eminence of Leicester in the Dissenting movement would suggest.

The main reason for this lay in the parochial structure of the town. Where in Leeds Dissenters could concentrate their efforts on one vestry which covered the whole Leeds township, in Leicester there were five parish churches, each with its own vestry organization. Though the overall dominance of Liberal Dissent might justify the epithet of 'Radical Leicester', Tory Anglicans could still maintain pockets of resistance in individual parishes where their strength was concentrated. This was exaggerated by local municipal developments which induced Liberals to use the vestries before municipal reform and the Tories afterwards. While the corrupt Leicester corporation was immune from assault the radical Dissenters fought the reform battle in the parishes, particularly in the vestry of St Margaret's. After 1835 the old Tory party was expelled from municipal office and parochial affairs were used as compensation for municipal defeat, especially in the Tory enclave in St Martin's. This was the parish which could levy church rates year after year and the ward from which most Tory councillors were returned. As always, parochial politics were determined by their relative position in the local political structure.

Initially the Dissenting assault upon church rates followed the familiar pattern. In the parish of St Nicholas rates were refused as early as 1833 and this was repeated in the years following. In 1836 after the rate was refused the vestry resolved that 'every religious denomination ought to support its own establishment'.[105] The two parishes of St Margaret and St Martin were much more difficult to capture. In St Margaret's the long reform struggle had led to the introduction by local Act of a select vestry whose composition was finally determined by the magistrates. While the bench was exclusively Tory the Church party continued to rule the parish, and this dominance was clearly threatened by the likely creation of Liberal magistrates following municipal reform. However, even in 1836 the Church party managed to carry its list and the rate was levied in an atmosphere of growing hostility.[106] It was in 1836 that Dissenters launched their own newspaper, the *Leicestershire Mercury*, and that year also witnessed the formation of a voluntary church society whose aims were clearly political.[107]

Albert Cockshaw, the proprietor and editor of the new paper, soon made it clear that Dissenters should not in conscience continue to pay church rates:

> If it be *wrong* to support a religious system which we believe to be founded upon unscriptural principles simply to avoid a considerable annoyance, all talk about doing so *involuntarily* is sheer nonsense . . . can we do right in supporting what we believe to be morally and religiously wrong?[108]

In this he was supported by the Baptist minister of Harvey Lane Chapel, Rev. J. P. Mursell, and they organized a refusal to pay rates at the end of 1836 by 22 parishioners including Miall himself. Church supporters were adamant that the defaulters must not be allowed 'to sneak out under the plea of *conscience sake*. Conscience indeed. Whoever heard of a dissenting parson's conscience. The rate must be enforced and we have no hesitation in saying that the present resistance to it is unconstitutional.'[109] So began the familiar Leicester story of distraint of household goods from protesters and the auction of these possessions to pay the defaulted rate. To moderate Liberals this taking of the pound of flesh exposed the Church's true nature which would hasten its demise; to radical Dissenters it was a further spur to action which stiffened the resolve to bring down the Church; to Tories it was a mere enforcement of the law.[110]

The short-term solution in St Margaret's was to get a Liberal select vestry and this was achieved in May 1837, which meant that there was no rate levied in the parish in that year.[111] There then began a two-year battle by the vicar and his churchwardens to enforce the levy of a rate by a writ of *mandamus*. In St Margaret's it was control over the vestry which really mattered politically and the possession of the office of church-warden was here not decisive. At the same time as defending their action in the courts the Liberal Dissenters, led by the radical printer J. F. Winks, were able to maintain political control over the select vestry in 1838.[112] The decisive vote came in 1838, for having failed in the legal battle to levy a rate the Church party's only hope was to regain control of the vestry. It was no walkover, for the Dissenting-Radical list was carried only by 920 to 812, a victory said to be based upon a union of 'Bastard churchmen, political dissenters of all grades, Roman Catholics and blaspheming infidels'.[113] It was sufficient to end the threat of church rates in this parish and to leave St Martin's as the last remaining Anglican stronghold.

One of the sources of Anglican strength here was the size of the parish, its ratepayers being less than a quarter of those of St Margaret's. For example, the vote for the church rate in St Martin's in 1836 was carried by 250 to 147[114] and the decisive poll in 1849 rejecting the rate also comprised just under 400 votes. These totals contrast with polls else-where which ran into thousands. This Tory island in the midst of a Liberal lake nurtured a virulent Tory Anglicanism which would accept no compromise in the enforcement of the legitimate rights of the church. Once St Margaret's had ceased to levy a church rate it was the par-ishioners of St Martin's who faced the distress warrants issued by the churchwardens and whose goods were publicly auctioned. At one such auction a near riot occurred in the market place which brought Tory censure on to the mayor and his fellow magistrates, whose failure to act had given 'encouragement to the ruffian conduct of the Leicester rabble'.[115]

Powerless to stop the levy of a rate, radical Dissenters relied on persistent refusal to pay. In Manchester and Bradford such action effectively ended church rates but in St Martin's Leicester Tory Anglicans were prepared to fight non-payment through the courts if necessary. This was not the doing of the vicar, who was a moderate Whig and wished for a compromise, but of his churchwardens, who represented the old Tory party which had lost so much of late and who were determined to exercise fully the powers they still retained. A draper, William Baines, a member of Miall's congregation, decided to take on the church in St Martin's. He refused to pay church rates or to recognize the ecclesiastical courts to which he was summoned and lost his case finally at Queen's Bench in June 1840, a victory signalled by the ringing of the bells of St Martin.[116]

The imprisonment of William Baines in November 1840 exposed the latent divisions within Leicester Liberalism. Many of the prominent middle-class leaders took the line of Buttrey in Leeds or J. E. Taylor in Manchester or Salt in Birmingham, that church rates as legal imposts had to be paid until Dissenting pressure upon Parliament secured their removal. John Biggs, the Unitarian leader of the local Liberals, certainly held this view and told a protest meeting on behalf of Baines, 'I do not concur in the course which has been adopted.'[117] This general approach found a mouthpiece in the Liberal *Chronicle*, edited by Thomas Thompson, who was severely criticized by the independent minister George Legge for his moderation and mocked as 'the Goliath of whiggery, the Gorgon Terror of the Tories, the Scorpion lash of the Chartists'.[118]

Thompson would not support Legge, Miall, Mursell and the *Mercury* in the frontal assault upon church rates personified by Baines. Liberals of all shades could unite to protest strongly against his imprisonment and the town council repeated its action of 1836 and petitioned Parliament against church rates and ecclesiastical courts.[119] The fiercest denunciation came from the radical Dissenters of the Miall school, one of whom composed a pamphlet of biblical censure which denounced

> a system which has for ages scorched and withered the nation – a system beneath the crushing weight of which the land has groaned, and men died and widows wept, and orphans lifted up their piteous cries – a system of oppression and murder – a system that has robbed heaven and peopled hell, stript families and crowded prisons – a system which never fails to pollute and injure its votaries.[120]

Baines became a national hero and there were meetings on his behalf all over the country. His martyrdom stimulated the national dissenting movement against the state church and played a big part in launching Miall on his national political career. While Baines was still in prison Miall left Leicester to launch *The Nonconformist* as the mouthpiece of the evangelical Dissenters.

The anonymous payment of William Baines's fine led to his release in May 1841 and ironically marked the end of the really active local struggle against church rates. This was partly because the Baines case itself indicated the need to attack the whole church establishment, a change of tactic confirmed by Miall's departure, and this inevitably reduced church rates to a minor position.[121] Church rates were also swamped by the issues of the moment which dominated Leicester in the 1840s, the suffrage, the Corn Laws and local improvement. Already in 1842 the *Mercury* was bemoaning the fact that there had been no real battle against church rates since the release of Baines.[122] This touched the paper closely, for its new editor H. A. Collier, secretary of the Complete Suffrage Association, had himself lost chairs, a table and an oakstand when he was distrained upon for non-payment.[123] All through the 1840s church rates were levied in St Martin's parish, a minor practical irritant to Dissenters but a major theoretical affront to the conscience. Baines and J. F. Winks continued with non-payment until in 1849 a decisive vote was carried by Dissenters at the vestry meeting and a rate was refused by 203 to 191.[124] With this victory in St Martin's, Leicester belatedly defeated church rates.

This review of the church question in cities of differing economic, social and parochial structure has indicated the importance of parochial affairs in urban areas. The office of churchwarden and its associated powers attracted the interest of urban political activists, some of whom began their political careers as wardens or as prime movers in vestry meetings. It was noticeable how many gentlemen of the press became parochial leaders: Baines, father and son, and Perring in Leeds, J. E. Taylor and Prentice in Manchester, R. K. Douglas in Birmingham, Bennett and Hicklin in Nottingham, Cockshaw in Leicester. The Church was at the heart of the polemical debate and activity in the vestry was a natural extension of the editorial battle of words. Since real issues of public concern were involved, parochial and editorial direction could reinforce each other to establish a claim to local political leadership. When Baines stood for Parliament Leeds citizens were urged to 'discharge that debt of gratitude you owe him . . . for having effected so many important economical reforms in the parochial affairs of our town'.[125]

Parochial achievement could thus lead to parliamentary rewards for they were but parts of a political whole. The personnel active in vestries were the same as those active in municipal, parliamentary and agitational politics. When the younger Baines protested at the leak from a private gathering on the burial question in Leeds he confirmed that the meeting comprised 'the gentlemen who usually meet at the private arrangements of the Liberal Party for Parliamentary, Municipal, Registration and Church Rate contests'.[126] In Birmingham the parochial leaders, Salt, Hadley, Pare, Douglas, G. F. and P. H. Muntz, were all prominent Political Union radicals whose names are familiar in the story of parliamentary reform.

The zeal with which such men entered the parochial fray was largely determined by two variables, the relative position of the churchwarden in the local political structure at a given moment, and the question of church rates. Greater interest was naturally shown in the office when other political avenues were closed and its potential power was considerably reduced once church rates had been in practice abolished. Thus the significance of the office of churchwarden may be precisely defined in time. It was during the second quarter of the nineteenth century that parochial affairs concerned with the status of the Anglican church were a significant component in the urban political structure. And in those years the office of churchwarden might become political because its status or power was highly regarded; because it was drawn into an all-embracing struggle for local control; or because it was deliberately utilized as a weapon in the conflict between Dissent and the Established Church.

3
The Poor Law

'*Political party feeling prevails to a mischievous extent at Leeds, the parties are nearly balanced and it is scarcely possible to take any step in Leeds Township without exciting strong party feeling.*' Charles Mott, Assistant Poor Law Commissioner, 24 August 1841

1

The Poor Law, contrary to a commonly held view, was both intrinsically political in itself and an important element in the urban political structure. Poor Law administration has normally been the province of social historians whose main interests tend to be methods of relief and social attitudes and who therefore ignore any political aspects. Much has recently been written on the nineteenth-century Poor Law but little light has been cast upon Poor Law politics. Similarly, recent interest in urban politics has steered clear of the Poor Law because of concentration upon elections, and so the Poor Law has been relegated to a sort of sub-political region. However, a great deal of local power was exercised within the Poor Law and the mode, aims and consequences of such execution of power was often controversial. The Poor Law provided a vehicle for local party combat and a contentious area of policy where rival interests and aspirations could conflict. Even the limited horizons of social administration were often politically determined, and this chapter will seek to reveal the ways in which the Poor Law was politicized.

Leeds, like many other large towns, had evolved a system of Poor Law administration in which the churchwardens were of central importance, a factor which heightened political interest in that office. The Leeds workhouse board comprised overseers appointed by the magistrates, and trustees and churchwardens elected by the vestry, providing a neat balance which 'contained the intelligence and philanthropy of men of all parties in the service of the town'.[1] In the workhouse board the churchwardens held the balance of power, so that when the Leeds Liberals captured the office in the late 1820s they also inherited control over the Poor Law. The concerted Tory attempt to regain power over the church-wardens (see above, p. 32) was as much as anything a means of resolving the political deadlock on the workhouse board, well described by Robert Baker who wrote that its members:

> have been squabbling for a long time amongst each other for prece-dence and place. The Boardroom has long been a sort of arena for party politics on a small scale . . . of late time politics have run high with us, the Trustees and Churchwardens chosen by the people in Vestry have been a little opposed to the overseers chosen by the magistrates and to such a pitch has this feeling been carried that public poor law business has been very much neglected and very bad feeling has existed.[2]

Having failed politically to regain control of the Poor Law, the Tories resorted to law in 1835 to prove that the tripartite composition of the workhouse board had no legal foundation, that 'Trustees sat on the Workhouse Board by courtesy, the Churchwardens by *usurpation*'.[3] The sole authority of the overseers was confirmed by counsel's opinion which indicated, in the words of the longest serving member of the board, that it possessed 'no authority in law to administer the Poor Laws . . . although their predecessors in office have for more than a hundred years performed all the acts necessary for the purpose'.[4] Tory exultation in exercising sole power via the overseers was short-lived, for municipal reform created a Liberal bench of magistrates who in 1836 appointed a majority of Liberal overseers. The Tories were further discomfited in 1837 when their partisan George Evers was dismissed as treasurer of the workhouse board and replaced by Christopher Heaps, himself a Liberal overseer, at double the salary.[5] The so-called 'Heaps job', the reverberations of which were to be heard for many years, and the appointment of the Anti-Corn Law League lecturer George Greig as registrar, indicated a political spoils system in operation.

The sole rule of the overseers, which even Liberals felt to be unsatis-factory, might have been ended by the introduction of the new Poor Law into Leeds which the Poor Law Commission in fact ordered. This put to the test the frequently expressed distaste for political battles in the parochial arena. Despite pious pronouncements about the irrelevance of politics in parochial questions, both parties, in the heated political atmos-phere of the 1830s, injected politics into the 1837 guardians' elections. That the Poor Law could not be isolated from its urban political context was demonstrated in Robert Perring's defence of a Tory party list: 'It is at all times desirable that party politics should be excluded from matters connected with parochial affairs but the grasping spirit of our political opponents has turned the election of every petty parish officer into a question of party.'[6] As if as an echo, the Tory list produced a Liberal list and Baines senior urged expedition upon the party agent 'so that we may at all costs have a liberal Guardianship . . . the Tories are working hard . . . I trust that our friends will not be less zealous nor less early in their movements'.[7] Little wonder that the dejected Assistant Commissioner reported that the election in Leeds 'has been made entirely a party question . . . and all the excitement and mutual jealousies of parties have been entertained here in a very strong degree'.[8]

Neither party could claim victory because, in a farcically inefficient election, defective election machinery made a result impossible and the attempt to form a union was abandoned. The attempt was renewed in 1844 as a means of forcing Leeds to build a new workhouse. Both decisions to form a union were conditioned by the refusal of vestry authority for the building of a new workhouse and the belief that the formation of a board of guardians would secure a new workhouse by bypassing the vestry.[9] The Leeds union was formed in December 1844 and the first election was fought mainly on the workhouse question, with the Tories implacably opposed to it. The Poor Law Commission could threaten, cajole and shame the new guardians but they would not build a new workhouse, though they would build an industrial school. The position was tersely put by the new clerk: 'the opinion of the Ratepayers on the subject was clearly shown by the overwhelming majorities by which the first members of the Board were returned, the question of a new workhouse or not being the principal point mooted at the first election.'[10]

In that election the Liberals had not gained one seat and Tories found that they could compensate for lack of success in the municipal field by controlling the mid-Victorian Poor Law in Leeds. During the quarter-century of the union's existence (until it was enlarged in 1869) there were only three years (1853, 1854 and 1859) when the Liberals had a majority. The political composition of the Leeds board of guardians has been analysed in tabular form, together with an analysis of how many of the eight wards were contested at each election (see overleaf).

The sudden reversal of fortunes in 1853 requires some explanation. Initial Tory control was made overtly political by the dismissal of the notorious Heaps together with two relieving officers and two registrars and their replacement by Tories, notably John Beckwith, assistant editor of the Tory *Leeds Intelligencer*, as clerk to replace Heaps. Some less important part-time posts and contracts were also politically distributed. The accusation was made that Beckwith and his colleagues had a vested interest in the maintenance of Tory control and that their manipulated election results 'renders the Board self elected'.[11] There was great scope

Table 2. Political composition of Leeds board of guardians, 1844–68

		Tory	Liberal	Contested wards
Dec.	1844	18*	0	8
April	1845	18*	0	1
	1846	16†	2	5
	1847	16	2	1
	1848	14	4	7
	1849	16	2	0
	1850	16	2	1
	1851	14	4	4
	1852	13	5‡	2
	1853	0	18	8
	1854	7	11	7
	1855	14	4	3
	1856	14	4	6
	1857	11	7	6
	1858	10	8	8
	1859	6	12	8
	1860	9	9	8
	1861	13	5	6
	1862	12	6	5
	1863	12	6	1
	1864	12	6	3
	1865	13	5	3
	1866	13	5	1
	1867	13	5	2
	1868	14	6	1

* Includes three Chartists.   † Includes one Chartist.
‡ Final result after Poor Law enquiry.

for abuse in an electoral system where the distributors of voting papers
'will always in contested elections be chosen if possible for their adhesion
to the party views of the clerk especially when his own happen to be the
reflex of those of the Board in possession, willing and perhaps anxious to
retain office.'[12] Liberal attacks, which concentrated upon the method of
election,* were hardly disinterested for in Leeds the Poor Law was a
Tory island in a Liberal lake or as one observer aptly put it, 'they do not
like the Clerk. Of course they don't, I believe his is almost the only Tory
appointment in the borough.'[13]

So vehement were Liberal claims about corrupt election results that
the Poor Law Board instituted an enquiry into the 1852 election. H. B.

* The method of election was unique to the Poor Law and involved delivering
voting papers to each house and collecting them when they were filled up. It
was a sort of secret ballot, but open to abuse.

Farnall, the local Poor Law inspector, was shocked by what he discovered, 'I have seen a great many electioneering proceedings but I never saw anything as gross as this.' Voting papers had been partially distributed; they had been altered; they had been destroyed; they had been filled up by Tory party agents.[14] The enquiry revealed to a shocked Leeds public that the guardians had not been 'the representatives of the ratepayers, they are in reality the representatives of a large . . . unexampled mass of frauds forgeries tricks and knaveries.'[15] In the circumstances it was hardly surprising that the Tory guardians were unseated in the disputed ward and more surprising that Beckwith escaped with no more than a censure for his negligence. The political result of the enquiry lay in the protracted 1853 election which led to the imprisonment of two Tory agents and produced a completely Liberal board of guardians.

Having proved their point the Liberals, securely in control of the town council, virtually resigned control back to the Tories after only a two-year reign when they nominated guardians for only half the wards in 1855. Nevertheless in the decade following the 1852 enquiry there was a high degree of political interest, particularly on the workhouse question. Indeed in the three consecutive elections from 1858 to 1860 all eight wards were contested in fierce party political battles and when the last ended in a tie Baines commented,

> The Board has been made political and the gentlemen who have now obtained seats there have done so as the representative of their respective parties. . . . It is not a question of politics or of no politics but simply whether the Conservatives or the Liberals are to have the power of giving the casting vote on all questions of public policy.[16]

Poor Law policy was thus regarded as essentially a political matter and it was only in the later 1860s that there was a marked drop in political involvement and that for the first time in over 30 years political party labels were not used in Poor Law elections.

The enlargement of the union coincided with the formalizing of ward political activity through more efficient party organization. Increased political interest led to more doubtful electioneering and so in 1870 a second Poor Law enquiry was held into electoral malpractices. The 1870 enquiry established the continuity in Leeds Poor Law politics, for the tricks of 1852 were still being practised. Parties were now better organized to cope with the increased electorate and the multiplicity of party agents who were active were merely the response of 'businessmen in conducting the election in a business way'.[17] The abuse as usual centred on the method of election with its use of distributors and collectors, and the clerk Henry Lampen, himself a political appointee on Beckwith's death in 1856, asked pointedly 'where am I as returning officer to get 100

men altogether free from political bias?'[18] Some understandably felt that
to appoint members of the Conservative ward committee as collectors
was going too far, especially when one of them was the son-in-law of the
candidate.

As in 1852, voting papers were not delivered to every house, they had
been filled up by the collectors, and they had been altered. When the
candidate's son was pressed very hard on whether he had filled up blank
papers the record revealingly reported 'the witness fainted'.[19] Perhaps
the most significant comment came from one of the paid electoral clerks
who was a supporter of Woodhead, the Tory candidate in the West ward.
He was asked,

> How came it that you, a distributor and collector, considered your-
> self one of Mr Woodhead's party? . . . I consider I was justified by the
> manner in which he (the liberal collector) was annoying voters saying
> 'vote for these three men' and in self defence I said 'vote for the other
> three'.[20]

The Poor Law could not be insulated from the political system of Leeds
and the resort to politics in self-defence was characteristic of the overall
political structure of the town in the Victorian years. The electoral abuse
revealed in 1852 and 1870 was a sign that political activists considered
the Poor Law a political spoil worth fighting for.*

The unseating of Woodhead on the issue of fabricating votes was a
temporary Liberal victory, reversed at the 1871 election when the
Liberals captured only 9 of the 31 seats on the enlarged board. However,
the Liberal caucus steadily increased its share of the board of guardians
in the early 1870s and in 1874 secured a prestigious conquest. William
Middleton, a retired pawnbroker, who had been a guardian for 20 years
and chairman of the board for 15, was defeated in North East ward. The
participation of organized political bodies was now overt and the Liberals
organized a horse-trading deal with the Conservatives. Only two years
before a guardian had been censured for introducing a political matter
and defended himself by saying 'politics were mentioned outside in
reference to the Board though he agreed very improperly'.[21] Now in 1874
a Conservative leader remarked: 'he did not blame the Liberal Association or the Liberal Party, they were quite right in using electioneering
tactics to get one of their party appointed vice-chairman.'[22] The Liberals
were by then on a rising tide and they captured 12 seats in 1874, 14 in
1875 and gained power with 21 in 1876, retaining their majority for the
rest of the decade. By the mid-1870s the caucus was firmly planted in
Poor Law affairs: as one activist put it, 'they did meet and would

* There were similar enquiries into electoral malpractice in Lancashire:
Clitheroe 1847, Bolton 1847 and 1861, Blackburn 1856, Haslingden 1871.

continue to meet and they would continue to be a power on the board'.[23]
The organization was new but the politicizing of the Poor Law was not.
This was a continuous feature of the Poor Law in Leeds throughout the
nineteenth century.

In Lancashire's major centres of population, Liverpool and the
Manchester/Salford conurbation, as in Leeds, many of the improvements
suggested in 1834 had been introduced before the implementation of the
new Poor Law. Liverpool's select vestry, dating from 1821, had appointed
eight salaried overseers and was already in the 1820s attempting to
distinguish between the deserving and undeserving poor. Expenditure in
poor relief was reduced despite population growth by screening all
applicants.[24] Economical administration and professional expertise
were the main planks in the Liverpool case to be excluded from the new
Poor Law, which was partially achieved by the revival of the select
vestry in 1842, only 18 months after the Liverpool union was formed.

Manchester, too, had professional relieving officers to enquire into the
bona fides of claimants, and the churchwardens and overseers, elected by
the vestry and confirmed by the magistrates, received special praise in
the Poor Law Report.[25] In particular the attitudes displayed by the
parochial administrators were those of the new Poor Law and in response
to a request for special relief in the midst of trade depression the churchwardens commented:

> Whilst this Board deeply sympathises with the suffering poor of this
> township they can never sanction the practice of indiscriminate relief
> and . . . they must . . . use their strictest endeavours to detect imposi-
> tion . . . it would be holding out a dangerous precedent to suppose that
> relief should be generally afforded from the parish fund because
> operatives may be reduced for a short period to the necessity of
> working only half time or may be temporarily unemployed.[26]

This gives some substance to the claim that the régime of the Poor Law
Commission was superfluous in Manchester and some point to the
Guardian's comment on the formation of the Manchester Union that 'the
change in Manchester will be extremely unimportant . . . the principal
difference consists in the mode of appointment of the administering
parties'.[27] Indeed the first board of guardians of 1841 found that the new
Poor Law 'in many particulars . . . much resembles the system heretofore
adopted in this town'.[28]

Political controversy was avoided in Manchester by the return of a
list agreed between the contending incorporation parties but in neighbouring Salford politics was a determining factor in Poor Law administration from the early 1830s through to the late 1840s. Some controversy
existed because of the magistrates' practice of ordering relief even if the

overseers had refused it, and in 1830 one of the parochial officials anticipated 1834 by suggesting that overseers should refuse relief to the
undeserving and that the workhouse test should be implemented.[29] It
was, however, overall political control and not the details of administration which came to be disputed in the early 1830s. The select vestry was
a central part of Salford's political and administrative structure.

The select vestry under Sturges Bourne's Act had survived only five
years from 1821 and was then allowed to lapse until 1832. The revival of
interest had much to do with the passing of the Reform Act and the
creation of one parliamentary seat for Salford. The political organization
necessary for the return of the Whig-Radical Joseph Brotherton, himself
a prominent parochial politician in the 1820s, was utilized in parochial
affairs after the victory had been achieved. The success in defeating a
Sturges Bourne poll on the question of public bellringing in Salford (see
above, p. 30) was but a parochial echo of the 1832 election, for the battle
lines were the same in both contests and it was reported that 'since the
termination of the election new vigour has infused itself into the Ley-
payers association and its importance has been greatly enhanced'.[30]

The most obvious manifestation of this 'new vigour' was the election
in 1833 of a Whig-Radical select vestry whose immediate achievement
was to reduce poor rates from 5s. in 1832 to 1s. in 1834. As Archibald
Prentice explained, 'overseers and a Select Vestry were chosen from . . .
the radical party – and truly the savings which they have effected entitle
them to that honourable appellation.'[31] J. B. Smith, one of Brotherton's most important supporters in 1832, used the election of a select
vestry in 1834 as a platform for the anti-corn law cause in which he was
later to achieve national fame.[32] Smith was an overseer, as was William
Lockett, a silk merchant, who had also aided Brotherton's election
campaign. Lockett was a prime example of the parochial politician
launching a successful career in urban life from a vestry apprenticeship.
First emerging as an overseer in the early 1830s, he became in the early
Victorian years Salford's most prominent political leader, dominating the
town's Poor Law, police commissioners and, later, municipal affairs. In
the mid-1840s he was both Salford's first mayor and for seven years
chairman of the board of guardians, thus straddling the town's two most
prominent governmental institutions.[33]

Lockett was the defender of the Whig-Radical régime at vestry meetings in the 1830s. In 1834 Anglican leaders had protested at the curtail-
ment of the chaplain's fee for preaching at the workhouse, and the
voluntary provision of unpaid Dissenting preachers had only fanned the
flames. In 1835 the Tories, in common with their compatriots in Leeds,
mounted a serious challenge to regain their former administrative empire.
In the spring of 1835 the Salford Operative Conservative Association had

been formed 'to regain the management of parochial and town affairs' at a time when, in the words of their secretary, 'every office in the town from the boroughreeve down to the collectors was filled with persons of (mis-called) liberal opinions'.[34] The participation of this new force gave added weight to the Tory attack at the 1835 Easter vestry, led by Lot Gardiner, who had in 1832 master-minded the campaign of William Garnett, the Tory opponent of Brotherton in that election.[35] The echoes of the 1832 election rang through Salford's Poor Law affairs in the 1830s with Brotherton's supporters running the revived select vestry and Garnett and his supporters leading a Tory counter-attack especially against the new Poor Law.

Gardiner's attack was aimed mainly at the parochial accounts and one of the radical vestrymen complained that a Tory clique was trying 'to disturb the harmony of the proceedings and the peace of the whole borough by their tory tricks . . . he believed some tories to be honest but still he would remind the leypayers not to be diverted from their points by any tory tricks whatever to regain power.'[36] The last phrase is significant: what was at stake in a Salford Poor Law contest was real local power, the exercise of which was deemed important by the contestants. For the moment the Liberal list was carried but it was recognized that this was only to be the first of many Tory strategic manoeuvres. In 1836 the Tories again used the Operative Conservative Society in the vestry but failed to get an adjournment to the Town Hall, which would have been advantageous to them as all non-electors had been excluded from the original meeting. The Liberals led by J. W. Harvey were again triumphant and their list included Lockett as overseer and Elkanah Armitage as a vestryman.[37] All three thus active in 1836 in parochial Poor Law affairs – Harvey, Lockett, and Armitage – came to be leading politicians in the Manchester and Salford area in later years.

By 1837 the possible introduction of the new Poor Law had become a matter of acute controversy and a bitter town meeting was held in January addressed by Oastler.[38] Lockett had to defend the select vestry against the charge of favouring the imposition of the new Poor Law in Salford. The well known anti-Poor Law and Chartist leader R. J. Richardson appeared at the Easter vestry meeting to urge the infusion of some new anti-Poor Law blood into the select vestry whose composition had been unchanged for several years.[39] Despite Richardson's oratory the Liberal list was carried and the anti-Poor Law feeling thus expressed no doubt persuaded Lockett and his friends against co-operation with the new régime of Somerset House. Although the Poor Law Commission did issue an order for the formation of the Salford Union in March 1837 it was soon rescinded owing to the refusal of the select vestry to organize districts for the new system. The anti-Poor

Law feeling generated at the vestry level exploded during the very bitter Salford parliamentary election of 1837. William Garnett, the Tory candidate, gave strong support to the attempt to prohibit the introduction of the new Poor Law in Salford. Conservatives warned that if the vestry chose overseers from their party they would pay the fine rather than serve as agents of the new system and Garnett encouraged such obstruction:

> Suppose the poor-rates were reduced lower than they are now – if there be merit in this why should we pay anything at all? But is this the spirit of Englishmen? Is this the conduct of Englishmen to their poorer fellow subjects? No I think not! An attempt has been made to resist the introduction of the law into Salford and I sincerely hope and trust that it will be successful.[40]

Indeed his Operative supporters made it clear that the Poor Law was the central issue in the election by urging Salford electors, 'if you value the rights of the poor – if you value the spirit of the 43rd of Elizabeth . . . vote for Garnett'.[41]

The anti-Poor Law frenzy was most widespread among non-electors and so the 1837 election went against the Tory-Radical alliance. Garnett's supporters did not have long to wait, however, and in 1838 they gained a spectacular coup by turning out of the select vestry the Liberal clique which had administered Salford's Poor Law for the previous five years. R. J. Richardson was again prominent at the vestry and he made it clear that he was putting his full radical strength behind the Tory attack. In Manchester the Tory-radical alliance fought the Charter: in Salford it fought the new Poor Law. Both sides blamed the other for politicizing parochial affairs and one of the Liberal leaders announced that 'as the meeting had been made a political one he would propose the reform list', while Richardson attributed the introduction of politics to the fact that 'a number of gentlemen had come down from the Reform Association to the Select Vestry and overruled the overseers'.[42] Liberals were successful at the meeting but for the first time for many years the Tories demanded a Sturges Bourne poll, amid Liberal charges of illegality. A Tory victory in 1838 with a majority of well over 100 was explained as due to 'the extraordinary activity of the tories who canvassed as for an election, carried up their voters in coaches and . . . paid the rates of a very considerable number of the poorer voters'.[43] The exercise of real local power was at stake and this explains Tory enthusiasm for parochial administration.

The achievement of control over the Poor Law had an unfortunate consequence for the Tory-radical alliance, since they had not captured the office of overseer which was not subject to a poll. The Liberal nominations had been accepted at the vestry and confirmed by the bench. A petty and squalid dispute then arose between a Tory-radical select vestry and a Liberal board of overseers which quickly brought Poor Law administration into an *impasse*. The vestry censured the overseers for making returns to the Poor Law Commission and rescinded authority for the overseers to act as treasurers to the vestry, while the overseers advertised in the press that they would honour only debts which they alone had authorized.[44] The imposition of the new Poor Law thus emerged as a means of resolving a political conflict which had undermined and strangled administration. The bizarre conclusion was that the 1838 select vestry was elected to oppose the application of the new Poor Law to Salford yet within three months presided over its introduction. Well might the *Guardian* draw attention to the 'comical gambols of the Salford "select".'[45] Once in power the Tories were reluctant to relinquish it and 'were determined . . . to make the election of guardians in Salford a political matter', refusing to compromise on a shared list of nominations.[46] In the event the Tory list was returned unopposed and within a matter of days Tory hostility to the new Poor Law mellowed. Possession of the power under the new Poor Law exposed the system in a new light for Tory eyes and Tories were soon boasting that the new Poor Law as administered by Tory guardians would be 'far less evil than the whig tyranny to which the township has been so long subjected'.[47]

One of the first actions of the new board of guardians in October 1838 was to dismiss one of the assistant overseers 'on the grounds of his being a partizan of the Reformers or Whigs' and appoint in his place one of their own men, Francis Wrigley.[48] Wrigley was a loyal party worker. He had been employed by the Tories in the 1837 election, retained by them to conduct a scrutiny of the result, and had been secretary for a Tory banquet in 1838, soon after which he had received his appointment by way of political reward. The potential controversy embodied in this appointment was indicated by the vestry's appointment of their own assistant overseer who was confirmed in office by the magistrates but not of course by the Poor Law Commission. Salford's parish funds were thus bearing the cost of two salaries.

What was later described by the local assistant commissioner as 'a most respectable board . . . a pattern to the district'[49] found itself subjected to a severe political challenge in 1840 after a mere two-year régime. The vestry called to elect overseers was highly charged, for as one of the participants said they were 'determined to make it a political question'. Rival Tory and Whig lists were proposed, with Lockett still subject to radical attack for 'adopting' the new Poor Law in Salford. R. J. Richardson was trying to rekindle past anti-Poor Law enthusiasm in reviewing 'the relative value of the whig and tory lists' and could not prevent the Operative Conservative list from being defeated.[50] The same political thrust also carried the offices of highway surveyor and Poor Law guardian into the Liberal camp, as these two elections also registered Liberal victories.

The new political masters of Salford's Poor Law now sought to avenge their ally who had been dismissed in 1838 by replacing the Tory nominee Wrigley. The prime mover in this was Smith P. Robinson, a keen Liberal activist, who made no bones about his political prejudices and indeed argued that the fact that members of the Poor Law Commission were of similar political persuasion to himself justified Wrigley's dismissal.[51] Wrigley's rueful exposition of the political motivation behind the attack can be well understood:

> I am sure it will not be overlooked that these charges are preferred by Mr. Robinson, – a most active and enthusiastic partisan – transmitted by him to Overseers who employed the Secretary of the Reform Association in arranging the lists of claims and objections to the franchise; – forwarded by them to the Board of Guardians; approved there by a majority every member of which was a Gentleman professing Liberal politics, . . . and that they were so approved upon the evidence of persons two of whom are in the pay of the Reform Association . . . it is obvious that the whole of these proceedings have been got up by the Reform Association.[52]

Wrigley certainly found himself upon a political see-saw, his elevation accompanying the Tory victory in 1838 and his demotion the result of the Tory defeat in 1840.

According to Charles Mott, the assistant commissioner, Wrigley had been 'a very good assistant overseer and his worst enemies cannot bring a charge against his conduct in the management of his official duties'.[53] It was, however, the using of his official power for political purposes that was the charge against him and William Lockett headed a committee of enquiry which found him guilty in February 1841. Despite Mott's advice that Wrigley should be merely censured the Poor Law Commission approved the dismissal on the grounds that Wrigley had 'perverted his office to political purposes'.[54] Wrigley's powerful friends now interceded on his behalf when Holland Hoole, the chairman of the late Tory board of guardians, and J. P. Bunting, a Conservative solicitor, visited the Poor Law Commission to plead Wrigley's case. As a result he was given a stay of execution pending a local enquiry by Charles Mott. A rather depressed Mott reported that the Poor Law Commission could not really win because any decision would give political satisfaction to only one side and he regretted how much Poor Law administration in Salford had been sacrificed to political partisanship. In the event a deal was agreed by which Wrigley resigned in return for the payment of full salary up to the date of the Poor Law Commission's final decision on the matter in June 1841.[55]

The Wrigley case confirmed the politicizing of Salford's Poor Law administration and a further dispute arose in the early 1840s which indicates a high degree of political involvement. A request that the appointment of rate collectors should be in the hands of overseers rather than guardians sounded an innocent enough administrative convenience. Mott however saw through this administrative device and concluded that it was part of the whole system by which 'the whole proceedings are managed with reference to political arrangements'.[56] It was perhaps significant that Mott's successor, less familiar with the devious doings in Salford, merely reported on 'the dislike of the Overseers to the mode in which the collectors hold their appointments'.[57]

Mott owed his perception to his knowledge of the history of Poor Law political disputes in Salford, but he was also fortunate in being given inside information by the secretary to the Salford guardians, John Hope. Hope was appointed by the first board and may have nursed a political grudge against his new masters or he may have felt that his loyalty to the Poor Law and its Commission outweighed his loyalty to his employers. For whatever reason it is clear that Hope 'shopped' the Salford guardians and opened Poor Law eyes to the political realities of Salford Poor Law administration. Hope explained that the matter of the rate collectors was concerned with insulating political activities within the Poor Law from Poor Law Commission supervision:

> If the true reason was known for wishing to have the collectors the immediate servants of the Overseers, I fear it would expose some abuse of the official position of those Gentlemen, and that of a Political Nature, they cannot, whilst they are under the protection of the P. L. Commissioners, use them for their own special purposes as they could wish. . . . A number of the Guardians and Overseers are much chafed at the interference of the Commissioners and our Chairman [Lockett] does not hesitate to say in the Board that he will have no communication with the Commissioners that he can possibly avoid.[58]

Lockett and his friends would have been upset to know that their clerk was revealing to Poor Law officials the ways in which the local Liberal party used their Poor Law powers to gain political advantage in various forms of local election (see below, p. 88). This revelation was much more significant than the local gossip that Lockett had his garden tended by paupers, a fact perhaps also leaked by Hope. Presumably Hope's embarrassing revelations were not laid at his door, for he survived in office until his death in 1844. Predictably, his successor was a political appointee, Philip Yandall, an accountant. Yandall had been for several years the secretary of the Salford Reform Association and as such had acted for the Liberals in the revision counts. He had in fact been a key witness in the enquiries regarding Wrigley's alleged improprieties. Lockett signed the contract of appointment and Yandall was a partisan from the Lockett stable. In confirming Yandall's appointment the Poor Law Commission also tied up the final loose ends in the Wrigley affair by confirming the appointment, six years after his vestry nomination, of John Watkin as assistant overseer.[59] The salaries of both offices, £150 *per annum*, were the same, an indication that the chief executive officers of the guardians and the overseers were deemed of equal importance, and by the mid-1840s both were firmly in Liberal hands.

Political controversy gradually subsided in Salford's Poor Law administration in the later 1840s but some dark shadows could still be cast. It was revealed for instance that one of the guardians was rated below £20 and therefore ineligible to sit and that Lockett and Yandall had offered to alter the rate books to put it right, an offer withdrawn when the offending guardian ceased to toe the Lockett line.[60] Yandall blotted the Lockett copybook by defalcating Poor Law accounts for which he was suspended and later dismissed.[61] The deficiency of £330 was first identified by Charles Mott, who was in 1847 the district auditor, and Yandall's exposure rather weakens Dr Midwinter's claim that the district audit system was largely ineffective.[62] Yandall's dismissal may have undermined Lockett, with whom he was closely identified politically, and Lockett withdrew from Poor Law affairs at the next election in 1848. Thereafter political interest in the Poor Law declined in Salford.

The minor offices of assistant overseer and poor rate collector became politically controversial in Salford and the same was true in Gateshead, though for different reasons. In Salford these offices were adjuncts of a ruling Liberal oligarchy where in Gateshead they became the means of opposing such a ruling clique. Gateshead's political affairs in the early Victorian years were very much under the direction of William Henry Brockett, a merchant and agent, who has been described as a sort of city 'boss'.[63] Brockett was for Gateshead what Lockett was for Salford and through his hands ran the channels of local petty patronage. Parliamentary, municipal, and parochial elections were organized by him and his associates, and he well merits his recent description of 'one of the original Disraelian tadpoles'.[64] Brockett never undervalued the local importance of the office of guardian and indeed fought very hard to establish his claim to sit as a guardian when in 1838 it was revealed that he was rated below the legal qualification. Though he was out of Poor Law office between 1843 and 1847, and though his control over council business may not have been as firm as sometimes suggested, Brockett still exerted the dominant influence over Gateshead's Liberal oligarchy.[65]

His main opponents were the old 'borough-holders' who had dominated the pre-incorporation years and had exercised power in the administrative areas now controlled by the Brockett empire. In 1849 an opportunity arose for a challenge to this empire within the field of parochial Poor Law administration. The dispute was not uncommon for the period and centred on the question of whether the appointment of the offices of assistant overseer and poor rate collector (two offices formerly performed by one man) lay with the guardians or with the ratepayers in vestry. The borough-holders, hoping to sustain their traditional parochial authority, argued that this was a vestry appointment: Brockett, preferring power to remain in a small body which he could control, argued that the guardians as the legal Poor Law authority should make the appointment. There was in fact a four days' poll of excitement as intense as that for a parliamentary election for these minor parochial appointments. The result was that two sets of rate collectors were appointed and ratepayers of the 'parish' party paid rates to the collector appointed by the vestry while ratepayers of the 'guardians' party paid rates to his rival.[66]

There was more here than a mere administrative duplication (which was not to be finally resolved until 1856), for this parochial Poor Law dispute enveloped the whole political structure of Gateshead in the mid-century. Predictably the next guardians' election, that of 1850, was fought on this issue. The party political lines were not those of Liberal versus Tory but those of parish party versus guardians' party. Upon a basic political conflict between superseded borough influence and a Brockett-managed political empire were built other political rivalries which cut across normal party divisions. Dr Nossiter has identified a radical shopkeeper resentment against Brockett's manipulation which emerged strongly in the 1852 election,[67] and the 1850 guardians' election, equally a challenge to Brockett, may have witnessed the first expression of this resentment. In any event Brockett himself was defeated, as were nine out of the ten sitting guardians in what might almost be termed a ratepayers' backlash. The elder Joseph Cowen was forced to stand down after 12 years as chairman of the guardians.[68]

Superficially the so-called 'clean sweep' election of 1850 was concerned with minor Poor Law appointments, but in essence the dispute involved the locus of authority and the exercise of power in an urban community. Since Brockett and his friends infiltrated all levels of political activity, parliamentary, municipal, and parochial, it was inevitable that this parish question would spill over into other institutions, for the Poor Law was but one element in the overall political structure of Gateshead. The 1850 mayoral election was fought on this parish question even though the dispute did not concern the office of mayor nor any aspect of municipal government. Brockett and the defeated guardians wished to reassert their authority against the parish party who now had four guardians sitting in the council.[69] Brockett's nominee was elected only with the casting vote of the outgoing mayor but the result is less significant than the fact that the 1850 mayoral election had been politicized by Poor Law affairs. Even the 1852 parliamentary election felt the vibrations of the parish question when Hutt, the Liberal candidate facing a severe radical challenge, found that he lost valuable votes owing to, as he put it, 'a parochial squabble . . . which . . . I do not understand'.[70]

The mid-century political excitement centred on Gateshead borough though this was only part of the Gateshead union. Indeed Walsham, the assistant Poor Law commissioner, had favoured a widely ranging union as he feared that Gateshead's ruling oligarchy would monopolize Poor Law affairs and he hoped that a rural hinterland would counter urban dominance. It soon became clear in Gateshead as elsewhere that in such marriages of urban and rural areas political interest was almost wholly concentrated on the urban centre. Dr Rogers has calculated that in the years 1836 to 1856 there were only two occasions when Gateshead itself did not have a contested election, whereas in the outlying districts there were only six contests in Heworth, four in Whickham, and one each in Winlaton and Stella.[71] A similar picture emerges from the large Bradford union in the 1840s. Between 1841 and 1847 Bradford township had a contested election every year except one, while Pudsey had four contests, Horton three, Allerton, Clayton Idle, Manningham, and Wilsden two each, Bowling Calverley, Hunsworth, and Shipley one each and the other eight townships staged no contested election at all. It was not uncommon for rural areas within urban unions to be short of nominations where the urban townships sometimes had a gross surplus of candidates, 53 for ten seats in Gateshead in 1850 or 28 for six seats in Bradford in 1845. The Salford result for 1846 was typical of many combined unions, with the outer townships of Broughton Pendlebury and Pendleton returning their guardians unopposed and 11 candidates competing for the eight Salford seats.

One of the consequences of this variation in pattern of political interest was that the issues which mattered to the central districts often determined the course pursued by the union overall. The parish dispute in Gateshead which was of no interest to the outer parishes convulsed the affairs of the whole union. Salford's political peccadilloes derived from the fierce political rivalries in the town, for which the rest of the union suffered. It was one of Mott's major criticisms of Salford's Poor Law affairs that the union officials were used for political purposes in the borough to the great detriment and annoyance of the other townships.

He suggested adding two extra townships to the union which would 'destroy that commanding majority from the township of Salford which has unfortunately been used entirely for political purposes'.[72]

In fact Salford had only half of the seats in the union and Gateshead only one-third. In both places the central township maintained its political control by better attendance. With so much tedious routine administration it was inevitable that only a minority of guardians would attend regularly and real power devolved upon them. Rural apathy contrasted with urban political interest which produced a higher rate of attendance from urban guardians, in Gateshead double that of the rural guardians.[73] Though in nearby Darlington there were no less than 50 guardians it could still be reported by the clerk that 'twelve of the Guardians work the whole union'.[74] Attendance was generally low in Poor Law administration but heavily urbanized areas tended to have better attendance records than growing townships with considerable rural spread. Dr Midwinter has provided attendance figures for one year at Haslingden to illustrate the low attendance in Lancashire.[75] From this one can calculate an average attendance per meeting of just under 4 guardians out of the total of 18, with a range of nought to 15 for individual meetings. This may be contrasted with a sample year from Manchester when 50 meetings were held in 1844. The range of attendance was 5 to 20 out of a possible 24 guardians and the average attendance was just under 12.[76] Semi-rural Haslingden had a 22 per cent attendance record while urban Manchester had one of 48 per cent. This would support a tentative conclusion, confirmed in Gateshead, that urban attendance was roughly double that of rural/suburban attendance.*

Though distance from the place of meeting must have played a considerable part, conflict of interest was probably more important, for often the interests of the central township and of the out-townships were incompatible. Union administration could easily become Poor Law administration of the central urban area, with minority interests of individual parishes or townships overlooked. Where, as often happened, economic and social stratification produced great contrast of function between different geographical areas within a union, then a corresponding centrifugal force was created. The interests of an industrial and commercial urbanised area were not those of its semi-rural and residential hinterland. Thus the parish of Handsworth with a larger area than Sheffield but with only 4 per cent of its population resented its subjugation

---

* Dr Boyson quotes different attendance figures from those of Dr Midwinter, which seem to be based upon different evidence or a different analysis. However, Boyson's figures reveal the same urban/rural contrast with urban unions as high as 57 per cent in Bolton or 52 per cent in Bury and rural unions as low as 34 per cent in Clitheroe or 26 per cent in Burnley.[77]

within the Sheffield union. In 1856 its inhabitants petitioned for release
from an urban bondage and for transfer to the neighbouring Rotherham
union: 'they would thereby be placed upon a par with the Ratepayers
of other Agricultural townships in the immediate neighbourhood and
be called upon to contribute only a fair amount towards the assess-
ments for the relief of the poor.'[78]

The hub of the discontent was financial; remoter areas within unions
frequently resented the high poor rates necessary to maintain the poor
of the central areas. That urban/suburban tension which was a strong
feature of municipal government also affected Poor Law affairs because
of the drawing of union boundaries. The question was not always as
simple as it appeared, for looked at in one way the out-townships often
contributed less to union funds than they should have done. One historian has calculated that within the Salford union the central township
contributed 78 per cent of the funds while only having half the seats on
the board, whereas Pendleton, which continually called for secession, in
fact had a quarter of the seats but paid only 13 per cent of the funds.[79]
The whole of Bradford's Poor Law administration in the middle and
later 1840s ossified around the dispute over union charges and the proportion to be borne by the out-townships. Bradford got itself into an
impasse in which there was so much peripheral resentment at the cost of
the central poor that the union had to be broken up with the seceding
townships forming the new union of North Bierley in 1848. Likewise
Prestwich forced secession from the Manchester union in 1850. Yet it
should not be forgotten that in Bradford the four urban townships had
half the population of the union but only 37 per cent of the seats. In the
Bolton Union the urban townships had about 60 per cent of the population but only 30 per cent of the seats.[80]

Within Bradford township itself Poor Law elections reflected the
fierce political struggle going on in the town in the 1840s and contests
were seen as part of the overall political battle for local control. The six
Bradford township guardians had been Tory from 1837 to 1844 but in
1845 the Liberals won two township seats on the board of guardians. In
1846 this was increased to three, in 1847 to four, and finally in 1848 the
Liberals captured all six Bradford township seats. Despite criticism by
the local Liberal journal of the politicizing of Poor Law elections,[81] in
Bradford those elections had become party contests, especially in years
of great political controversy in other fields. Though, as the Poor Law
Commission reported, most guardians' elections were uncontested,
nevertheless urban unions frequently produced political contests.
Interest could certainly vary considerably even from one year to the next.
In the Bradford union Allerton had contests in 1842 and 1843 but could
get no nominations at all in the next two years, while in Darlington a

fiercely contested election in 1841 was followed by a year of insufficient nominations to fill all the seats on the board. Even allowing for severe fluctuations in political interest it remains true that politically contested Poor Law elections were a feature of the early Victorian urban scene.

The experience of Leeds and Salford has already been explored and other examples may be cited. In Birmingham R. K. Douglas admitted that the so-called Blue List which had been nominated for the 1837 election was overtly political: 'it is a Reform List and never was meant to be otherwise;' and three years later he was bemoaning how Liberal apathy had produced a Tory walk-over: 'here is reaction, three years ago the Tories for their exclusive list were able to muster no more than 120 votes now they muster 1000.'[82] Naturally the evidence of Tory reaction was enthusiastically welcomed by local Conservatives, as once again parochial elections assumed great political significance: 'the people are growing tired of the reign of Radicalism, with the terrorism and all the other *isms* with which it has been accompanied. . . . Birmingham has achieved a glorious victory . . . has set an example to the nation by declaring for Conservatism.'[83] In the partisan political atmosphere of early Victorian Birmingham the Poor Law provided but one more context in which political victories could be registered.

In Leeds, Tories used the Poor Law as a compensation for loss of municipal office and a similar development occurred in Leicester. It has already been noted (see above, p. 50) that the Tory corporation party used the vestries as enclaves of continued Tory power in the face of a Liberal municipality, and the Poor Law was part of this strategy. Entrenched in the parishes of St Margaret and St Martin, Leicester Conservatives took advantage of the multiple voting system to control the Poor Law guardians from the formation of the union in 1836 until a determined Liberal effort was successful in defeating them in 1845. In that first decade Poor Law elections and appointments were part of the political struggle between Liberal and Conservative, and Mott's comments on Leeds and Salford were echoed by Assistant Commissioner Edward Senior who claimed that everything in Leicester was made a political question. Elections were fought on party lines and the same deceit which characterized Leeds elections was evident in Leicester with the usual story of voting papers not delivered or collected, false proxies and the like. Tory party faithful were rewarded with Poor Law appointments, the most spectacular of which was the offer, later vetoed by the Poor Law Commission, of the clerkship to Thomas Burbidge, the discredited ex-town clerk of the corrupt unreformed corporation. His son was eventually appointed and was later joined as relieving officer by H. J. Wilkinson, former editor of the scurrilous and rabidly ultra-Tory *Leicester Herald* which had ceased publication in 1842.[84] Once the

Liberals had gained control the intensity of party feeling within the Poor Law weakened somewhat but did not entirely disappear.

Straight party political contests could be found in places as diverse as Nottingham in 1846 and Beverley in 1869,[85] and wherever local political rivalry was intense the Poor Law was likely to become a vehicle for party contests. The case studies discussed so far, Leeds, Salford, Gateshead, Bradford, Birmingham, and Leicester, were all in this category with the political interest deriving from the local political situation rather than from Poor Law policy itself. In this sense the Poor Law was a political institution as part of an overall political structure and most urban political interest emanated thus.

2

However, Poor Law policy could sometimes become so controversial as to generate of itself a political struggle over the way in which the intrinsic authority of the Poor Law ought to be exercised. In such cases, and they tended to be intermittent rather than persistent, the political excitement was generated from within the Poor Law administration and often spilled over into other areas cutting right across normal party lines. The whole anti-Poor Law movement which greeted the imposition of the new Poor Law in the later 1830s was of this genre. It was not so much an extension of the normal party warfare as a popular resistance to the machinery and methods of a new system of poor relief.[86] It may be noted here that in most places the movement reinforced the Tory-Radical alliance which had been developing under the auspices of the Operative Conservative societies. Where such bodies had not been formed the anti-Poor Law agitation provided the materials for the alliance, so that at Leicester the imposition of the Poor Law was quietly received in 1836 but the onset of severe depression in 1838 produced fierce resentment. It was the opposition to the Poor Law which launched the career of the local Chartist John Markham, and his pleas on the distress of the framework knitters were supported by the Leicester Conservative press which condemned 'the horrible operation of the workhouse system . . . (which) has given them a prison discipline, a severed family and a desolated hearth'.[87]

Operatives, likely to experience the new régime at first hand, naturally concentrated their attack upon the 'bastilles' and the abolition of outdoor relief. It has often been pointed out that such people soon deserted the anti-Poor Law movement either because they became Chartists or because they found that the theoretical aspirations of the new system were not fulfilled in practice. As one perceptive observer commented 'the new Poor Law is in fact only fit for seasons of prosperity and must in a

great measure be abandoned in times of adversity'.[88] In the depressed
years of 1838 and 1839 the workhouse test was simply not practical in
urban areas.

Those better placed, who were more likely to be dispensers rather than
receivers of relief, had certainly joined the attack upon the inhumanity
of the new Poor Law and sympathized with the condition of depressed
workers. Yet for many the essential objection was to central control.
Leicester Tories might support the framework knitters and remind them
that their true friends still cared for their plight, but above all they
resented

> the tyrannical and arbitrary power of the Central Board of the
> irresponsible Commissioners which completely nullifies and destroys
> the representative system . . . and places the individuals whom the
> people may elect to regulate their affairs entirely and helplessly
> subject to the baneful coercion of government hirelings.[89]

Recent research suggests that such judgements require much qualification since in practice considerable local autonomy remained in the absence
of ultimate central sanctions. Even so the fear of central direction at the
outset can be readily understood and contemporaries persisted with such
fears long after the initial popular resentment at the workhouse test had
abated.

Successful resistance to central direction, only achieved by stubborn
persistence, did not convince local people that high-handed assistant
commissioners or their London masters had abandoned centralization as
a policy goal. Thus Rochdale, which successfully resisted central authority
from 1837 to 1845, still found itself fighting the anti-centralization
battle in 1852. One of the biggest meetings ever held in Rochdale heard
John Bright argue the case for independent local government in opposition to central control. The feeling of the assembly, gathered together to
protest against the Poor Law Board's prohibitory order, was summed up
by one of their local magistrates:

> He felt a degree of jealousy of orders like those issued by the poor law
> board because he thought a body of men like the guardians were best
> able to judge the necessities of paupers. If they allowed them to insert the
> thin end of the wedge they would drive it home and where that would
> be God only knew. . . . One great evil of the present times was central-
> isation, to which he did not object, if kept in its proper place. He had
> no particular relish however for a system which placed the body in
> Lancashire and the head in London.[90]

Local feathers had been ruffled in Rochdale by assistant commissioner
Farnall's repeated request that a new workhouse be built, and the

building of new workhouses came to be both the most obvious manifestation of central direction and the most controversial political question to emerge out of Poor Law policy itself. In the welter of criticism of the workhouse test it was often forgotten that in Chadwick's phrase, 'a well regulated workhouse' was central to the new Poor Law for the classification of non-able-bodied paupers. As the assistant commissioners inspected their districts and told local guardians that their workhouse was 'the worst they had ever seen' it became clear that not only were workhouses unsuitable for implementing the test, they were also grossly inadequate for the separate treatment of the different categories of 'impotent' poor, the old, the infirm, the lunatic or the widow and orphan. It was frequently as a means of getting rid of unsuitable general mixed workhouses that central pressure was brought to bear upon the question of the erection of a purpose-built new workhouse.

Where the question of a new workhouse emerged at an early stage in a new union's development, then the controversy tended to merge with the general popular attack upon the new Poor Law. This is what happened at Nottingham where from 1837 the board of guardians became an important political forum and where the building of a new workhouse became the key political question in the town's affairs in the years 1840 and 1841. It was in June 1840 that the predominantly Whig guardians of Nottingham announced in public that a new workhouse was contemplated, and within a month a ratepayers' meeting had condemned the proposal.[91] When this popular opposition did not divert the guardians from their course a second more militant meeting was held which launched a Tory-Radical attack upon both the workhouse and the new Poor Law.[92] This was faithfully reproduced in the disposition of the local press with Richard Sutton's radical *Review* and John Hicklin's Tory *Journal* attacking the proposal and Thomas Wakefield's moderate *Mercury* defending it. The proposal was deemed inappropriate not only because of the depressed state of trade but also because the site of the new workhouse was to be outside the town. Sutton rallied the anti-workhouse ratepayers:

> We ask the ratepayers to come forward and resist the attempt to increase the local burdens and add to the miseries of the poor and show the Board of Guardians that this is *not* the time for a few individuals to increase the rates of the town in opposition to the parishioners without advancing a single step in the cause of humanity or justice.[93]

It seemed amazing to Sutton and his friends that 13 guardians could thus bring the Poor Law into disrepute by riding roughshod over the ratepayers' wishes as expressed in two lively meetings. Even the town council seemed to go along with the proposal for a new workhouse, though the decision to erect it outside the union was reversed.[94]

The political seeds thus sown were to bear the fruit of dissension in three separate elections in the winter and spring of 1840–1. First the municipal election of November 1840 was contested in many wards on the workhouse question which injected much political excitement into the party struggle. Sutton concluded simply: 'we were not wrong in describing the feeling of a majority of the ratepayers to be in opposition to the erection of a new workhouse',[95] while the Whig defender of the guardians forecast optimistically,

> next year the high state of feeling among the townspeople will have passed away when they see the benefits that will be conferred upon the deserving poor by the new building and the discouragement that will be given to vice and immorality and they will again rally round their party.[96]

Such a rally would perhaps be needed, for the Conservatives captured four Liberal council seats on the workhouse question. Two wards were particularly spectacular for the Conservatives. In Castle ward a sitting Liberal guardian was defeated, while at St Ann's one of the leading Liberals of the town, Samuel Bean, chairman of the anti-corn law association, was beaten by John Hicklin, editor of the *Journal*.[97] Hicklin was also successful in the 1841 guardians' elections in which he came top of the poll in St Nicholas's parish and in which the workhouse supporters were routed.[98]

The Poor Law election coincided with the mortal illness of the sitting Whig M.P., so that a by-election was imminent in which Tories made it clear that the Poor Law would be the focus of a new political alliance: 'Throughout the town there is a strong feeling against the obnoxious Poor Laws, affording a centre of union round which those whose opinions upon other subjects are widely different may harmoniously rally.'[99] It was hostility to the Poor Law which brought Chartists and radicals behind the Tory candidate John Walter, proprietor of *The Times*. There was a specific connection between anti-Poor Law philanthropists and Walter for he was proposed by the ex-mayor William Roworth, who was one of the most prominent figures in Nottingham charitable circles and who had been presented with silver plate just before the election by his working-class beneficiaries. As Sutton remarked of Walter, 'his colour *blue* is worn by the very children in the streets not as a Tory but as an enemy of the new Poor Law', and all local political observers ascribed the Tory victory in April 1841 to the Poor Law question.[100] Indeed, most went further and cited the building of a new workhouse as the main cause of the Liberal defeat and one leading Nottingham politician blamed the loss of the seat on the Liberal clerk Absolem Barnett, who had done most to push the workhouse question through. Thus the question of a new Nottingham workhouse had altered the political composition of the board of guardians, had lost four seats to the Conservatives on the municipal council, and finally had led to the return to parliament of the first Tory member for Nottingham since 1807.

The timing of the workhouse issue in Nottingham had much to do with the virulence of the dispute, as the new Poor Law was in 1840 still a relative novelty. By the mid 1850s much of the controversy had gone out of Poor Law administration and the building of a new workhouse then might be less contentious than 15 years earlier. The story of the Sheffield workhouse in the mid-1850s however indicates the persistence of Poor Law disputes over the exercise of administrative powers. Sheffield had for some years avoided contested elections by holding prior meetings to approve lists of guardians in order to save the cost of a formal election. In the early 1850s the main Poor Law dispute in Sheffield concerned the role of the clerk, John Watkinson, who was reprimanded by a Poor Law inspector for using pauper labour on his own farm and who frequently reversed guardians' decisions on his own authority.[101] There had been a running battle for several years over the inspector's insistence that a new workhouse was necessary, confirmed by a report in 1855, but the guardians refused to budge. In 1854 a new clerk was appointed, Joseph Spencer, who occupied that post for over 40 years, and in 1855 a new chairman of the guardians was elected, Robert Younge. This new régime disturbed the calm of the Sheffield Poor Law.

Younge, a self-made silver plater and a prominent philanthropist, had entered Poor Law affairs with a great sympathy for the pauper which was undermined by the influence of two key Poor Law officials, Farnall the inspector and Rogers the master of the workhouse. These three between them concocted the scheme for the new workhouse which became appropriately known as 'the Farnall, Rogers and Younge monster'.[102] At the end of October 1855 Younge launched the plan for a new workhouse. So great was the local opposition that he was forced to adjourn a decision until public meetings had been held and a deputation had waited on the guardians. Two public meetings, a vestry meeting, a deputation to the guardians and a petition to the Poor Law Board failed to shake Younge's resolve and he got the scheme approved with the lowest possible vote, eight out of the 15 on the board.[103] The new workhouse had become 'very properly the all engrossing subject for the Sheffield public; ratepayers, shopkeepers, tradesmen and mechanics'.[104]

Events moved quickly in the early months of 1856. Younge knew he had to get the scheme so far advanced before the next election that the next board could not escape the obligation to build a new workhouse.

Treading carefully because of his slender majority and privately activating Poor Law wheels behind the scenes Younge, and his clerk Spencer, managed to so arrange matters that a site was quickly chosen and a deposit paid for its purchase. Each step was accompanied by critical vestry and public meetings and Younge was accused of manipulating the situation in a dictatorial way. The correspondence with the Poor Law Board certainly justifies this accusation. Predictably in the light of public opposition, all eight pro-workhouse candidates for Sheffield township were defeated in the 1856 election, being outvoted in the region of eight to one.[105] One of the main opponents of the workhouse had already anticipated that a dispassionate review of the question would be impossible because after the election 'they would come like a parcel of bigots pledged to one side'.[106]

The new anti-workhouse board now sought to put the question on ice and the committee appointed in April 1856 to enquire into the exact position did not submit its brief one page report until April 1857, on the last day of the board's régime. As one of the members later admitted 'we agreed to taboo this affair' and while this seemed sensible at the time it was later much criticized, for 'as soon as elected they did not appear to care what became of the ratepayers' interests'.[107] The board of 1857, also elected to oppose the workhouse, found itself in a legal quandary since the date for completion of the purchase of the site had passed and the vendor was pressing them. They were told they could not resell the site or let it and their hackles rose when a second medical enquiry in August 1857 confirmed that a new workhouse was necessary.[108] By October 1857 relations between the guardians and Poor Law Board were so bad that the former resolved to have no dealings at all with the Board and even refused conciliation offers from the town council. In January 1858 the guardians bowed to legal necessity and purchased the site, still refusing to build a new workhouse on it. They offered to alter the existing workhouse in the summer of 1858 and the tension was further exacerbated by the Poor Law Board closing 16 rooms as unfit in the autumn.[109] The dispute dragged on messily until in 1859 alterations were approved. Younge's beloved new workhouse was not built until the 1870s.

An analysis of the Sheffield workhouse dispute reveals the familiar popular distaste for increases in public expenditure. At the outset Sheffield's leading journalist Robert Leader proclaimed: 'The combined influence of heavy taxation dear food and bad trade is to make men shrink from any new burdens . . . a time of depression is not the time for inviting the ratepayers to enter upon expensive improvements.'[110] When the election took place in 1856 it was argued that the ratepayers would be saddled with a debt of £60,000 if the scheme went ahead and when the proposal was renewed a year later one of the guardians refused to support those 'who only want to get their hands a little further into the public purse'.[111] The financial question never became the central issue, though it remained an underlying and predetermining cause of opposition. The dispute also had some elements of class conflict, with many larger rate-payers supporting a workhouse and the less wealthy opposing it. It was noticeable that when Younge's party were invited to stand for re-election in 1856 the requisition was signed by 'a great number of our first merchants manufacturers and shopkeepers' which indicated, according to Farnall, the Poor Law inspector, 'the interest which the large ratepayers of Sheffield take in the question'.[112] Farnall's successor Mainwaring, commenting on the low class of the 1857 board of guardians, confirmed that 'the more respectable and higher rated inhabitants of the union are generally in favour of a new workhouse'.[113] Yet class was never the whole answer, for Younge's main opponent and successor as chairman of the board was Alderman T. E. Mycock, who had been for the first 20 years of its life chairman of the watch committee and whose respectability was unimpeachable.

Financial and class questions were absorbed into a complex dispute which revolved around three main issues; first, whether final authority rested with the guardians or the ratepayers; second, what the role of the workhouse should be in Poor Law policy; third, the question of centralization. There were special local reasons why the workhouse dispute in Sheffield should resolve itself into a conflict of authority. The whole public life of Sheffield in the early 1850s was impregnated with the issue of ratepayer democracy which had been opened up by the radical Isaac Ironside and his supporters. All public institutions in Sheffield in the 1850s were subject to close popular control in the 'Ironside era' (see below, p. 108) and when Younge showed his disregard for the general will Isaac Ironside was well to the fore in taking up the constitutional issue. The question in this light was essentially one of consent since Younge would be saddling posterity with a tax that had never been publicly approved. In the opinion of the citizen who had forwarded the petition to the Poor Law Board, the plan had been 'to thrust the new workhouse down the throats of the people without their consent and concurrence'. Ironside was even more pointed and argued that if the ratepayers were of no consequence and were to submit to the levy of new taxation without consultation then 'it was time they ceased to call themselves free men and put on chains and called themselves slaves'.[114] Ironside, as the nice constitutional lawyer, saw the need to arm the anti-workhouse party with some *legal* authority and it was he who introduced the vestry motion instructing the overseers not to levy or disburse any rate for the building of a workhouse.[115]

In the context of Sheffield in 1855 it was predictable that Ironside

3 The Poor Law

would argue the case for ratepayer democracy; it was not predictable and perhaps hence even more significant that Younge would defend himself also on the grounds of authority and the exercise of power. It soon became clear, as one anonymous letter writer observed, that Younge would 'not submit to the pressure from without'.[116] He vigorously criticized the attempt of ratepayers' meetings or deputations to dictate to the board of guardians and proclaimed boldly that he would use his discretion independent of public pressure:

No public meeting in Sheffield should deter him from his duty, which he would perform respectfully but firmly . . . He looked upon the present movement as nothing more than an attempt to influence the actions of the board of guardians . . . If there were any guardians there . . . who would have their judgment put in swaddling clothes by a public meeting they were proper men to be re-elected to the next board, always to sit as the delegates of others and decide upon their opinions and not their own.[117]

In fearlessly doing his duty Younge's actions did give some substance to the charge of dictation. He and the clerk Spencer dealt with correspondence which even other guardians did not see and behind-the-scenes instructions went to the Poor Law Board unknown to Younge's colleagues. When worried about carrying with him one of his precious majority who had agreed to the workhouse scheme only if its implementation were delayed 12 months, Younge secretly advised the Poor Law Board to issue 'a peremptory direction that the Board shall *immediately* proceed to *select and secure* a site on which the future building shall be erected'.[118] When pressed he admitted that he hoped to bring about a situation where the future guardians could be compelled to build a new workhouse so that even an election would not thwart the scheme. Little wonder that with the Crimean War in mind one of his opponents should remark 'Mr Younge was a complete despot – talk about Russian despotism – we had Sheffield despotism'.[119] Here was a minor provincial echo of Burke's debate about the exercise of power – was Younge a representative or a delegate? At the heart of the workhouse question lay a purely *political* dispute about how power should be exercised on behalf of the electorate.

The precise function of the workhouse was itself at issue. There were two main planks to the case for a new workhouse – the needs of the deserving poor, and of classification. Perhaps because of the influence of the master of the workhouse and the local Poor Law inspector Younge became convinced that a large mass of paupers were fraudulent or indolent or both. As one of his opponents put it 'instead of finding that the poor were oppressed and the officers tyrants he found that the poor were imposters and the officers martyrs'.[120] Younge was much influenced by the paradox that the deserving poor struggled on manfully to resist the moral taint of the workhouse while the undeserving flocked to the guardians for relief, having made no provision for disaster themselves. The workhouse party argued that a high proportion of the poor rate was expended upon

> persons who have never been in any club, have made no provision against 'the rainy day' and who on the first appearance of difficulty apply for relief at the workhouse, where on the hard earned money of the Poor Ratepayers they live month after month without making the slightest effort to get their own living. . . . Pauperism is eating its deadly way into the vitals of your prosperity. The idle and dissolute crowd your workhouse.[121]

The concern over indiscriminate relief had an 1834 ring about it and equally the concern for the evils of a general mixed workhouse was Chadwickian. The great boon offered by a new workhouse would be the proper accommodation and treatment of the non-able-bodied poor, what Younge's requisitionists called the 'real comfort and happiness of the unfortunate poor'. The pro-workhouse handbill quoted above identified the pernicious tainting influence of the existing building in which 'the asylum is too small, the infirmary is too small, the infection wards are too small . . . the bad corrupt the good'. Few gave Younge any credit for generous motives but he did believe that opinion might be converted when people saw that in a new workhouse

> the aged and infirm are more carefully tended – the invalid has a better chance of recovery – the idle and vicious are properly employed – the general texture of society strengthened and improved – and the hard earned money of the poor ratepayers applied to mitigate the distress for which it was designed not to encourage pauperism.[122]

Such noble aspirations cut little ice with Ironside and his friends who quickly revived the anti-Poor Law language of the 1830s. There was a strong local tradition here, for in Samuel Roberts Sheffield had produced the most prolific anti-Poor Law pamphleteer and the propaganda of the 1850s was very much in the Roberts' tone. Ironside denounced the whole 'blasphemous, atheistic and materialistic' new Poor Law with its 'unheard of cruelties and tortures such as never disgraced even the Spanish Inquisition' and vigorously opposed the building of 'a huge workhouse prison properly designated a Bastile'.[123] One of his supporters criticized the idea of 'bastiles with cells for the incarceration of their unfortunate brethren' while another claimed the aim was to stop outdoor relief and drive the old into the workhouse where 'they would meet with cruel cold looks and actions'. Alderman Mycock, on a lighter vein commented on Younge's discovery of the new workhouse as 'a sort of universal vegetable pill which was a panacea for all the ills which afflicted mankind'.[124]

Perhaps two themes stood above this familiar abuse of the new Poor Law. Sheffield was going through a trade depression and there was a growing awareness that in such an economic climate a deterrent Poor Law with its punitive streak for the undeserving was wholly inappropriate. It was in fact 'as unjust as it is tyrannical. They propose to punish a man who unfortunately requires parish relief, from bad trade or other circumstances by putting him and his family into the workhouse. They want to treat him as a criminal and make his poverty a crime.'[125] In this context it was argued that the desire to inculcate a spirit of self-reliance would be better met by personal solicitations among the poor to join sick and benefit clubs than by rigorously applying the workhouse test.

In addition to this concern for the involuntary pauper there was, secondly, a suspicion that there was a deliberate attempt here to manipulate the labour market, reviving the Oastlerite idea that the factory system and the new Poor Law were in alliance to crush labour. As one of the speakers at a protest meeting explained, the comfort of the poor was not the main aim; 'but a model prison they wanted to build in order to get the working classes under the finger and thumb of the arbitrary and avaricious manufacturers: and then they would be obliged to work for what the masters chose to give, or go into the model prison.'[126] In such notions class conflict was most prominent. The propertied were concerned about saving rates swollen by the fraudulent abuse of poor relief; the propertyless were worried by the insecurity of employment in a fluctuating labour market. Such were the extrapolations from a situation which originated in Younge's seemingly innocent desire 'to secure to the ratepayer less taxation and to the poor more comfort'.[127]

The dual issues of the exercise of power and the role of the workhouse were largely overtaken as time went on by the third question of centralization. Once an anti-workhouse board had been elected it became clear that ratepayers' opposition to the new workhouse was fully reflected in board policy and concurrently the pressure for a new workhouse came more and more from the Poor Law Board itself. From the first there were those who saw the whole plan as nothing but a 'crude cruel dictatorial scheme of the Poor Law officials'[128] and once Younge and his allies had been removed from office the centralization implicit in the demand for a new workhouse became overt. The election of 1856 raised the question 'whether the Poor Law Board was to ride over them and enforce the erection of the new workhouse in the face of such a majority as there is here in opposition to it'.[129] When procrastination by the 1856 board brought a reprimand from London Ironside put the question clearly in its centralization context:

> The busybodies of the Poor Law Board have shown their official insolence this week by sending a letter to the Sheffield Guardians, telling them to get on with their work and send it up for examination. . . . The Guardians know that no workhouse is necessary, and 8000 ratepayers have voted them into office on that knowledge. The Poor Law Board know all this and the more they are told to mind their own business and be idle, the better for those who have to pay their salaries. We can manage our business in Sheffield without their insolent dictation and we mean to do so.[130]

When the question was revived in 1857 the Poor Law Board was advised by its inspector Mainwaring to take a very strong line and to warn the guardians that if they refused to proceed then 'the Board will feel compelled to take the necessary steps to oblige them to do so'.[131] Mainwaring argued that the purchase of a site, which could not be resold, gave the Poor Law Board a cast-iron case for compulsion, though his superior argued that this was not possible since plans had not been adopted. Despite this Mainwaring pressed very hard on the guardians, instituting a medical enquiry in the summer of 1857 and ordering the closure of rooms in 1858. Relations deteriorated alarmingly after the 1857 report had again condemned the workhouse and the Sheffield board resolved 'we the Guardians hereby resolve to have no further correspondence on the subject of a new workhouse with the Poor Law Board or to take any steps in the matter either to complete the purchase of the land . . . or of proceeding to the erection of a new workhouse'.[132] This stone-walling was itself mild compared to the earlier threat that 'the whole town would rise up in mutiny'.[133]

A town meeting on the workhouse question was not necessary because in the last resort the Poor Law Board was powerless to compel the Sheffield guardians to act against their will. The site had to be purchased, the unfit rooms were closed, the inspector could pull rank and stand on his official dignity but ultimately the Board had to accept the compromise of altering the existing building: the site was sold and no workhouse was built. As a perceptive observer remarked of the Poor Law Board, 'They are well aware that their authority lies in words and threats rather than deeds . . . and that they can do nothing effectual if the Guardians and ratepayers of Sheffield be united in their opposition to the arrogance of office and the force of centralisation.'[134] Precisely the same conclusion had been reached in Leeds in the 1840s when the central authority showed itself equally powerless to enforce the building of a new workhouse.[135] Since Sheffield had so enthusiastic a disciple of Toulmin Smith as Ironside it was no surprise that the centralization battle should be thus joined and in the event won.

The centralization issue linked the Poor Law with other areas of contemporary social and economic policy and in the realm of elections there was a formal connection. The whole electoral process originated in Poor Law machinery, for all elections, parliamentary, municipal, even parochial, were conditioned by a rate-paying franchise. No potential voter could exercise his franchise unless his poor rates had been paid and the only official who could provide a list of actual paid-up citizens was the overseer. Hence the lists worked on in the revision courts were produced by overseers who might in practice have a degree of discretion about who ought to be listed. The complicated question of compounding with its attendant discounts to landlords was a fruitful mine of party dissension and the overseer was also privy to the names of persons who had missed a quarter or half year's rates in the period preceding an election or a revision. Where party rivalry was fierce the control of the overseers' electoral machinery took on political significance.

Urban political propaganda frequently concentrated upon the partisan abuse of the overseer's powers but in the nature of the case hard evidence is much rarer than accusations. In so delicate an operation little documentation would have been used and so sometimes inferential evidence has to suffice. It may be assumed that a conscious effort by contending parties to neutralize the political role of the overseers by power-sharing was both an admission that abuse existed and a statement of intent that the political advantage should not lie all on one side. Such a development occurred in Leeds and Liverpool in the 1840s.

In Leeds in 1842 the creation of Tory magistrates, the passing of the Improvement Act and even the 'plug riots' led to a cooling of partisanship and a desire for amicable relations in essentially non-political areas. The Poor Law seemed appropriate and Baines Senior argued 'the sooner they got rid of party the better and the more they attended to the fitness of men for parochial duties and the less they attended to the particular colour men might wear the more fitly they would discharge their duties'.[136] Forgetting party altogether was impossible in the Leeds situation but an equal sharing of the overseers' posts was the next best thing and when this occurred in the early 1840s the Tories welcomed the compromise since 'party has, after many years of injustice, been at length put on such an equilibrium as must to all reasonable ratepayers give satisfaction'.[137] The guardians continued to offer scope for political combat but the overseers' power was neutralized and when the second Reform Act placed even more onerous burdens on the shoulders of the overseers they were confident that their powers could be exercised impartially.[138] This was because, as they had reported in 1859, 'to preserve unity of feeling and to avoid any political bias the magistrates have elected an equal number of persons professing opposite political sentiments and the harmony which has existed among the overseers has never been broken'.[139]

In Liverpool Poor Law affairs had never generated the political interest that was displayed at Leeds and the revived select vestry was a largely unchallenged Tory monopoly. By the mid-1840s two processes converged which did politicize the Poor Law for a brief period. First there was a campaign in the press led by John Smith, editor of the Liberal *Liverpool Mercury*, against extravagant expenditure on officials whose appointment smacked of favouritism, against the ineffective treatment of sick paupers and in favour of greater publicity for the activities of the vestry. In this Smith disclaimed political motives since he deemed politics inappropriate 'in works of charity public government and public improvement'.[140] His campaign heightened interest in the 1845 parochial elections which were politicized by the registration concerns of the Liberals. The Anti-Monopoly Association, the Liverpool branch of the Anti-Corn Law League, had recently assumed registration responsibilities for the borough and its secretary Charles E. Rawlins junior, decided that the time had come to end the abuse of the overseers' power which had long given the Tories an unfair advantage. The electoral lists had been drawn up by a full-time assistant overseer who was a faithful Tory servant of his Tory masters.

Liberal political concern for the register superimposed itself on an awakened public interest in the vestry and so the 1845 parochial contest soon 'assumed more the shape of a Parliamentary election', with the original list of candidates mostly Conservative and the amended list mostly Liberal. The Anti-Monopoly Association made a deliberate and concerted political effort to neutralize a party which had 'used its power for the purpose of tampering with the registry'.[141] The main ploy had been for the assistant overseer to supply the Tory party with the names of Tory ratepayers who were behind in payment and whose rates were then paid from Tory party funds to ensure that they remained on the register. Free traders were rallied by the attempt to purify the register and the Tory membership of the vestry was reduced from 25 in 1844 to 18 in 1845. Rawlins was proud of the achievement and promised that they would go further and gain half the seats in 1846. This they did, again fighting a parochial Poor Law election on the issue of partisan registration. By sharing the seats on the select vestry the Liberals had produced an 'annihilation of party in one of our great local bodies'.[142] Again power-sharing had neutralized the political advantage implicit in control over the Poor Law and later the Liverpool select vestry could be cited for 'the great absence of all party bias from its proceedings'.[143]

In Leeds and Liverpool the inference from political action taken indicates the potential and actual abuse of Poor Law powers. Two other examples give clearer indications of the sort of trickery that was possible, in Salford in the 1840s and in Preston in the 1860s. The Salford experience revolves mainly around the case of the dismissed assistant overseer, Francis Wrigley, which was discussed earlier in the chapter. It has already been explained that Wrigley was dismissed for perverting his office to political purposes and the precise charges concerned his handling of the electoral register. In the official enquiries into Wrigley's activities much was revealed of the devious methods of manipulating the electoral process. The prevailing partisanship which led both sides to corrupt the register induced Wrigley to make extensive admissions in the belief that he and his party could not equitably be singled out. Indeed Charles Mott did his best to exonerate Wrigley by reference to the mitigating circumstances in which Wrigley 'was placed in a situation of some difficulty between two violent parties, when more than two thirds of the suggested votes were disputed'.[144] Though the Poor Law Commission did not accept the recommendation that Wrigley be merely censured, it was acknowledged that 'a strong contest was going on of a political character in which the payment of rates constituted the qualification of the voters'.[145]

That two-thirds of Wrigley's provisional list of voters should be challenged was an indication of the lack of public confidence in his handling of the register. The initial Liberal accusation concerned the familiar payment of rates by the Tory party which had occurred at Liverpool. In the enquiries Wrigley admitted this but reported that both sides resorted to this tactic and his supporters repeatedly argued that Yandall of the Reform Association had paid rates on behalf of Liberal voters in order to win a recent churchwardens' election. In view of the dubious nature of this question, where both parties were guilty, the Liberals switched their attack to a specific abuse, namely the pre-dating of receipt of rates. Whether paid by individuals or not the rates had to be received by a specified closing date, usually in the summer with a revision in the autumn. Once the final date had passed no retrospective payment could enfranchise a defaulter but it was a simple matter to date the receipt of the money within the qualification period. This was exclusively a Tory ploy, for Wrigley and the guardians were Tories, and while Liberals might pay rates only the Tories had the opportunity to pre-date the receipt. In the event it was this specific abuse which led to Wrigley's dismissal for it was this which 'effected a fraud upon the franchise of the duly qualified ratepayers'.[146] It is equally clear that in the matter of the rate collectors, also discussed earlier, the Liberals had in mind some similar abuse of rate payment.

Liberals could adopt an attitude of outraged innocence at this abuse of official powers but when in control themselves they derived the full advantage from power over the Poor Law. Again the revelations of John Hope, secretary to the guardians, were instructive. It appears that in 1842 Lockett, chairman of the guardians and leader of the Liberals, deliberately delayed the actual levy of the poor rate lest Liberal voters be disfranchised by non-payment. Instead of levying the rate a bank over-draft financed Poor Law administration. Initially Hope assumed this was merely the work of Lockett but he explained, 'I afterwards discovered that the Overseers themselves were equally anxious to delay the rate for the same reason'.[147] Lockett repeated his action in 1847 when he was again able to persuade the overseers to delay the levy of the rate in order to prevent disfranchisement for non-payment.[148] This seemingly minor variation in Poor Law administration was in fact of great political significance because of the important connection between the Poor Law and the electoral process, which is so often overlooked.

The Salford situation revealed itself through the Poor Law; that in Preston emerged from the candidature of George Melly, the wealthy Liverpool merchant who wished to enter Parliament.[149] Melly, while nursing the seat, kept in close touch with Preston's political leaders and in particular with Edward Ambler, a printer and stationer, who was a backstage party manager. Ambler's reports on the progress of the Melly cause reveal the important connection between elections and the Poor Law and the ways in which control over the Poor Law could yield political advantage.

Ambler was himself a Poor Law guardian and he felt that guardians' elections, often fought on party lines, were themselves a guide to Melly's electoral prospects. Thus when reporting his own victory in the 1863 Poor Law elections, Ambler commented that the success showed that his ward 'will yet tell a better tale than it did at the election last year'.[150] Being a guardian was considered to confer upon Ambler 'position and what is of more importance *influence*' and Melly appreciated this, requesting that Ambler should stay on as a guardian in 1864 which would serve Melly's cause.[151] Perhaps, as Ambler claimed, he could influence poorer voters but more important was his access to vital information which could be used in the revision courts. As a guardian he was able to know who was in receipt of poor relief. This was important in Preston where there remained a considerable number of old franchise holders qualified to vote as freemen, many of whom sold their votes to the Tories. Ambler felt that in 1863 'there is a larger number of old franchise recipients of relief on the other side; if so they must go'.[152]

Using privy information of the Poor Law he could substantiate successful objections to Tory voters in the revision courts. Ordinary non-freemen voters were equally vulnerable, for Ambler was able to get hold of information through the Poor Law of the real rental paid by each voter, vital information for a successful registration campaign.*

Above all Ambler could use the Poor Law to improve Liberal chances even before the revision court sat by ensuring that, as in Liverpool and Salford, arrears of the party faithful could be made up. Only through Poor Law influence and control could party activists gain the essential information on which ratepayers were in arrears. Once this was known the previous poll book and the canvass information yielded the political leaning of the voter. Ambler reported on those who were in arrears on 20 July 1863, the qualification date:

> Our opponents of course have been permitted to drop off, and are done with for this year. In the cases of well known and thoroughly reliable *friends* . . . I have been advised of all cases on our side and have in a number of instances guaranteed payment of rates, by this means retaining their names unopposed on the list of voters.[154]

Melly was, in short, financing the manipulation of the list of voters produced by the overseers and those whose rates were paid by Ambler would appear like any other ratepayer on the list. Implicit in Ambler's arrangement must have been the pre-dating of the receipt of rates as practised at Salford.

In the following year Ambler got the vital information before the qualification date and suggested to Melly that he follow the same practice:

> A friend of ours in the overseer's office has informed me that a considerable number on both sides are in arrears for Poor Rates and has promised me a list of our friends in that position. Don't you think I had better do as I did last year . . . to pay the rates to keep *good men* on the books for votes? . . . We shall have this advantage, that the other side will not have a similar chance of saving this class of voters.[155]

In both years Ambler's Poor Law connection enabled the Liberals to gain registration advantage for in each case Tory unpaid arrears would lead to a loss of the franchise while Liberal votes would be protected. It may well have been in reference to such dealings that Ambler reported to Melly, 'I have had some difficulty in keeping what has been done a

---

* Data on ratepayers was always considered one of the bonuses of local power and as a Leeds politician put it in 1870, 'You know very well that if the party in power whether in the Corporation or Guardians want it they will get the information.'[153]

secret. If it oozes out there will be an explosion.'[156] There can be no
doubt that the manipulation of lists of ratepayers was explosive. As the
evidence from Leeds, Liverpool, Salford, and Preston indicates, Poor
Law administration could yield electoral dividends.

What emerges from this analysis of the political aspects of Poor Law
administration is that there were three strands to the politicizing of the
Poor Law. First, and most often, the Poor Law was but one aspect of an
overall political struggle for power as political activists sought to make
manifest their supremacy over their rivals. Second, controversial issues
within the Poor Law, such as the building of a new workhouse, were
politicized in disputes over how power ought to be exercised. Third, the
Poor Law was politicized by its formal involvement with the electoral
process. It is not contended here that the Poor Law provided a continuous vehicle for political excitement. When there was no dispute over
the exercise of Poor Law authority, when the personnel, methods, goals,
implications, and consequences of the Poor Law were uncontentious,
then politics faded into mere administration. It did not, however, take
much to re-kindle political interest – sometimes within the party system,
sometimes across it. Within the urban political structure the Poor Law
could at times generate considerable political excitement and it should
not be forgotten that the Poor Law remained well into the twentieth
century a *separate* political institution. The political excitement of
Poplarism in the 1920s was but a twentieth-century example of a
nineteenth-century involvement.

4
The improvement commissions

'In some instances the separate and conflicting authority of the commissioners is avowedly used as a check and counterbalance to the political influence of the Corporation.' First Report of the Royal Commission on Municipal Corporations (1835), XXIII, 43

From the mid-eighteenth century it became increasingly common in both incorporated and unincorporated towns for there to be established bodies, variously titled, for scavenging, watching, lighting, and draining the streets. Whether called street, sewer, water, or police commissions these bodies were but forms of a statutory authority for improvement which is generally known as the improvement commission. It was very rare for improvement functions to devolve upon the corporations and so even in corporate towns the improvement commissions were the main agency for sanitary reform. In the early nineteenth century these bodies multiplied and no less than 300 were created between 1800 and 1830. The improvements commissions were generally of three types. The most common was the mirror image of the self-elective corporations where named commissions were empowered by private local Acts to perform improvement functions and to fill vacancies by co-option. Perhaps the most famous oligarchy of this sort was the street commission of Birmingham which became in effect a sort of self-elected substitute corporation. The second type of commission, very common in the years 1820 to 1835, involved the election of commissioners by ratepayers, of which Leeds is a prime example. The third type enabled all ratepayers rated at a given level to qualify automatically as commissioners: the most famous example was the commission operating in Manchester and Salford from 1792.

Though often overtly non-political the improvement commissions assumed a political role in two main ways. First, they were part of that complex web of overlapping authorities whose inertia and vested interest hampered the progress of public health reform. Improvement commissions often frustrated Chadwick, for the existence of statutory authorities with even minimal powers of environmental control made the creation of powerful health agencies extremely difficult. The question of which body should exercise such powers was often as politically controversial as the question of whether the powers should be created at all. Second, in the administrative sphere the improvement commissions constituted a body which rivalled the local corporations. In corporate towns before 1835 and in all towns after that date improvement commissions were sources of alternative authority to that of the municipal council. The essentially political question of the relationship between commissions and councils had to be resolved in the early Victorian years.

In Leeds such a question was resolved in 1842 by incorporating the improvement powers into the municipal council and allowing the improvement commission to lapse. Before municipal reform it was clear that the improvement commission in Leeds was a political rival to the corporation and it was reported in 1835 that 'the commissioners are opposed to the majority of the corporation in political principles and collisions might be apprehended'.[1] Indeed the 1835 municipal report cited the politicizing of the Leeds improvement commission as one of the pernicious consequences of a closed corporation:

> The ill effects of the present exclusive system are rendered strikingly apparent from one circumstance in this borough. In cases where the election is popular as in the choice of the Commissioners under the local acts the persons selected are all of one political party professing the opposite opinions to those entertained by the majority of the corporation: which is accounted for by the necessity of balancing the influence of the corporation at the same time it is said to show the inclination of the majority of the town. This choice of Commissioners exclusively from one party is admitted to be undesirable but is justified as being resorted to in self-defence.[2]

There were a number of Tories elected but, without ever becoming a matter of fierce political contest, it was usual for about 15 of the 18 commissioners to be Liberals. It lay in the logic of the political situation in Leeds that the improvement commission's affairs should become more political in the 1830s in view of the Tory attempts to regain political ascendancy and to compensate for loss of municipal power. It was the question of Leeds water which brought the political rivalry to a head when an ill-fated public water supply scheme raised technical, financial, and ideological issues which were difficult to resolve. The politics of improvement are discussed fully later on (see below, Chapter 7) and it need only be recorded here that local Tories, largely on political grounds, favoured the provision of water by a joint stock company. Where public control meant Liberal control then Tories argued the advantages of private enterprise. So in Leeds in the 1830s embryonic collectivists were Liberals while free market individualists were Tories. The political vagaries of Leeds water were a parallel to those of Manchester gas (see below, p. 98).

The water question politicized the elections for improvement commissioner in an unprecedented scramble for this minor office. Using the Operative Conservative Society to pack the vestry the Tories managed to capture the Leeds improvement commission for the first time in 1837, a victory repeated in 1838 and 1839 when there was only one Liberal commissioner.[3] The 1840 election was expected to be especially embittered because the Tory commissioners had in 1839 begun to rate poor cottage property, which had traditionally been exempt.

Political contests for the offices of improvement commissioner seem somewhat bizarre, for as one Liberal remarked, 'surely the office of sweeping the streets and lighting the lamps or of superintending these operations has not much to do with either politics or religion'.[4] Yet early Victorian commissioners' elections in Leeds were fiercely fought because of the local political structure. Tories had been deprived of power in the parish, in the Poor Law and in the council, and the improvement commission offered some political compensation. Therefore the office acquired a temporary political value far beyond its intrinsic status. The Tory editor and local political leader, Robert Perring, roused his followers not by the attraction of the office itself but by what it represented in the overall Leeds political context: 'Some persons may think the Improvement Commission is not worth contending for . . . The affair is part of a plan to get possession of all local elective offices. The Conservatives should therefore bestir themselves – assert the rights of property and crush a coalition . . . the object of which is the acquirement of local power.'[5] In a similar vein he confirmed, 'the prize contended for is of no value in itself . . . the question is, shall the Whigs and Whig-Radicals be permitted to monopolize everything?'[6] The politicizing of minor offices of township administration is explained thus.

Although in 1840 Liberals with Chartist support were able to defeat the Tory list in the vestry, it later appeared that an adjournment for a poll was illegal and so the 1839 commission remained in office during 1840.[7] These 'usurping commissioners' ignored repeated vestry demands to resign and dwindled in numbers because ratepayers refused to elect replacements. The legal subterfuge only delayed the inevitable and in the 1841 poll the Liberal list was carried by 2,220 to 1,790. Some Chartists were included in the 1841 commission and in 1842, as part of a general programme in Leeds of Chartist participation in local government, the

Chartists carried their own list.[8] It was an important accession of power and represented a defeat for the Liberals.

Joshua Hobson, the Chartist printer who led the commission, found that his friends had inherited office at a crucial period of the commission's history. Inspired partly by Robert Baker's revelations in a statistical survey published in 1839 and partly by fear of the impact of general public health bills under consideration by Parliament, the Leeds improvement commission had launched a new improvement bill which was now to be exposed to the Chartist vision. In a series of vestry meetings in the early months of 1842 the Leeds Chartists attempted to mould the bill into a measure that would make working-class participation in local administration really meaningful. Powers were to be vested in commissioners elected directly by the vestry with no participation by magistrates or councillors; there was to be no financial qualification for commissioners, only a residential one; separate authority would be required from the ratepayers for all improvements costing more than £500; all meetings were to be at 7 o'clock in the evening instead of the normal 12 noon; houses under £10 were to be rated at one-third the rate of houses about £50.[9]

The minutiae of an improvement Act raised general questions about authority and the exercise of power in urban society, for here in the very workings of administration was an attempt to democratize local government. Popular control would be maintained through direct election; working men would not be disqualified by a financial qualification; financial control would be effected by the £500 limit; working-class participation would be facilitated by evening meetings; progressive taxation would lay the main burdens on the wealthy. No longer were the politics of the improvement commission concerned merely with a party battle between Liberal and Tory. These suggestions laid bare the fundamental distribution of power and the methods of its exercise. Some Tories, fearful of Liberal monopoly of municipal power, supported the preservation of vestry authority,[10] but most prominent political leaders recoiled with horror at this slice of democracy.

Predictably the previous alliance of forces in support of the bill now collapsed. The council, the magistrates, the legal agents of the commissioners and those who had agreed to finance parliamentary expenses, all withdrew their support. Hobson and the commission could only accept the inevitable and drop the bill themselves, for no parliament would pass such a measure in the face of powerful local opposition. The vestry accepted Hobson's motion that no local Act was acceptable which did not contain the Chartist suggestions, thus hoping to prevent any section 'using their party political and legislatorial influence to procure the passing of the bill in a shape to suit their own party and class interests but in a shape objectionable to the majority of the inhabitants'.[11] It was a last desperate effort to retain the principle of real popular control. In fact the 1842 Leeds Improvement Act abolished the commission and vested all powers in the council. The municipal leviathan was on the march.

Manchester, unlike Leeds, had no corporation in the early nineteenth century and so there was no rivalry between the so-called police commissioners and an unreformed corporation. However, there could have been conflict within the local administration, which was a complex mixture of manorial, parochial, and civil authorities. This was avoided by the sharing of office among a small Tory Anglican oligarchy which monopolized the posts of churchwarden, constable, boroughreeve, and police commissioner. Nevertheless, the police commission was a potential focus for political rivalries because of its open structure. Under the 1792 Police Act any citizen at £30 rental or above* could act as a police commissioner so in the event of increased political interest there would be ease of access. The Manchester police commissioners were active agents of improvement and, as the Webbs noted, there was a direct relationship between the administrative zeal of commissioners and the level of political involvement since a 'widened range of activities attracted popular interest and gave scope for discussion of general principles, the conflict of interests and all the excitement of political partisanship'.[12]

When radical opposition to the Tory oligarchy developed after the Napoleonic Wars it did not necessarily focus immediately on the police commission. Since the entrenched oligarchy had enveloped all of local administration, then an attack upon any of the parts was in effect an assault upon the whole monopoly of power. Hence the riotous vestry meetings to scrutinize the constables' accounts or to limit the churchwardens' expenditure (see above, pp. 26 and 37) were part of the general radical conflict with the governing élite headed by Thomas Fleming. The ease of access to the police commission did eventually politicize that body, and on an improvement issue. The Webbs' improvement-politics ratio was well illustrated by the Manchester gas question in the 1820s.

The police commission had launched the first municipally controlled gas company and this pioneer social utility in the public sector received parliamentary approval in 1824. It was immediately a profitable concern and a dispute arose over the utilization of the profits. Many police commissioners believed that improvements to the streets could be financed out of gas profits which would benefit all ratepayers. On the other hand, many consumers of gas felt that the price of gas should be reduced and improvements financed out of rates levied on all ratepayers. A minor question of local administration soon became a major political

* Such was the difference between rent and rates assessment that many rated at under £25, and even a few at under £15, were able to qualify as commissioners.

controversy which polarized along class lines. The majority of gas consumers were small shopkeepers, craftsmen, tradesmen, publicans and the
like who were politically radical, while the majority of the police commissioners were large-scale manufacturers or merchants who were Tories or
respectable Whigs. The politics of the Manchester gas question exposed a
fundamental issue of nineteenth-century urban life – by whom should
improvements be financed. The larger ratepayers derived the greatest
potential financial benefit from improvements financed out of gas profits
since they were thereby relieved of potential rates; the gas consumers
resented what was redistribution in reverse by which those of middling
incomes were subsidizing the wealthy. As Archibald Prentice explained,
'the taxed shopkeeper was the radical and the untaxed warehouseman
was the conservative'.[13]

The political interest generated by the gas question led to greater
numbers qualifying as commissioners, 600 at one meeting in 1826, and to
stormy meetings at which the transaction of business was impossible.
Led by William Whitworth and Archibald Prentice, the radical commissioners vigorously challenged the close control of the old oligarchic
commissioners and meetings of 800 were common. When a contentious
meeting in January 1828, which was to have discussed the price of gas,
ended in uproar after a four-hour dispute over who should take the
chair, the traditional governors of Manchester decided that they must
get a new Police Act to alter the composition of the police commission.
The 1792 Act had by 1828 become unworkable as the gas dispute was
gradually overtaken by a generalized political conflict over who ought to
rule the town of Manchester. It was wholly typical of the spirit of those
who wished for a change in the constitution of the police commission that
the instigation of the new Act was voted on at a parochial meeting under
Sturges Bourne's Act.[14] The aim of the proposals, as of the Act itself, was
to restore to property its rightful influence over affairs.

The new proposals involved both a fundamental change in the police
commission (which was now to be an electoral office) and a Tory attempt
to exclude lower-rated citizens from both voting for and acting as
commissioners. Parliament was asked in 1828–9 to define the nature of
authority in urban affairs, to decide who ought to exercise power and on
whose behalf. Manchester gas had brought to the surface a fundamental
conflict in urban life which all towns were forced to resolve in the mid-
nineteenth century. Should urban government be a close province of the
propertied or should it be a form of open democracy? Prentice isolated
this facet of the complex dispute over rating and he reported that those
who had formerly dominated town government 'did not find it work so
pleasantly as when a few conservative gentlemen had the business all in
their own hands' and that they wished to restore 'quieter times, when

humble men did as they were bidden by men in higher commercial station than themselves'.[15] By 1828 the police commission was virtually a lost cause for the Tories and two meetings of commissioners in March resolved to petition against the new bill. The only chance of avoiding radical domination was to change the rules of the game.

The eventual compromise by which £16 ratepayers could vote and £28 ratepayers* could act as commissioners superficially gave something to both sides. The radicals got a more democratic franchise than that which had been proposed, while the Tories eliminated the lower rate-payers from the police commission. In reality it was a victory for the Tory-Whig coalition and though radicals had controlled the commission in 1828 they were effectively squeezed by the 1829 régime. The rate-paying qualifications and the distribution of commissioners between districts emasculated radical strength. It has recently been calculated that the more democratic franchise still only provided about $2\frac{1}{2}$ per cent of the population with the vote. The electorate varied between 58·7 per cent of the population in a rich district and only 0·5 per cent in a poor one. There was one commissioner for 270 people in the former district and one for 2,390 in the latter.[16] Such facts as these preserved Tory rule into the 1830s.

The gas question had politicized the police commission's affairs and this issue continued to raise the political temperature in the 1830s, after the constitutional disputes had been resolved by the 1829 Police Act. In 1830 Prentice, supported by the radical James Wroe and the Whig-Liberal Thomas Potter, unsuccessfully attempted to limit the gas directors to their original borrowing powers and to insist on ratepayers' consent before amending legislation was proposed. Three years later he was again unsuccessful in proposing a scale for reductions in the price of gas.[17] Though not because of radical demands, prices were reduced in the 1830s at the same time as subsidies continued for street improvements. Between 1834 and 1837 the price of gas was reduced by just over 20 per cent while the overall total granted for street improvement went up from £10,000 to £16,000.[18] The relative merits of relieving gas consumers and subsidizing ratepayers continued to be a running sore throughout the 1830s and there was as much need for the police commission to proclaim its principles in 1841 as there had been 15 years earlier. The gas committee recommended the transfer of funds for improvement

> so as to confer relief on all classes of the Ratepayers from the highest to the lowest instead of making a further reduction in the price of Gas and thereby conferring the advantage on the Gas Consumers alone who form but a part of the general body of ratepayers . . . improvements

* Equivalent to approximately a £40 rental qualification.

... not only tend to raise the character of the Town but materially contribute to the prosperity of all classes by promoting the general health.[19]

As late as November and December 1842 Abel Heywood, one of Manchester's leading radicals, was pressing for further reductions in gas prices while the commission reaffirmed its policy 'to appropriate the profits in Public Improvements in which all participate'.[20]

The gas question raised two interesting corollaries: the principle of public control, and the question of the clerk's salary. During the 1830s police commission affairs came more and more to be dominated by middle-class Liberals who were soon to be pressing for incorporation. Though traditional Tory leaders such as Thomas Fleming still acted, and indeed sat as chairmen of important committees, Liberals such as William Neild, Thomas Potter, and Jeremiah Garnett were becoming more prominent, while a minority of radicals led by Heywood, Wroe, and Prentice were also a scourge on the Tories.[21] Despite the temporary respite granted by the 1829 Act Tories could not look forward to continuous power in the police commission and so when in 1834 the possibility was raised of selling off the gas company into private hands many Tories supported this on political rather than ideological grounds. Where public control meant Liberal control Manchester Tories preferred private enterprise for gas, just as Leeds Tories had preferred private enterprise for water. It was an indication of the havoc which politics could wreak in the ideological debate that the stoutest defence of the public control of social utilities came from Thomas Hopkins, a leading Liberal of the Manchester school.[22]

Attacks upon the clerk's salary were part of a radical drive for economy which frequently characterized nineteenth-century urban government. In Manchester it appeared that gas consumers were not only subsidizing the ratepayers but also financing excessive salaries. In fact Thomas Wroe received £200 as clerk to the police commission, £100 as comptroller to the gas directors and £50 as clerk to the improvement committee.[23] When the radicals attacked the salary in 1837 the gas directors merely recited the statistics of reduced prices and increased grants for improvement.[24] The case was even stronger when the economists' attack was renewed in 1842, for the directors could quote a 30 per cent reduction in the price of gas and a trebling of the surplus transferred to the improvement fund since Wroe's appointment.[25] Though Prentice was able in July 1842 to limit Wroe's re-appointment to three months, his amendment in August that Wroe's salary was 'more than is warranted by the strict economy which ought to be observed in the management of public property' was easily defeated.[26]

Just as in the 1820s the gas question was overtaken by the constitutional issue, so too a decade later this became the major question. The police commission was clamped between two contending forces. The radicals never abandoned the attempt to democratize the commission. In January and February 1838 James Wroe proposed the extension of the suffrage to all those who paid the police rate and in May Edward Nightingale moved for 'a new appointment of commissioners to the several districts in proportion to the population therein'.[27] Radical demands for an extended suffrage and proportional representation were contemporaneous with Liberal demands for incorporation, and the granting of a charter in 1838 put the very existence of the police commission under a cloud. Once the new council was in being a fierce rivalry grew up between it and the commission which was based upon both an administrative and a political conflict. Anti-incorporation Tories not only used the churchwarden's office (see above, p. 41), but also the police commission, the politics of which finally came to represent a struggle between old and new forces of urban government.

The police commission elections in 1838 resulted in Tory control of the main committees, largely because Liberal attention was focused on the first municipal election. This meant that for much of 1839 the Tory-controlled police commission could frustrate the new corporation. The commission refused to disband itself and continued to levy the watch rate for police expenditure. Two important votes in 1839 illustrated the Tory control. In July the finance committee resolved to levy the watch rate in view of the doubtful legality of the charter, and an amendment by the Liberal Thomas Hopkins and the radical Prentice that watching should be omitted was defeated. The same issue was raised the following month when J. E. Taylor and Jeremiah Garnett asked for relief from paying the police rate because of the illegal inclusion of watching which was now performed by the council. Again Hopkins was defeated in a vote which confirmed the reality of Tory power.[28] This was neatly symbolized in the refusal of the commission in January 1839 to grant the council the use of the town hall.[29]

The authority of the police commission was undermined by the imposition of the government's own police commissioner and then the Tory grip on power was loosened by the 1839 elections. Incorporation Liberals were now aware of the continued importance of the police commission and Liberal supporters were urged to reverse the setback of the previous year in order to advance the cause of the charter.[30] The town hall question now became a symbol of Liberal predominance. In January 1840, one year after refusing the council permission to use the town hall, the police commission reversed its decision and defeated a Tory amendment to charge rent.[31] Eighteen months later an even more pointed Tory

amendment wished to refuse the mayor the right to call meetings in the
town hall 'in as much as the office of mayor is in no way connected with
the office of Commissioner of Police'.[32] This too was defeated, for Liberal
control had indeed forged a firm connection between the commission and
the council. Once the legality of the charter was confirmed the amalgamation of the police commission into the council was only a matter of
time. Political controversy faded away and the commission carried on
quietly with its routine work until its demise. In 1843 the body which had
for half a century been the strongest administrative institution in
Manchester tamely succumbed to the new political master of urban
government.[33]

By 1843, Salford too was moving towards incorporation which would
eclipse the town's police commission, which had separated from the
joint commission with Manchester in 1797. Salford police commission,
like that at Manchester, used gas profits to subsidize town improvements,
especially after 1840. The gas question in Salford never assumed the
political proportions which it had across the Irwell and the main political
interest focused on the composition of the police commission. From 1832
Liberals came to dominate the commission, leaving Tories in the old
manorial offices of boroughreeve and constable, and this was part of an
overall assumption of Liberal power which included the Liberal select
vestry and the election of Joseph Brotherton in 1832 (see above, p. 62).
The new all-powerful improvement committee of the police commission
was chaired by a series of Liberals who were to dominate Manchester and
Salford affairs for a generation; J. B. Smith, later of the Anti-Corn Law
League, Elkanah Armitage, a future mayor of Manchester, John Kay, a
future mayor of Salford, and of course William Lockett, Salford's chief
Liberal politician.[34]

It was through the police commission that Lockett and his friends, in
the absence of a corporation, assumed political control over a town
whose economy they dominated. Effective local power and status confirmed the social pre-eminence of this urban élite which used the available
institutions as political battlegrounds. Indeed some felt that politics
played too great a part in the choice of commissioners and Thomas
Bateman the constable advised electors in 1839 'that, instead of looking
to the politics of the men whom they elected, which he was afraid had
hitherto been the case, they should be careful to select men who would
work. If this were not done, he was afraid that the business of the town
could not be carried on.'[35] The same sort of plea was echoed by Edward
Baines when he urged the appointment of overseers on non-political
grounds (see above, p. 85).

Despite Tory success in the select vestry in the later 1830s the Liberals
maintained their control over the police commission and were only

involved in any serious political controversy at the very end of the police commission's existence. A major conflict had arisen in 1843 over the proposed incorporation of the borough of Salford and the same Tory-Radical alliance that opposed the charter also opposed the improvement bill sponsored by the police commission. The major dispute concerned the legitimacy of the commission's action in introducing legislation without first consulting the ratepayers. This was a live issue, for incorporation had also been instigated by the commission without public consultations. Once more the nature of authority and the exercise of power in urban society was called into question.

The opposition to the bill was grounded not on its merits but on its mode of introduction. Local chartists, who were active on this question, took a narrow legalistic view of the limited mandate given to the police commission; as one leader explained, 'the commissioners had no right to go to Parliament for such a bill, they were elected merely to carry out the provisions of the Police Act and had no right to be soliciting new acts of Parliament, unless they first applied to their constituents'.[36] Here was a ripe harvest for the waspish talents of the radical R. J. Richardson, who saw the proposal as a means of enlarging the powers of a local oligarchy which he described as 'a greedy grasping junto like those in Spain – some twenty of them kept all the power in their own hands'.[37] Above all the mode of proceeding conflicted with the radical-Chartist belief in real popular control. Those who would pay for improvement had not been consulted and this fact raised broad general political principles. At the final unsuccessful attempt to halt the improvement machine a leading orator clarified the issue:

> He opposed it on the principles of radical reform for which he had been contending for thirty years – the meaning of which was the people should govern themselves. If a measure were a good one he would not have it thrust upon them. He was fond of pudding but he would not have a piece thrust down his throat without his consent.'[38]

As in Leeds the minor question of improvement was overlaid with great political issues.

In Salford the degree of public consent and control was controversial but in Birmingham these were non-existent, for the town's street commission was a self-elected oligarchy. In fact the street commissioners were as exclusive and select as any unreformed corporation and became for Birmingham a kind of substitute corporation. Originally set up by an Act of 1769, the Birmingham street commission had done much valuable work in the improvement field. It was never explicitly political but its composition was predominantly Whig and élitist.[39] When Birmingham was granted a charter a more overt political rivalry was established in two ways. First, implicit in the fact of incorporation was the eventual amalgamation of powers within the council and one of the reform leaders had urged his supporters to fight 'until every oligarchical system throughout the town was utterly abolished and all its rights powers and authorities were transferred to the Town Council'.[40] In short, the very existence of a self-elected street commission was an affront to the council. Second, that council was overwhelmingly radical and its members were politically hostile to the moderate Whigs of the street commission. Thus whereas in Manchester from 1840 there was a close political relationship between police commission and council, in Birmingham there was party political hostility. There was, for instance, only about a 20 per cent overlap in membership between the two bodies.[41]

In Birmingham as elsewhere self-elected bodies ran counter to the radical principles of popular control and R. K. Douglas bitterly criticized the street commissioners who were 'working in the dark unseen by the public eye, irresponsible to the public voice, appointing their own officers, levying taxes at their pleasure and distributing them, without check or control as their inclination shall determine'.[42] Another radical, T. C. Salt, introduced a motion into the council in November 1843 for removing the commission but this produced no action.[43] The public was only roused on this issue when J. A. Jaffray took over as editor of the *Birmingham Journal* in 1844 and began a sustained campaign for amalgamation of powers in the council.[44] The street commission was largely unmoved and in 1845 even proposed to extend its own powers with a new Act. The abandoning of this proposal opened a period of growing acceptance of the need for amalgamation which was brought into sharper focus by the public health issue (see below, p. 173). Nevertheless the commission could still frustrate health reformers by preventing the imposition of the 1848 Public Health Act, regarding which Jaffray commented acidly 'the disinterestedness of the commissioners is strong enough to divert the whole current of legislation into their own particular little sewer'.[45] Though the street commission gave way gracefully in the 1851 Improvement Act there were still just over a quarter of the commissioners who petitioned *against* the incorporation of their functions into the council.[46] As late as mid-century there were those who were unwilling to abandon the traditional institutions of the old élitist society to the political power of the elected municipalities. Township administration gave way only reluctantly to municipal government.

5
The highway surveyors

'*Members of highway boards had always taken good care to look after their own property and it always would be the case if the ratepayers did not look after them.*' William Harvey, a Sheffield democrat, *Sheffield Times*, 29 March 1851

This review of parochial and township institutions may be concluded by a brief glance at the political role of the boards of surveyors of highways. The highway surveyor was the least attractive of the local offices of parish administration and in view of its relatively low status did not normally command any great political interest. However, the surveyors were responsible for levying highway rates and where public expenditure was involved there was some potential popular concern. Whereas churchwardens were to a large extent prevented from levying rates during the early Victorian years, the surveyors continued to spend public funds well into mid-century. Three West Riding examples, those of Bradford, Leeds and Sheffield, illustrate the ways in which even this humble office could become politicized. In Bradford the highway surveyors were sucked into an all-embracing party political battle for total local control. Leeds provided a case study of political interest generated by men whose social status made access to superior offices difficult. Finally Sheffield was perhaps a unique case in using the highway surveyors as the lynch-pin of a theory of local self-government.

Leeds and Manchester witnessed their bitterest political struggles for local power in the 1830s; Bradford experienced its traumatic contests in the 1840s. As in the two larger towns, Bradford's struggle involved a revolt against traditional manorial and parochial modes of local government dominated by old Tory Anglican families. New men who had made their economic mark in the worsted industry, Liberals and often Dissenters, wished for local political power to confirm their positions as natural leaders and to provide that social status which mere wealth did not bring with it. In the absence of a corporation proscribed Liberals looked to the Poor Law or the improvement commission for opportunities to challenge the old oligarchy and in similar vein political interest developed in the highway surveyors.*

Part of the challenge in Bradford involved the abandonment in 1843 of the old manorial surveyors in favour of a board elected under the General Highway Act which the town adopted. In March 1843 the first board elected comprised ten Liberals and only three Tories and it began energetically to fulfil its duties.[1] This Liberal board was fearful, however, that its grasp on power was tenuous and could easily be loosened. It told the 1844 Health of Towns Commission:

A party of ratepayers alive to the importance of having better regulations in the town, assembled in the vestry and elected the present Board, several of whom have taken a great interest in the good management of the town. . . . Nevertheless, by the present constitution of the Board the whole of the surveyors will have to retire from office at the end of the year, and though re-eligible, they are aware that at the ensuing election a stronger party may assemble and elect an entirely new Board, who may be either totally ignorant of their duties or who being averse to the plans of the present Board, may suspend the improvements now going on and prevent those that are in contemplation. From the loose wording of the Act, also, it is not clear whether, when a Board is once formed, the vestry shall have the power to revert to the old mode of management.[2]

Having made the highway surveyors political the Liberals feared a Tory counter-attack either in electing a new board or in persuading the vestry to abolish the office entirely. The solution offered was instructive for it involved a reduction of direct popular control through the vestry with the adoption of a municipal or Poor Law franchise instead of open vestry election. Despite their fears Liberals remained in control after the 1844 election.[3]

A Tory counterblast was not long delayed and it grew out of Tory-radical opposition to the proposed charter of incorporation. This is exactly what had happened in Manchester in 1838 when the anti-incorporation radicals led by Wroe and Nightingale had opposed the nomination of a Liberal list whose most prominent figure was William Neild.[4] Tory-radical opposition to the charter in Manchester used the highway surveyors' election to register a blow against incorporation and

* This politicizing of the highway surveyors as part of an overall battle embracing all local institutions had similarly occurred in Salford in 1840 when at a time of great political tension the chairman of the Operative Conservative society had unsuccessfully opposed a reform list in a straight party contest for the office.

the same happened in Bradford in 1845. Besides the incorporation issue there were other activities in Bradford in the mid-1840s which made a Tory-radical alliance likely. The sanitary movement which had begun with the woolcombers enquiry was predominantly, though not exclusively, supported by Tory Anglicans and it brought into partnership well-known Chartists like George Flinn and prominent Tories.[5] Opposition to incorporation and a concern over the sanitary condition of the town forged a strong Tory-radical link which expressed itself in a packed vestry in 1845 which elected a Tory board of surveyors. The incorporation issue was not entirely irrelevant for the 1844 surveyors had petitioned in favour of a charter thus identifying themselves firmly with the incorporation Liberals and exposing themselves as a legitimate target for their opponents. The working-class element in the opposition was confirmed by George Coates, the Tory agent, who said at the vestry meeting that it was 'highly necessary the Board of Surveyors should be formed from men of business who would study the interests of the working class'.[6]

The sole Liberal on the 1845 board could not prevent the surveyors disowning the previous pro-incorporation petition and substituting a counter-petition against the charter. The Tory surveyors and their supporters were highly elated when in August 1845 the Privy Council rejected the proposal for a charter. Despite Liberal disappointment renewed strength was found to fight the 1846 elections for highway surveyor and the 1845 defeat was decisively reversed.[7] The success in re-establishing Liberal control over the board of surveyors in March 1846 was a springboard for a renewal of the incorporation campaign in October. Once again the surveyors nailed their colours to the mast by petitioning in favour of a charter, which was finally granted in 1847. The political interest in Bradford's board of highway surveyors was thus generated by issues external to highways and was part of a general campaign which carried the improvement commission, the board of guardians, and the surveyors into the Liberal camp. Similarly the Tory victory in 1845 was more concerned with the wider question of incorporation than with the intrinsic importance of the office of surveyor. The politics of township administration made sense only in the context of the overall local political structure.

It was in 1843 that Bradford's highway surveyors first attracted political interest and the same was true in Leeds, but for very different reasons. The loss to the Chartists by the abolition of the improvement commission in 1842 (see above, p. 95) caused them to seek other areas of administrative control. So in 1843 William Brook led his Chartist supporters into the vestry to capture the board of surveyors of highways. This was elected by the vestry usually without a poll and was far more accessible to Chartist influence than either the council or the board of guardians. It was widely acknowledged that vestry meetings could be swamped by non-ratepayers whose influence was nullified by a proper poll.[8] The Leeds Chartists were demonstrating that they, as relatively humble men, could manage public affairs as efficiently as any other social groups, and they were proud of their economical administration which enabled a surplus to be passed on each year. Through the 1840s the Chartists received votes of confidence from the vestry and their authority was not really challenged until the election of 1852.[9]

From 1850 Brook had ceased to use the term Chartist and referred to his surveyors merely as members of the working classes. When the expenses of a deputation to London were challenged by R. M. Carter, himself a Chartist surveyor, Tory interest grew at the possibility of a division in the ranks. Much was made of the trip to London, 'a bootless errand unless it was to see the Great Exhibition without making much demands on their own pockets', and on the suspicion of jobbery Tories wished to make a change in 'the ultra liberal, democratic or chartist character of the board'.[10] In a noisy vestry meeting reminiscent of contests 20 years earlier, William Brook asked for and obtained middle-class Liberal support against the Tories. This was doubly significant. First, a similar request to maintain Chartist control of the churchwardens had fallen on deaf ears and indicated the superior importance by 1852 of the surveyors. Second, the Liberal-Chartist alliance was a reverberation at a minor level of the national unity forged in 1852 between middle- and working-class reformers for a further extension of the suffrage. In what was simply referred to as a Liberal versus Tory contest the former were victorious by about 2,600 to 700.[11] Three years later another row, this time over the canvassing activities of a man employed on the stone heap, led to a similar alliance against a Tory attack and another Liberal victory in a two to one poll.[12]

The victories by poll in 1852 and 1855 confirmed control in the hands of ex-Chartists and radicals of somewhat inferior social status. Tories took little interest in subsequent elections and when contests occurred which used the euphemism 'old' and 'new' surveyors they were invariably Liberal attempts to graft a more respectable membership on to the board. In 1854 the Liberal magistrate and former mayor of Leeds, Darnton Lupton, openly admitted that his list of nominations contained respectable property owners, but the ex-Chartists remained in office.[13] Six years later a very confused situation arose when a number of 'new' respectable Liberals were elected but the 13 'old' surveyors refused to co-operate with the new blood and there was a squabble over the legality of the elections.[14] This could not finally be resolved until the 1861 election which was again characterized by disputes over expenses. Once more a prominent Liberal proposed a 'new' list which, he claimed, would carry on the surveyors' work 'with efficiency and economy' and his list was carried on a show of hands in the vestry. However, the old radical surveyors proved unwilling to give up without a fight and asked for a poll which confirmed them in office.[15] Thereafter until highway powers were absorbed into the council under the 1866 Improvement Act radical control was uncontested.

Middle-class concern over Chartist control is understandable in view of the not inconsiderable sums involved: during the 1860s £12,000 or £13,000 *per annum* were spent by the surveyors. Yet there was never any serious questioning of the administrative ability displayed and indeed the radical leader R. M. Carter argued that only plain folk could run highway affairs since 'the gentleman part of such bodies did not do the work and would not do the work. No the work must be done by plain practical hardworking men like himself . . . the barristers the lawyers and the physicians were the worst attenders on any committee.'[16] Whether true or not, the facts were that the Leeds board of highway surveyors was, from the time of Chartist accession in 1843 until its demise in 1866, the political resort of the humble. The 1845 board comprised 13 retailers and 6 craftsmen or tradesmen while that of 1846 included 11 retailers and 8 manufacturers or craftsmen, of whom 2 might have been middle class. The final board of 1866 was in no way different, with 9 craftsmen or tradesmen, 8 retailers all involved in food and drink and just 2 professional men. Typical of the men whose social status made the office of surveyor politically attractive was William Parker, owner of a well-known temperance hotel and a Chartist councillor from 1851 to 1854. Wishing to continue his municipal career as a radical he was an unsuccessful municipal candidate in 1854 and 1856 and in the mid-Victorian years found the board of surveyors a politically acceptable alternative. Men would fight the good fight in whatever institution was accessible to them.

In Leeds there was an element of Hobson's choice about the politicizing of the highway surveyors, as men deprived of participation elsewhere looked to the board as the only avenue of political advancement. This was in sharp contrast with Sheffield where in the early 1850s the highways board was consciously used as the central organ for implementing a general political philosophy. Isaac Ironside, the ex-Chartist accountant, organized a party of 'democrats' which attempted to democratize local government in the image of the great anti-centralization pundit Joshua Toulmin Smith.[17] Toulmin Smith has so often been associated with opposition to the 1848 Public Health Act in defence of local self-government that it is sometimes assumed that he saw all-powerful local councils as the ideal. In fact he went much further:

> Local self government does not then consist as many imagine in
> having local bodies elected or otherwise and leaving the exclusive
> management of everything in their hands. Its essence consists in this:-
> that . . . arrangements also exist by which regular fixed frequent and
> accessible meetings together of the freemen themselves shall take
> place; at which all matters done by the representative bodies local and
> general shall be laid before the folk and the people, discussed and
> approved or disapproved.[18]

This was the democratic local self-government which Ironside tried to
plant in Sheffield and he organized so-called 'ward-motes' to facilitate
real popular participation. These ward-motes, directed by Ironside's
Central Democratic Association, were mid-Victorian examples of what
are now called community politics and they claimed the right to vet
parliamentary candidates, to submit nominations for local offices in a
kind of pre-election and even on one celebrated occasion to elect under
Ironside's guidance their own aldermen.

In this context of respectable anarchism Ironside sought to use the
highways board as the agent of what he called 'the science of direct
legislation', relying on popular assent as the sole authority for executive
action. The board of highway surveyors was none too promising for so
elevated a function. It was a byword for jobbery and inferior service. In
the 1840s its sole employee had been unable to read or write, and surveyors had authorized work done near their own properties without the
knowledge of their colleagues.[19] In 1851 it was reluctantly acknowledged
by one of the democrats that in the absence of public interest and control
surveyors would look after their own property and an irate ratepayer
complained of a surveyor who had ordered the improvement of one side
of a street but not the other:

> He had improved Duke Street as far as his own property and a little
> beyond it; but when a man's range of vision did not extend beyond his
> own property he was not likely to do his duty satisfactorily in a
> general way . . . There was a nice little party assembling at the Robin
> Hood that concocted these things. They say 'if you'll serve my turn
> I'll serve your turn'.[20]

Ironside was determined to put an end to this self-seeking petty
jobbery and make the highways board a useful institution for practical
reform. By the time of the 1852 elections he was in full control of the
vestry and the ward-mote scheme was well advanced.[21] The assumption
of democratic control of the board under Ironside's chairmanship in
1852 was both a party political victory for the radicals over the Liberals
and a fundamental change in the interpretation of authority and the
exercise of local power. Ironside embarked upon an ambitious sewerage

scheme for the town for which a previous board were advised they had no powers. The 1852 board looked to the ratepayers rather than Parliament for authorization.

In September 1852 the highways board put the sewerage scheme to the ratepayers in vestry and brushed aside the view that they lacked legal powers to proceed. Ironside, quoting Toulmin Smith as his authority, insisted 'that anything that this meeting might resolve upon would be thoroughly legal ... the highway board was advised that a vestry meeting could confer all the requisite powers'.[22] He was bitterly attacked for having recently been responsible for the abandonment of a promising improvement bill sponsored by the council, an event described as 'one of the greatest misfortunes we have known happen to Sheffield'.[23] Ironside's defence of his opposition to the bill is instructive, for he claimed that 'it disfranchised a large number of ratepayers and introduced the property qualification by abolishing the popular and simply elected highway boards and transferring their powers to the Town Council'.[24] Sheffield democrats, like Leeds Chartists, knew the political advantage of popular vestry elections. Ironside's local democracy and his personal ascendancy were only possible where the central authority of the municipality was severely limited. Even within towns centralization had to be opposed.

Since pitifully few ratepayers attended the September vestry meeting Ironside agreed to adjourn. He was disappointed at the public apathy and as the second meeting approached he extolled the legal and moral virtues of vestry authority:

> Why are the people so unwilling to avail themselves of the powers they possess? We cannot divine except it be that they have been so long accustomed to have things done for them that they are afraid to act for themselves. If a vestry can levy rates for fire engines why not for drainage?[25]

Ironside re-affirmed at the adjourned vestry meeting that if authorized by the vestry the highways board could proceed since 'the jurisdiction of the vestry was anything that was for the public good'.[26] Oblivious to the renewed criticism of his actions over the improvement bill Ironside, armed with vestry authority, proceeded expeditiously to organize the laying of deep sewers in Sheffield streets. Although his critics claimed that public money was being illegally expended they had to admire his industry in getting the project completed over the next two years. The board issued clear orders that no property owner should be allowed to put his drainage into the sewers until he had paid his share of the costs, that failure to contribute would lead to a surcharge under the Highways Act, and that even owners in private streets would be compelled or induced to get the streets in proper order.[27]

It is clear that in strict law the highways board was not empowered to lay deep sewers but sewers were laid and since Ironside, so to speak, got away with it he no doubt convinced himself that vestry authority was all-powerful. When he extended this to the controversial Consumers Gas Company which he was sponsoring he found he had overreached himself. This new gas concern had not received any parliamentary sanction for its activities but Ironside had insisted that laying gas pipes could be authorized by the highways board. The gas company was intended to be, in the words of one historian, 'a triumphant assertion of the power of the local highway boards their authority grounded on the decisions of vestry meetings'.[28] Because the gas question was so controversial it dominated the 1853 election in place of the sewerage issue which had become a *fait accompli*.

In the few years of his supremacy Ironside had generated powerful enemies who now combined to attack him on the gas question. The propaganda at the 1853 surveyors' election concerned the rival merits of the two gas companies and the vote was said to be a vote for or against laying gas pipes with only vestry authority.[29] Yet coming more and more to the fore was a revolt against Ironside's personal authority. His opponents attacked 'the spirit of dictation' and convicted Ironside in the light of his own theories:

> Local self government taught them that the right of the people was a voice in the choice of their representatives . . . Then why should a certain party select men privately for highway men . . . It was nothing but a farce when one man dictated to them what they should do. That was their local self government.[30]

Robert Leader, the mouthpiece of Sheffield middle-class liberalism, soon jumped on the bandwagon and broadened the attack to include the monopolistic tendencies of the whole democratic movement which had 'aimed to set up a dictatorship . . . to engross all offices in the hands of subservient nominees of the moving power'.[31]

Ironside beat off the attack in 1853 and proudly referred to the unity of feeling at the board on the sewerage question when he was re-elected in 1854.[32] By then however his empire was collapsing along with the gas company which did require parliamentary authority and which eventually merged with its rival. Ironside had alienated many of his own supporters by his awkwardness (in 1854 he refused to allow reporters into board meetings) and in 1853 and 1854 he was defeated in the municipal elections. The democratic schism within Sheffield liberalism gradually healed and by the end of 1854 the highways board had returned to the political oblivion from which the remarkable career of Isaac Ironside had raised it.

Ironside's fall from grace and the consequent reaffirmation of municipal over vestry institutions is an appropriate terminal point to the first section of this book. The case studies have revealed a lively area of political interest and activity at the minor parochial and township level. The institutions became political bodies by a complex process which, for the most part, comprised four elements. First and most common of all, party political rivalries at one level of political life affected the whole political structure and so parochial and township institutions became political foci as an extension of general contests for local power. Even Ironside's unique activities at the vestry level had their counterpart in his nomination of Toulmin Smith as a parliamentary candidate for Sheffield in 1852. Second, these institutions were politically attractive to men who were denied alternative political participation, sometimes by proscription, sometimes by the electoral process, sometimes because of their social status. Third, men fought for political control at this level because of policy, in order to get the power to put into operation some desired policy goal, perhaps the abolition of church rates or the building of a workhouse. Finally, parochial and township administration raised broad general questions, not easily resolvable along party lines, about the nature of authority and the exercise of power in the urban community. Increasingly such urban authority was to be exercised through municipal rather than parochial channels.

Part Two
Municipal Government

6
Council politics

'Every year there will be that delightful agitation which I love to see – an election of one common council man for every ward – just enough to remind the other two, if they don't behave themselves that their turn is coming . . . I tell you in all frankness that I think the Corporation Act the most democratic measure upon our statute book.' Richard Cobden, 1838

1

The predominant endemic political rivalry in early Victorian cities was not the potentially explosive conflict between bourgeoisie and proletariat but a struggle for supremacy within the urban middle class itself. The larger cities were characterized by a diverse and fragmented social structure which produced a rather amorphous class of superior craftsmen and tradesmen, retailers and providers of a variety of services who blurred the class lines between the owners and servants of capital. In a sense these groups together with the embryonic proletariat were spectators to a struggle for power among their social superiors and were invited to side with one or other of the contenders. The battle lines were drawn along three contours. Family was of crucial importance in English social organization and the urban struggle for power was often a rivalry between traditional long-established ruling families and newly-founded dynasties, commonly the product of go-ahead migrants to the town. This new-man/old-man conflict was exacerbated by religious divisions, for the traditional ruling families were almost exclusively Anglican and the rising newcomers predominantly, though not exclusively, Dissenters. Political affiliation confirmed the contest for power and the traditional Tory urban establishment found itself opposed by Whig-Liberal or radical challengers. Family, religion, and politics produced a battle between the insider and the outsider, the ins and the outs.

Proscription from closed corporations prevented Dissenting Liberals from participation in municipal government in the early nineteenth century and we have seen in Part One how this transferred the political battleground to parochial and township affairs. Municipal reform in the

1830s enabled men who had made their mark in the local economy to enter the municipal arena and achieve a position of political leadership appropriate to their economic station. Successful businessmen sought to legitimize their role as social leaders through political office and from the 1830s a new area of political participation was opened up. The municipal council became the focus of a power struggle between rival élites within the bourgeoisie. Seats on the council, the aldermanic robe, and the mayoral chain became the yardstick for measuring success in the battle between a traditional Tory-Anglican establishment and a new Liberal-Dissenting economic élite. It was a struggle for the very soul of the city.

The traditional oligarchy of merchants and gentlemen had mono-polized urban government through closed corporations, many of which were corrupt. Leicester corporation, for instance, had become a byword for political partisanship, private peculation and gross venality and was in the words of its historian 'at best capable of only a spasmodic concern for the good regimen of a community of which it could in no effective way be considered representative'.[1] The municipal corporations commis-sioners indicted many corporations for abuse of their powers and for neglect of local administration. Yet not all corporations were tarred with the same brush. Leeds corporation, lacking large funds and properties, had no political influence to exercise and had administered justice efficiently. Indeed one official reported, 'Every person whom we con-sulted agreed so remarkably in eulogising the present corporation of Leeds that we cannot doubt that the town is well governed through their means and it appears that the defects usually attendant upon their method of election are almost neutralised by the circumstances of their possessing little or no property.'[2] Similarly, despite the notorious venality of its freemen and despite mercantile complaints over town dues and dock administration, Liverpool had been on the whole well governed by its unreformed corporation. The commissioners concluded that, 'in the main, the Corporation have evinced economy and good management in their affairs; that as magistrates they are attentive to their duties, and careful of the due regulation of the Borough; and that, as its governing body their conduct seems to have been materially influenced by a desire to promote its welfare.'[3]

Although the corporations of Leeds and Liverpool did not altogether share the defects of many of the corrupt bodies, they were characterized by the one overwhelming evil which in the minds of municipal reformers damned all unreformed corporations. They were exclusive self-elected close corporations, the absolute negation of open government. The largely harmless Leeds corporation reinforced the oligarchy of woollen merchants who dominated the local economy and offered no access to the rising Liberal Dissenting groups who contributed so much to the economic development of the town. Edward Baines complained bitterly that the corporation had 'been characterised by the most rigorous exclusion of all persons differing in politics or religious creed from the favoured few' and the commissioners confirmed that it was a closed shop:

> The close constitution of the corporation is obvious, all vacancies in each branch of it being filled by the Select Body, gives to that body absolute and uncontrolled self-election. Family influence is predominant. Fathers and sons and sons-in-law, brothers and brothers-in-law succeed to the offices of the corporation like matters of family settlement.[4]

The same political and religious exclusiveness marred the achievements of Liverpool corporation and the emergent élite of newer Dissenting merchants was denied corporate honours. The same family network enveloped urban administration as 'they were not only a self-elected body but a family party . . . the immense patronage at their disposal was too often considered as the heirloom of the Corporate families'.[5] Egerton Smith, Liverpool's leading Liberal editor, explained the situation clearly:

> The simple facts are that the members of the Common Council elect each other – that they consist of a round of sons, brothers, and cousins – that they are an exclusive body both in religion and politics – that no merchant, however eminent, no Dissenter, however distinguished for his talents character and services has the most remote chance of obtaining a place in that privileged body.[6]

Only occasionally, as in Newcastle's complicated method of election, or Nottingham's junior council, or even in Liverpool's riotous and venal mayoral elections, was an element of popular participation allowed to seep into the unreformed system. Only municipal reform could dislodge the monopolists of corporate power, entrenched in close corporations. Where, as in Leicester, the corporation showed itself brazenly partisan by, for instance, creating hundreds of non-resident Tory voters to sway elections, municipal reform became the most pressing local political issue. The 1832 Reform Bill was seen in Leicester as being the only way to answer a simple question, 'does the Corporation exist for the Town of Leicester or the Town of Leicester with its forty thousand inhabitants for the benefit of the Corporation?'.[7] Largely because Leicester corporation's 'foul and filthy corruptions have stunk in the nostrils of the whole nation',[8] the town's reformers played a prominent part in the campaign for municipal reform. It is significant to cite also condemnation of its neighbour in abuse at Nottingham:

The avenues of office are effectually closed against the admission of
rank, respectability and talent unless they possess the necessary
passport – a full accordance with the political views of those who bear
the mace of authority . . . the most zealous defender of Corporations
cannot . . . support the exclusive plan of self-election, the employment
of municipal power for electioneering purposes or the non publication
of the receipts and expenditure of trust property.[9]

Political exclusion, electioneering and financial abuse were common
indictments, but this attack on Nottingham corporation came from a
Tory pen. Since Nottingham had the rare distinction of boasting a
corrupt Whig corporation all the enthusiasm for municipal reform there
came from the Tory side.

It is right to view municipal reform as a parallel to 1832 and not
simply because it was an extension of a vague belief in representative
government. One of the main aims of the Reform Act had been to
legitimize influence, both by removing its corrupt exercise in the domains
of the landed gentry and by creating in urban areas spheres of influence
for the aspiring middle class. Municipal reform in 1835 provided an
institutional framework within which the political influence of social and
economic leadership could be legitimized. It was widely recognized that
this would create a transfer of power locally not so much between socio-
economic as politico-religious rivals. As Dr Hennock has shown, there
was no great difference in the social composition of the old and new
Leeds corporations.[10] It was simply that ambitious and frustrated outsiders had supplanted traditional insiders, and defenders of the old
system mocked the political exclusiveness of the new:

> Indeed the Rads are working hard
>   Each in his own vocation
> To get a finger in the pie
>   Of a *party* corporation
> The 'Local' lies – it lied before
>   But oh! what an alteration
> It now lies *for* what it lied *against*
>   A *party* corporation.[11]

If the old élite within the urban middle class had legitimized its role as
natural leaders through closed corporation, the new élite would attempt
the same process through political control of freely elected municipal
councils. Municipal reform created the setting for the battle between
rival middle-class élites and called into question the forms and composition of traditional social leadership in the city.

The same sort of process could be seen in the unincorporated towns

where in such places as Manchester, Birmingham, or Bradford Whig-
Liberal Dissenters had to obtain a charter as a first act of defiance
against the traditional oligarchy. In Manchester that oligarchy had not
only been challenged in its control of parochial and police commission
affairs but had also allowed the traditional vehicle for its authority, the
manorial institutions, to become effete. As Cobden put it so forcibly, 'the
old state of the government of Manchester is so decrepid and worn out,
that it has actually fallen to pieces and gone to the death'.[12] Because
there was general dissatisfaction with outmoded manorial institutions
wholly inappropriate to Manchester's needs in the 1830s, it was widely
agreed by all parties that some changes would have to be made. Hence
the incorporation struggle was preceded by suggestions for police reform
from the Liberal Quaker William Neild, which foundered on radical
opposition.[13]

When Cobden's unhappy experience of manorial government inspired
him to attempt to generate a municipal reform movement he went for the
straightforward plea 'incorporate your borough'. Cobden's case for
incorporation was grounded on a simple fact, that Manchester's 'Chief
Municipal Officers should be a body popularly chosen instead of being
nominated by the Lord of the Manor's Court Leet'.[14] In his view the
essential aim of the Municipal Reform Act had been to end close government, 'to deprive the oligarchy of their power in two hundred and
fifty of our large towns and to put that power into the hands of the
people themselves'.[15] More specifically, the middle-class Liberal Dissenting élite wished to supplant the old oligarchy as the natural governors of
Manchester and a municipal charter was assumed to be the best way of so
doing.

What was in reality a blatant struggle for local power between rival
groups of similar social status within the upper ranks of the middle class
was clothed in language which would appeal to the spectators of that
power struggle. Both Liberal incorporators and Tory anti-incorporators
made a bid for those numerically greater though economically weaker in
order to give weight to the party band wagon. Cobden's pamphlet
Incorporate Your Borough (1837) and his speech to launch the application
for a charter in 1838 aimed to capture two specific groups, the artisan
and working-class radicals and the so-called 'shopocracy'. The failure to
win over the former was outweighed by success with the latter whose
option in favour of a charter proved decisive.

Radicals were tempted by the essentially democratic nature of the
new system. This was not mere specious window dressing from Cobden
(though not all Manchester Liberals were as keen on extending the
suffrage as he was) and many middle-class leaders across the country
saw open free election as the main virtue of municipal reform. But the

emphasis placed upon the democracy of incorporation was clearly a bait
to the radicals:

> Every man's vote, however humble his circumstances may be, is of
> equal value with his wealthiest neighbour's. There is no Clause
> borrowed from Sturges Bourne's Act, giving six votes to the rich mill-
> owner and only one to the small shopkeeper. The banker or the
> merchant, though worth a million, and though he ride in his carriage
> to the polling booth, can only record the same number of votes as the
> poor artisan, who walks there perhaps slip-shod and aproned from his
> garret or cellar.[16]

Cobden reminded the large audience at the first incorporation meeting
that the municipal system was 'universal suffrage, annual parliaments,
vote by ticket if not by ballot' and his main supporter confirmed that 'it
was not Sturges Bourne's Act, no bricks against brains'.[17]

Archibald Prentice, whose radical credentials were as good as any,
professed amazement that radicals should opt to retain the Sturges
Bourne Act which had frustrated popular wishes so often and that they
preferred 'Sir Oswald Mosley's government without any suffrage at all'
to the broad suffrage of the municipal system.[18] Despite the apparent
incongruity, the radical leaders James Wroe, Edward Nightingale, and
Elijah Dixon bitterly opposed the incorporation proposals and refused to
swallow this democratic bait. The Tory-radical alliance already forged
on the Poor Law question was strengthened by the incorporation
struggle. Wroe and his friends intuitively recognized what Cobden's
party sought to hide, that this was an attempt to reinforce economic and
social dominance with political authority. While Liberals saw the police
and Poor Law propaganda as red herrings, the radicals found these
issues all too real. They feared that wealthy manufacturers who already
dominated the local economy would control the working class with a more
efficient police force, subjugate the masses by the 'bastilles' and sit in
judgement on them as new magistrates. As a Sheffield anti-incorporation
radical explained, 'by means of a corporation you will be raising up an
aristocracy among you and also creating a set of masters over you' and it
was just this which Edward Nightingale feared when urging Manchester
men, in a significant phrase, 'to resist the tyranny of the bloated rich'.[19]
Cobden's second, C. J. S. Walker, claimed that their aim was not 'to take
power from one party in order to put it into the hands of another' (which
was exactly what it was) and as if to fulfil the radical prophecy Walker
not only became an alderman for the first 18 years of the corporation's
life but also was chairman of the Poor Law guardians during the 1840s.
This would not have surprised Wroe, who perceptively identified the
Liberal aim as 'to transfer the management of the town to sixty four

wiseacres of the new school'.[20] This was exactly the line taken by Dixon at the vestry in 1840 (see above, p. 42), for radicals saw the Liberal middle classes seeking power for selfish ends. Once this 'tyranny of the bloated rich' with its 'turtle-fed aldermen and cotton lord mayors' was established by a charter there would be little hope for ordinary folk. In the struggle between élites the radical crowds backed the traditional oligarchy as the Tory-radical alliance held firm.

Cobden had equally appealed to a second identifiable group, that wide band of neither poverty nor riches, which included skilled craftsmen/ retailers, specialist and general shopkeepers, purveyors of food and drink and sometimes accommodation, who were characterized by their dominant segment the shopocracy. In order to establish government by a middle-class élite the Liberals needed to arouse the political conscious-ness of the shopocracy. Thus Cobden reminded them of their inferior status in the old system and defined a political role for them in the new:

> It is, of course, very well known that hundreds of respectable and wealthy *shopkeepers* reside within the township of Manchester but it is not equally notorious that it has always been a maxim, at the election of municipal officers that no retailer was eligible to fill the office of boroughreeve or constable! . . . But in the city of London, where you will find no manor court-leet diffusing its tone of feudal insolence and slavish servility, there is a corporation renowned for its liberal character; and more than a moiety of its common council men, and several of the aldermen, are shopkeepers. . . . The shopkeepers, to a man, will support the plan because its immediate operation will tend, as has already been shown by the example of London, to elevate them to their proper level in the social scale, and afford to the public spirited individuals of that influential class an enlarged field of usefulness.[21]

In the crucial opening phase of the campaign the support of these middling ranks of the middle class was absolutely vital and Cobden admitted that the Tory-radical alliance threatened defeat for the Liberals but that 'the *shopocracy* carried the day'.[22]*

Carrying the resolutions to launch the charter application was but the beginning of a bitter, complex and protracted struggle which was ended only by the decision in the *Rutter* v. *Chapman* case in 1841. Tory-radical resistance to the charter was virulent and we have already seen how the anti-incorporators used both the churchwardens and the police commis-sion to frustrate the charter. When police commissioner Sir Charles

---

* Evidence of their role may also be found in the social composition of the first council where no less than 18 of 64 members were in the retail trade. The comparative figure for Leeds was 8.

Shaw was imposed upon Manchester by the government he was shocked
by the bitterness of party rivalry: 'I found local party animosity carried
to an incredible height, the feelings of hatred to each other being so
rabid as not even to be exceeded in civil commotions of Portugal and
Spain . . . in Manchester public good was forgotten.'[23]

This venomous power struggle was complicated by a number of factors.
First, there was opposition from out-townships, particularly Chorlton,
against incorporation with Manchester. Chorlton had in fact resolved
against joining Manchester as early as 1833, since incorporation within the metropolis 'would tend not only to depreciate the value of property
there but also burthen them with additional rates'.[24] Second, there was
the private interest of the old office holders, particularly the omnifarious
clerk, Oswald Milne, who had personal reasons to fight the anti-charter
battle. Indeed some years later Alderman Alexander Kay described the
prime motive of the anti-incorporators as 'to continue to three public
officers the large fees and emoluments they had been accustomed to
receive'.[25] Third, there was the crucial question of forged signatures for
and against the charter. Wrongdoing was by no means the province of
one party here, and in 1838 Cobden reluctantly authorized corruption in
imitation of his opponents:

> we shall have much trouble over this dirty odious business. It is this
> kind of work which makes public matters about as pleasant as
> scavenging and not so cleanly either. But since we have begun there is
> no help but to go on . . . we must not begrudge a few pounds to the vile
> instruments of the Tories. They will pay and there is no alternative for
> us but to do the same.[26]

What finished up in the seedy world of venal party hacks had originated in a much higher vision, for Cobden had placed incorporation in a
wide political horizon. His pamphlet had opened with an explanation of
the way incorporation could aim a blow at the aristocracy; it was littered
with anti-aristocratic references; it sought to establish a zone of urban
authority which would 'place for ever the population of our town and
neighbourhood beyond the control of a booby squirearchy'. The whole
exercise was aimed at beginning a new era for Manchester 'when it
shakes off the feudal livery of Sir Oswald Mosley to put on the democratic garb of the Municipal Reform Act'.[27] More than this, Cobden took
up Attwood's ideas in Birmingham that councils would become legalized
permanent political unions, officially active in political agitation:

> The new corporations are trades unions in opposition to the corn law
> tyrants – the *'landed interest;'* they are normal schools of agitation
> for the education of orators and patriots; 'they are,' (to use the

words of Thomas Attwood . . .) 'real and legal political unions in every borough . . .'.[28]

There was no doubt that in the opinion of Cobden and Attwood municipal corporations would be overtly political institutions with highly political functions to perform. Yet many were prepared to challenge this and a running battle went on throughout the nineteenth century over the question of whether politics ought to enter the field of municipal government. Initially such views came mainly from the Tory side, but in the face of Liberal enthusiasm over municipal reform and likely Liberal electoral success the 'no party' cry was a predictable Tory ploy. As one Liverpool observer remarked, it was all very well for Tories to stand as non-political candidates,

> but we cannot disguise from ourselves that those gentlemen are put forward on account of their politics – that to carry them is a political and party object and that their election will be hailed not as the return of so many sensible and respectable men to the council but as the defeat of the Reform Party . . . under these circumstances the contest unavoidably assumes a political character.[29]

A typical Tory view was that expressed by a Bradford conservative councillor who, on the occasion of the first aldermanic election, explained 'that he did not look upon the matter as a political question – and he trusted that all colours be they yellow green or blue would be wholly disregarded in the council room'.[30]

Tories soon had to accept the political realities, since Liberal monopoly of municipal power could only be terminated by effective counteracting political activity. Liberal political partisanship confirmed that Tories would also take on political stances and so politics became firmly embedded in municipal affairs. A Tory editor explained the situation well in 1838:

> In treating Municipal matters we should wish to avoid as much as possible all reference to politics and to parties but that dissenting and discontented politico-religious body which by the cast of the die obtained a temporary ascendancy in the Council Chamber at the first election has been so immediately governed in all its acts and appointments . . . by party distinctions and political predelictions that any attempt on our part to discard politics when treating of Municipal affairs would be utterly futile.[31]

Even in the mid-Victorian years when some Liberals began supporting the idea that political affairs were no part of municipal business there was still strong advocacy of the old Cobden/Attwood line and, for instance, in

1866 a Leeds alderman of 25 years' standing countered the notion of a
non-political municipal council:

> this was a political body: the very first act that was done in sending
> gentlemen into the Council was a political act and the Councillors were
> elected because they had certain political opinions. . . . To suppose that
> gentlemen were sent there merely to make sewers, to light lamps and to
> cleanse the town was to take a very poor view of the duties devolving
> upon the council.[32]

It was startlingly clear that within this overtly political context
municipal reform was a huge Liberal accession of power. Whatever
subsequent elections produced, the first municipal election in most
cities recorded an overwhelming Liberal success. Table 3 illustrates the
initial Liberal/radical hegemony in eight towns.

Table 3. Results of first municipal elections

Town	Date	Councillors elected	
		Liberal	Tory
Leeds	Dec. 1835	42	6
Liverpool	,,	43	5
Leicester	,,	38	4
Nottingham	,,	27	15
Manchester	Nov. 1838	48	0
Birmingham	Dec. 1838	48	0
Salford	July 1844	18	6
Bradford	Aug. 1847	30	12

The aldermanic seats which were thus in the gift of Liberal majorities
merely reinforced the Liberal hold on municipal power. How far such
initial success was sustained can only be established by studying
municipal affairs in individual cities.

2

In Leeds, municipal reform opened up the council at a time of fierce
political rivalry for total control which had engulfed all local institutions.[33] It was therefore a pious hope that politics could be excluded
from municipal affairs: Leeds council was run on party-political lines,
even though the party contest did slacken in the mid-Victorian years.
Table 4 gives the bare bones of the party contests in Leeds from the first
election through to the first major ward boundary revision in 1881.

The table indicates a serious Conservative challenge in the early years

Table 4. Political composition of Leeds council, 1835–80

Year	Councillors Liberal	Tory	Aldermen Liberal	Tory	Whole Council Liberal	Tory
1835–6	39	9	12	4	51	13
1836–7	37	11	12	4	49	15
1837–8	33	15	12	4	45	19
1838–9	27	21	16	0	43	21
1839–40	20	28	16	0	36	28
1840–1	16	32	16	0	32	32
1841–2	23	25	16	0	39	25
1842–3	26	22	16	0	42	22
1843–4	31	17	16	0	47	17
1844–5	34	14	16	0	50	14
1845–6	38	10	16	0	54	10
1846–7	36	12	15	1	51	13
1847–8	33	15	16	0	49	15
1848–9	35	13	16	0	51	13
1849–50	39	9	16	0	55	9
1850–1	41	7	16	0	57	7
1851–2	40	8	16	0	56	8
1852–3	40	8	16	0	56	8
1853–4	39	9	16	0	55	9
1854–5	35	13	16	0	51	13
1855–6	32	16	16	0	48	16
1856–7	34	14	16	0	50	14
1857–8	39	9	16	0	55	9
1858–9	41	7	16	0	57	7
1859–60	41	7	16	0	57	7
1860–1	41	7	16	0	57	7
1861–2	42	6	16	0	58	6
1862–3	40	8	16	0	56	8
1863–4	36	12	16	0	52	12
1864–5	32	16	16	0	48	16
1865–6	31	17	16	0	47	17
1866–7	34	14	16	0	50	14
1867–8	36	12	16	0	52	12
1868–9	37	11	16	0	53	11
1869–70	37	11	16	0	53	11
1870–1	37	11	16	0	53	11
1871–2	31	17	16	0	47	17
1872–3	25	23	16	0	41	23
1873–4	18	28	16	0	34	28

Table 4 (contd.)

Year	Councillors		Aldermen		Whole Council	
	Liberal	Tory	Liberal	Tory	Liberal	Tory
1874–5	25	23	16	0	41	23
1875–6	33	15	16	0	49	15
1876–7	35	13	16	0	51	13
1877–8	37	11	16	0	53	11
1878–9	36	12	16	0	52	12
1879–80	37	11	16	0	53	11
1880–1	38	10	16	0	54	10

of the reformed Leeds corporation. The inaugural mayor had argued that parties 'were useful in exciting a spirit of competition and vigilance and had the effect of bringing a greater degree of energy into the service of the public',[34] and that certainly occurred in Leeds where there was an intense party struggle until the early 1840s. Both sides relied upon organized activity and both had registration societies which fought out the preliminary battles at the annual revision courts. Indeed so intense were these that the revision of 1840 could not be completed because of the number of claims and objections, and the election of that year was fought on the 1839 register, leading to many contentious disputes about the right to vote.

In addition to registration activities Liberals needed to organize council business, partly in order to disburse the spoils of power, and there were frequent criticisms of the way Liberals ran the council. Quite early on a Tory councillor complained, 'if gentlemen were to come there with measures cut and dried it was all a farce coming there to discuss them', and the Tory press urged independent members not to stand for the domination of a caucus.[35] The campaign against 'the *Caucus* which meets . . . to dictate the measures of the whig majority' was stepped up in the later 1830s and Robert Perring asked whether it was right 'to hold a little caucus in the "Reform Registration Office" and there to appoint delegates under the name of aldermen to counterbalance the votes of councillors elected by the Burgesses'.[36] The same propaganda was a feature of the 1860s and Henry Price, an aggressive Tory doctor who sat in the council from 1861 to 1870, was a frequent critic of prior organization, 'the business having been done in the back room in Bond Street out of which many things emanated which had better not see the light'.[37] He was particularly critical of prior Liberal meetings to choose a mayor:

Instead of meeting in the Council Room to transact their business they went to Mr. Baynes' Reform Association offices and there determined amongst themselves in what way the majority were to deal with the minority. . . . Nobody could expect fifteen or sixteen gentlemen would come into the Council Room to be treated like automata.[38]

The caucus of the 1870s was thus not a new phenomenon but an updated version of a long Leeds tradition.

The caucus was itself only an expression of a fierce party contest for municipal power which was also a long-term characteristic of Leeds. When the Tories were increasing their representation on the council in the later 1830s two issues fanned the flames of party warfare, the cost of the new system and the alienation of the borough fund. It was likely that displaced Tories would make much of the alleged increase in local burdens consequent upon municipal reform, and at the very outset a radical observer predicted Tory strategy:

> We well know that there is a party which, having always opposed popular interests, seeks to delude the people to its support by professing to advocate a system of the most miserly and niggardly kind: a party which never found out that a lavish list of Tory sinecurists and pensioners was extravagant and iniquitous, but which *when out of office* seeks popular favour by a hypocritical whining about economy whenever a public improvement is proposed.[39]

So it turned out, with Tory propagandists juggling the figures to show how cheap the old system had been and how expensive the new one was becoming. Particularly at election time the town was placarded with bills about increased rates, and such propaganda clearly delivered many seats into Tory hands. All Liberal policies were judged extravagant, especially the newly uniformed day police ('the day parades of dandy policemen'), and the building of Armley gaol which was voted on many times.

Tory hackles rose over finance, and Liberals were angered by the decision of the old corporation to give away all its funds to Anglican churches and charities. This obviously partisan insult aimed at the new corporation was the most important reason for the continuance of bitter party warfare after 1835. The Tory case was that the money was private property derived from fines paid by members of the old corporation; the Liberal case was that there had been a gross misappropriation of public funds. The Liberals in the new corporation began a suit in chancery for recovering these funds and where Tories argued that the suit could only end in robbing charities Liberals saw the original alienation of the fund as robbing the burgesses. The legal dispute took five years to settle and the Liberals had to face the growing legal costs of the suit and frequent Tory motions for its abandonment. When the case was finally decided in 1840 it was a victory for Liberal resolve in the face of severe difficulties and the money was restored to the new corporation.[40] The chancery suit was as important for Leeds as *Rutter* v. *Chapman* was for Manchester, for both represented a legal challenge to the authority of the new corporation. The chancery suit victory was a great triumph for municipal reform in Leeds.

What had made the continuance of the chancery suit doubtful was the increased number of Tory councillors who were elected each year. Indeed the Liberals were forced to rely on the aldermanic vote to maintain control and the pacific gesture in 1836 of giving the Tories four aldermen (itself intensely unpopular among the Liberal rank and file) was not repeated in 1838. After the 1840 election the Tories had two-thirds of the elected members and during 1841 the council was absolutely balanced 32–32. Increased Tory representation had substantially improved the Tory attendance record and since in 1840–1 it was superior to that of the Liberals there was *de facto* Tory control (see table 5).

Table 5. Council attendance, Leeds, 1836–41*

	Per cent attendance		
	Whole council	*Liberal*	*Tory*
1836–7	59·4	66·6	33·3
1838–9	70·0	69·5	73·0
1840–1	76·5	73·9	77·2

Because 1841 was a year of aldermanic election and the Liberals would thereby be deprived initially of the votes of the eight retiring aldermen, it was confidently predicted that 1841 would see a reversion of municipal power to the traditional Tory élite. Yet in a desperately close election, in which four seats were won by a total majority of only 12 votes and in which the Tories were just four seats short of overall control (prior to the aldermanic election), the Liberals narrowly managed to hang on to power. The Tories, undermined by losing victory at the last gasp, fell back as if exhausted and by 1845 had only ten seats on the council. It was another 30 years before an effective Tory challenge was mounted again.

From the mid-1840s there was a decline in the bitterness of party rivalry, partly because permanent Liberal control was assured, partly because of a new concern over improvement. Indeed the coincidence of a vote on sewerage and the gesture of giving Tories one alderman in 1846 was hailed as

a moral sewerage . . . a first step towards draining off that accumulation of party feeling which has been hitherto suffered to infect and paralyse party bodies. Mad political party hate is beginning to be an

* Calculated from Council Minutes, vols 4–6 (Leeds Civic Hall)

old fashioned vice. It is unavoidable it should be so, the moment there springs up a real earnestness about the public good.[41]

There was something more happening to the council towards the end of the early Victorian period: its social composition was gradually changing. Though social categories can never be precise, an attempt has been made to analyse the social composition of the whole Leeds council from its inauguration until 1851–2. The analysis divides members of the council into four broad groups: Group I, gentry and professional; Group II, merchants and manufacturers; Group III, craftsmen and retailers; and Group IV, the drink and corn interests. The full figures are given in table 6.

It was part of Tory propaganda to assert in the early years of the council's life that its social composition had declined as compared with the unreformed corporation. An address to municipal electors in 1837 looked to the time 'when rank and station, education and moral worth, will resume their proper places in society' and in the following year an Operative Conservative confirmed that men of wealth, learning, and

Table 6. Social composition of Leeds town council, 1836–52 (whole council 64 members)

	I		II		III		IV	
			Mchts & Mfrs					
		Profes-	Tex-	Non-		Re-		
	Gentry	sional	tiles	textiles	Craft	tail	Drink	Corn
1836	6	9	30	8	1	4	4	2
1836–7	6	10	30	9	1	4	3	1
1837–8	6	11	26	10	2	3	4	2
1838–9	4	14	25	8	2	4	4	3
1839–40	9	10	21	10	3	5	3	3
1840–1	10	12	20	11	4	3	2	2
1841–2	9	7	22	15	5	3	2	1
1842–3	8	10	22	10	6	4	3	1
1843–4	9	7	21	8	7	7	2	3
1844–5	6	8	17	8	5	12	4	4
1845–6	6	6	18	6	9	9	5	5
1846–7	5	7	22	8	6	9	3	4
1847–8	4	7	21	9	7	9	4	3
1848–9	4	5	19	7	13	11	3	2
1849–50	6	5	12	9	14	12	3	3
1850–1	6	3	12	11	15	13	1	3
1851–2	9	4	14	11	9	14	2	1

respectability had been replaced by 'political mountebanks, bankrupt tradesmen and potato carriers'.[42] Edward Baines rejected this view and argued that no change had taken place: 'The Old Corporation was very much in respect to station like the new Corporation. He saw no difference. There was a great many respectable merchants and tradesmen in both.'[43]

Table 6 confirms Baines's judgement. During the last years of the old corporation there had been 9 in Group I, 26 in Group II and 2 in Group IV, there being none in Group III. The new corporation was dominated by men in Groups I and II just as the old had been.

The overall interpretation of municipal reform representing a struggle between rival middle class élites is reinforced by this analysis of social composition. The men who took power in Leeds in 1835–6 differed in politics and religion from the old oligarchy, but they were no different socially. The council was sometimes called the 'Leeds House of Commons' and it was as though the government had fallen and an opposition of similar social composition had taken over. If one looks at individuals one sees the change of like for like as outsiders became insiders. Tory wool merchants of the old corporation such as Henry Hall and Thomas Motley were replaced by Liberal wool merchants such as George Goodman and Joshua Bateson; Tory bankers such as William Perfect gave way to Liberal bankers such as William Williams Brown; Tory solicitors such as John Upton were succeeded by Liberal solicitors such as T. W. Tottie and Matthew Gaunt; Tory doctors such as William Hey were supplanted by Liberal doctors such as Robert Baker and James Williamson; J. R. Atkinson and Anthony Titley were flaxspinners in the old corporation, Thomas Benyon and John Wilkinson represented the same occupation in the new; the old corporation had an ironfounder in John Cawood, the new in Richard Jackson. The list could be extended, illustrating the way in which the new echoed the old, for the new elected élite was just as respectable as the old oligarchy.

However, during the 1840s Tory accusations about a lowering of the quality of councillors had more substance and by 1848 the Tory view that municipal offices 'are now shunned as a nuisance by the class which of old eagerly sought them as a prize' was being supported in the Liberal press: 'the higher classes of our townsmen as a body have not only withdrawn from offering themselves as willing candidates for the honours of the Council . . . they have even manifested a contemptuous sneering indifference to the constituted authorities.'[44]

The evidence is to be found in table 6 which indicates that during the 1840s the numbers in groups I and II were falling while numbers in the other two groups rose steadily. The change in social composition is starkly illustrated by comparing the situation after the second election in 1836 and that in mid-century after the 1850 election. In 1836–7 groups I and II comprised 86 per cent of the council where in 1850 this had fallen to half. In particular the numbers of professional and gentlemen had virtually halved while the numbers of craftsmen and retailers had increased more than five-fold. The same picture emerges when comparing the bench and the council. When natural social leaders were active in municipal affairs there was a good deal of overlap between the two institutions, and of 22 magistrates appointed in 1836, 15 were members of the council either then or soon after, while 8 of the 9 appointed in 1842 were so. Yet of the whole bench made up to 29 in 1848 only seven were in the council.* The social élite still wished to sit on the bench but its desire to sit in the council was waning.

Some argued that this downward social tendency was inevitable since an aspirant to the council would regard it as a means of association with his social superiors: 'he is one who feels the official status into which he desires to step to be superior to that which in his private capacity he is entitled to. To no other would the object be one of personal ambition ... Thus the corporation barge soon dips its sides so low in the water as to be easily boarded by the smallest wherry.'[45]

In fact in the 1850s and 1860s there was no substantial lowering of the quality of aspirants for council membership, which can be seen from table 7, an analysis of the social composition of all candidates in the three decades from 1841. The downward trend of the 1840s was reversed to some extent in the 1850s. The 1860s were a carbon copy of the 1840s, with an identical number of candidates and an almost identical distribution. In all three decades over half of the candidates were from groups I and II.

Table 7. Social composition of municipal candidates, Leeds 1841–70
Candidates falling in each social group – annual elections only

	I		II		III		IV	
	Per cent	No.	Per cent	No.	Per cent	No.	Per cent	No.
1841–50	18	(43)	39	(94)	33	(81)	10	(24)
1851–60	23	(51)	37	(86)	30	(70)	10	(24)
1861–70	17	(42)	39	(94)	34	(83)	10	(23)

Though council *membership* did not always necessarily reflect it, professional men continued to offer themselves to the electors in the mid-Victorian years and, for instance, in 1859 alone there were six medical or legal candidates for municipal office.[46]†

* Hennock *op. cit.*, p. 226 gives the later situation as 6 out of 42 in 1861, 4 out of 25 in 1871, and 4 out of 41 in 1881.
† A study of *candidates* rather than council members may give cause to qualify views about attitudes to the council. Dr Hennock, *op. cit.*, p. 204, has drawn

During the 1860s there was a revival of party competition, a sure sign of which was the increase in bribery and treating at election times. Public concern was sufficient to lead to a council committee of enquiry which found itself powerless to act effectively in the current state of electoral law.[47] The high point for the Tories in the mid-Victorian years was 17 seats achieved in 1865, but by the early 1870s they were on a strong upward swing. Most cities experienced fierce party contests in the 1870s, now often organized on a caucus system, which has led to the idea that this was a new feature of municipal affairs.[48] That it was merely a part of a well-established Leeds tradition is well illustrated by the comments of one political observer who had the contests of the 1870s very much in mind:

> a member of the Leeds Town Council is seldom returned on the simple grounds of personal fitness; he must be pronounced and definite in his party views and sympathies to be acceptable to the ratepayers and so the struggles which are gone through each November are fought under the rival flags, sometimes with a bitterness and always with an intensity of effort which the Municipal interests of the ratepayers alone will scarcely account for . . . this habit . . . has obtained the strength and force which long continuance in any habit whether good or bad does obtain; and it appears today to be as likely to last as in any by-past period.[49]

Tories were encouraged by the capture of one parliamentary seat in 1868, which breathed new vigour into their ward organization, and they benefited from reactions to government policy. A so-called alliance of 'beer and church' (hostile to Gladstone's licensing and Irish church policies) stimulated Tory energies for the municipal battle. The conjunction of parliamentary and municipal politics was now well established. It had always been the case that the same registration and ward organization was used in both parliamentary and municipal elections and it was widely acknowledged that 'the names of Liberal and Conservative are accepted by both sides as embodying a distinct policy in municipal as in Parliamentary government'.[50] Because of this it was assumed that party fortunes would be affected by success in one sphere or the other. Thus the main plank in Liberal propaganda in 1873 was that a Tory victory would encourage them for the 1874 parliamentary election, while in 1879 it was

attention to 'the total disappearance of the professional men' from the Leeds council in the 1870s, but this was not a voluntary withdrawal. In fact most municipal elections in the 1870s had some professional candidates, e.g. two in 1874 and 1878 three in 1875 and 1876. The overall distribution of candidates for the decade 1871–80 does show an increase in groups III and IV but also in group I. The figures are I 21 per cent (55), II 27 per cent (73), III 39 per cent (103), IV 13 per cent (36).

felt that the 'municipal elections will afford trustworthy data upon which the future action of the two great political parties may be based'.[51]

Election results in each sphere, however, did not necessarily run parallel. A narrow Liberal victory 9–7 in the 1873 municipal election could not prevent the capture of two seats for the Tories at the 1874 general election, with the spectacular defeat of Baines. This victory, coupled with the fact that 1874 was a year of aldermanic election, provided an excellent Tory opportunity to end a 40-year Liberal rule. Tories needed an 11–5 victory in 1874 to capture the aldermanic vote and total power, but renewed Liberal organization and enthusiasm produced an 11–5 Liberal victory with the council comfortably in Liberal hands 41–23.[52] The increased interest of the early 1870s may be gauged by the larger numbers voting in elections.

Table 8. Estimated numbers of municipal voters casting votes, Leeds 1872–4

1872	1873	1874
23,084	25,746	32,535

Fifty per cent more people voted in 1874 than in 1872 on a marginally increased electorate.

At this point of increased public interest it is worth enquiring whether the social composition had fundamentally changed. Despite the absence

Table 9. Social composition of Leeds town council, 1874–5

I		II		III			IV
Gentry	Profes-sional	Mchts & Textiles	Mfrs Non-textiles	Craft	Retail	Drink	Corn
8	0	16	13	10	10	5	2

of professional men, groups I and II still contributed over half the council. Perhaps the most significant feature were the five members of the drink interest, the largest number for 30 years. All but one of these were Conservative, but the strength of the Conservative drink interest could not prevent the continuance of Liberal municipal control for another two decades. The prophecy made in the early days of the reformed Leeds corporation, 'that the conservatives have been thrown back for six years and perhaps for sixty', proved true and Tories did not take over the 'Leeds House of Commons' until 1895.[53]

Liverpool Tories did not have so long to wait, for it was a mere six years before the Liberal régime there was ended. When at the first election the Liberals won an overwhelming victory and dominated the council by 58–6 it seemed that, as at Leeds, a long period of Liberal power was assured. The traditional families had been ousted and the alternative Liberal Dissenting 'merchant princes', the Rathbones, Holts, Earles, Hornbys, had taken their place. Party animosity was fierce and it was generally accepted that council elections would be hotly contested party struggles: 'the struggle between the rivals for civic honours will . . . be more fierce and acrimonious than the contests we have hitherto witnessed at our general elections . . . the elections will be so many petty civil wars.'[54] So acrimonious were relations on the council that the formal vote of thanks to the mayor in 1841 was opposed by Conservative councillors and it could only be passed after they had withdrawn. Evidence of the political controversy implicit in the early years of Liverpool's reformed corporation may be found in the extraordinary number of contested elections. In the first six annual elections only 6 out of 96 seats were filled without a contest, where even in the highly politicized atmosphere of Leeds 20 out of 72 seats were uncontested (see table 12, below). Tory regeneration owed something to superior organizing ability and to a willingness to involve those of lower social status in the Tradesmen's Conservative Association, a less energetic Liberal copy of which was later formed under Joshua Walmsley. However, the Tory revival rested firmly upon a Protestant backlash against the educational policy of the Liberal majority. In this context municipal policy had a direct influence upon political affairs in Liverpool for much of the nineteenth century. The decision of the Liberals to open corporation schools, previously exclusively Anglican, to pupils of all denominations was to have far-reaching consequences. In the short term it allowed the Tories to gain party advantage by rousing Protestant opinion against the council majority. In the longer term it shaped the contours of political opinion in Liverpool, with the Liberals indelibly marked as the party of the Irish Catholics and the Tories by contrast a Protestant party with a strong anti-Catholic, no popery, working-class following.[55]

Liberal educational policy was not specifically pro-Catholic but the composition of Liverpool's population ensured that this was how it would turn out. By the late 1830s there had been a massive withdrawal from corporation schools by Anglicans and 58 per cent of pupils were Catholic, whereas within a year of the Conservative return to power with its reassertion of Anglican exclusiveness some 73 per cent of pupils were Anglican. This anti-Anglican Liberal image was reinforced by the legal process begun for the recovery of £105,000 invested by the old corporation to pay the salaries of Anglican clergy. The return of this money, as at Leeds, was a great victory for municipal reform, but in Liverpool it added fuel to the Protestant anti-Liberal flames. Tories hit upon the clever ploy of carrying a Bible at their meetings and processions, asserting that the authority of the Bible was being challenged. There is perhaps much truth in the contemporary view that Liberals were motivated by a genuine belief in mixed education whereas Tories merely used education as a political weapon. Certainly Tories took advantage of fanatical anti-Catholic sentiment, stimulated by an Ulster minister Rev. Hugh M'Neile; Joshua Walmsley recounted the story of how an Anglican minister watched his wife teaching from the Authorised Version of the Bible yet preached on the following Sunday against the radical council which had banished the Bible from its schools.[56] Such specious party manoeuvring which tended to defile religion sickened some Tories, and, for instance, it was mainly on this issue that Robertson Gladstone defected to the Liberals in the 1840s, thus anticipating in a municipal arena the even more significant assumption of Liberalism by his brother in national politics.[57]

The schools issue yielded impressive electoral dividends and the Tories won eight seats in 1836, four in 1837, six in 1838, nine in 1839 and no less than eleven in 1840. By that date they were within sight of actually capturing the council, since the Liberal majority was only sustained by the aldermanic vote and eight aldermen would retire in 1841. Amazing as it would have appeared years earlier, Liverpool seemed to be returning to what one Liberal activist called 'their old vomit of toryism'.[58] The Liberals needed to retain only nine of the 16 seats vacated in 1841 but were disadvantaged by the large numbers of rate arrears settled on the Tory side. In the event, Liberals won only three seats in 1841 and the Tories returned triumphant. Many corporation reformers were disgusted that the opponents of reform should do so well in Liverpool, especially as they had also returned two Tories at the 1841 general election. That result may have been biased by the freemen but that excuse could not apply to municipal elections and as James Mellor, the Liberal councillor for Exchange Ward, explained:

> They had to chuse between tories and reformers, the former had done everything in their power to prevent the people ever having a vote to give and had spent large sums of the *Corporate Money* in deputations etc to London for that purpose – whilst on the contrary the reformers had laboured for years and spent large sums of their *own* money to obtain for the people the right of voting for corporate offices – and yet we see the people prefer the Tories – . . . Liverpool I consider ranks intellectually lower than any large town in England . . . the people are devoid of all genuine political integrity or principle.[59]

That Mellor should cite both parliamentary and municipal evidence for the defection of Liverpool from reform principles was an indication that in Liverpool political fortunes in both fields ran in concert, each mutually reinforcing the other. It was thus logical to use the same electoral organization for both types of elections, and when the Tradesmen's Reform Association was launched in 1837 it set out specifically to return reformers to both Parliament and the council.[60] Yet there was always one influential Liverpool voice raised against combining municipal and parliamentary politics and that belonged to Charles E. Rawlins Jun., who was secretary of a succession of Liverpool's Liberal organizations in the mid-nineteenth century. When the Anti-Monopoly society wound up in 1846 and Liverpool Liberals were seeking a basis for a new organization, Rawlins spoke out against a combined operation: 'I am opposed to the union of local and national defects in one association. In other words I wd. divide the revision of the Municipal from that of the Parlty Register. . . . Is it well to accumulate all the personal and party bickerings from every year's local struggle and encumber great national questions with the heap of rubbish?'[61] A decade later when Liberals were discussing the propriety of a greater political involvement in council affairs Rawlins confirmed that he had always 'opposed the union of an agitation for Parliamentary reform with Municipal reform. He was not an advocate for returning members to the Town Council upon political principles at all.'[62]

Both in 1846 and in 1858 Rawlins was overruled by Liverpool Liberals, who not only returned councillors with party labels but also viewed municipal affairs as inextricably bound up with the relative strength of parties in parliamentary contests. In 1861 a party worker, urging greater activity upon George Melly and other social leaders in Exchange Ward, commented:

> Let us but carry Exchange Ward and we could easily so change the political feeling of this town as to secure not only Mr. J. C. Ewart's seat for Liverpool but also a second member. Neglect this opportunity and as sure as I write we shall lose the chance of having a liberal member for Liverpool at all. I assure you this is as I say. This election, if we are successful in Exchange Ward, would be a fatal blow to Toryism.[63]

It was said that the Liberal aim in 1862 was to elect aldermen and their own mayor for 'if we secure possession of the Town Hall . . . we return two members for Liverpool and dumbfound Lord Derby'.[64] Party activists looked to municipal election results as a guide to prospective parliamentary performance, much as politicans now look to opinion polls. It was therefore in keeping with this tradition that a Liverpool politician in 1878 could argue that the year's municipal election results would show 'the feelings of the people in regard to the Imperial policy of the country', and that the good Liberal performance in 1879 was viewed

Table 10. Political composition of Liverpool town council, 1835–67

| | Councillors | | Aldermen | | Whole council | |
	Liberal	Tory	Liberal	Tory	Liberal	Tory
1835–6	43	5	15	1	58	6
1836–7	38	10	15	1	53	11
1837–8	34	14	15	1	49	15
1838–9	31	17	16	0	47	17
1839–40	30	18	16	0	46	18
1840–1	23	25	16	0	39	25
1841–2	15	33	7	9	22	42
1842–3	11	37	6	10	17	47
1843–4	10	38	6	10	16	48
1844–5	10	38	0	16	10	54
1845–6	13	35	0	16	13	51
1846–7	14	34	0	16	14	50
1847–8	14	34	1	15	15	49
1848–9	15	33	1	15	16	48
1849–50	17	31	1	15	18	46
1850–1	19	29	3	13	22	42
1851–2	18	30	3	13	21	43
1852–3	18	30	2	14	20	44
1853–4	17	31	2	14	19	45
1854–5	18	30	2	14	20	44
1855–6	18	30	2	14	20	44
1856–7	21	27	1	15	22	42
1857–8	21	27	1	15	22	42
1858–9	26	22	1	15	27	37
1859–60	27	21	2	14	29	35
1860–1	26	22	2	14	28	36
1861–2	26	22	2	14	28	36
1862–3	24	24	2	14	26	38
1863–4	28	20	2	14	30	34
1864–5	22	26	3	13	25	39
1865–6	25	23	3	13	28	36
1866–7	24	24	3	13	27	37
1867–8	24	24	3	13	27	37

as an indication that Liberals could carry both seats for Liverpool and for South Lancashire in the 1880 general election.[65]

Since parliamentary and municipal fortunes moved together it is not surprising that the largely Tory-dominated parliamentary seat of Liverpool should have a Conservative town council. The figures for the period down to the second Reform Act are given in table 10, which shows that although Liberals came near to regaining power on several occasions, they could not reverse the 1841 result. By the mid 1840s the Liberals had only a handful of seats, as the disillusion of defeat spread apathy, and the later 1840s were marked by local issues discussed in the next chapter.

For nearly two decades after 1841 the council was dominated with ease by the Tories and it was their leading personalities who made the running. There were only two Liberal mayors in those 20 years and council affairs were largely organized by prominent Tories such as Sir Thomas Brancker, John Bramley Moore, James and G. H. Lawrence, Samuel and James Holme, and Francis Shand. Two Tory political careers planted in municipal politics flowered in the parliamentary arena. T. B. Horsfall, who was alderman from 1844 to 1850 and mayor in 1847, was elected M.P. for Liverpool in 1853 (when Bramley Moore was an unsuccessful Tory candidate), 1857, 1859, and 1865. In the last year his partner was Samuel R. Graves, who was also elected in 1868 – and Graves had been elected a councillor for Pitt Street ward at three successive elections in 1857, 1860, and 1863, and was mayor in 1860.

This catalogue of Tory achievement should not, however, hide the fact that the decade prior to 1867 was one which saw a fierce Liberal challenge; in the ten years from 1858 there was only one (1864–5) when the Liberals did not have at least half of the elected seats on the council. It is important to correct the impression given in a pioneering municipal history of Liverpool that the party system collapsed between the 1840s and the 1870s. B. D. White builds much upon this contention and has written that 'in the sixties ... the Tory majority was so secure both in the council as a whole and in most of the individual wards that the party system had become almost inoperative'.[66] As has already been shown, the Tory majority was certainly not secure and a brief review of the 1858–67 municipal struggle will indicate how active the party system was.* The revival of Liberal interest may be dated from 1857 when in the annual report of the Liverpool Reform Association William Brumfitt, the ex-barber who acted as paid secretary, recommended that 'the time has now arrived when a class of men will again be returned who from their

---

* It may also be noted that throughout Mr White's *History of the Corporation of Liverpool* (1951) he assumes that the Tories regained power after the 1842 elections, whereas it was of course after the 1841 election. Corrections are important since in the absence of municipal histories researchers have used Mr White's work for comparison and on occasion have been led up a false trail. See by way of example R. A. Church, *Economic and Social Change in a Midland Town, Victorian Nottingham* (1966), 206, commenting on Mr White's deductions from his view of the middle decades of the century as years of political stability lacking party controversy.

position ability and integrity are qualified to take part in the government of this great commercial town'.[67]

Brumfitt's remarks were themselves stimulated by two spectacular
victories for radical-Liberals in the 1856 election. J. J. Stitt was elected
for Everton ward, and even more important, J. R. Jeffery a self-made
drapery tycoon, entered the council for Lime Street. Jeffery was to prove
a scourge of the Tories, a fierce party propagandist and an energetic
local administrator. Though there was some complaint that Liberal
gentry refused to come forward, the Liberals only narrowly failed to gain
sufficient seats to nominate the aldermen in 1859 and in the next few
years a Liberal majority was a distinct possibility. The 1862 election,
with another aldermanic vote pending, was fiercely fought in certain
wards, especially Lime Street where Jeffery's re-election was deemed
crucial 'not simply because of his individual ability but because of its
issues for years to come'.[68] The Reform Association gave £150 to help
with Jeffery's campaign (with a warning to spend no more) and £100 for
Stitt in Everton where the previous election had cost him £500. Jeffery's
eventual defeat was much regretted and even a critical observer admitted
'no other man has done so much for the town'. Though Stitt was returned,
despite the siting of polling booths to the Tories' advantage, the two
Toxteth wards were won by Conservatives after vigorous appeals were
made to employers to influence the votes of their workpeople. The
bitterness of the campaign was resuscitated when Stitt's defeated
opponent Joseph Hubback was 'pitchforked' straight on to the aldermanic bench.[69]

Liberals had talked confidently of nominating their own mayor and
aldermen in 1862 but this optimism had not been shared by Robertson
Gladstone who felt that the campaign at best 'may bear its fruits and
take shape in improved organisation for the future.'[70] His was a judicious
prophecy and far from it being the case that the party system was dead
in the 1860s, that decade was to witness the elevation of municipal
party politics to a quite new level of intensity. In 1863 a municipal
reform association was formed which was nothing less than a fully
fledged municipal caucus, anticipating the Birmingham caucus of the
1870s. Its objects were the total organization of Liverpool Liberal
politics: 'to have control of municipal matters . . . to win all the wards,
elect the mayor, make the borough magistrates and return to Parliament
almost whom they liked.'[71]

A caucus of sorts had existed to disburse spoils, as at Leeds, and was
seen in action when Walmsley's claims to the mayoralty were rebuffed
at a prior Liberal meeting in 1838. Ward organization had been very
strong from the 1830s and the Reform Association of the 1850s confirmed
the need for a ward system of political activity.[72] The ward organization

of the 1850s was in turn the basis of the caucus system of the 1860s and 1870s. Robertson Gladstone had felt that the Liberals on the council could only be held together by a caucus and Brumfitt referred to the meetings of such a body in 1862.[73]

What was new in the 1860s was the willingness to challenge even tried and trusted Conservatives in an all-out party battle and the desire to organize municipal politics, 'to think for the electors and act for them too'. The result was a renewed injection of party fervour: 'Liberals and Tories will stand against each other and Liberal and Tory voters will vote for those candidates with whom they coincide in opinion . . . politics are thus made the shibboleth in local affairs.'[74] This intensification of party politics was the strategy of Joseph Robinson, elected councillor for Scotland ward in 1864 and 1867, and he had urged this on the Liberals as early as 1858.[75] It was he who directed the so-called 'cellar clique' (nicknamed thus because they met in a basement in contrast to the 'garret clique' of Conservatives) and the secretary of the organization was J. D. Fisher. The 'cellar clique' of younger, more radical Liberals was as much a challenge to the richer aristocratic Liberals as to the Conservatives, and the two organizations, the Reform Association and the 'cellar', were never fully merged.

The more vigorous 'cellar' policy yielded five gains in 1863 and, for only the third time since 1841, a liberal mayor. In 1864, when for a time the parties were exactly balanced, the 'cellar' was active ('they give their mind to the business and they know what is best for the welfare of the town') and the year's municipal elections were fought with unprecedented virulence. Jeffery, who had returned to the council in 1863, was widely tipped as the next mayor, and it was the premature revelation of this which was blamed for the Liberal defeat in 1864, which undermined belief in the new methods of party dictation. Indeed, the new strategy rebounded upon the Liberals, for in addition to rejecting Jeffery as mayor the Conservatives came with prepared committee lists and so 'the whole municipal administration will be virtually seized and retained by the Tory party'.[76] There were reports in 1865 that the 'cellar' had been closed down with debts of £800 but in fact it was still active at the municipal elections of that year. By the later 1860s municipal reformers had reached a position whereby the Tory majority needed the aldermanic vote to remain in power. Though there was much criticism in 1869 of 'miserable cliques of pothouse politicians', nevertheless many Liberals by now believed in the effective management of the council by parties and these methods survived into the 1870s.[77] By a further development of organized municipal politics, Liberals once more got within one seat of victory, but no further, in 1880.

That Liverpool Liberals could never quite achieve municipal control

in the nineteenth century, despite the new organized methods of the
1860s, was puzzling, especially since the potential appeared to be there.
As one observer put it, 'Liverpool can be whenever the liberals are really
in earnest a thoroughly liberal borough'.[78] The restraints upon Liberal
municipal success originated in the nature and structure of the Liberal
party itself. As elsewhere, the basic political struggle in Liverpool was
between two very wealthy rival élites of merchants and gentlemen.
Attached to the respective élites were groups of tradesmen, craftsmen
and retailers (which the Tories quite clearly integrated more successfully
into their party) and below this a mass following, largely Catholic and
Irish on the Liberal side. Two basic problems grew out of the socially
stratified Liberal party.

The first was a moral diffidence on the part of Liberal merchant
princes to 'pull out all the stops' in the political battle. When the 'cellar'
announced its decision to contest municipal elections more fiercely
William Rathbone, the natural leader of Liverpool Liberalism, wrote: 'I
hope it is not the intention to contest all the wards chance or no chance
or even to try to unseat *valuable* and *independent* candidates who by
their faithful and efficient discharge of their duties are entitled to the
renewed expression of confidence by their respective constituencies.'[79]
Even where they did contest seats, Liberals would not sully their con-
sciences with any doubtful acts of electioneering and in fact one of the
raison d'êtres of the 'cellar' was to imitate Tory methods to which Liberal
gentlemen would not stoop. Charles Melly vowed he would not pay a
single sixpence for a vote, while Philip Holt was even more puritanical
and proscribed 'the hiring of cabs, placards, an organised canvass hiring
of committee rooms refreshments etc . . . I will not have people teased
worried or cajoled into voting for me . . . I will only be returned by the
free and unsolicited votes of my supporters, if I find other means are
being resorted to on my behalf I will most certainly retire from the
contest'.[80] Needless to add, Tories were not so squeamish and reaped the
dividends in the results.

The second difficulty grew out of the first. Aristocratic Liberals were
suspicious of organization, bribery, and so on because they inhabited a
political world where they naïvely believed only opinions mattered.
Hence they underestimated the value of menial electoral *work*. It was the
perennial complaint of ordinary party workers that the real Liberal
leaders were remote and inactive, or as one put it to George Melly, 'if our
big men don't turn out . . . we shall certainly lose'.[81] One of Jeffery's
supporters in the crucial 1862 election isolated the problem then (as now):

unless Mr Jeffery's committee of organised workers can be materially
and immediately increased the election will be lost . . . we had an

excellent meeting and we have a long list of committee men and on the day of election there will be swarms of sympathisers to a certain extent but what we want is half a dozen steady efficient canvassers suitable for any class of electors . . . we have the votes to win with if we can only procure them by work.[82]

When George Melly and his brother Charles failed to attend their local ward meeting in 1869 their cousin chastised them with the reminder that 'the perpetual complaint . . . is that the gentlemen in the ward hold aloof' and in a significant phrase reported that their absence 'disheartened the workers much'.[83] The dichotomy between leaders and workers was also manifest in the financing of Liberal politics. It was truly remarked that a handful of old Liberals were 'the milch kine of the local party . . . Radicalism roars but doesnt pay'.[84] The merchant princes paid up* and hoped the party faithful would do the work, but too often they forgot that, in the words of Louis Greg, 'the liberal party throughout the town requires keeping together and that is not to be done without the sacrifice of time and thought on the part of the leaders'.[85]

3

Municipal affairs in Leeds and Liverpool were thus characterized by a heightened political involvement, and other towns displayed similar characteristics. In Birmingham, as in Manchester, the application for a charter was the occasion for an intense party battle between the supporters and opponents of reform. The latter, entrenched in the traditional fragmented institutions of town government, were convinced that municipal reform was a synonym for Political Union radicalism. As the corporation's first historian explained, 'it was no wonder that the Corporation – the realisation of the hopes of one side and the aversion of the other – became the symbol of party', and every seat was contested by Conservatives at the first election in December 1838.[86] The Political Union via the incorporation committee had attempted a caucus system at the outset by nominating candidates without even consulting ward meetings, and this had produced some compromise lists. Even so, the radical-Liberal interest achieved a total victory, winning all seats and controlling all the aldermen. The political nature of the triumph was confirmed by Tory discomfiture.

* Precise details are hard to come by but Melly Papers 2383 contains a balance sheet for the 1864 municipal election. Melly collected about £1400 to fight the elections, of which £900 was subscribed by ten families contributing between £50 and £150 each. The balance sheet also reveals that despite the high moral tone taken by Charles Melly and Philip Holt, mentioned above, 50 of their friends donated £420 to fight the contests in Exchange and Abercromby wards.

Its aim and object was to shut out from all possible participation in the administration of our local civil affairs those who largely contribute to the coffers of the town: to bring a once peaceable population into an arena of never ending strife turmoil and animosity: to make party politics everything and never to consider what are the talents, the character or capacity of an individual for any office but merely what are his politics.'[87]

Time might cool the passions of Birmingham municipal politics but at the outset the creation of a 'legalised political union' was a development of major political significance.

Nottingham's reformed corporation, like those at Leeds and Liverpool, was socially just as respectable as its unreformed predecessor and politically similar too. Whig-Liberals dominated both old and new corporations and when the creditable first showing of Conservative success in 1835 was unrepeated the declining Tory membership presaged a solidly Liberal municipal future. However the Nottingham workhouse question (see above, p. 76) revitalized Toryism so that by 1844 Conservatives were within one vote of capturing control of the council.

Table 11. Political composition of Nottingham council, 1835–40

	Liberal	Tory		Liberal	Tory
1835–6	36	20	1840–1	46	10
1836–7	36	20	1841–2	44	12
1837–8	39	17	1842–3	39	17
1838–9	45	11	1843–4	36	20
1839–40	50	6	1844–5	32	24

As so often the crucial year was one in which half the aldermen retired and after a bitter and expensive election the Liberals needed the casting vote of their own mayor to nominate aldermen and hence retain control.[88] Thereafter municipal Toryism withered and the Nottingham council was run by a Liberal caucus throughout the mid-Victorian years. Leicester and Bradford were also safe Liberal havens in mid-century, with Conservatives never having more than a handful of seats.

The big omission from this catalogue of municipal politics is of course Manchester, which in view of the bitterness of the charter controversy, seemed destined to have a lively council battle. In fact, Manchester distinguished itself by being the prime example of a non-political municipal council. The *Guardian* certainly put its authority behind the move to keep politics and parties out of the corporation:

Having witnessed for many years past much of an oblivion of mere political feeling in everything that concerned the municipal and parochial offices of the town of Manchester we cannot bring ourselves to believe that any such feeling will hereafter and under a new form of government be permitted to interfere with the election of officers or the discharge of functions of a purely municipal character and wholly unconnected with political considerations . . . it will be with great regret that we shall see the election of a town council converted into a party struggle.[89]

Such moralizing was common in the urban press but was usually powerless to quench the flames of party warfare. In Manchester the crucial difference was that the Tory strategy involved disputing the whole legality of the charter and hence a total boycott of municipal elections.[90]

The idea of a total withdrawal by Conservatives was flirted with in many towns. In Leicester this tactic was used temporarily in the hope that the new Liberal council would become so discredited that municipal power would drop into Tory laps: 'let the radicals manage affairs a little while longer and the growing disgust of the inhabitants at the measures they adopt will do more to annihilate the faction than the return of any minority of conservatives, however respectable.'[91] In Birmingham, after contesting all seats in 1838, the Tories fell back on the illegality of the charter and refused to acknowledge the validity of the elections. Only in the mid-1840s did Birmingham Tories seriously challenge for municipal seats and by 1846 there were eight Conservative councillors.[92]* Bradford Conservatives also threatened a boycott but were chastised by one of their number, 'it would ill behove such of you as are conservatives to stand aloof and neglect the best interests of your fellow townsmen'.[93]

It was only in Manchester that the Conservative boycott took a real hold upon local affairs and had a long-term impact. When the charter was confirmed, a number of overt Tory candidates were proposed (one in 1842, three in 1844, five in 1845) and a handful of Conservative councillors were returned (between four and seven in the middle 1840s). Temporarily party labels were used but this was soon overwhelmed by pressing financial and rating questions and by 1848 the *Examiner* could identify a distinctive Manchester municipal image:

candidates are measured not by the extent of their devotion to toryism whiggism radicalism or chartism . . . political feeling . . . formed so small an element in the contest that a political classification of the candidates would afford no index here as it does in many other places to the political views of the great body of the electors.[94]

* Further evidence of the relationship of municipal and parliamentary elections may be seen in the fact that it was in 1844 that Birmingham Tories won both their first council and parliamentary seat.

In Manchester 1 November passed without those displays of party feelings which characterized so many corporate towns. Though occasionally a party political contest occurred, such as that in St James' ward in 1853 'between the narrow and broad cloth, between effete toryism and radicalism',[95] it was far more common to find men fighting on the passing issues of the moment. It was wholly in keeping with what became a Manchester tradition that the Cheetham election of 1857 was contested on whether bands should play in the parks on Sundays.[96]

Local tradition was a powerful influence in determining the nature of political activity. It is clear that the traditional party political rivalry of Leeds affected politics right through the nineteenth century, that the traditional image of a pro-Catholic and anti-slavery Liverpool Liberalism was still important in the late Victorian years and that the traditional Whig Dissenting belief in corporate service elevated council membership in Nottingham as a legitimate political ambition in mid-century. Equally in Manchester the absence of that intense party rivalry and political contention for power in those early years established a tradition of a non-political municipal council which survived the nineteenth century. The deleterious effects of such a lack of political sparkle were commented on frequently and Lady Simon was only the latest in a long line of observers to remark that some found 'in those councils which are run on party lines . . . a greater sense of responsibility both in office and in opposition than can exist in Manchester'.

The lack of political involvement produced some paradoxical situations. For instance, Manchester town council refused to petition on behalf of Cobden in the 'personal responsibility' issue with Peel in 1843 while other councils with less connection with Cobden did so. Public apathy towards council affairs (common even in political councils) was more marked and in 1851 it was claimed, 'hardly any of them care a rush who is to fill a vacancy in his ward'.[97] Evidence may be found in table 12 which lists the numbers of contested elections in four towns, including Sheffield, which had on occasion some lively political disputes. That Manchester had a rate of contested elections of half that of towns with political councils is an indication of the relative public interest in council business. Only half as many Manchester people were sufficiently interested to offer themselves as council members as those in Leeds, Liverpool, or Sheffield where party politics ruled.

Party was the means by which disputes between rival élites were resolved and the spoils were both rewards for the victors and a measure of the extent of triumph. In all towns there was an exhilarating effusion of party appointments when municipal reform transferred power from one élite to another. In Leeds the old town clerk was manoeuvred into resignation and replaced by Edward Eddison, who had acted as agent for

Table 12. Contested municipal elections, 1835–67 (annual elections only)

	Leeds	Manchester	Liverpool	Sheffield
Total no. of wards	12	15	16	9
		Number of wards contested		
1835	11	–	16	–
1836	2	–	16	–
1837	8	–	15	–
1838	12	1	12	–
1839	8	1	15	–
1840	11	0	16	–
1841	9	1	13	–
1842	10	3	13	–
1843	10	3	13	9
1844	7	3	10	4
1845	5	4	6	6
1846	3	9	12	9
1847	10	4	11	9
1848	6	10	8	6
1849	4	6	8	6
1850	5	8	8	4
1851	5	2	7	3
1852	7	5	9	4
1853	7	7	5	5
1854	6	3	7	8
1855	5	3	7	2
1856	6	5	5	3
1857	6	4	8	0
1858	7	2	5	7
1859	11	8	9	4
1860	7	7	4	4
1861	6	9	7	4
1862	7	6	5	5
1863	5	4	8	3
1864	9	5	11	3
1865	10	2	7	4
1866	10	3	5	4
1867	7	5	4	5
% of wards contested	61·1%	29·5%	58·1%	53·7%

the Liberals in the revision courts. When Eddison resigned through ill health in 1843 he was succeeded by John Arthur Ikin, first secretary of the West Riding Reform Registration Association. Another solicitor who had acted as Liberal agent, James Richardson, was appointed clerk of the peace (succeeded on his death in 1861 by his son) and Baines got the corporation printing contract. In Birmingham, where Tories had been warned that offices 'will be the gift of the council – of the majority of the council; and the majority of the council will not give their gifts to neutrals much less to opponents',[98] some of the political appointments became highly controversial. The first two town clerks, William Redfern (1838–40) and Solomon Bray (1840–52), belonged to the firm of Liberal solicitors which dealt with all the election and incorporation affairs for the party. Two other appointments were more startling. The veteran radical George Edmonds was appointed clerk of the peace and R. K. Douglas, editor of the *Journal*, was made registrar in the mayor's court. To have a member of the Chartist National Convention in an official law enforcement position was anathema to many, especially in view of the Bull Ring riots, and both Edmonds and Douglas received scathing notoriety from Peel when he criticized the policing of the town.

Manchester corporation, despite its non-political character, still gave its chief office to a partisan, for Joseph Heron, probably the most distinguished town clerk of the nineteenth century, had been a member of the incorporation committee and had been chosen by activists even before the granting of the charter.[99] In Liverpool, the barrister who had acted for the Liberals in the municipal enquiry, Richard Radcliffe, was appointed town clerk, and his deputy G. W. Crooke was also a reformer, as was the treasurer John Wybergh. In view of these political appointments which involved a purge of the municipal administration, it was no surprise that when the receivership of town dues fell vacant in 1849 the Tories used the vacancy to reward one of their party faithful, Sir Thomas Brancker, who had been alderman from 1841–7. Predictably in view of the bitter municipal struggle in Leicester, Liberals there used a spoils system to oust Tories and reward radicals,* while in Bradford J. A. Cooper, secretary of the incorporation committee, was appointed town clerk, succeeded on his sudden death by John Rawson, also a Liberal.

This partisan distribution of the fruits of office had been widely anticipated and Joseph Parkes, the *eminence grise* behind municipal reform, had freely acknowledged: 'Liberals are naturally looking to the Municipal patronage – county attorneys to Town Clerkships – Liberal bankers to

---

* Cf. *Leicester Journal*, 24 August 1849: 'Among the Radicals there is a sort of "family compact" which throws all parochial pickings, offices, emoluments, honours, distinctions pleasures into the Radical lap.'

treasurerships etc. etc. . . . . it is human nature.'[100] Yet this spoils system gave substance to the Tory attack upon the motives of municipal reformers. It was understandable for a Leeds Tory, seeing the unrelenting flow of offices in one political direction, to view reform as simply 'the robbery of one party in order to pamper another with the spoils'.[101] In the light of the political appointments in Birmingham one could hardly quarrel with the judgement that reformers were primarily motivated by a desire for 'personal aggrandisement . . . power and influence and some share of the loaves and fishes of official rank'.[102] When Bradford Liberals sought to enlarge the council's powers with an improvement Act an anonymous Tory critic was prompted to offer a lucid interpretation of what was really involved in liberal incorporation: 'Violent political changes had not given them all the patronage which profit and pride had hoped for. A corporation offered an easy means of placing everything in their grasp.'[103] There was one overwhelming defence against these indictments and it lay in the exclusive Tory Anglican monopoly of patronage in the pre-reform system. Small changes became symbols of the existence of a new world and when Edward Baines obtained the printing contract for Leeds council it ended an association of over half a century when the *Intelligencer* office had been as close to the corporation as that of the town clerk. Baines offered an all-embracing defence that was appropriate for all new councils:

> Almost everywhere the Lords Lieutenants, the County Magistrates, the Clergy, the Police, the functionaries of our law Courts from the Judges on the bench to the humblest officer and all the endless train of dependants on each including the publicans, the *employes* of the Corporations etc. have within living memory been of the Tory party.[104]

Liberals, attempting to remedy this imbalance, found the exercise of power and patronage sweet and could themselves look to the offices of alderman, mayor, and magistrate as due political reward. The positions of aldermen, which were recognized as an élite within an élite, were allocated almost always on the basis of political control. Occasionally generous non-partisan gestures were made but they rarely became a general pattern. When Leeds Liberals on the advice of Baines allowed Tories to have one-quarter of the aldermanic bench in 1836 they were bitterly attacked by their own supporters and the gift was not repeated. Two moderate Liberal solicitors, T. W. Tottie and J. Hope Shaw, preached the need to share the spoils of power in the 1840s but the sum of their achievement was one Tory alderman elected at a by-election. In Leeds, there was no Tory alderman for half a century from the mid-1840s (see table 4). In Liverpool, partisan appointments were the rule in the first decade and thereafter a gentleman's agreement allowed two or three reformers to become aldermen, which gave Liberal leaders enormous difficulties in reconciling the claims of rival activists[105] (see table 10). Political control of the aldermanic seats was often decisive in maintaining a council majority during years when the annual elections were going in favour of the opposition.

The mayoralty, particularly in the early years, attracted a very special kudos for men long denied access to honorific posts. Again this was allocated primarily on political grounds and where one party had a secure majority it was rare for the minority to participate in the honours. There was no Tory mayor in Leeds for 60 years after 1835, only one in Gateshead between 1836 and 1856, none in Leicester for 40 years after 1836, while on the other side there were only three Liberal mayors of Liverpool in the half-century after the Tory victory of 1841. Perhaps the most striking feature of the mayors in the first decade of municipal reform was the predominance of Dissenters, whose religion had been a primary cause of prior exclusion. Leeds was not untypical and the sequence there was a Baptist, an Independent, a Roman Catholic, three Wesleyan Methodists and four Unitarians. In particular, the political role of Unitarians was of significance far beyond their numbers and in many towns their chapels, Mill Hill in Leeds, Cross Street in Manchester, Renshaw Street in Liverpool, High Pavement in Nottingham, and the Great Meeting in Leicester, became a kind of 'mayors' nest' as centres of municipal dominance.

If the mayoralty offered status to previously proscribed religious groups it also enshrined economic leadership with a very special confirmatory imprimatur. The civic chain appealed especially to self-made, first-generation entrepreneurs, often migrants, who looked to the mayoralty to legitimize their economic achievement. Compare the disdain with which Thomas Benyon and W. W. Brown, already half-way to being Whig country gentlemen, refused the Leeds mayoralty in 1836 with the avid enthusiasm and ambition in Liverpool of Joshua Walmsley in the 1830s and J. R. Jeffery in the 1860s. Walmsley and Jeffery were men of humble origin who had made good financially but who felt the need of civic honours to confirm that they were socially acceptable. Both men were opposed on social grounds.[106] They looked to the office of mayor much as did the little-known James Watts* in Manchester, described by Mrs Gaskell as 'a new man and a new mayor unknown to most people here as most of our mayors are; they, being principally risen men who are willing to give two or three thousand pounds for the privilege of being mayor, and *the power which it gives them of getting into society*'.[107] Joshua Walmsley found that a career already well-launched

---

* James Watts, merchant, *d.* 1878, councillor St James 1848–56, alderman 1856–65, mayor 1855–7.

by wealth and marriage flowered after his mayoralty, while it may be no coincidence that Saltaire was only started after Titus Salt's mayoralty had confirmed the social leadership of a new and somewhat insecure Bradford worthy. The mayoralty was also often a final accolade for political careers which had served long apprenticeships. The Manchester radical Abel Heywood had begun as a police commissioner in the 1830s but it was only after 20 years on the council that his increased wealth aided him to the mayoralty in 1862 and 1876, while in Leeds Peter Fairbairn, the self-made Scottish engineer, matched his soaring business career with upward progress in local politics, first as churchwarden, then councillor, then alderman, and finally mayor in the year when the queen opened the town hall. Royal visits reinforced the ceremonial tendency of chain, mace, and robes, and Cobden and Bright were highly critical of the snobbery and mummery to which the Manchester corporation became addicted.

Mayors and aldermen held temporary positions and the really permanent evidence of social leadership lay in a seat on the bench. The power to nominate its own magistrates had been cited by Cobden as one of the main attractions of incorporation as a means of freeing Manchester from the thraldom of the county bench.[108] When Liberals assumed control of town government in the 1830s their leaders in each town occupied the majority of places upon the newly-created borough commissions, the so-called Russell justices. In the tense political atmosphere many Conservative gentlemen, some of whom had previously acted as magistrates, were omitted from Liberal nominations and this produced howls of protest. Birmingham and Leeds deputations of Tories went to see Russell to intercede on behalf of the wealth and respectability which had been overlooked.[109] Marginal changes were made in the lists proposed, but the wholly Liberal Manchester list was accepted *in toto*. Political appointments were common throughout the nineteenth century and the first four commissions in Leeds reflected the politics of the government of the day.* When the second round of incorporations took place the same political appointments occurred and at Bradford three-quarters of the new borough magistrates were Liberal, as Salt and his friends received their final colours. By the late Victorian years political appointments were the norm and it was no surprise to find Gladstone's second ministry creating eight new Birmingham magistrates in 1884, of whom only two were Tories.[110]

Political reward and the confirmation of status were thus involved in

* The figures were: 1836, 19 Liberals, 3 Conservatives; 1842, 8 Conservatives, 0 Liberals; 1848, 7 Liberals, 4 Conservatives; 1855, 8 Liberals, 6 Conservatives. Members of Parliament were also channels for demands for seats on the bench, for which see below, p. 180.

the creation of magistrates and it was in the interests of good administration that Liberals should have their share. In practice magistrates
might act fairly, yet as the Liverpool merchant prince and county M.P.
William Brown put it, 'we ought to have on the Bench gentlemen of all
religious and political opinions, that the Catholics and Dissenters . . .
may not consider that justice is all on one side'.[111] Moreover, magistrates
did have important political functions. In Leeds the new Liberal bench,
by appointing Liberal overseers, made possible Liberal control of the
Poor Law. The Liverpool 'cellar' politician Joseph Robinson bitterly
criticized Conservative magistrates being 'dragged up to do the dirty
work of the Tories on the licensing bench when any particular job has to
be worked', and an Oldham Liberal, faced with a bench loaded 15–4 in
the Tories' favour, complained that 'unless we get the Bench more equal
no justice can be done in political matters'.[112] Abuse was, as ever, not the
sole property of one side and the radical J. R. Jeffery was on one occasion
brought to task over his refusal to confirm the appointment of a Tory
overseer with the plea, 'let Jeffery the parochial politician be quite
distinct from Jeffery the lay justice'.[113]

The role of party in the distribution of spoils was a powerful factor in
ensuring that councils would be overtly political institutions. This was
especially true in the early years when previous policies of proscription
had to be corrected. In time the imbalance was rectified and other forces
tended to weaken the control of parties in running council business.
Where one party, usually Liberal, had an unchallenged supremacy, then
inevitably party discipline was weakened and party unity threatened.
Without the challenge of an alternative political force, parties found the
differences within their own ranks more compelling than the no longer
vital battle with an exhausted opposition. Disagreements over policy
inside the majority party then produced new groupings within and
across parties for the conduct of council business. These groupings
fluctuated widely as different issues produced combinations of different
interests and they often became the dominant factor in council politics.
Councils which had an established ruling party thus often gave the
impression of not in fact being run on political lines even though the
fragmentation of the majority was itself evidence of overwhelming party
dominance. This sort of process occurred in Birmingham, Newcastle, Bradford, Nottingham, Leicester and of course Manchester, which though an
overtly non-political council was overwhelmingly Liberal in composition.*

* Demonstrated by the following facts; there were only four Conservatives
nominated as aldermen in the first 30 years of the corporation's history;
between 1838 and 1870 there were only three years of Conservative mayoralty;
and of all council members between 1838 and 1900 only 30 per cent were
Conservative, and this includes the later years of Conservative revival.

At certain times Liverpool and Leeds were also prey to the break up of a majority party.

The earliest and most obvious issue accelerating such cross- and intra-party disputes was that of 'economy', which appeared in some guise in every corporation. Sometimes the cry for economical administration focused not on a profound and fundamental act of policy but on a symbolic issue of minor financial significance. Such was the case in Leeds when for a decade the town clerk's salary became a political football booted about between the parties year after year. Though Tory propaganda was based exclusively in the late thirties upon the 'extravagance' of the Liberal council this did not prevent some Tories from opposing and some Liberals from supporting cuts in the salary. Leeds experienced bouts of 'economist' activity in the early and late 1840s, the early 1850s and the late 1860s. All these were nervous public reactions to sudden increases in powers and expenditure and they were also found in Leicester and Salford in the 1840s and Birmingham in the 1850s.

Demands for economy and retrenchment were the only issues to impart any real political interest in Manchester council affairs in the 1840s. Such feelings first emerged when 'salary levellers' were victorious in two wards in 1843 and they recurred in greater strength three years later when a ratepayers' association was formed to oppose high salaries, a new market and an increased police force. In 1846 many wards were contested for the first time and there was more interest than ever before with, again for the first time, the use of placards, canvassers, coaches, committees, the general bustle normally associated with elections. Ratepayer candidates did not prosper, for the president of the association, Caleb Davenport, was beaten by the radical Abel Heywood in Collegiate Church ward and the secretary, James Hibbert, was defeated at Exchange both in 1846 and 1847. However, the 'economists' had managed to inject some life into a municipal election which survived to some degree until the following year when lower rates was again the main issue.[114]

There had been nine contests in 1846 and in 1848 this was exceeded with ten, the highest number of contests at any mid-century Manchester municipal election (see table 12). In all the contests economy and retrenchment were the shibboleths and candidates were assessed not as Liberals or Tories but according to their devotion to municipal economy. James Hibbert was successful at the third attempt at Exchange ward and there was a particularly fierce battle at St George's where 'cars, coaches, canvassers, squibs exhortations, damaging hints and innuendoes – all the material and even some of the spiritual weapons of a tough election were brought into requisition'.[115] As so often elsewhere, this negative 'economist' activity, based upon no real policy other than retrenchment, soon faded away and by the early 1850s the pattern of public apathy was restored to the Manchester municipal scene.

Yet what lay behind a public desire for municipal economy was of deeper and more lasting significance. As councils tried to widen their functions, moving from politics to administration, so they were confronted with problems associated with their role, function, powers, and purposes. In one way or another these concerned the fundamental question of how the urban experience could be improved. Here the problems were not those of parties, which could be resolved by a caucus or a partisan distribution of the spoils, but the problem of policy. The politics of 'who's in and who's out' perforce gave way to the politics of improvement.

7
The politics of improvement

*'The advocates of the dry earth system and the fluid method
of deodorisation fight as bitterly as did the partisans of the
Neptunian against the Vulcanian philosophers who
theorised upon the original formation of the world.'*
Liverpool Courier, 5 August 1870

The first fruits of municipal reform had been popular participation in
local government and the creation of a political role for previously proscribed social groups. The exercise of such political power was, however,
never deemed an end in itself. It was valid to ask 'what boots it to the
people whether a fool wear a blue cap or a yellow one?' and to state one's
indifference to mere politics, 'I care nowt what colour they wear; its not
blue nor yellow 'at makes 'em better or warse'.[1] Corporations, in order to
justify themselves, had to contribute to the welfare of the urban community. As the first reform mayor of Leeds put it, their aim was to
'effect a material improvement in the condition of the burgesses . . . and
promote those objects which would tend to their happiness and prosperity'.[2] It was significant that when Manchester council had served its
seven years' apprenticeship mayor Alexander Kay chose to review its
achievements in terms of the improvements made on behalf of the local
community. He particularly emphasized that 'we have largely increased
and have every intention of still further increasing the funds destined to
improve and embellish this, the metropolis of the great manufacturing
district of England. We have acquired the power . . . of promoting the
health and comforts of our population'.[3] The provision of new markets
and water supply figured in his programme for the future. Hence while
a coherent municipal gospel did not emerge until the age of Chamberlain
there was a general acceptance in early Victorian cities of the socially
useful role of municipal corporations in the field of improvement. The
assumption of the goals of improvement did not, however, mean an
abandonment of politics. As indicated in the headpiece of this chapter,

conflicts over improvement issues could raise political passions just as much as the normal disagreements over political philosophy.

The political battles which raged over the water supply of Leeds provide a classic example of the politicizing of an improvement issue.[4] There was general agreement by the mid-1830s that, in the words of the promoters of the eventual act, Leeds water was 'bad in *quality* and deficient in *quantity*, being taken from the River Aire which is greatly defiled by the refuse from the mills and dyehouses and by the common sewers and drains of the town'.[5] That the solution to this problem lay in a publicly controlled water supply was equally agreed and Robert Perring, editor of the Tory *Intelligencer*, was expressing the general view when he argued that the town should not be supplied by a joint stock company 'whose sole object would be a large percentage on the capital employed'.[6] When the improvement commission set about drawing up a scheme for an extended water supply in January 1834 there seemed no reason why there should not be a speedy application to Parliament on what appeared a non-controversial improvement issue.

In fact the scheme was delayed and finally abandoned largely because of professional disagreements between engineers. Well-meaning laymen found it difficult to judge between alternative sites for reservoirs, variable routes for piping and the advantages of a 36-inch fall of water as against one of 15.[7] All these technical questions became important as the commissioners polarized in support of rival engineers, whose schemes in truth depended upon St Swithin, for 'whether the rain which falls equally upon the just and the unjust will vary in quantity and quality as the changes of the engineer is a question of importance'.[8] A major political struggle ensued between the supporters of the rival engineers which frustrated attempts at progress and made for delays which had important consequences.

By the summer of 1835 Leeds Tories had lost control of the vestry with its power over the office of churchwarden and over the Poor Law and were faced with an imminent loss of power because of municipal reform. At a time when Liberals were championing their suitability as municipal governors the failure to settle the water issue took on a political significance. There was political capital to be made out of the collapse of the improvement commissioners' scheme, which induced growing doubt about the efficiency of public control. Perring, previously a supporter of public control, now began to question the advisability of having water supplied by 'a fluctuating body of Town Commissioners to whose management no capitalist will entrust fifty pounds', and he soon came out clearly in favour of private enterprise: 'It is time to give over this wretched farce. Let the Commissioners stick to their sweepings and their drains and leave *pure* water alone because this is a soilable article.

In a word Leeds can only be properly supplied by a Joint Stock Company'.[9] This new enthusiasm did not cause the company idea to prosper and neither this nor a compromise of half-public and half-private control got off the ground. Two years of indecision left Leeds still without an adequate water supply.

Municipal reform proved an important turning point in the history of Leeds water. The first reform mayor George Goodman, a Baptist woolstapler, chaired a council committee which strongly recommended a public water supply under the control of the council and financed by a contingent rate upon property. Finance from rates was perfectly appropriate according to Goodman because of public needs:

> the object is not only to supply individuals with a sufficient quantity of good water for their domestic purposes but also to promote the health and safety of the inhabitants at large by a better service of Water for removing impurities in the public streets and Drains of the Town and a more available supply in case of Fire.[10]

Goodman's views brought a quick response and by the autumn of 1836 a tripartite management had been agreed between magistrates, improvement commission and council. The so-called united committee got vestry approval, launched a subscription list and blazoned the virtues of rate support and public control.

The contingent rate revived the fears of those suspicious of public control, particularly since the rate would be levied on all property owners whether they required water or not. Those who had always quarrelled with the policy of taxing the many for the benefit of the few were now accused of the equal injustice of taxing the few for the benefit of the many. Leeds water exposed an ideological conflict between rampant individualism and embryonic collectivism and an unknown hand inscribed the case of the propertied:

> Baines jr. says the water works should be better managed under the Town Council than Joint Stock Company because the public would have combined stability with responsibility. Let those people *who say a property tax* won't be wanted come forward as subscribers to a Joint Stock Company at 4 or 5 p.c. and no more and shew their philanthropy. I believe not one of 'em will take a single share. All they want is to expend other people's money and get popularity by letting what *they may call poor* have the water for nothing and also accommodating themselves and tenants at other people's expense . . . I have 10 Thd. pounds worth of property and have been at considerable expense in getting water − my neighbour has the same and his property will be considerably benefited by having water brought to it and mine can't

possibly be benefited at all – is [it] just that I should be made to contribute a yearly sum towards furnishing his estate with water and increasing the value of his property 15 or 20% and taxes me $1\frac{1}{4}$.[11]

Such fears of redistribution, grounded on principle and backed by self-interest, swiftly resuscitated the idea of a joint stock company which attracted support from property owners who had natural supplies of water or who had already paid for an artificial supply.

An ideological battle was thus joined between supporters and opponents of the public control of social utilities. In favour of the joint stock company it was argued that there was greater justice to those who did not require water because its income would derive from water rents paid by consumers, that lacking the power of general taxation the company would of necessity be more efficient under the watchful eye of shareholders, and that the institutions which had served the nation so well in the provision of canals and railways could be trusted for the supply of water.[12] Collectivists supported the simple proposition that the town's water supply should be in control of the town since private enterprise was inappropriate for water supply by its very nature: 'The Joint Stock Company is just a scheme for throwing the Town of Leeds bound hand and foot into the power of these men to do as to them seemeth good. The public have over them no control and their scheme is just a monopoly of one of the necessaries of life.'[13]

The ideological debate was underpinned by a political rivalry. Men did not simply view public control in a vacuum and it was recognized that public control in the Leeds of 1836–7 meant Liberal control. To displaced Tories it seemed that an élite of Liberals, having captured all parochial and municipal power, was now seeking to enlarge its sphere of influence by more power and patronage. Leeds water became an issue in municipal politics and the joint stock company became increasingly a Tory riposte to Liberal monopoly. The political division was manifest in the rival bodies, with the united committee overwhelmingly Liberal and the larger shareholders in the joint stock company predominantly Tory. Indeed the 1837 election for improvement commissioners was fought on the water question, Tories standing in support of the company and Liberals in favour of the united committee.[14] To add even more spice to a complex argument the rival engineers of the previous dispute were again retained and they once more threw their technical differences into the political cauldron.

Leeds faced a costly parliamentary dispute with rival bodies contending for rival schemes and were only saved from this by the avuncular intervention of the Earl of Harewood, from whose land the water was required. Adopting a 'plague on both your houses' attitude he adamantly refused to proceed until the two sides had settled their differences. A compromise was arranged by which management of a new waterworks would be vested in a board half elected by shareholders and half nominated by the council, with a council option on purchase after 12 years. The nominations under the 1837 Leeds Waterworks Act reflected what had become a political rivalry, with all six council representatives being Liberal and five of the shareholders' directors being Tory.[15] Well might the 1837 Act be described as 'an act of compromise . . . a compact, a covenant, under which two parties who had long been engaged in personal strife and animosity should cease their opposition and think and act together for the attainment of a great and public good'.[16] It was rare indeed in the politics of early Victorian Leeds for such a concert to be enacted.

Yet social reformers whose only aim had been to try and provide water for Leeds found that they could not yet get up from their bed of nails. The new company, so delicately balanced between public and private control, was threatened by the final convulsions of the engineering disputes which had dogged Leeds water from the outset. A rump of shareholders retained their faith in the controversial engineer around whom all the previous arguments had revolved and who had been dispensed with by the new company. His merits and the defects of the new engineers were paraded in public and once more Leeds opinion was asked to decide on technical issues, the significance of a 24-inch pipe, the role of peat in a reservoir, the nature of evaporation, rainfall and dew.[17] After so much tribulation the directors decided to make the issue one of confidence and if the disgruntled engineer were to be forced upon the company then the board would resign and the company collapse. Well-meaning political activists found that they were still being frustrated in achieving an agreed social objective. As the Liberal doctor, alderman James Williamson, explained in 1838:

> he regretted deeply that the question of the Leeds Water Works too long alas of angry discussion of . . . party feeling – of feelings of acrimony and personality by which their proceedings had been so much embarassed and the execution of their project so long delayed – should still excite hostility among parties who could only have one common object in view – that now when they had hoped all occasion for such discord had ceased there should be a spirit of division on most important points.[18]

The 'apple of discord' was a real threat to what had been achieved but a greater threat was the imminent collapse of the company. The crisis passed and the company survived to get on with the real task of getting water into Leeds.

That task was difficult enough and the company faced recalcitrant landowners and further technical problems. Eventually ten years after the vestry had first raised the matter Leeds got its water and within a further decade the number of houses supplied increased seven-fold. Such was the voracious thirst of growing towns for water that before the end of the 1840s new sources were needed as the company faced criticism over the declining quantity and quality of water supplied. It was decided after much argument to attempt to use the Washburn as a new source and this required the co-operation of Francis Fawkes, a veteran West Riding Whig squire. Fawkes, like a latter day Welsh nationalist, refused to acknowledge the urban entitlement to rural water and denounced the Leeds water pirates and their 'six months perseverance... in a course of the most unnecessary indefensible and insulting mode of attempting a more nefarious appropriation of private property than ever Railway saturnalia conceived'.[19]

The intransigence of Fawkes in 1851–2 helped to swell the tide in favour of full municipal control which was being suggested from 1848 onwards. Once more Tory voices were raised in favour of private enterprise which was reputed to be more efficient in such matters. The cost of buying out the company was frightening and the old fears about rates were again revived.[20] Opinion of all political persuasions displayed reservations about the municipalization of water supply and the man who took up the question, the Liberal solicitor alderman John Hope Shaw, had a formidable public relations task. He did not shirk the questions but patiently answered them first in a long and able report in August 1851 and then in two further reports in which a council committee chaired by himself recommended the purchase of the company at its original valuation.[21] Hope Shaw finally undermined his opponents in a two-hour speech in April 1852, arguing that 'the Town Council was the proper body to manage the supply of water and that no principle of trade would be violated by their management of such works'. When the purchase went through in November 1852 at the staggering cost of £227,000 George Goodman, since 1836 a supporter of municipalization, confirmed that 'the Corporation would carry on these works far more efficiently than a limited proprietary could do and from this important movement he anticipated great and lasting benefit'.[22]

The benefit which undoubtedly accrued to the Leeds community was always tempered by the political controversy with which the Leeds water question seemed indelibly marked. In the mid-1850s there was a fierce dispute over whether the extended water supply should be taken from the Washburn or the Wharfe, with the council deciding by 28–17 in favour of the Wharfe against Hope Shaw's advice.[23] A decade later criticism from the Privy Council inspector forced Leeds council to reconsider and the Washburn came to be chosen after all in 1866. The new scheme was enacted by the 1867 Leeds Waterworks Act, the cost and ethos of which once more raised political difficulties. There were still those who opposed municipalization, now with the evidence of a 15 years' experience of council control. One of the corporations' own engineers argued that corporations were by their nature inappropriate:

> Almost the entire of their attention is devoted to objects of a political party or personal nature . . . involved in continual rancorous contests they have neither the time the inclination nor the ability to devote themselves dispassionately to the subject of local improvement . . . I feel impressed with the importance of witholding the power of becoming traders in or distributors of public necessity or public utility from the hands of a body so incompetent so ill informed and so unstable as Municipal Corporations.'[24]

Such belated anti-municipal feeling could not prevent the passage of an Act which combined with the Leeds Improvement Act of the previous year raised the borough debt to £800,000 and the rates to 3s. 4½d.[25] Water, highways, a new bridge, a new library, a park, a major slum clearance programme, all merged together in the late 1860s to produce a ratepayers' resistance movement against further expense. As G. A. Linsley, the pawnbroker who led these 'economists', put it: 'the desire for public improvement is becoming almost a mania',[26] and many municipal elections of the late 1860s and early 1870s were fought on the economist ticket. It was the ratepayers' economist movement which gave birth to the political career of the celebrated fruit merchant Archie Scarr, a man anxious for working-class welfare but unwilling to finance the municipal programme necessary to achieve it. By the 1870s water supply had become merely a plank in the general improvement question, which had itself become the central issue in the municipal politics of the day.

Liverpool's water supply also engendered a celebrated case of contentious disputes over improvement when the so called Rivington Pike debate inserted its fissiparous tendencies into local politics in the later 1840s.[27] The politics of Liverpool water raised four issues of general principle as the battle between rival schemes was fought out. First, there was the question of whether water supply should be in public or private hands: second, the dispute involved a resolution of complex technical issues; third, there were financial considerations, and not solely those of economy, which called into question whether Liverpool ought to plan for its present or future needs, whether with a parochial or regional horizon; finally, water supply focused on the general role of municipal government involving in effect a searching examination of the nature of municipal power, how it should be exercised, by whom controlled and with what goals. Liverpool water raised the political temperature and sparked that moral indignation which was so characteristic a feature of Victorian urban politics.

The shortage of water in the 1840s first provoked interest in the question and it was immediately clear that while extra sources of water were urgently required the overlapping and to some extent competing jurisdictions of interested parties would have to be rationalized. There were two private water companies and three administrative bodies with elements of public jurisdiction, the commissioners of sewers, the highway board and the council. In the mid-1840s the water supply question resolved itself not so much into a search for new water but into a debate over the merits of private control. The private water companies were severely pilloried although they had some defence. Cisterns which could compensate for intermittent supply were lacking because of cheeseparing landlords, although public censure was reserved for the private companies.[28] Private enterprise had served the town well, often without great profit, and even collectivists admitted that 'those who have invested the capital in water works have rendered a most essential public service'.[29] The private companies were championed by one of their directors who sang their praises: 'It is the spirit of private enterprise which has called public works into action and rendered them by persevering industry, whether the result has proved losing or profitable to the capitalists engaged in them, sources of benefit and convenience to the community at large.'[30]

Gratitude for past services did not reduce the demand for some form of public control which was the theme of the memorials on the subject. The strongest case for a public water supply was put by Samuel Holme in a decisively important pamphlet, *Want of Water* (1845). Holme, a builder, had been an organizer of the Tradesmen's Conservative Association and sat in the council from 1842 to 1845, from 1846 to 1849, and again from 1850 to 1864, being mayor in 1852 and alderman from 1853. He was a prominent Conservative activist and he took up a clear collectivist stance, promulgating a coherent argument for public control of water supply.

> The public body is under public control. It is answerable to a constituency for its acts. It has no private interests to serve and all its deliberations are under the public eye . . . A private company on the contrary has a pecuniary interest at stake . . . its deliberations are with closed doors . . . self interest is the ruling motive and the smallest supply at the highest rate produces the most satisfying dividends. I do not say that a public body ought therefore to become the butchers and bakers of a community but . . . water is as necessary to the health

and welfare of a community as air . . . *public bodies must not be permitted to trade* . . . but in this case they will purchase [the private companies] for public benefit only and it will be as proper for them to do so as it is for them to tax us for our local government or to make our public sewers. The health of the town demands it.[31]

Holme's views found a receptive audience and both the special committee appointed by the highway board and the health committee of the town council recommended public control.[32] The highway board itself drew up a bill for a more extensive water supply which was only deferred because of the major sanitary bill being proposed by the council in 1846. After the passage of the Liverpool Sanitary Act it was clear that it would be the council which adopted the requisite powers for the purchase of the two existing companies. This was done in 1847 at a staggering cost of £537,000. It is necessary to keep in mind that all further disputes were conditioned by this massive expenditure to which the council was already committed by its water policy. That further expenditure would be necessary was agreed by all since the half-million spent upon taking the water companies into public control had not added one drop of water to the deficient supply in which the dispute had originated.

The adoption in two council votes in March and April 1847 of the Rivington Pike scheme began a controversy which was to engulf all other political questions in Liverpool's municipal government. A host of distinguished engineers and geologists had pronounced on the virtues of a series of reservoirs to be built at Rivington Pike near Chorley which would more than adequately supply Liverpool's water needs. By the spring of 1848 a fierce battle was in full swing which cut right across party lines and raised almost unprecedented bitterness.

As elsewhere a major undertaking of civil engineering raised technical questions which the interested layman was incompetent to judge. Essentially the anti-Pikist argued that the hitherto accepted judgement, that local sandstone sources were inadequate to supply the town's needs, was erroneous. The first of the many official reports on Liverpool water, that of the 1845 special committee, had stated clearly that 'this locality will not admit of a continuous supply to the inhabitants at large'.[33] It was this belief which led Liverpool further afield and hence the Rivington scheme. Its opponents reopened the local supply aspect by adducing technical evidence to show that local sources could provide sufficient water. Figures abounded as engineers exchanged insults over whether local sources could yield 3, 8 or 12 million gallons daily. The council members, not being technically competent, had a difficult task of verification when one set of engineers assured them that more bore holes would yield more water while another said that they would merely

deprive existing wells of supplies. The public also had to judge the role
and quality of condensing water, salt water, soft and hard water.
Questions of engineering and geology merged into those of good house-
keeping when one Pikist urging the virtues of the soft Rivington water
reminded housewives, like some latter-day detergent promoter, that
'cloth washed in hard water becomes sooner rotten . . . this also destroys
the beautiful clear white of linen and gives that faint dun yellow'.[34]

Much of the technical argument over the merits of Rivington and the
local sandstone sources was in reality a rationalization of an essentially
financial concern, and as one participant explained, 'much of what has
been said in the newspapers and elsewhere in favour of the quality and
yield of our present wells has arisen from apprehension of the cost
attendant upon the new undertaking and consequent fears of increases in
the rates.'[35] Financial concern was understandable when in addition to
the half-million already spent, Thomas Hawksley, the well-known
engineer, estimated the cost of the Rivington scheme at £450,000. It was
not only the anti-Pikists who realized that 'no estimates are more
uncertain than estimates of the cost of bringing water from a distance',[36]
and the final cost was three times that of Hawksley's estimate. The alternative local sources had the attraction of not involving the outlay of the
Rivington scheme, and anti-Pikists estimated that the initial and annual
costs of Rivington would be 50 per cent greater than those of an extended
local supply.

Pikists never accepted that the financial equation was as simple as that
and they mounted a mind-boggling juggle of figures to get at the 'real'
cost involved. It was argued that in fact the Rivington scheme was
cheaper proportionally in terms of the extent of its supply, by a calculation of the cost of a notional local supply equivalent to that projected at
Rivington. It was maintained that the cost of softening local water (i.e.
bringing it up to the quality of Rivington water) would be equivalent to
the interest charge for nearly the whole Rivington expenditure. Looked
at another way, the cost of an adequate provision of cisterns (to create
that continuous supply locally which Rivington promised) would pay a
quarter of the interest on the larger scheme, or yet again it was held that
two-thirds of the interest could be met by savings consequent upon more
efficient street cleansing.[37] As always, statistics were a fickle instrument
and could serve the purposes of either camp. In truth much of the
financial controversy derived from the economists' view that the
Rivington scheme was unnecessary since it would in fact over-supply the
town. Anti-Pikists were content to plan for 20 years where Pikists looked
beyond this.* The former were at pains to point out that if Rivington

* Planning for prospective water needs was always a controversial urban
question and in Manchester caused tension in 1850. Cf. *Manchester Guardian,*

yielded the 16 million gallons per day for Liverpool which was predicted the town would have a gross surplus. The notion of a regional water strategy in which the Liverpool works serviced other towns had no appeal for parochial anti-Pikists.

These technical and financial issues provided the weapons in a sanitary civil war which lasted for more than two years from the spring of 1848, involving numerous petitions, pamphlets, meetings, council votes, and municipal elections. Town water became *the* question of the day as 'by degrees "Rivington Pike" became a party cry on which for many years all elections and town squabbles turned'.[38] This party cry cut right across normal political lines. Pikists included many of the wealthy Liberal élite such as William Rathbone, George Holt, and William Earle, yet also comprised leading Tories such as Samuel Holme, G. H. Lawrence, T. B. Horsfall, and above all John Bramley-Moore, mayor in the crucial Rivington year of 1848–9. The anti-Pikists were led by J. R. Jeffery, the radical later to be a prominent Liberal leader, and John Smith, the editor and proprietor of the Liberal *Liverpool Mercury*. Yet these two Liberals found allies inside the council among the most extreme Tories such as William Bennett, who sat for St Ann's for four years from 1846 and was an alderman for the two decades from 1850, James Procter, councillor for Abercromby in 1844–7 and alderman for six years thereafter, and the arch-economist H. G. Harbord who sat for Great George from 1847 until his death in 1850. Given the general political views of, for instance, Harbord and Jeffery, the anti-Pike alliance took on the character of an ultra-Tory/radical coalition.

Such a coalition was already active before the 1848 elections which were fought mainly on the question of dock rating, an issue which entwined itself within the Rivington controversy. It was found that many of those wealthy merchants who had enlarged views on a public utility like water supply were not so accommodating when it came to contributing towards municipal expenditure by the rating of the docks and corporate estates. Dock rating, by leading in 1848 to the defeat of Rathbone and Earle and the withdrawal of Lace and Evans, deprived Rivington of some of its most influential council supporters.[39] The economic depression now began to turn the tide against the Pikists and, though they survived two hostile motions in November 1848, a motion for a further enquiry (virtually a motion of no confidence) was carried in January 1849. A new and hostile water committee was appointed and engineers were retained to produce an overtly anti-Pike scheme.[40]

The 'stop the Pike' movement was at its height in the early months of 1849 and a huge excited public meeting in February voted against the

26 October 1850, with its critical editorial on 'an expenditure that might have been more wisely limited to *present* wants'.

Pike, though according to George Holt all the argument was on one side and merely votes on the other.[41] The public meeting had taken up an issue which had been aired at the November elections, namely whether the council should be immune to public opinion. From an anti-Pike position it appeared that a high handed council was in need of 'a salutary lesson. It is vain to attempt to ride roughshod over a determined people ... on any question involving, at a time of great depression, the expenditure of thousands – it may be millions of money.'[42] The water question had exposed a wider concern over the nature of municipal power and the role of the electorate in having a direct influence in the determination of policy. That influence appeared to have triumphed by the summer of 1849 with the adoption of an alternative scheme involving expanded local supply and the abandonment of Rivington, and with H. G. Harbord firmly in control of the water committee.

The economist face of the anti-Pike party must not be allowed to hide the genuine concern which anti-Pikists had for sanitary reform. This was not a negative obscurantist campaign for economy, as John Smith explained:

> the Pikemen would fain make it appear that they only are influenced by sympathies for human suffering and that those who oppose their views are the enemies of the poor and the abettors of pestilence and disease from a niggard spirit of economy. But we contend that those really are the philanthropists who desire to give to the town an immediate large addition to their supply of pure springwater.[43]

There is really no place here for the picture sometimes dispensed of social reformers frustrated in their enlightened policy by intransigent, insensitive, selfish economists. Both parties wished to provide water for Liverpool. The inadequacy of supply was never in doubt nor were the deleterious effects of water shortage upon the social and sanitary condition of Liverpool's poorer citizens. Jeffery's commitment to working-class social welfare could not be doubted, yet he led the anti-Pikists in their desire to oppose unnecessary extravagance and provide a social utility in the most efficient and economical way. They wished to end the water hysteria which had grown out of the water crisis of the 1840s, well described by an anti-Pikist engineer: 'A clamour was got up: more water was wanted and it was really thought that more water was not to be had. People's minds were so possessed by this idea that they actually went mad upon it. We all went mad and lost sight of the main points.'[44]

Unfortunately for the anti-Pikists one of these 'main points' was that by the time they gained their council ascendancy the Rivington scheme was already advanced and preliminary contracts had been signed. When, because of a writ of *mandamus* from Rathbone and his friends, a special committee was appointed to report on the current position, the pro-Rivington chairman George Holt was able to cite one compelling financial statistic. The costs to which the council was already legally committed amounted to some £200,000 and this together with the cost of local supply would exceed the cost of proceeding.[45] This is what we may now perhaps call the 'Concorde argument' – so much money has been expended that the costs of cancellation outweigh the cost of continuing. The eventual adoption by the council in August 1849 of this pro-Rivington report only further confused a complex situation in which the council's water committee was pursuing a policy which the whole council had now rejected.

Though the anti-Pikists had suffered a reverse they came back strongly in the 1849 municipal elections, when all eight contested seats were fought on the water question, with six of them between members of the same party. The results were rendered in Pikist terminology with four anti- and 12 pro-Rivington councillors retiring and no less than 14 anti- and only two pro-Pike supporters returning.[46] The pro-Rivington special committee was disbanded and an anti-Pike water committee re-appointed on the tide of electoral success. Yet the anti-Pikists were now floundering in a current of perplexity from which they could not escape. There was for practical, financial, engineering, and legal reasons no real alternative to a completion of the Rivington scheme. It was merely a statement of the obvious when in 1850 the engineer Robert Stephenson reported strongly in favour of Rivington,[47] and though further twitch-ings of anti-Pike muscles were felt during 1850 the Rivington scheme was now safe. It was a measure of the insatiable thirst of growing cities that in the 1860s even Rivington was found to be deficient and the urban search for water began once again.

Water supply also featured in the improvement schism which rent Leicester Liberalism in the 1840s. Leicester Liberals had a near-total monopoly of municipal power once the old corporation oligarchy had been vanquished and by 1845 signs of political fragmentation were clear which the improvement question exaggerated. The low-lying older parts of Leicester were particularly insanitary and in great need of an efficient drainage system. The revelations in the Chadwick report and in that of the Health of Towns Commission awakened opinion to the sanitary question. Until the mid-1840s, however, the corporation's financial position was too weak to contemplate a major programme of improve-ments.[48] Locally the Whig-Liberal *Leicester Chronicle* fought a prolonged campaign in 1843 and 1844 on the drainage question, arguing that 'something more than mere counting house merit is required in municipal matters' and expressing the hope that the reformed council would be distinguished for 'philanthropy public spirit and enlightenment'.[49] The general agreement over the needs of drainage and water supply was disturbed by the intrusion of the Chadwickian joint stock company idea for sanitary reform. William Biggs, who with his brother John led the Liberal party in the town, spoke out strongly for leaving drainage, water supply, and a cemetery to the joint stock companies while reserving council attention for physical improvement such as new markets and a new town hall.[50] Joseph Whetstone, chairman of the finance committee and leader of the more moderate Whigs, was horrified at the costs of these latter improvements and wished to give priority to sanitation. A battle ensued within the Liberal party between Biggs and his so-called 'improvers' or 'expenders' and Whetstone's 'economists'.

This Liberal schism on a local matter of improvement did not develop in a vacuum. It was partly a manifestation of a deeper potential split on general political questions, and there had already been tension about the Church, corn laws, and above all the suffrage. As elsewhere, there was some difficulty in holding the Whig and Radical wings of the party together and on the improvement question the more radical elements tended to support Biggs, the more Whiggish Whetstone. This was itself a reflection of a generation gap, for Whetstone was one of the older Whigs who had fought the unreformed corporation while Biggs represented younger Liberals who were now supplanting the Whigs in Liberal leadership.* Such was the way with improvement disputes, however, that radicals and Conservatives were to be found on both sides. The personalities issue between two members of the same Unitarian chapel was refined and developed in the press where battle was joined between the Liberal *Chronicle*, supporting Whetstone, and the Biggsite radical *Mercury*.

The *Mercury* had a greater circulation than the *Chronicle* and Biggs commanded more council votes than Whetstone, so the council adopted Bigg's improvement bill with its costly embellishments to the town and its exclusion of drainage and water supply. There was much public disquiet but petitions had no effect on what was becoming a Biggsite dictatorship. The failure of public concern to sway the council led some to question the very nature of municipal reform where a Liberal oligarchy had merely changed places with a Tory one. Ratepayers no longer had a legitimate political role: 'They must not interfere with their local governors. They must give up the antiquated notion of petitioning against what they do not approve of. They must trust the benevolent despotism of the town council. . . . They must not think

---

* A vivid image capturing this conflict was that of the Whetstone party as 'the old coachee' which put on a drag at the first hint of an incline and the Biggs party as 'the new coachee' descending the hill without a brake so as to take the next slope more easily: *Leicestershire Mercury*, 16 May 1846.

for a moment that they have any other part to fulfil than that of submission.'[51]

Much of this public opposition stemmed from financial fears and the £50,000 loan (small by Liverpool standards but frightening locally) with its inevitable improvement rate worried 'economists'. Yet it would be a gross distortion to view Whetstone's 'economists' as hostile to public expenditure *per se*. They were not so much opposing expenditure as questioning what the money was to be spent on. The dispute centred not on whether £50,000 should be spent but whether drainage or a town hall should have priority in the allocation of scarce resources. When in 1844 James Thompson, editor of the *Chronicle*, produced a list of six improvements he placed drainage at the head of the list and a town hall at the bottom.[52] Biggs and his 'expenders' had appeared to reverse the priorities. For their part they argued that the town would get the benefit of both sanitation and improvements and at a smaller financial outlay since joint stock companies would bear the expense of sanitary reform.[53] Such arguments not only increased the controversy by raising the contentious issue of whether social utilities should be in public or private hands, they also failed to convince the 'economists' who continued to pose the stark contrast between mortality and embellishment: 'Fever may enter your dwelling and strike to the earth your life's partner, it may attack *you* and prostrate you on the bed of sickness for weeks or months or it may rob you of some of your little ones . . . what then? Have you not a great Market Place and a beautiful Town Hall to look at?'[54] Whether the town wished it or not they were to be blessed with 'magnificent "Brummagem" town halls'.[55]

Both in 1845 and in 1846 the annual municipal elections were fought on the improvement question and by the latter date it was being contended that there was no longer a split within one party but two distinct and separate parties – 'economists' and 'expenders'. The 1846 election became virtually a vote of confidence in Biggsite leadership, particularly calling into question William's motivation.[56] This was a murky area but even a neutral observer admitted that 'plans founded upon humanity and for the real benefit of the town have not always originated in patriotism or philanthropy'.[57] Perhaps there was some point to the veiled criticism that drains were below ground and hidden from view whereas rebuilding was open to the public gaze. Had the plans of William Biggs matured the town would certainly have taken on a different appearance and had it not been for the Liberal schism Leicester might indeed have been 'tattooed, bruised, turned upside down, removed from north to south, twirled from east to west by Act of Parliament'.[58]

Aspersions upon William Biggs's sincerity continued to flow and 'economists' reiterated the charge that he was more interested in creating a personal reputation than in caring for the needs of the inhabitants who lived in such insanitary conditions. Perhaps there was some justification for Thompson's remarks on Biggs in the 1846 campaign: 'he did not care to meddle with the "dirty work" of Town Drainage. There was no glory to be gained in "washing sewers with cold water", laurels were only to be won by the builder of Town Halls.'[59] Biggs genuinely believed that by his scheme the town would be both drained and beautified but he certainly did display more enthusiasm for embellishments than for sewers. He apparently had notions of copying Florentine princes or emulating Caesar 'who found Rome built of brick and left it built of marble'.[60] Events turned out otherwise and only part of his scheme was proceeded with, and the joint stock company collapsed leaving sanitation no further advanced than it had been in 1844. During the 1849 election the remnants of the 'economist' party sadly contemplated a civic improvement budget of £46,000 of which not a penny would be devoted to the drainage question first aired by Whetstone five years before.[61] The 'economist-expender' battle had not solved the town's sanitary problems and the Liberal schism was not healed until the 1860s.

During the 1840s improvement became in Leicester a significant political question and the same was true in Salford and Birmingham, where improvement centred on the question of amalgamation, in Salford of townships, in Birmingham of institutions. We have already seen how the proposed Salford improvement bill of 1844 had aroused controversy because of the failure to consult ratepayers (see above, p. 101). The improvement issue was closely related to that of incorporation itself and the Tory–radical alliance opposed both incorporation and the improvement bill. It was no surprise therefore that the threat of major improvements in Salford was the central issue in the first municipal election in 1844.[62] One of the anti-improvers expressed the uncertainty of many when he remarked 'My wonder is that anyone will reside in Salford overhung as it is with railways on the one hand and threatened with a complete unsettling of property by a so-called Improvement Bill on the other.'[63]

Even before the charter of incorporation had been granted a major dispute had arisen over the boundaries of the new municipality. William Lockett and the Salford Liberal élite wished the municipal borough to be coextensive with the parliamentary constituency and thus include the townships of Broughton and Pendleton. Opposition in the latter led by Stephen Heelis, the Tory solicitor who had acted for Garnett in the 1832 election, prevented the union of the three townships. Heelis feared a Liberal monopoly in which Pendleton's rates would be increased to finance Salford's social policy.[64] The union of the three townships made

sanitary sense, and increased awareness of sanitary needs through
government reports and the like increased the prospect of amalgamation.

In 1847 the question was raised again largely because of the desires of
some Broughton ratepayers to introduce effective local government.
Even William Garnett, the most respected Salford Tory, who was himself no friend of the Lockett clique, admitted that the township must
find some way, through incorporation, amalgamation, or statutory
regulation, of governing itself properly. Such views could not allay
familiar Tory centripetal fears based mainly upon finance. When
Broughton held a protest meeting on the proposed amalgamation with
Salford these financial fears were brought into the open. One speaker
referred to Salford Liberals as snakes in the grass only waiting to pawn
the township, while another, suspicious of Salford's sudden affection for
Broughton, claimed that 'considerations of pounds shillings and pence
were mixed up with her virgin love'.[65] When the 1847 proposal was laid
low the Tory press clarified what had really been at issue:

> it would be a mighty comfortable sort of thing to ease its own burdens,
> by inducing the 'purple and fine linen' gentlemen of Broughton and
> Pendleton to contribute, out of their worldly stock, somewhat to help
> pay the police of Salford keep the streets in repair and make improve-
> ments in thoroughfares *and* property. We congratulate Pendleton and
> Broughton on having escaped the trap that was laid for them.[66]

This interpretation of amalgamation was to recur in the final successful
phase which led to full incorporation in 1853. By that date powerful
forces in the field of sanitary reform were making amalgamation of the
three townships a logical step. The Public Health Act forced the townships
to consider some form of sanitary institution and Robert Rawlinson's
reports on the two townships provided extra evidence, especially in
Pendleton, of the needs for sanitary regulation and ultimately for
amalgamation. Under the guiding hand of Joseph Brotherton, Salford's
Liberal M.P., an act of amalgamation was steered through Parliament in
1853 and was confirmed by ratepayers' votes.[67] There was a last-ditch
resistance from Broughton Tories who used all the old arguments to
resist Salford's clutches. As ever beneath the genuine separatist fears of
Broughton lay a political reality, for amalgamation in 1853 meant an
enlargement of *Liberal* municipal power in Salford.

In his remarks upon Pendleton Rawlinson had commented that 'the
leading principle of the Public Health Act is consolidation of power in
one representative local body',[68] and it was the search for such a consolidation which dominated Birmingham's municipal affairs in the
1840s. There the question of amalgamation involved the incorporation of
powers of diverse local institutions within the town council. In fact the

amalgamation issue was but the first stage of a three-tier development in the politics of improvement in Birmingham. This first period ended with the Improvement Act of 1851; the second was dominated by the constraints of 'economist' control of the council which lasted throughout the 1850s and into the late 1860s; the third and most productive phase was that of the civic gospel of the Chamberlain era.

The confirmation of the legality of the charter in the early 1840s ought logically to have opened a phase of active improvement in Birmingham municipal affairs. That it did not was a consequence of the fragmented authority of the council which shared its jurisdiction with nine parochial or township institutions of the pre-reform era. These were not, as in Salford, outside the borough but within the municipality and as we have seen (above, p. 101) the most important was the street commission. Amalgamation of powers did not become a live political issue until J. A. Jaffray succeeded Douglas as the editor of the *Journal* in 1844 and launched a campaign on amalgamation which he sustained for the rest of the decade. Financial extravagance and administrative inefficiency were themes of Jaffray's attack upon the 'Babel of confusion' which characterized Birmingham's 'mob of municipal governors'.[69] Yet underlying these familiar themes was a concern for sanitary reform, which could never be effectively brought about without amalgamation. Improvement was a more important goal than the party dominance for which Birmingham town council was noted. 'To lead the van in the regeneration of the condition of his impoverished townsmen is well worthy of the ambition of any of our Corporation and the public voice will infinitely more readily sanction such an undertaking, than an aggrandisement of one political party or the discomfiture of another.'[70]

Once the amalgamation issue caught the public imagination an interesting political formation developed, for amalgamation was assailed from opposite sides. The old institutions themselves were unwilling to play the part of sacrificial lambs to a municipal leviathan and continued to assert their independence. As if to show amalgamators that these institutions still had an important role, both the street commissioners and the commissioners of Duddeston-cum-Nechells promoted their own bills in 1845 to give themselves increased powers. Neither bills were enacted but the Liberal monopoly of power encouraged some to support the township institutions, which, though self-elected, had in fact been 'composed of and represent every important party and interest in the borough'.[71] From the opposite side Liberal amalgamators were opposed by radicals unhappy about the suffrage aspects, and the council majority was split on this question.[72] Complete suffrage radicals were unwilling to extend the powers of the council until the municipal suffrage was widened. Without such a safeguard total power would be placed 'into the

hands of the wealthy and leave the poor without the slightest means of
protecting themselves against local oppression'.[73] Here was that fear of
the 'tyranny of the bloated rich' which had expressed itself through
radicals in Manchester in 1838. Birmingham radicals resisted what was
seen to be an 'insidious attempt at centralisation' and favoured not the
amalgamation but the liberalization of township institutions, wishing to
see smaller discrete units of local government in place of municipal
despotism.[74]

Town meetings, council debates and even the 1845 municipal election
mulled over the amalgamation question. Progress was not made in the
mid-1840s because amalgamation was gripped in a vice of political
opposites, well described by Jaffray:

> While one party strives to maintain authority for the few, another
> class would refer all power to the many. The old political aristocracy of
> the town decry the Town Council as a popularly elected body; an
> extreme section of the liberal party will allow no responsibility or
> independent action to their municipal representatives, and denounce
> the burgess roll as a limited and incapable elective body. Thus while
> our ultra-Conservatives bewail the flood of Democracy let in by our
> Charter, the ultra-Radicals contend for . . . the veto of public meet-
> ings.[75]

Such a stalemate pushed amalgamation off the political stage for most of
1846 although it was still an issue at the 1846 municipal election when
candidates were warned by a normally neutral observer that those who
could see no difference between elected and self-elected bodies 'are not
exactly the parties to be placed at the head of a corporation'.[76] Interest
revived in 1847–8 with the debates over Morpeth's public health proposals in Parliament and the 1848 Public Health Act was in the event an
agent for amalgamation in Birmingham. Amalgamators supported even
the 1847 bill because it made consolidation of powers likely, while anti-
amalgamators came to the defence of commissioners who were to be
summarily superseded.[77]

By the end of the 1840s there was general concern in Birmingham over
sanitation, despite the town's relatively healthy situation because of
certain natural advantages. The passing of the 1848 Public Health Act
forced Birmingham to consider how best to implement improvement
policies which were generally desired. Amalgamators in the council
favoured an order under the new Act by which many, though not all, of
the existing powers would pass to the corporation as the local board of
health, while the street commissioners were even more convinced that
they should get their own Act for sewerage and drainage. The advantage
of the latter course was that it avoided central supervision and strong

fears on the centralization question only delayed amalgamation further. Some felt the incongruity of Birmingham, having resisted the Duke of Wellington in 1832, willingly submitting to 'a base and a more degrading and enduring slavery' than even he had attempted. The objections of anti-centralizers were powerful but as Jaffray remarked they did not deny that 'the borough is deficient in public and private drainage and we have no powers for remedying the evil'.[78] The very real drainage needs of the town were reiterated by amalgamators as the compelling evidence for consolidation. Again here as elsewhere, sanitary reformers were on both sides of the question, for anti-amalgamators were not hostile to improvement. They merely questioned the forms, powers, and channels through which improvement would be effected. They in fact refused to accept what amalgamators regarded as self-evident logic:

> It may be taken for granted that until the control of all parts of the borough shall be vested in one governing body no efficient system of drainage can be established and that all partial efforts in this direction may and in some cases must lead to useless expense. The Corporation cannot do one half of the work and the Commissioners the other.[79]

Anti-amalgamators did indeed believe that there was a role for both council and commission.

While the council pursued its goal of an order under the 1848 Act, the resistance of the street commission was unrelenting. Once the council became persuaded that a local Act could give all the advantages and none of the disadvantages then a union of forces was possible. The threat of centralization in the Public Health Act finally persuaded the street commission to surrender its powers to the corporation. That amalgamation lay at the heart of the question was confirmed in the preamble to the 1851 Improvement Act which stated, 'it would be attended with great public advantage if the sewerage, drainage cleansing lighting paving supplying with water . . . were placed under the control of one governing body'.[80] The Birmingham town council now had the potential for becoming a major agency of town improvement.

The process by which the council finally fulfilled its potential in the 1870s is well known and has been frequently described by historians.[81] From 1852 to the later 1860s municipal government in Birmingham was constrained by economists of two broad schools. During the mid-1850s the council was dominated by the negative public parsimony of Joseph Allday, formerly the editor of a Tory-radical periodical which had been a vehicle for scurrility. Political battles in this decade resembled somewhat those of Leicester in the 1840s and the main improvement issues were fought out between the 'economists' and the 'extravagant' parties. Allday secured some notable coups which frustrated sanitary reformers and held the council in a financial straitjacket. The withdrawal of Allday presaged a period of more enlarged views in the 1860s but even then the council came under the influence of Thomas Avery with a variation on the 'economist' theme. Avery was aware of the wastefulness of negative parsimony which resulted in administrative inefficiency, but at the same time he was unwilling to see the municipal budget grow substantially. On the controversial loan question he put his authority behind those who wished to restrict municipal finances.

During Avery's ascendancy the seeds of the civic gospel were being sown by the ideas of George Dawson and R. W. Dale. From the end of the 1860s a more elevated view of the role of the council combined with increased awareness of the sanitary and educational deficiencies of the borough to produce a revolution in Birmingham's municipal affairs. In the Chamberlain years of the 1870s the issue of improvement in its various forms, educational, sanitary, physical and social, became central to Birmingham politics. The very existence of the corporation was now to be justified by its role as an agent of improvement and Chamberlain identified the important goals of municipal government: 'There is no nobler sphere for those who have not the opportunity of engaging in imperial politics than to take part in municipal work to the wise conduct of which they owe the welfare the health, the comfort and the lives of 400,000 people'.[82] Through the politics of improvement Chamberlain was able to substantiate his abiding faith in municipal institutions as organs of social reform.

To this list of Leeds, Liverpool, Leicester, Salford, and Birmingham may be added others where likewise the politics of improvement became a significant local issue. In Nottingham the improvement question resolved itself into a dispute over the enclosure of the common fields with a familiar cross-party conflict. Bradford's improvement bill of 1851 provided an opportunity for an extension of the incorporation battle, with Tory-radical anti-incorporators opposed to the vastly increased powers the Liberal élite would acquire. Sheffield's improvement programme was complicated by the activity of Isaac Ironside, whose decisive change of heart led to the defeat of the improvement bill in 1851. Later in the decade radical 'economists' of the Ironside school elevated the 1858 improvement bill into the most violent political conflict. That political groupings could follow normal paths was demonstrated in the 1860s when the Sheffield water company was pilloried after a reservoir disaster. Partly because the main shareholders were Liberals, Tories began campaigning for municipalization and the politicizing of the issue was reinforced by the vigorous defence of the water company by the

Liberal M.P.* Because of the local political structure Sheffield Tories in the 1860s were in favour of that municipal control so vigorously opposed by Leeds Tories in the 1830s.

Such paradoxes were common in the history of the quest for urban improvement. In the same town and on the same question it was possible for divisions to be both along and across party lines. Improvement raised both party and non-party political issues. To venture into the field of improvement was to encounter complex technical, financial, and ideological disputes in which the angels were to be found on both sides. It was often not the goals but the means and modes of municipal policy which were at issue. The nature of municipal authority hence became a factor in the politics of improvement. Faced with the unprecedented strains of urban growth, municipal councils were impelled towards policies of environmental control. Such policies forced men to define the role of corporations and the limits of their authority. In so doing political activists found that the spheres of influence of Parliament and of the municipality merged in the area of improvement. The politics of improvement came to be inextricably linked with the parliamentary politics which were at the very centre of the urban political structure.

* This gave extra bite to the Tory attack upon the sitting Member and so in 1865 one strand in Sheffield's election campaign was this controversy over municipal control of water.

Part Three
Parliamentary Elections

8
Elections and society

'One of the great evils of a general election is the "democratisation" it causes.' E. H. Greg to G. Melly, 28 April 1859

Both contemporaries and historians have accorded to parliamentary elections the premier position in the field of political activity. An election was an occasion for a symbolic act of identification where, at least until 1872, the voter had to stand up and be counted. It provided an opportunity for the assertion of class, interest or group loyalty. In some situations the vote was merely an expression of a deferential social context in which the voter responded to the influence of an élite which made the initial political choice; in others it was a conscious decision in support of a particular political viewpoint. Many historians would see parliamentary elections as the essence of political history. The timing of elections gives some perspective to this view. In the quarter-century before the second Reform Act there were only five general elections. Indeed between 1832 and 1880 there were only a dozen. By-elections increased the opportunities for voting; but can we really accept that the casting of a dozen votes over half a century constituted the total political experience of the average citizen? Clearly parliamentary elections did not represent the voter's total political diet, yet it was generally agreed that the parliamentary election was the cream of the political milk. It was a cohesive force retaining loyalty for other levels of political activity. Conversely a parliamentary contest could reflect or instigate a schism in the local political system. The parliamentary election was but one strand, albeit a prominent one, in the local political structure.

Though in large cities a parliamentary contest was an exciting occasion, swaying the passions of both voters and non-voters, there were always some who doubted whether such an election was the best avenue for local improvement. It was not lost on a citizen that a churchwardens', guardians' or municipal election could have much more significance for the local community than the return of an M.P. to Westminster. A seat in Parliament was an attraction to a natural social leader, but often more could be achieved in his own local empire:

> We are always thinking there must be some beautified land beyond those distant mountains, while we will not cast a look upon the flowers that are growing around our own door. . . . In the House of Commons you know all the while that you might just as well speak to the benches or the dead walls that are around you. Who listens? Who is moved? Who is convinced? . . . What can you do? What result achieve? – nothing. . . . But for *real good to be done* . . . [we] may do more *in our own place* – by working in our own field among those who, after all, are at the bottom and foundation of everything.[1]

George Wilson was positively advised by John Bright against taking a seat since he believed Wilson's influence would be *reduced* by entering Parliament. Others however retained their faith in the supremacy of Parliament whose power could so vitally affect the general welfare, and viewed a seat as the most prestigious honour:

> It is a high personal honour for a man who commenced life in a very humble station . . . to fill the first station in the land that a commoner can fill independent of court favour. . . . Independent of the honour, there is given by a seat in Parliament a power of doing good to the people of Great Britain and Ireland, and to all their dependencies; and not only of doing good to the present age, but to after ages, and that to an extent cannot perhaps be done in any other situation.[2]

To be an M.P. for a large urban constituency was certainly no sinecure, for in addition to general parliamentary affairs the local electorate expected three essential functions from their representative. He was expected first to manage local business, second to act as a channel of patronage, and third to give a lead to local opinion, to create the right sort of image for the town. The pressure of local business certainly grew from mid-century onwards as the number of local Acts multiplied with the increasing complexity of urban administration. M.P.s were responsible for overseeing through Parliament railway, judicial, sanitary, improvement, burial and parochial legislation of specific interest to their constituencies. Such bills were often tedious and time-consuming and weighed heavily upon a conscientious representative. It was this feature of an M.P.'s life which would soon take the lustre off the great personal achievement of gaining access to Parliament, and an ambitious Liverpool politician was warned; 'once there the drawback to the life would become very marked particularly as members for large places and when your attention was taken from national questions by the Liverpool Parliamentary business . . . [you become] really wearied with the life, the rushing back and forward to Liverpool and endless correspondence.'[3]

Because local business was deemed so important, familiarity with local conditions was considered a vital asset for a parliamentary candidate. It was not mere political petulance which caused Yorkshire Tories to criticize Macaulay in 1831–2 for being in need of Oastler's 'first lesson on Yorkshire slavery and the trade of Leeds' or to attack Molesworth in 1837 for knowing 'as much about the West Riding of Yorkshire as a West Riding pig knows about the German flute'.[4] Local knowledge was invaluable in fulfilling an essential role of an urban M.P. and much of the initial opposition to Milner Gibson, a Suffolk squire standing at Manchester, was due to the view that 'for such a place as Manchester it would be desirable to have one better acquainted with commerce'.[5] Similarly when Lord Lincoln was canvassed as a candidate in 1846 Bright commented 'Manchester electors will hardly like to be handed over to a son of the Duke of Newcastle'.[6]

A fair proportion of the 'endless correspondence' of an urban M.P. comprised begging letters of one sort or another from would-be office holders or their sponsors. While it was usual for local parliamentary business to be non-partisan, the channel of patronage was an essential nexus in the local party system. A successful M.P. was expected to provide a *quid pro quo* for those who had helped him obtain his seat. In the wider context an urban M.P. was vitally placed to aid the fortunes and honours of his party in general. It was perfectly natural for Russell, finding himself in 1836 badgered by disgruntled Leeds Tories over Liberal nominations for magistrates, to turn to Baines, the local M.P., for guidance. It was equally natural that Baines, while acknowledging the merits of the odd Tory, should remind Russell of the need to reward a young merchant 'whose services to the Liberal party in Leeds have been valuable'.[7] Similarly the election of the Tory William Beckett in 1841 provided a natural connection between Leeds and the incoming Peel ministry, whose fruits were to be seen in the exclusively Tory addition to the Leeds bench in 1842.

In Liverpool the Liberal M.P. Joseph Ewart deliberately cultivated the channel of patronage in the 1850s and 1860s in order to strengthen his own political position, and one critic complained: 'he has virtually nominated a number of magistrates all of whom feel bound to support him.'[8] Yet it was always a delicate business and Ewart found himself in the midst of a torrent of complaints in 1864 and 1865 from aggrieved aspirants to the bench. Even candidates were expected to smooth the upward path of frustrated local leaders and while George Melly was cultivating the Preston constituency he was appealed to on behalf of the Liberal mayor who felt that 'he has been overlooked and when he can see old friends who have worked with him for the liberal cause and who started the world at the same time made JP he feels it'.[9]

It was the county bench to which the mayor of Preston aspired and county M.P.s with substantial urban support acted on behalf of the towns. This was particularly true of South Lancashire and the West Riding, where Liberal members were regarded as specifically the representatives of urban interests. Alexander Henry, the overtly urban nominee for South Lancashire in 1847, viewed his own election as an opportunity for urban Liberals to redress the political balance in the matter of land tax commissioners: 'as I believe that those which were put in by the tory party exercised their power in many instances in a very unfair spirit, the liberal party in the different Boroughs in the southern division of Lancashire have now an opportunity of putting in men of their own way of thinking'.[10] Even the short-lived Derby administration of 1852 had swamped the Lancashire bench with Tories and William Brown, the Liverpool merchant who sat for South Lancashire from 1845 to 1859, offered to apply the corrective. Tory ministers, he complained, had 'rejected respectable liberals . . . and made many tories much less fit', and so he asked George Wilson to 'procure for me the names religion and politics of our County and Borough magistrates that I may see how they stand and use the argument if necessary to increase the liberals'.[11]

Cobden soon found that many in the West Riding welcomed his election as an urban enclave in a field dominated by landed influence. He was urged, for instance, to remedy Liberal deficiencies on the Huddersfield bench by rewarding Liberal partisans. Rumours of proposed nominees to the Huddersfield bench shocked a leading activist who told Cobden: 'If we must have new magistrates why not select men of uniform consistency? Men who have sacrificed time and treasure in defence of our principles . . . [who] in point of Education Intelligence and property are quite equal to any the other side will suggest.'[12] In short the spoils of office were regarded as the normal rewards of political activity and an M.P. was expected to make the wheels of political patronage turn smoothly in his own party's interest. Where a town had two M.P.s of conflicting politics then the pull of patronage operated simultaneously in opposite directions. Thus in Halifax the Whig-Tory coalition of 1847 led Charles Wood to seek a clerkship of customs for the nephew of a Whig family who had 'always been active friends to the cause in the Riding', while his fellow M.P. Henry Edwards was packing the Halifax bench with Tory nominees in the interests of a prominent Tory solicitor who wished to become clerk to the justices.[13]

The spoils of the political system were relevant only to the local political élite, for whom the expectation of office was a strong motive in supporting a party candidate. The channel of patronage was a cohesive force binding natural social leaders to an M.P. and his party, who paid the price of political loyalty with the coin of honorific reward. To retain support of the wider electorate, however, something more was required of an urban M.P. The larger electorates of the towns could never be managed simply through the influence of an élite personally rewarded by seats on the bench and so an M.P. had to give a lead to local opinion and create the right sort of image for the town in the country at large. In order to sustain the tedious duties of the electoral machinery or even to command consistent loyalty at the polls the urban M.P. had to convince his constituents that he and they were working in the same political cause. His speeches and votes in Parliament were carefully watched and he flouted local opinion at his peril. Charles Wood, for all his Whig landed connections, could not afford to offend Halifax dissenters and one of his supporters advised discreet absence on the Maynooth question: 'a number of your constituents will deem your supporting it a sin not to be forgiven. But I think you were aware of the views of this section of the party and I hope may have been otherwise engaged on that evening.'[14]

The political image of a town depended partly on the character of its M.P.s and Edward Baines had this very much in mind when he launched T. B. Macaulay for Leeds in 1831–2. Baines argued that it set just the right tone to have one local textile manufacturer together with one talented politician with a national reputation. When Baines himself replaced Macaulay in 1834 he set out to support those causes which were most dear to his own constituents, municipal reform, justice to Dissenters and the like. It was because he did not satisfy the political objectives of local radicals that Baines was scathingly criticized by some electors who sought a new candidate more acceptable to their opinions.

The Leeds experience with that candidate, Sir William Molesworth, well illustrates the importance of this political relationship between the views of electors and elected. When Molesworth was launched, following radical ward activity, the Whig-Liberal élite of Leeds was aghast. Molesworth's social status as a Cornish landed gentleman was perhaps inappropriate for an industrial city, but it was his radicalism which was his main defect in Whig eyes. Much of the normal Liberal leadership of Leeds could not willingly accept a candidate in 1837 who would not even pledge himself to support the Whig government. For an important section of the Leeds electorate Molesworth would not be giving the sort of political leadership required. Conversely Baines, for the same reason, did not satisfy Molesworth's supporters. Ironically, in the event, Molesworth proved unsatisfactory even for the radicals, since he did not deliver the political goods. By 1840 Leeds radicals were once more searching for a candidate who could remedy Molesworth's main deficiency his lack of political leadership for the town: 'Sir W. Molesworth will not do for the Leeds people. They want an active man – one who will say and do something to advance their principles.'[15]

A Leeds M.P., then, was expected to promote the causes in which his constituents believed and Edward Baines junior found that, like his father, his moderation lost him support. His equivocation on political reform in the 1860s finally left him high and dry as a moderate Whig, defeated in 1874. Conversely the more extreme views of the Birmingham radical Joseph Sturge were the prime cause of his failures in the 1840s (Nottingham 1842, Birmingham 1844, Leeds 1847). An election registered in one sense, the degree of political agreement between candidate and constituency. Activists interpreted the results as indicators of the political character of their town and of its image outside. Hence Birmingham Tories welcomed their victory in 1844 as an indication of 'the rapid increase of Conservative principles in this town and the firm determination to rescue Birmingham from becoming an hereditary borough'. The vanquished Liberals gained their revenge three years later when, for them, the return of William Scholefield signalled 'the future political regeneration of Birmingham'.[16] As always the political perspective varied according to the colour of the observer's spectacles.

Since urban communities were themselves fundamentally divided between rival élites struggling for local power, it was clearly impossible for an M.P. to satisfy everybody's notion of what public face the town should wear. Milner Gibson's lukewarm reception among Manchester Liberals derived partly from the image the town would have under his stewardship. As Cobden said, 'Manchester has now a reputation as a commercial place all over the world. I mean a reputation for bold and sound views on commerce and political economy, and if possible I should like to see the borough represented by a man of similar established reputation.'[17] The town's reputation lay in the hands of its representative who had to be in tune with its essential character. Again events turned out unexpectedly. Cobden was perhaps surprised to find Gibson become a faithful disciple of the Manchester school, while the élitist families led by the Potters, who thought that a Suffolk squire would impart a bit of tone to Manchester, were disappointed by Gibson's apparent subservience to George Wilson and the Newall's Building political machine. The Whig-Liberal revolt which built up in the mid-Victorian years against Gibson and Bright was a protest against the political leadership they had given and the consequent political image Manchester had acquired (see below, p. 203). Though the bourgeois élite might be overtaken numerically as the electorate increased, it still claimed the right to represent the real Manchester: 'If in Manchester Abel Heywood is sent in by the $\frac{2}{3}$ of the lower voters does not Bazley or Ashton, sent in by the $\frac{1}{3}$ merchants, leading men of wealth and standing, stand quite on a footing and represent all that makes Manchester Manchester as Abel Heywood sent in by the $\frac{2}{3}$.'[18] The urban M.P. had the task of satisfying both property and population.

The M.P. who could thus manage local parliamentary business, oil the wheels of patronage and provide the right sort of leadership and image stood a good chance of a renewed mandate from a large urban constituency. If we turn from the M.P. himself to the electorate we find a different perspective on parliamentary elections, whose significance has been much discussed by historians recently. Professor D. C. Moore has found in the operation of the county franchise a powerful agent in preserving the cohesion of 'deference communities', in which voting operated on parameters determined by social influence in a vertically structured local society. Professor J. R. Vincent's analysis of poll books casts much light on the relationship of occupation and voting and on the nature of the political structure. He argues for a class interpretation of voting, though class is defined in a very special, certainly not Marxian, way. Technically more sophisticated than either, Dr T. J. Nossiter has evolved programs for the computerization of election data for large numbers of elections and constituencies and has analysed in depth the politics of the North East. From both Dr Nossiter has derived a picture of politics in which elections were the product of three factors, the market, influence, and agitation, with special emphasis on the first two.[19]

These scholars and others have perceptively illuminated the nature of politics in Victorian England. Their conclusions in many ways reflect the England they had in mind. Moore's work is specifically related to county and village society in which landed influence predominated. He freely admits that his approach based on 'deference communities' is inappropriate for urban society:

> Since local political agreement is found most often where landowner-ship was concentrated in the hands of a single individual it is not surprising that diversity of local political expression should be found most often in those communities, among which most of the larger towns must be included, where several interests were focussed. These considerations will explain why the use of borough poll books for a study analogous to the present one could hardly be contemplated.[20]

Moore's England is that of the broadacres, still of course important in the mid-century and still firmly in control of executive government. But it is not the England within which a large proportion of the electorate operated.

Vincent's poll books cover a wide range of constituencies but he also admits that the larger cities are under-represented in his survey, partly because fewer poll books survive from these places. He explains that the bias of his study is 'strongly towards the medium-sized constituency of 10,000 to 50,000 people, normally a market, county or cathedral town rather than a manufacturing centre . . . the pollbooks throw little light on the politics of great cities'.[21] He is right to point out that the actual political system was weighted towards these smaller constituencies, a salutary reminder to those who predate the dominance of metropolitan England. Yet again Vincent's England is not that of Cobden and Bright, Attwood and Baines. Nossiter's work does include a study of one provincial metropolis, Newcastle, which was however not quite on a par with Birmingham or Manchester. Northumberland and Durham contained that mix of agriculture and industry which characterized England as a whole. Yet the overgrown villages of the North East set within the framework of landed influence and the industrial interests of landed proprietors combined to produce powerful and solid interests such as land, coal, and shipping which underpin Nossiter's emphasis upon the role of market and influence. These factors were of less importance in the multiplicity of interests found in the larger cities.

As before and after, there was not one England in the mid-nineteenth century. None of the historians cited above can grasp the essential England in his hand. All tell part of the story but it is a different part from that which is attempted here. The England of this analysis is the England of the great cities, particularly those linked in the minority clause of 1867 as being distinctively metropolitan – Leeds, Liverpool, Birmingham and Manchester. Despite Cobden's propaganda urban England was no more the real England than was Moore's England of the county squire. Yet the great cities were the forcing house of social change and harbingers of the predominantly urban England of the future. Moreover they were communities in which politics could operate more freely than perhaps anywhere else. What *The Times* said of the West Riding to a greater or lesser extent applied to the larger cities: 'with its 30,000 voting men and its unequalled concentration of interests [it] is beyond the reaches of all influences but those which appeal to the conscience and the mind of man. No threats, no frowns, no quarter day, no Christmas bills, no money or money's worth can avail to corrupt so vast a legislative army. Here if anywhere is a free election.'[22] The venality of Liverpool freemen, themselves a relic of the pre-reform system, qualified but could not blur the picture of a relatively free exercise of political choice in the newly created urban constituencies. When these are allowed to occupy the centre of the analytical stage the parliamentary election appears to be a function of three variables: organization, ideology and the local social and political structure.

2

Belief in the importance of organization was promoted by both the nature of urban society and the nature of the new electoral system. Organization became something of a distinctive mark of urban society. The face-to-face rural society with its natural social cohesion had no need of organization as a binding force. As Baines junior explained to a newly-formed political association, rural England comprised:

> for the most the dependants and almost the vassals of a number of larged landed proprietors . . . you have not that natural connection together which exists among the tenants-at-will of a large landowner – by means of the steward, by means of the landowner himself, . . . they have this mode of connection among themselves but you in a very considerable measure want that connection.[23]

Organization supplied the deficiency and was a means of re-establishing some order out of the chaos of social relationships consequent upon industrialization. Through organization urban society could itself cohere and establish the identity of the new society, countering the values of the old. It was organization by which 'the influence of the press and of public opinion will be substituted for the traditional influences of landlordism or of feudalism'.[24]

Citizens became 'accustomed to associate and organise themselves for a great variety of public objects'[25] and so clubs, groups, associations and organizations multiplied in the city. Some, like trade unions or literary societies, reinforced the class consciousness of a society fast becoming horizontally structured; others, including political associations, were geared to preserving vertical links in a complex society. As England became more akin to an urban industrial society so organizations flourished as mutuality challenged individualism as the basic social tenet. By 1867 the trend was clear: 'there never was a period when the principle of fellowship was so fully recognised and so extensively embraced as in these days of Commercial Treaties, International Exhibitions, Co-operative Societies, Limited Liability Companies, Amalgamated Railways and Trade Associations. The world appreciates the value and utility of combinations'.[26]

This tendency towards organization, implicit in the urban experience, was reinforced by the political system within which the city operated. Even if enough natural social connections had existed the urban electorate would not have been manageable by mere personal solicitation. At the outset the size of the electorate put it beyond rigid control by either money or influence. In the period between the first two Reform Acts the larger constituencies were ranged between 5,000 and 15,000 voters, in round figures. It would have needed a very long purse indeed or an infinitely ramified economic and social connection to deliver a majority in such an electorate. If voters were to be managed at all then some organizational structure was essential.

Furthermore the very rules of the political game confirmed this necessity. It soon became apparent in the early 1830s that the registration clauses of the Reform Act made organization mandatory upon any party aspiring to electoral success. Events in Leeds in 1834–5 made dazzlingly clear the truth of the proposition that elections could be won in the revision courts. Leeds Tories gained a spectacular victory at the 1834 revision by successfully objecting to the Whig compounded ratepayers on the register of electors. Compounders offended against the Reform Act in two respects: they did not pay their rates personally and the discount given to landlords meant that the full rates had not been paid. The compounded ratepayers were a mine of political controversy until well beyond the second Reform Act. The great advantage of the system lay in the field of rate collection, as a Liverpool politician explained to a puzzled parliamentary reformer:

> The beauty of the compound system which exists here not only legally up to £6 but by arrangement up to £27 or £30 is this – That every man who lives one week in a house has paid 1/52nd part of the taxes of Liverpool on that house. He may die or bolt or migrate every Monday, we have got his 1/– or 1/3 for that week and every other householder has that much less to pay.[27]

In Leeds, Liverpool and elsewhere compounders complicated the electoral process and parties needed to be adequately prepared either to steal a march on opponents or to counter their ploys. When Leeds Tories were able to fight and win the 1835 election on the register they had doctored the previous autumn, it became clear that seats could be insured before election day.

Apart from compounding there were a whole host of technical objections which could be sustained and parties exploited these to the full in the 1830s as the lesson was painfully learned that there was only one qualification to vote, namely actually to be on the register. It soon became common for revision courts to be required to adjudicate on more claims and objections than there were on the original electoral list. Parties were committed to a bed of nails, involving mountains of tedious registration minutiae, unwilling to relax for fear of giving ground to their rivals. Year after year the same cases were heard. Hamer Stansfeld, a Leeds cloth merchant, was objected to six years running on the same grounds and a Rochdale Liberal had to defend his right to vote every year from 1832 to 1846. For this sort of party warfare an adequate organization was vital and it was for this that money was required, for the manufacture rather than the purchase of votes.

It was a numbers game and the real professionals knew how to play it. Bright, with a sensitive ear for murmurs of opposition, continually urged Wilson to ensure by registration that his Manchester seat would be immune from attack.[28] The registration organization was an essential tool in the political battle and when a local schism occurred it was of fundamental significance which side inherited the political machine. Whig-Liberals in Leeds and the West Riding were powerless to fight the voluntaryists who controlled both borough and county registration in 1847–8. On the other hand, if the political machine became too remote from its political community, the machine could be taken on and defeated, as in the 1857 Manchester election.

Registration not only altered the nature of urban political activity, it also altered the character of the urban political activist. What sapped the vital energies of leisured gentlemen, the tedium, technicality and regularity of registration, nevertheless had to be suffered by someone if the political battleground was not to be meekly surrendered to the enemy. The wealthy coughed up the money and the *menu peuple* gave time and energy for the common political cause. If anything, the role of the humble became more important than that of the élite:

> The time has been when a grand excitement at an Election would do all that was needful by putting Reformers on their mettle. It is quite otherwise now. The system of registration has changed it all. Regular persevering systematic effort is the thing wanted under the Reform Act. A plodding shopkeeper on a committee who sees that the registration is attended to does more good than a dozen wealthy squires who reserve all their energy for the Election itself.[29]

It was a sign of the new political era when the merchant princes of Liverpool retained an ex-barber as paid secretary of their organization.

Much of the tactics of registration-based political activity emerges only from the cases publicly heard in the revision courts. Occasionally a fragmentary source casts light on the actual Tadpole and Taper world, such as the canvass return of a Leeds out-township in 1838:

John Brook	im Self not been long nuf.
Benjamin Davidson	im Self he as none freehould but is Brothers
Thomas Goodworth	prentis Boy not Upper Wortley but more side and not had it Long in Nuf.
David Greenwood	he as none freehould but what he occupyes
Joseph Hirst	Wife ses he hase freehould houses but only one house

John Naylor	not his but is mothers
William Atkinson	Onley paise 9–0–0 rent.
Wm. Burnell	made assinment to crediters and gave Possesan
James Milner	dus not pay ten pounds onley 9–15
Thos Goodworth	lets one Room of.[30]

A great deal may be deduced from this extract. The cramped, un-tutored hand and the deficient spelling indicate the poor education and low status of the author. Yet this unknown minnow was clearly of crucial importance in his local party and his importance illustrates the role-finding aspect of political organizations. He had found a niche in the superstructure of the new society appropriate to his education, income and status. Politics and its particular Victorian structure defined a role which encouraged self-respect and, because of the value to the local party, earned the respect of others. Political organization played its part in redefining and re-establishing urban social relationships.

Additionally, the extract confirms the detail necessary to win elections. Much painstaking effort and local knowledge was needed to obtain the requisite information on rates, rents, ownership, tenancy, status and occupation. Insight may be derived into the nature of political activity in the mid-nineteenth century where elections could never be wholly left to the expression of political opinions. Organization was always a key factor in urban constituencies, although the success of organization varied with the intensity of the political commitment of party workers. Like today's committee room envelope sticker and canvasser, the nineteenth-century registration hack gave of his time and energy according to the level of his political involvement at a particular point in time.

A brief review of organization in practice will illustrate its importance in urban politics. In Leeds the die was cast by the very first prolonged election campaign of 1831–2 in which the political forces were ranged by organization. The two Whig candidates were supported by the Bainesite Leeds Association and the more popular Leeds Political Union, while the Tory-radical alliance behind Sadler was manifest in the combination of the True Blue Constitutional Association, the Committee of Operatives and the Leeds Radical Political Union.[31] It was the Tory barrister Robert Hall who first saw that registration was akin to annual elections which required permanent organization and Liberal registration machin-ery was created in response to initial Tory moves. The needs of registra-tion soon altered the character of political organizations. These had been pioneered by Edward Baines and his Leeds Association whose aim had been 'to organise the dispersed elements of popular strength and per-petuate by system and by prudent counsels the advantage gained by enthusiasm'.[32] The Leeds Association was a private prime mover working behind the scenes to generate the spark of activity on behalf of a Liberal political programme. The loss of one seat in 1835 because of a registration defeat signalled the demise of the Leeds Association and its replacement by a Reform Registration Association. In one form or another it survived for several decades but was always prey to Liberal divisions. In the late 1840s on the education question and in the 1860s on further parliamentary reform the Leeds Liberal organization was threatened by schism.

Liverpool Liberals, like those at Leeds, had much to learn about organization from their Tory rivals in the 1830s. Initially the Liverpool Conservative Association, formed in August 1832, was merely a counterpart to the two existing Liberal agencies, the standing Committee of Reformers and the Parliamentary Reform Union. Similarly in 1835 the formation in February of the Liverpool Reform Association was followed three months later by the Conservative Registration Association.[33] Yet the Tories were quicker to see the implications of the structure of the Liverpool electorate. The rival élites of merchant princes needed to harness less wealthy voters to their cause and Liverpool Tories successfully married the organizational needs of the new system with the traditional rank and file Toryism in the town. In 1836 they launched the Tradesmen's Conservative Association to organize popular Tory support. The corresponding need on the Liberal side was apparent from 'the want of an association constructed on popular principles, embodying and concentrating the scattered elements of power'.[34] Joshua Walmsley's Tradesmen's Reform Association, in emulation of the Tories, was very successful and soon stole much of the thunder from the more respectable Reform Association. Yet throughout the middle decades of the century Liverpool Liberalism found it difficult to harness together élite Whiggism and retail and artisan radicalism.

The opposition to Walmsley's candidature in 1841 symbolized the conflict within the Liberal party and his organization withered away on his departure from the town. The Liberal élite was not fully equipped to take advantage of this and in 1845 the Anti-Monopoly Association took over registration activities from the Reform Association. At the end of the 1840s the Liberals were floundering, unable to find a basis for a unified political organization. In the early 1850s a more fruitful relationship was established and in 1852 the Liverpool Reform Association was launched with a paid secretary, the ex-barber William Brumfitt, and a supporting ward organization. The election of J. C. Ewart in 1855 was a result of the more efficient organization on the Liberal side. The emergence of more radical spirits led by J. R. Jeffrey and the increased political challenge in the municipal arena, which was not wholly popular with the merchant princes (see above, p. 141), led to renewed dissension in the early 1860s. The effect of a débâcle in the 1864 municipal poll and the collapse of the so-called radical 'cellar clique' left the Liberals in a weak position for the 1865 poll. Ewart's defeat led to yet another organizational change, this time more permanent. The Liverpool Liberal Association, formed in 1865, survived until 1885. Despite this a local Liberal leader could still complain in 1869 of the loss of vigour between elections: 'they allow all the energy which had been developed in the election and all the machinery which had been got into working order with so much trouble to fall again to pieces and they retired to their callings and forgot all about politics until the next election.'[35] Dull routine registration could never replace political excitement as a prime mover.

Manchester did not initially place as much emphasis on organization as Leeds or Liverpool. However, the closely-run election of 1839 convinced many Liberals that a permanent organization was required and the nephew of William Neild, a prominent Liberal leader, wrote to Wilson:

> The result of the election I hope has convinced a good many of the friends of good government here that it is highly expedient that some systematic arrangements should be made immediately (for) concentrating all the force we can command and having that force organised in the best possible manner . . . the formation of an efficient association which shall have for its object the preservation of my native town from the fangs of its worst enemies.[36]

A sub-committee was formed and rules drawn up for a Liberal association which was apparently in existence in 1840 searching for a new candidate. However, for the next two decades Liberal organization tended to be subsumed in the Anti-Corn Law League, a tendency confirmed when the League went into registration in a big way. After the demise of the League the Newall's Building machine continued to dominate Liberal politics, spreading its influence beyond Manchester into Lancashire and Cheshire. Its strength lay in its control over registration and when the 1857 Whig-Liberal revolt was mounted Abel Heywood confirmed that 'the simple object of those who sat in Newall's Building was to maintain the register of electors.'[37]

The 1857 schism savaged Liberal organization which could not quickly be rebuilt. One Manchester Liberal commented sadly in 1859: 'we are disorganised, split to shivers and I fear demoralised . . . we cannot get a dozen people to walk across the street to save the liberal party.'[38] Neither the Lancashire Reformers' Union nor the Manchester Reform Association, both launched in 1859, could reimpose unity on a divided Liberal party and at both the 1859 and 1865 elections the radical Abel Heywood stood against the official Liberal candidates. The demolition of

Newall's Building in the mid-1860s was a symbolic removal of a perennial source of tension and in 1866 the United Liberal Party was formed as a loose confederation of the various sections of the Liberal party. Its cohesive influence was seen in the return of Jacob Bright in 1867 and in the nomination of three candidates in 1868, one from each of the sections of the party. Partly because of the minority clause and partly because Ernest Jones was too radical for some moderates the United Liberal Committee could not carry all three seats in 1868. The surrender of a second seat in 1874 led to the establishment of the Manchester Liberal Association, modelled on Birmingham but never completely in the Birmingham image.[39]

The Birmingham image was that of the caucus of the 1870s.[40] The town earlier had had a very similar experience of political organizations to that elsewhere. At the time of the Reform Bill the Birmingham Political Union, like the League in Manchester at a later date, took charge of Liberal organization. Thereafter both parties launched registration societies in the 1830s, the Reform Association for the Liberals and the Loyal Constitutional Association for the Tories. There was no fundamental change in the pattern until the Birmingham Liberal Association was founded in 1865. Within a decade this had become the Birmingham caucus, which evolved to meet three new circumstances.

First was the problem of the increased size of the electorate, large even before 1867. How was leadership to be imposed upon an electorate of perhaps 50,000, in which 'a whole suburb could be out-voted by a couple of streets'?[41] Second, and more important, was the minority clause, which posed an acute challenge if majorities were not to be wasted. (The larger cities were given an extra seat in 1867, but voters were restricted to two votes as before, in order to give an unrepresented minority adequate opportunity to be represented.) Liverpool Liberals could see no easy answer and George Melly posed the question neatly for Gladstone, unconsciously anticipating the Birmingham solution: 'how can a committee so *direct* the votes of 40,000 persons as to ensure the return of 3 members even if their opponents only number 6,000 or 8,000 and how can any liberal advocate a procedure based upon the despotic obedience of thousands to a central head?'[42] Control of the school board was the third challenge which the caucus was devised to meet. The school board was significant both because control of it was a natural ambition for the National Education League which captured the Liberal Association, and because its cumulative voting system posed problems similar to those of the minority clause.

We have already noticed the use of the word 'caucus' from the 1830s onward to denote a party committee operating privately to organize political activity. The Birmingham caucus was more much than this, but how revolutionary was it? Its two distinctive marks were the ward organization which built up the party from the grass roots, and its politicizing of minor institutions (council, school board, board of guardians) which sustained political commitment between parliamentary elections by marking out areas of political ambition and reward for party activists. Neither of these was a complete novelty. It has earlier been argued that the politicizing of minor institutions began in the 1820s and 1830s rather than the 1870s, for which much evidence had been cited. Party politics in municipal affairs was not new in the 1870s, though its intensity seemed novel in places such as Manchester, which had been non-partisan, or Birmingham itself, where a large one-party majority had cooled party political conflicts. Boards of guardians had been part of the party political struggle in the 1830s and 1840s, while at other times specific issues had raised political controversy. In politicizing the Poor Law, the caucus was reviving earlier tendencies rather than opening up new areas of urban politics. The school board was of recent creation, but again the politicizing of a minor institution in the interests of Dissenters' grievances was as much a feature of vestry politics in the 1830s as of school board politics in the 1870s. In all three institutions the caucus was intensifying earlier developments by formalizing connections between the different levels of politics.

Similarly, ward organization existed before the 1870s. Even in Birmingham, ward committees were common at election time in the 1830s and 1840s. In Leeds in the 1830s something like the administrative structure of the Birmingham caucus existed, as was revealed by the emergence of Molesworth in 1836. His name was first canvassed by ward committees set up in the out-townships, and when enough support was gained in this manner his radical nominees put his name forward to the Whig leadership of the party. A delegate conference was called to discuss the candidature in which each ward sent representatives to a central committee. In 1836–7 Molesworth's candidature reversed the normal procedure in which a nomination was agreed by the party leadership and then put to the wards for adoption. In this case the initiative was taken by the wards themselves.[43] In Liverpool also there was some continuity in that the ward organization of the 1870s was based upon that of the 1850s, which in turn was founded upon that used in the 1830s.[44] It was clear that Liberals appreciated the advantages of a ward organization and in 1857 William Brumfitt, secretary of the association, was advising all reformers to attach themselves to a ward committee.[45]

A point that is often made about the strength of the ward system of the caucus is that it worked so well because the ward was the unit of activity at the municipal level. Annual elections for councillor thus kept the political machine in good working order and maintained the continuity of political involvement. Using exactly the same line of argument, the highly politicized municipal contests of Leeds or Liverpool stimulated the growth of something akin to a caucus system before the 1870s. Again, evidence has been cited of the close relationship of municipal and parliamentary elections from 1835 onwards. The essential novelty of the caucus ward system was its permanence, for even where ward committees existed their activities revolved around the actual election, with only a skeletal organization on standby for registration. In the 1870s the caucus used permanent standing ward committees as the basis of its organization. Its methodology involved the rationalization, systematization and regularization of earlier developments in order to meet the challenge of a changed political system.

One further and more debatable element of continuity may be mentioned. In one sense the caucus established political control by a very small élite within the local Liberal party, and this is not so very different from the practice operating earlier whereby perhaps 20 or 30 families dominated the party informally. In both situations an élite governed by consent. Melly, cited earlier, referred to 'the despotic obedience of thousands to a central head' and much of the anti-caucus propaganda was based on the image of a dictatorial clique crushing independence. William Harris, Schnadhorst and Chamberlain were quick to defend the democratic basis of the caucus, allowing free expression and influence to the humblest follower. It was a step towards participatory democracy. Conversely, the submission of wards to central direction and the delivery of blocs of votes according to prior instruction cast a familiar oligarchic shadow over the caucus. Whether a caucus system existed or not, the emphasis upon organization in larger constituencies originated in the belief that 'the party by which the materials are best used will be the winner. Organisation and management will beat the strongest party that ventures to rely upon political principle and personal zeal.'[46]

Yet political principle underpinned the strength of an organization. Chamberlain could deliver the vote but, as he explained, the caucus could not 'turn Conservatives into Liberals or secure for a Liberal minority a representation to which its numbers do not entitle it'.[47] Organization could not in the last resort overturn political preferences and nor for that matter could money or influence. As Professor Vincent has written, 'an underlying genuine political preference may shine through against all that gold and influence could do . . . it is doubtful whether influence alone controlled any important group of urban voters . . . Croesus fought many elections, but he never made shoemakers into good Tories or butchers into good liberals'.[48] In the larger cities what made good Liberals or good Tories was a genuine commitment to a political ideology. In the cities, at least, opinion mattered.

Because this was so, elections in the larger towns were seen in terms of political ideology and this was true even when, as in 1859, the national debate involved in a general election was obscure. Issues of national or local policy characterized urban elections, with towns often establishing their own distinctive mark on a campaign. In 1847 the Leeds election focused almost wholly on education whilst the Birmingham contest centred on radical reform. With a high proportion of seats contested (and even where there was no contest there were always rumours of secret candidates) each election took on the character of a trial of rival opinions. One or more of the great questions which activated the mid-nineteenth century mind enveloped each election campaign – parliamentary reform, the ballot, municipal reform, the Established Church, education, administrative reform, financial reform, free trade, pacifism, temperance, the Poor Law. These and others gave to urban elections the characteristic element of a genuine political choice between policy options. Election results were a victory for a body of opinion as much as for a coalition of interests.

Clear-cut occupational or class interests were difficult to discern in the urban political scene. That Sadler, standing at Leeds in 1832, had the support of nearly all factory operatives was not in doubt. The converse did not follow, since Marshall did not have the support of nearly all factory owners, a fair minority of whom were Tory. The relationship of occupation and voting does not suggest, except in special cases, that men in the same economic interest thought the same way politically. A profession, trade or industry might tend one way or the other but the political inclination was rarely overwhelming. Political partisans, both Liberal and Tory, could be found in almost all occupational groups. Certainly among the élite contesting power in the great cities there was no economic, social, or occupational difference between the rival groups. Where, as in the case of the Toryism of the drink interest in the 1870s, there was a close correlation between occupation and voting, this was clearly brought about by very special circumstances in which an economic interest found itself threatened by the public policy of one party. Its great rival, the temperance interest, was not a uniform economic or social group. The provincial middle-class strand running through temperance did not give it a coherent class identity.[49] Temperance reformers were bound together by a common political view not by a common relationship to the means of production.

No doubt it was true that poor men tended to vote in a more radical way than rich men, who tended to vote in a more conservative way. Yet many poor men were Tories and many rich men radicals. The widespread

Operative Conservative movement has been found anomalous by both historians and contemporaries, and one radical artisan marvelled, 'why a poor devil depending on his day's work and obliged to give a portion of that to the support of the Church and other Institutions should rank himself as a Conservative Operative is rather astonishing'.[50] This movement should not be seen, as is sometimes argued, as merely a revised version of Sadlerite Tory-radicalism of 1832. Operative Conservatism was strongly anti-radical and adamantly refused to be drawn into the factory question.[51] Oastler was mortified at what he deemed a desecration of Sadler's memory by the separation of Toryism from the cause of the factory child. The strength of Operative Conservatism must at the very least admit the possibility of a deferential Church-and-King Toryism among the humble. Even if we accept that Operative Conservatives were for the most part in the employ of Tory manufacturers and were subject to duress, then this demonstrates that many manufacturers were Tory. The apparently iron link between the industrial bourgeoisie and Liberalism turns out to be flexible.*

Sectional or class unity could never be assumed in urban elections. As one activist ruefully admitted, 'that a Baptist working man is nominated does not make it certain that either the Baptists or the working men will care about him'.[52] Operative Conservatism gave the lie to the notion of a 'natural' working-class radicalism, and religion, though a fair predicter of political preference, was never an invariable determinant. There was a very close connection between Dissent and Liberalism, a less close but real one between the Church and Toryism. This did not prevent the Tory Methodist or even the Tory Unitarian (as in Sheffield) being a common phenomenon. The large number of politically active Liberal Anglicans, at whose head stands Cobden, deny that religion was ever the whole answer. Indeed, on an issue which involved religion itself, men did not necessarily divide on denominational lines. When Baines split the Liberal Dissenters of the West Riding on the education question in the 1847 election his second-in-command was Francis Carbutt, a Unitarian from that same Mill Hill chapel which produced many of the local state education leaders and, in J. G. Marshall, the state education Liberal candidate. Marshall's experience in the 1847 Leeds election was a further indication that the assumption, derived from the counties and small towns, that a great economic interest carried natural electoral influence, could not be applied to the great cities. Dod proclaimed the great manufacturers of Leeds as the dominant electoral influence but Marshall's large factory in Holbeck could not prevent his coming bottom of the 1847 poll in that ward.

* Cf. Cobden on electoral prospects in North Lancashire where the opponents

Marshall's economic influence was weakened by the structure of his work-force (largely women and children) and of the electorate (pre-dominantly non-proletarian). Perhaps even more important, Holbeck was strongly radical and Marshall was opposed by a radical candidate. In a situation where voters would place their own political views above the economic and social influences bearing upon them, the personality and opinions of the candidates were always vital. Urban constituencies would not tolerate a weak and shadowy candidate and this was why Fitzwilliam's young son, the 'Wentworth cub' as Cobden called him, fared so badly in the West Riding in 1848. He had to withdraw because he had no real political opinions of his own and relied solely on his family's influence. Sometimes, in view of the difficulties of finding local candidates with the leisure and income to cope with parliamentary life, a local candidate of very limited talents and views might be acceptable, but he would be expected to mouth the right slogans in acknowledgment of the primacy of political commitment.

The issues were mirrored in the personalities of the candidates. The Leeds election of 1832 expressed through the candidates the various facets of that election's key issue, factory reform. In Marshall was personified economic self-interest, in Macaulay ideological commitment to *laissez-faire*, and in Sadler philanthropic social paternalism. A candidate in an urban constituency stood on a platform based upon policy. A vote for the candidate was a vote in favour of the policies he espoused. The cry supporting William Garnett, Tory candidate in Salford in 1837, was characteristic of urban contests: 'Electors of Salford – if you value the institutions of your country – if you value the rights of the poor – if you value the spirit of the 43rd of Elizabeth ... vote for Mr Garnett.'[53] A vote for Garnett was a vote against the new Poor Law; a vote for Abel Heywood in Manchester in 1859 and 1865 was a vote for radical parliamentary reform; a vote for Muntz in Birmingham in 1847 was a vote for currency reform; a vote for Beckett in Leeds in 1847 was a vote for state education; a vote for Turner in Liverpool in 1852 was a vote for no popery and the Church.

In the pre-reform or county seat an aspirant needed the right pedigree and status; in the urban constituency a candidate's credentials were his opinions. When Molesworth was being considered for Leeds in 1837 a pamphlet was published reviewing his past actions and printing his recent speeches.[54] Urban voters were keen to vet the opinions of the candidate and this was why Roebuck, ideal in all other respects, was unacceptable to the Leeds Dissenters. As Smiles informed him, 'But for that confounded Sabbath question which would be carefully raked up

of the League 'relied upon being able to beat us, with the aid of the Tory manufacturers'; R. Cobden to G. Wilson, 11 February 1845, Wilson Papers.

there would be no fear of success . . . the influence which it might have on the mind of the less informed Methodists and Dissenters would no doubt be very considerable.'[55] Similarly when the Leicester Liberal, William Biggs, approached George Wilson for a possible candidate the requirements were clear:

> there is one condition which is a sine qua non, that the member to be invited is one who will advocate separation of Church and State (Nonconformist view of it) and universal suffrage and I think beyond this the voluntary principle in Education in opposition to a government scheme . . . these extreme views are not mine but we are honourably pledged to a section of the radical party here to find a second candidate who supports these views.[56]

The landed patron sought personal and social status in his nominee; the city boss looked for the right catalogue of political opinions.

Biggs, in searching for a radical second candidate, was engaged in that delicate exercise, which all Liberal constituencies had to perform, of keeping the Whig and radical wings of his party together. Elections were a resolution of issues and through them local opinion fought out the public battle between 'the old coachee' of moderate Whig-Liberalism and 'the new coachee' of radicalism. Cracks in the Whig-radical edifice of Leeds appeared as early as 1834 and every election between 1837 and 1874, in one way or another, involved aspects of Whig-radical tension and the attempts to contain it. In Manchester this boiled over in the frontal assault upon the rump of the League in 1857, and in the candidature of Heywood in 1859 and 1865 and Ernest Jones in 1868 the dispute rumbled on. The only time that Birmingham surrendered a seat to the Tories between 1832 and 1880 was in 1844, largely as a result of a Liberal-radical split. In the mutual recrimination the intransigence of the radicals ('Joseph Sturge and no compromise') stood out and even distant observers remarked on Sturge's apparent death-wish. Bright commented, 'he and his friends seem struck with something like madness', while another League crony called Sturge a goose, for 'if he wanted to drive from him the Whigs, the timid and the cautious he has succeeded to perfection.'[57] Strong views would often brook no containment.

Since the views of both elector and elected were so closely involved in contests, it was natural for partisans to deduce the state of opinion in the town from the result. A Tory victory in a Liberal town was deemed an indication of the growth of Conservative views there; a Liberal victory a confirmation of the norm. The election gave the town a chance to state its view and decide its course. Hence when the Tory Richard Spooner sought re-election for Birmingham in 1847 it afforded Birmingham the opportunity to answer a simple question – 'are the majority of the men of Birmingham committed to Chartism or will they rally round the throne and constitution?'[58] What seemed to Tory eyes a contest between the Charter and the constitution assumed in Liberal circles more the beginning of a major turning-point in opinion. The prickly refusal of G. F. Muntz to march in concert with the second Liberal William Scholefield was a symbol of the growing public doubt about the Birmingham currency orthodoxy, which Muntz had inherited from Attwood. Within two months of the election the major Liberal journal in the town was dismissing Muntz's currency dogma with contempt and pouring scorn on a town petition inspired by him: 'We . . . disavow the Birmingham memorial. Our taste dissents from its rhetoric and our reason from its logic. It is absurd as a composition and utterly contemptible as an argument.'[59] The eclipse of the Birmingham School in Birmingham, though less spectacular and sudden than the eclipse of the Manchester School in Manchester, was of great significance. It was a prerequisite for the radical leadership of John Bright. By 1858–9 Birmingham had abandoned Attwood's ends (currency reform) in favour of Attwood's means (parliamentary reform).

The full extent of the growing rejection of currency reform in Birmingham was hidden by the 1847 result in which Muntz and Scholefield were returned. In that result we may see shining through the ultimately and intentionally political judgement of the electorate. Only $5\frac{1}{2}$ per cent cast their votes across party lines (the rest either plumped or split between candidates of the same party) and this in an election where there were circumstances encouraging a cross party vote. Muntz refused to coalesce with Scholefield and though Liberal party meetings adopted them jointly there was no official alliance between the candidates. This gave strength to the Tory move encouraging voters to return the sitting members (Muntz and Spooner), especially since the Liberal press and party leadership were critical of Muntz, who was praised in Tory papers. Yet despite all this the ordinary voter saw through the manoeuvring and voted according to his normal party preference. The comments of a very moderate and normally objective Tory are extremely instructive:

> The most heedless observer of the signs of the times must see that the progress of Free Trade and a more free and expansive view of many other political and religious questions – whether for good or for evil cannot be retarded. . . . It was therefore scarcely to be expected that Birmingham which has always been the first to advance what are called 'liberal' opinions, of whatever kind, should return a member pledged to an opposite course of policy.[60]

An endemic Liberalism, demonstrated by the town's election results over half a century, is here admitted by a Birmingham Tory. Implicit in this local judgement is something of more general significance. The Birmingham result was discussed in the context of other large towns and it was expected that urban elections would be closely related to movements of opinion. In the city an election recorded the genuine political will of the electorate, not the power of money or influence.

Inevitably the voter operated in a social context which determined how freely he might exercise his political judgement. Landlords, employers, patrons, customers, even mobs might bring pressure to bear upon a voter whose intellectual judgement could also be swayed by beer and money. Bribery could always be punished by a parliamentary enquiry but undue influence was more problematical, as Cobden explained: 'intimidation whether by landlords priests mobs or customers does not constitute grounds for unseating a member . . . but in its various disguises forms nineteen twentieths of the evils of our electoral system.'[61] The standard Liberal answer was the ballot and the faith of Liberals in the ballot was a confirmation that their ideal political world was one in which the voter could vote freely. The city approximated more closely to that ideal than anywhere else. For all the talk of beer bribery and influence there was only one contested return in all the four large provincial cities (Manchester, Birmingham, Leeds and Liverpool) between 1832 and 1867 and this was the Liverpool election of 1852.*

The volume of propaganda issued at election time, especially in Manchester and Leeds, is evidence of the premium placed on rational choice. Electors were fed the usual diet of squibs, cartoons, broadsides and doggerel but also a considerable amount of densely packed political argument. This propaganda was reinforced by a combative and rhetorical newspaper press and in all towns the political battles were fought in and shaped by the editorial columns of rival journals. In Leeds the 'Bainesocracy', which ensured that a Baines represented the town for 29 out of the 40 years from 1834, was a remarkable tribute to the power of the press. The influence of the Baines family confirms that the press could guide opinion and that the electorate was responsive to rational persuasion. Even in Liverpool where freemen expected to be paid, money often strengthened a genuine political preference. The persistent Conservatism of Liverpool is more a reflection of a popular dislike of pro-Catholic Liberalism than of Tory gold.

Money did vitally affect Preston where poor men were forced into using the votes as a rare capital asset. Bribery carried its own code of ethics and George Melly's coterie was found wanting in 1862:

> well after O I'd rather voet for Melly bur they'll give us nowt or
> I'd voet for him. . . . They went for one old *lame* man to vote . . .

---

* The cost of prosecuting a petition against an election may have deterred further contested returns in Liverpool. That of 1852 cost the Liberals £20,000.

offering him his money, which was due to him for twelve day's service but when he *had* voted, he was forsaken instantaneously and had to get home as best he could. Is this Liberalism. No there was not one piece of money stirring at all. If there was money it was 'bottled' and *still is* 'bottled' for I at least can't get my fee. . . . It was nothing but natural that a poor half-clad starved clammed man with a wife and children having a vote will barter his principle for money.[62]

Liberals had to accept the powerful local tradition and pay up. More important they had to recognize that the composition of the electorate in Preston, with many potwallopers, made bribery more likely than in the newly created £10 franchise. The half-clad, starved weaver did not have a vote in most large cities. As always the social and political structure bred its own political culture.

The relationship between the two was subtle but real. It has been argued that the regional variations in both the parliamentary reform movement and Chartism derived from the local economic and social structure.[63] The artisan radicalism of Sheffield clearly owed something to the structure of the town's economy, described by John Parker, the local M.P.:

There is not that marked line of difference between the rich man and the poor man which is becoming annually more observable in other places. The middle ranks are 'nearer' both to the upper and the lower. The trade here is, as it ought to be, republican and not an oligarchy: it is in the town and not in the hands of a few enormous capitalists.[64]

Cobden found that Birmingham had 'a greater faith in democratic principles' than Manchester and put this down to the essential sociological differences between the two:

In Birmingham where a manufacturer employs his three or four hands only and sometimes but an apprentice or two, there is much more cordial and united feeling among the two classes. In fact the social steps connecting one class with another are so gradual that instead of the great gulf which separates masters and workmen in Stockport or Manchester it is difficult to know where the line which divides the two is to be found.[65]

It now seems likely that Cobden ought to have distinguished between Manchester and its surrounding single-industry cotton towns like Stockport. Manchester as a commercial capital in fact had a smaller proletariat, a larger middle class and a more variegated and crowded class between them than did the cotton towns with their extensive factory system. It was the highly developed horizontal social structure which sustained the apparently proletarian political domination of Oldham, recently identified by Dr Foster.[66] By way of contrast, Leeds, with a variegated social structure similar to that of Manchester, produced a political system in which both working and middle class were politically fragmented in a battle fought by an alliance of working-class Operative Conservatism and middle-class Toryism against one of working-class Chartism and middle-class radical Liberalism.

The politics of elections were vitally affected by the social structure and by the local political structure which grew out of it. Parliamentary elections could not be immune to the sparks flying from battles fought at other levels in the political structure. A parochial dispute or a municipal schism could determine the course of an election as effectively as could a fundamental disagreement between political movements. The whole political system of Liverpool was affected by the mid-century fissure in the fabric of the town's élite, created by the twin disputes over dock administration and water supply.* Often these parochial or municipal disputes raised issues about the nature and exercise of urban authority, and an election result in one sense encapsulated at a given point in time what best expressed the power structure of the urban community. Political authority ran along channels determined by the social structure, which gave to the political system a natural hierarchy. Cobden received a sharp rebuke from a Huddersfield bigwig for bypassing the normal political leadership and appealing for funds directly to the working men of the town: 'it is a very doubtful policy to call for money upon the working classes through new and in our district unknown agencies, in the present state of political affairs. . . . I have no doubt that the working classes will respond enthusiastically to the call of their former leaders.'[67] Politics were supposed to strengthen rather than weaken the nexus of social authority in the city.

The role of the social and political structure in determining political action is a complex one. In some ways it could run counter to the political direction suggested by the workings of organization and ideology, already cited. The social structure acted as a sort of matrix or mould within which organization and ideology combined to mix the stuff of politics. The key variables of ideology and organization operated within parameters determined by the social structure. This elusive element in urban politics is perhaps best illustrated by looking at one constituency in some detail and the relationship of social and political structures is neatly displayed in the politics of Manchester in the 1840s and 1850s.

---

* Cf. Robert Mather to G. Wilson, 27 January 1850: 'The political feeling in Liverpool is I fear very backward especially among the rising generation and very much distracted by local questions.' (Wilson Papers.)

3

Manchester Liberalism had been given an appearance of firm unity in the early Victorian years not by the League but by the struggle over the Charter. The proscribed élite gradually defeated the prescribed élite in vestry, commission and finally corporation, to provide for itself the institutional framework for the exercise of natural social authority (see above, p. 120). Though the industrial and commercial interests of Manchester which comprised this Liberal élite supported free trade, the League never wholly spoke for the town. The League was not supported by the *Guardian* and in 1845 the controversial expulsions from the Manchester Chamber of Commerce (see below, p. 243) openly split the local Liberal party. Some might see origins of this Whig-radical tension as far back as 1832 with the moderate Whig support for S. J. Loyd who stood in the first election against the official reform candidates. However, it was the formation of the rival Commercial Association in 1845 which created a focus around which anti-radical forces could group. The launching of the *Manchester Examiner* in 1846 signified that Manchester Liberalism would speak with two voices rather than one.

In the heady success of the repeal of the Corn Laws the schism was obscured but the approach of a general election brought some differences out into the open. Mark Philips wished to retire and his obvious successor was Cobden, whose reputation and popularity in 1846 were so over-whelming as to silence any doubts about unity. But Cobden played a rather equivocal game in 1846–7 and his repeated refusals to stand at Manchester were not accepted at face value by the more respectable Liberals. Cobden declined to accept nomination for Manchester and also declined to provide a public recommendation for Bright, although privately he wrote of him, 'how truly it is to be desired that he should have his obvious ambition to sit for Manchester gratified'.[68] The opposition to Bright from some of the élite families such as the Potters was somewhat puzzling. In 1843 Bright's expenses at Durham were met by Sir Thomas Potter and since T. B. Potter had been vice-president of the Complete Suffrage Association Bright naturally commented 'Tom can surely have no objection to extreme opinions.'[69] Bright assumed that the opposition was on social grounds. He was not in the big league financially and when the Peelite Lord Lincoln was suggested he mocked 'the poor sneaks who prefer a Tory lord to a man of their own rank whose chief fault with them is that he is wanting a social position'.[70] It was more likely that men who themselves aspired to be an urban aristocracy resented Bright's virulent anti-aristocratic views.

Despite the support of the *Guardian* and of many Whig-Liberal Leaguers, Lord Lincoln did not proceed with his candidature. His with-drawal enabled Bright and Milner Gibson to be returned for Manchester unopposed in 1847, apparent proof of the unchallenged supremacy of the Manchester school and of the Newall's Building machine which lived on after the demise of the League. One small fact symbolized the incipient malaise of Manchester Liberalism in its hour of triumph. William Neild, the wealthy and powerful supporter of Cobden in the Charter battle, declined to be a member of C. P. Villiers's election committee for South Lancashire.[71] One of the leading Liberal families of the town gave notice that it would not toe the League line.* An oligarchy had finally confirmed its status of authority and leadership and was announcing 'thus far and no further'. Wealthy but excluded families like the Neilds (Quakers) or the Potters (Unitarians) had been radical in the 1820s and 1830s in vestry and township affairs. They had ended their religious inferiority by neutralizing the vestry and abolishing church rates; they had ousted the 'broad cloth' in the government of the town and confirmed their own leadership with the stamp of municipal authority; they had secured their own economic position by the acceptance of free trade. They had no remaining quarrel with the aristocracy and saw no virtue in further reform. They merely awaited the opportunity to allow their natural social influence to find political expression. This élite wished the image of Manchester to be stamped with their authority rather than that of the League.

In the growing prosperity of mid-Victorian Manchester small, sometimes very small ripples, disturbed the political calm. During John Potter's mayoralty the corporation introduced the civic pomp of robes and hospitality which so disgusted Cobden – 'a Mayor of Manchester importing the obsolete sensuality of the Cockney Corporation, which, like Smithfield, has outlived its time and ought to be equally the subject of sanitary reform'.[72] Also during Potter's term of office the queen visited Manchester, conferring a knighthood on the mayor, and encouraging the corporation, in Bright's words, 'to lose its senses and its character'. Potter's third year of office (1850–1) took on political significance. There was already a tradition of giving mayors a second year and Sir Thomas Potter, William Neild, Alexander Kay and Elkanah Armitage had all been once re-elected. John Potter, no doubt feeling himself something very special, wished to serve a third term and this was much resented by the radicals. Were there not others worthy of the office, asked the *Examiner*, which also enquired whether the extra honour was for Potter's public service or merely in deference to his private status. Abel Heywood's spirited opposition to Potter in the council predictably fell on deaf ears and the relatively weak radical municipal

* Neild and Garnett, editor of the *Guardian*, were the only two to vote against Bright's adoption by the Reform Association in October 1846 (G. Wilson to J. Brooks, 14 October 1846).

position was indicated by Heywood's eight votes in the 1850 aldermanic poll against Potter's 51.[73]

These municipal trivia have to be seen against the background of political opinion in Manchester at the time. When the *Examiner* and *Times* merged in 1848 it was made clear that the paper was committed to a radical extension of the suffrage in order to break once and for all the power of the aristocracy.[74] Nothing could have been nearer to Bright's heart and the Manchester school moved closer to radical reform and shifted its power base to a lower social level. There was much dissatisfaction with Gibson for his compromising relationship with the Russell government* and neither Bright nor Cobden could be relied upon to deal with the Manchester parliamentary business. There was widespread talk of Potter standing at the next election and already by 1851 a Liverpool ally could regretfully refer to 'the unfortunate schism that has taken place in Manchester amongst the Liberal Party'.[75]

If the social structure had been the only determining factor in parliamentary elections then John Potter would have stood against the Manchester school Liberals in 1852. He was fresh from his knighthood and his three-year mayoralty, during which he had arranged meetings between Whig and Tory leaders. Potter was apparently seeking a fusion of the elements of the town's élite, no longer divided by municipal battle, and this seemed a useful preparation for the reassertion of political authority by the wealth of the town. Yet not even Potter could defy the logic of political ideology. The threat to free trade posed by the Derby administration led to the revival of the League and the general election was called on the issue of a return to protection. The possibility of a Whig revolt was made even more remote by Tory moves, inspired by the Rev. Hugh Stowell, vicar of Pendleton, which involved fighting the election on Anglican, no popery lines.[76] Potters, Neilds and their followers could hardly be a party to an election campaign on behalf of extreme Protestantism and protection. Bright and Gibson secured a comfortable victory over the weak Tory candidates Loch and Denman because the issues involved in the election imposed a political logic which the social structure was powerless to defy. Again the Manchester school emerged unscathed. In 1847 the lack of a contest and in 1852 the character of the contest hid the true state of Manchester Liberalism.

Thereafter the tide ran steadily against Cobden and Bright, largely because of foreign policy considerations. Their pacifist views during the Crimean War left them in a very exposed and weakened position in the

* Gibson was vice-president of the Board of Trade from 1846 until he resigned in 1848. He got the worst of both worlds for he was a disappointment to the radicals in not achieving more economic reform while in office and to the Whig-Liberals for resigning from the ministry and then moving hostile motions against it.

town. Many former lieutenants now deserted the League banner, most notably Absolom Watkin, whose defection was likely following his support of war on the Kossuth issue in 1851. It was Watkin who confronted Bright in December 1854 at a meeting called to protest against the M.P.'s public letter confirming his pacifist opposition to the war. When a requistion for the meeting was launched Bright contemptuously denounced its signatories as merely Tories or *Guardian* men, commenting sadly, 'what brutal ignorance prevails in Manchester even after all our labours'.[77] Cobden, as ever, was more realistic and was very worried about the outcome, advising Wilson to

> send out a few thousand circulars to the most reliable supporters of Bright and Gibson of the electoral class and tell them that the requisition is chiefly signed by Tory Protectionists. . . . If there is any of the old spirit which we used to have when 10 years ago you and I used to make similar appeals you will not fail to beat your opponents. The war spirit must be mad indeed if you cannot beat them by these means.[78]

The war spirit was mad and Bright was shouted down and attacked by crowds in his own constituency. The £29,000 collected by Manchester for the Patriotic Fund was almost equivalent to a Palmerstonian election chest and when in November 1856 Palmerston visited the town he received a great public display of support.[79] That the Cobden motion brought down Palmerston made it inevitable that the election would be fought in Palmerstonian terms. In 1852 the electoral issues ran in favour of Gibson and Bright where in 1857 they ran against them.

The 1857 Manchester election (along with that of 1847 in Leeds) was the most fascinating of all mid-nineteenth century urban contests. Indeed in composite form it displayed all three factors – organization, ideology and social structure – which have been here cited as the crucial variables in urban elections. The defeat of Gibson and Bright by Sir John Potter and J. A. Turner in 1857 was intricately bound up with the question of organization and its proper role in urban politics. The registration and electoral agency known as Newall's Building run by George Wilson, former president of the League, controlled both borough and county registration and sponsored a clutch of candidates in Lancashire and further afield. Newall's Building was the centre of a network of M.P.s which included in mid-century James Heywood in North Lancashire, William Brown and Alexander Henry in South Lancashire, Cobden in the West Riding, J. B. Smith in Stirling, and a considerable number of Liberals sitting for Lancashire boroughs. By 1857 there were many in Manchester who found the domination of Newall's Building galling. The arrogance with which the Wilson men declared that they could carry whoever they pleased among the candidates they carried in their pockets sickened even J. B. Smith, who complained about 'the Wilson clique whose intense selfishness and vanity have entirely disgusted us as well as a host of others'.[80]

The *Guardian* had perceptively foreseen in 1846 the potential dangers of a powerful electoral agency. It warned in its tribute to the League, 'A combination with such funds at its command engaged in superintending the creation of votes, conducting the registrations and acting at elections, might, if ill-directed, become most dangerous to the peace and good order of the community.'[81] The following decade convinced the *Guardian*, some Liberals and most Tories that the political machine had been 'ill-directed' and would have to be destroyed. Manchester had become a sort of pocket borough in the power of an organization which was 'striving to maintain a permanent yoke where we gave it only temporary allegiance'.[82] Manchester wished to rid itself of the stigma imprinted upon the town's image by Newall's Building, a wish expressed by both Liberals and Tories. The latter supported Liberal candidates for one main reason, 'to destroy the dictatorship of the League in this city', while moderate Liberals joined the *Guardian* in attempting to break the League stranglehold: 'They are trying to rule us by a clique, a family party, which, having been permitted to erect a powerful system for one purpose which they have triumphantly gained, keep it standing ready upon any occasion to be thrown into gear for others, to operate even against those who originally helped to provide it.'[83] When the defeat had been sustained many Cobdenites were prepared to admit that too much power had been retained by a self-perpetuating clique. Wilson was advised that Manchester needed a new, broader-based organization which should 'afford larger opportunities than have heretofore existed for the development of the political genius of its citizens'.[84]

These citizens showed in 1857 that in addition to resenting the domination of political organization they also disagreed with the Manchester school on matters of opinion. Bright emphasized that they were not faced by a Tory challenge but by one mounted by 'those who make a profession of our principles and who would, if in Parliament, sit on our side of the House'.[85] These *quondam* reformers, including the Potters, Neild, Jeremiah Garnett, J. A. Turner, Oliver Heywood and Jonathan Pender, all disagreed with the Manchester school on ideological grounds. Their views were not those of Gibson and Bright and so they opposed them in an election. They disagreed on foreign policy, on the leadership of Palmerston, on what policies best served both Manchester and the nation. Though some might argue that there were no real political issues at stake, merely a question of commercial policy, even here opinions differed and the election contest expressed this divergence of view. Beyond the overt Palmerstonian issues lay the nature of Palmerstonian Liberalism and its Conservative character. Implicit in the opposition of the Potter party was a rejection of the radical parliamentary reform of John Bright:

> Is there a man among them who can point to a solitary address delivered on any public occasion in which that measure of reform is advocated. Such men as Mr Aspinall Turner and Mr W. Neild are all astir when their commercial interests are threatened . . . but who ever heard from either of those gentlemen . . . a single hearty address in favour of reducing the taxation which presses upon the working man or advocating his admission to the rights of a British citizen.[86]

The 1857 Manchester election was a dispute between the radical and the Palmerstonian view of Liberalism.

Underlying these issues of organization and opinion lay the social and political structure of Manchester and the question of how urban authority should be exercised. The candidature of Sir John Potter (and of J. A. Turner when Robert Lowe declined the invitation to stand) involved an assertion of authority and pre-eminence by an élite whose social status was secure but whose political power had always been limited. This wealthy connection could nominate aldermen and mayors with impunity but political developments decreed that the representation of the town should not be in their gift. The election, though fought on Palmerstonian issues, revolved around the question of whether the town ought to be represented by one of its wealthiest sons or by a nondescript political tradesman from Rochdale. The social hierarchy of Manchester was seeking to assert its natural authority by throwing weight of property against that of mere population. This essentially social challenge was given its cutting edge by the changing view this élite had of its own economic interest.

Dr V. A. C. Gatrell has convincingly argued that a fundamental shift in the pattern of exports in mid-century underpins the assumption of Palmerstonian attitudes by the commercial élite of Manchester.[87] The increased investment and increased production in the cotton industry during the 1850s required new markets. The bigger growth in cotton exports occurred not in traditional corn-growing areas but in places such as the Levant and China where Palmerstonian policies produced economic dividends. An aggressive foreign policy which opened and protected new markets was therefore in the interests of Manchester cotton and Turner's Commercial Association argued the Palmerstonian case against the free trade non-interventionist League orthodoxy. Palmerston, as the Don Pacifico episode proved, would protect the trader and in him patriotism and economic sense joined forces. The Manchester school thus represented both an affront to the social position of the commercial élite and a betrayal of its economic interests. Potter in asserting social authority was also ensuring the economic wellbeing of his own class.

A revolt, inspired by the social structure and fanned by changing economic circumstances, could still only be successful if it took into account the political structure of Manchester. During the second quarter of the century the fundamental political division of Manchester was that between rival political and religious élites. The Anglican Tory élite had been vanquished yet remained a sizeable minority in the Manchester political community and even in the unfavourable climate of the 1852 election the Tories could command about 43 per cent of the vote. All élites, by definition a minority, need a power base of numbers responding to the leadership of the élite through economic, social, or political influence. When, in the decade from the mid-1840s, the commercial élite lost (one might say rejected) its power base amongst the radical shopocracy, it was deprived of an essential component in the exercise of political power. Its only alternative, while the Manchester School controlled the radical crowds, lay in the Tory electorate. The absence of a contest in 1847 and the issues of the 1852 election prevented the commercial élite from appealing to Tory rank and file on those occasions, although such a coalition had been recommended by the Tory press as soon as Bright was adopted in October 1846.[88]

In 1857 the issues were more appropriate for such a move and Cobden realized he was fighting 'a combination of tories and moderate Liberals'.[89] Had Manchester Toryism stood aloof in 1857 and allowed the two Liberal factions to fight it out there is little doubt that Potter and Turner would have been defeated. They could count on only about a quarter of the Liberal electors and without Tory support social influence alone would not have been enough. Toryism gladly accepted the chance of vengeance for which it had been waiting for 20 years. The defeated élite of the 1830s took its belated revenge in the rout of the Manchester school in the 1850s. The official party made no move but as individuals the Tories acted. The Tory William Entwistle, now on the same side as Mark Philips who defeated him in the 1841 election, seconded Turner's nomination and some 6,000 Tory voters nailed the coffin of the Manchester school.[90]

When Liberals surveyed the charred battleground they subconsciously voiced the three themes of the election. They acknowledged both the strengths and weaknesses of their organization and some admitted the legitimacy of their opponent's aim 'of level-ing the debris of the old League'.[91] They recognized that in the rejection of Gibson and Bright (and of Armitage at Salford and Cobden at Huddersfield) there was a rejection of the opinions and ideology for which the Manchester school stood. As Bright put it bitterly, 'the "school" may be said to have shut up – at least for a vacation, the discipline being too severe for the scholars'.[92] Above all Cobden and Bright saw in the 1857 defeat that which lay at its heart, the assertion of authority by an urban aristocracy. Deference to an élite was what was wanted in the manner to which the municipal hierarchy had accustomed the town, and this Gibson and Bright would not provide. The latter wrote: 'I think it was in Potter's reign at the Town Hall that the Corporation put on robes of office. It would be most appropriate that in his time also the representatives of Manchester should begin to wear plush. Gibson and I are kicked out because we would not wear livery.'[93] Having scaled the economic heights the commercial élite wished publicly to mark the gulf between respectability and the *menu peuple*. Prosperity had, as Cobden explained, 'tended to strengthen the aristocratic influence and render the democracy unfashionable. What so natural as that your genteel people should kick down the ladder by which they rose.'[94] That 'tyranny of the bloated rich' which radicals had feared in 1838 was finally manifest.

The anti-aristocratic sentiment which became so controversial in Manchester figured strongly in a further dimension to urban politics (which can only be briefly outlined here). Parallel to the political struggles that occurred within cities there was a wider conflict between town and county in the rural hinterland of each city. In urban elections there was a clash between rival views of the city's image; in counties the struggle was increasingly overlaid with whether the region should be stamped with a commercial or a rural die. Especially in the counties within reach of the great provincial cities, Lancashire, Yorkshire, Staffordshire and Warwickshire, there developed a town versus county tension which dated from the early nineteenth century.

In the great Yorkshire election of 1807 the towns were fully mobilized in a contest between two prominent county houses, Wentworth Woodhouse and Harewood. Leeds and the *Leeds Mercury* were very important components in the contest, though very much in the service of the county. It was perhaps in 1812 that towns, particularly unrepresented ones, began to assert their interests against those of agriculture. The theory that county M.P.s were responsible for urban interests broke down when Birmingham found local M.P.s wanting on the matter of the Orders in Council. It was from 1812 in both Staffordshire and Warwickshire that county politicians had to acknowledge the importance of the city in choosing M.P.s. A further development was the overtly urban candidature of Richard Spooner in the 1820 Warwickshire election. Spooner, though a Tory, received even radical support in an unsuccessful urban assault upon the county.[95] An important turning point elsewhere was the election in Yorkshire of John Marshall in 1826, a tribute more to his wealth than his social status but an admission that the urban élite was acceptable to county society. The greatest coup of all in this nascent urban-rural trial of strength was the imposition of Brougham upon Yorkshire in 1830, following sharp action by Baines and the urban Dissenters.[96] This was the most strident assertion of urban self-consciousness thus far experienced in any county politics.

The enfranchisement of the large cities naturally turned political attention inwards and county elections in the 1830s were largely in the hands of traditional families, with urban activists playing a supporting role. The needs of registration brought the town and county into closer partnership by the late 1830s; much Liberal strength lay in the towns and urban activists undertook much of the tedious work of registration. There were in any case large numbers of urban voters who had voting qualifications for both town and county. Urban involvement in county politics came to a head in the 1840s with the invasion of the urbanized counties by the Anti-Corn Law League. Initially in 1844 the League suffered a great reverse in its own back garden by the defeat of William Brown in South Lancashire at the hands of William Entwistle, a Manchester Tory. Further attention to the register and the manufacture of 40 shilling freeholds made the free traders invincible and Brown was returned unopposed in 1846 and again the following year with C. P. Villiers, who preferred to retain his seat at Wolverhampton. Villiers's successor, Alexander Henry, acknowledged that he was the nominee of 'the Gentlemen connected with League rooms'.[97]

When the League methods were imported into other counties they were by no means popular and in North Warwickshire the Birmingham press criticized methods that were not 'in accordance with good policy or fair and legitimate strategy'.[98] In the West Riding much greater doubts were raised by the League registration campaign. The financially weak registration organization in the county needed an infusion of fresh blood, but the social and political implications of a League takeover shattered the aristocratic image of how the county should be run. Earl Fitzwilliam responded to financial appeals in fear of the future and wrote, 'indeed I shall do so *con amore* if the alternative be a registration by the League – this wd. be destructive of everything'.[99] A running battle went on between Cobden, who wished to abandon the Whig gentry, and Baines, who wished to create a partnership between town and county.[100] The latter managed to hide the full extent of urban control and it was a member of the traditional élite, Lord Morpeth, who first benefited from the League activity, by his uncontested return in February 1846. There was no gainsaying Cobden's claim that but for him 'Lord Morpeth might still have been rusticating at Castle Howard'.[101]

The efficient registration organization for Leeds and the West Riding, run by Thomas Plint, had by 1847 created a clear free trade majority on the register, which activists were anxious to make use of. As a Yorkshire free trader explained, 'when we have spent so much money in buying Forty Shilling Freeholds we ought to have an opportunity of exercising our franchise in the Free Trade cause'.[102] Traditional social authority wanted an uncontested return of the existing landed members but the towns were anxious to assert themselves, with assistance from Lancashire. Indeed, urban free traders were engaged in a dual drive against the landed interest by putting up Cobden in the West Riding and Villiers in South Lancashire. The uncontested return of these two, as Villiers said, 'for such constituencies as Yorkshire and Lancashire has nearly accomplished all the good of which they are capable by manifesting the strength of opinion on the subject of Free Trade'.[103]

The West Riding triumph of 1847 was followed by the disaster of 1848, for the urban-rural conflict had become intermingled with the voluntary question (see below, p. 271). The former ensured the withdrawal of the Fitzwilliam cadet but the latter, through Whig abstentions and transfers, presented a seat to the Tories. Baines, though the cause of the voluntaryist split, and Sir Charles Wood, though a confidant of Fitzwilliam and the landed interest, between them pieced together a Whig-Liberal unity in the West Riding. There was no contested election between 1848 and 1859 but by the time of the 1859 contest Liberal urban and Whig rural interests had worked out a compromise by each having a nomination and agreeing a policy of mutual support at the polls.[104] In the county as in the town an election reflected the balance of social and political forces in the community.

By the 1850s most urbanized counties had conceded a proper political role to the towns. In South Staffordshire the shift of power from rural to urban was clear, as one of its leading gentry noted in 1853; 'The patronage for the seats in the southern Division is passing into the hands of the Traders in the chief towns. In my earlier days they neither thought of it or were thought of by others – the chief County families settled the matter among themselves.'[105] In North Warwickshire there was a close connection between town and county especially on the Tory side. Richard Spooner was able to retreat comfortably into the county seat in 1847, after having been defeated in Birmingham in the same election. Five years later one of the reasons assigned by Joseph Parkes for the town's reluctance to contest Spooner's county seat was that 'some Birmingham men fear if he retired from the county he would re-visit and bother the borough'.[106] Parkes, despite great efforts and begging letters to Manchester for much needed funds, could not 'plant' North Warwickshire in 1852, as he put it. His efforts illustrated the balance of interests within the county, for he needed the support of the traditional gentry with their natural influence over voters, as well as that of the towns which would provide organization and money. Second only to money for indemnifying the candidate was the need for a *persona grata* in both town and county. Parkes had such a man primed from 'a most deservedly popular family of influence' who would also 'vastly please Coventry and Birmingham'.[107]

North Warwickshire remained elusive to the Liberal grasp but North Lancashire allowed the towns one safe seat. James Heywood, a wealthy manufacturer, sat for North Lancashire from 1847 to 1857. When the leaders of urban liberalism in the county heard of his likely retirement in 1857 they buzzed around in the search for a new candidate so as to forestall the county Tories. The comment of Ashworth, the Bolton magnate, was instructive, for he wrote, 'I should be sorry to see Lancashire send a military man . . . or a Squire who had not direct connexion with our trade interests'.[108] By 1857 the urban activist proscribed two of the social groups, the army and the gentry, which had traditionally provided county representatives. By such changes did the political system record the wider social consequences of industrialization.

9
Electoral analysis

'Allow me most strongly to press the importance of a classification of the voters . . . which I think may be published with great advantage to our cause. . . . An important moral *and* intelligent *majority I am sure we can establish in our favour . . . you can exhibit our defeat as "an abstract" victory!'* Thomas Bazley to George Wilson, 28 May 1844

At a time when statistics were first coming into their own Thomas Bazley, quoted above, recognized their fundamental characteristic. Statistics are a fickle servant in the cause of any master, exhibiting a variety of truths dependent upon the degree and nature of their manipulation. The student of nineteenth-century elections is bedevilled not only by the general difficulties of statistics but also by severe problems in relation to the data he wishes to quantify. The two-member seats which were found in the large towns are unresponsive to straightforward psephological analysis and the surviving poll books whose coverage of constituencies is partial raise as many handling difficulties as the elections which produced them. Problems of sampling and of occupational analysis make poll books less easy to work on than they at first appear. As always in historical studies the data is never quite recorded as we would wish. Nevertheless some attempt must be made to quantify political developments, as reflected in election results and, as elsewhere in the book, the aim here will be to indicate a methodology and establish its credentials rather than to exhaust the subject. Particular attention will be devoted to the role of municipal elections, the computation of parliamentary election results, and the provision of a social dimension to voting.

Thus far little or no note of municipal elections has been taken by political historians. It cannot be sustained that such exclusion of local elections rests on their non-political character for, as we have seen, the wholly non-political council like Manchester was very much the exception. Indeed, municipal elections do provide opportunities for developing an extra dimension in our understanding of urban politics, particularly in towns and periods when party rivalry was fierce. The municipal electorate was not so very different in composition from the parliamentary electorate (Leeds was an exception here) though in many cases it was smaller, despite the more democratic appearance of the municipal franchise. Ratepaying and residential conditions took their toll upon municipal voters, especially those below the £10 parliamentary qualification. The municipal election is particularly useful in refining the political picture revealed by the parliamentary electoral process and it has two main advantages. First, the municipal election was fought annually and therefore can provide a much more accurate chronological analysis of political preference. Second, the election was fought in wards rather than in the borough as a whole and so a more accurate geographical analysis within towns can be derived.

To give an indication of the potential here an analysis is attempted of municipal elections in Leeds and Liverpool, both of which had highly political town councils. The political composition of and number of contests for the councils here and elsewhere have already been discussed (see above, Chapter 6) and now the main emphasis is upon a ward analysis. Fortunately the ward boundaries drawn up in 1835 were not amended in either town in the period under review (see maps). In Leeds there were eight wards in Leeds township with double representation for Mill Hill and West, largely justified by property valuation rather than by population. The ten out-townships were organized into four wards: Hunslet, Holbeck (Holbeck and Wortley), Bramley (Bramley, Armley, Farnley, and Beeston), and Headingley (Headingley, Potter Newton, and Chapel Allerton).

The annual elections for each year from 1835 and 1880 have been analysed and the share won by Conservatives computed. The evidence has been displayed in the form of a diagram which immediately reveals a wide range, for the Conservatives captured 82 per cent of seats in Headingley but only 3 per cent in Holbeck. It is interesting to relate these results to the number of contests to see how far the political character of a ward dissuaded opponents from entering the field. Table 13 shows some correlation between non-contested seats and a

Table 13. Percentage of non-contested municipal elections, Leeds 1835–80

Ward	%	Ward	%
Mill Hill	33	Kirkgate	15
West	27	South	58
North West	42	Hunslet	38
North	33	Holbeck	20
North East	22	Bramley	42
East	29	Headingley	55

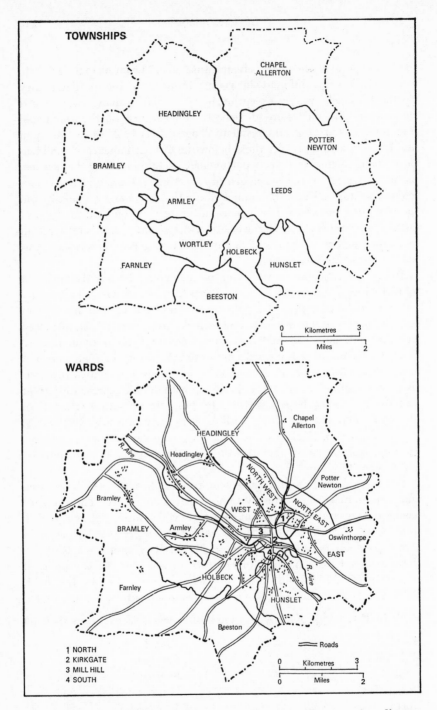

Map 1. The townships and wards of Leeds; with accompanying diagram showing the percentage share of seats won by Conservatives in Leeds municipal elections, 1835–80, by wards.

high degree of political identification in particular wards. The two wards with the highest rate of walkovers, South and Headingley, were two of the most committed politically, with South returning 94 per cent Liberal councillors and Headingley returning 82 per cent Conservative. Similarly the next two ranking wards, with 42 per cent of elections non-contested, North West and Bramley, were solidly Liberal. It is not surprising that the minority parties in these wards should abandon their cause as near hopeless on many occasions. On the other hand the figures also reveal that the second most Tory ward in the borough, Kirkgate, had the highest number of contests and the strongest Liberal ward, Holbeck, had the second highest. In these wards, though a strong predeliction in favour of one party was evident (in Holbeck overwhelmingly so), the successful parties nearly always had to fight it out.

The question which naturally arises is whether there was any relationship between these wide ward-based variations in political support and the wealth of wards. It is not easy to devise a wholly satisfactory scale for measuring the wealth of wards but a guide is provided by the rateable value. Table 14 computes rateable value *per capita* for 1841 and 1871 to establish a rank order of wards in order of wealth in these two years (only Hunslet slightly altered its position between the two dates). The table also gives the position of the ward ranked in order of Conservative support, derived from the diagram below. There is indeed some correlation between wealth and voting, as seen in the fact that the three richest wards, Mill Hill, Kirkgate, and Headingley, were the three most successful for the Conservatives while two of the poorest, Hunslet and Holbeck, were overwhelmingly Liberal. Nevertheless the overall correlation using Spearman's coefficient was only 0·40 and there was little difference in either rank order or percentage share of support between Mill Hill, the richest ward of Leeds, and North East, the poorest. Both the richest and the poorest wards of Leeds inclined to the Liberals and when the richest

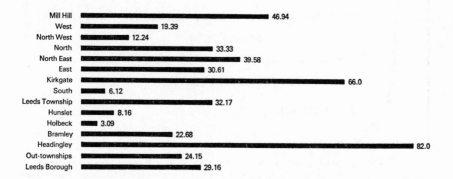

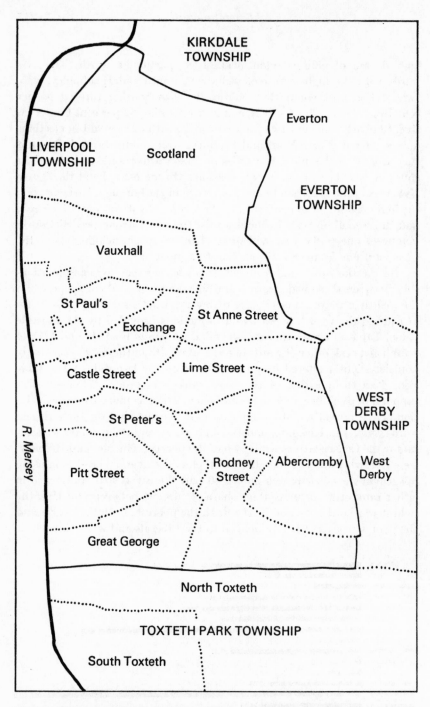

Map 2. The townships and wards of Liverpool; with accompanying diagram showing the percentage share of seats won by Conservatives in Liverpool municipal elections, 1835–67, by wards.

Table 14. Wealth and municipal voting in Leeds

Ward	Rateable value per capita in £		Rank order of Conservative support
	1841	1871	
1 Mill Hill	11·94	23·69	3
2 Kirkgate	7·52	11·21	2
3 Headingley	6·27	4·39	1
4 South	3·82	3·94	11
5 West	3·67	3·33	8
6 Bramley	2·82	2·78	7
7 North West	2·78	2·37	9
8 North	2·24	2·16	5
9 Hunslet	2·23	1·92	10
10 Holbeck	2·11	2·20	12
11 East	1·83	1·67	6
12 North East	1·49	1·38	4

and poorest wards could return about the same number of Conservative councillors over nearly half a century one must beware of forging iron links between municipal voting and wealth.

In Liverpool, as in Leeds, there was a combination of township and out-townships and there were 12 wards in Liverpool parish, each returning three councillors and a further four wards in the out-townships, West Derby, North Toxteth, South Toxteth and Everton with Kirkdale. Liverpool council was, of course, predominantly Conservative in the mid-nineteenth century and any comparison with Leeds must take this into account. Again a diagram is used to show the Conservative share of council seats in the years from 1835 to 1867 and, as at Leeds, there is a

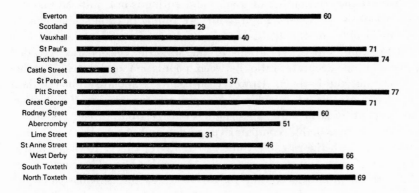

considerable range, between 8 per cent at Castle Street and 77 per cent at Pitt Street. As before the number of contests has been calculated and these figures include all elections, those caused by deaths, resignations, and disqualifications as well as annual vacancies. Table 15 shows that the safest ward in the borough, Castle Street, had the lowest number of contests and though the Liberals had an easy run there, the other five Liberal wards were all contested more often than they were not. The two wards with the highest number of contests, St Anne Street and Vauxhall, returned almost the same number of Liberal councillors, indicating a pretty stiff contest for power in those wards. On the other side the safest Conservative ward, Pitt Street, was contested more often than not, but the second safest, Exchange, was second only to Castle Street in the number of no contests.

Table 15. Percentage of non-contested municipal elections, Liverpool 1835–67*

Ward	%	Ward	%
Everton	41	Great George	41
Scotland	44	Rodney Street	55
Vauxhall	29	Abercromby	51
St Paul's	33	Lime Street	38
Exchange	58	St Anne Street	21
Castle Street	65	West Derby	47
St Peter's	46	South Toxteth	38
Pitt Street	47	North Toxteth	36

* Source: R. W. Davies, *Municipal History of Liverpool* (1868).

To test the relationship of wealth and voting is not quite so easy for Liverpool as for Leeds. Figures for *per capita* rateable value can be obtained only for the 12 Liverpool parish wards and not for the four out-township wards. Variations in the way the census was recorded preclude an accurate ratio between population and rateable value throughout the borough. However one can extrapolate from the data available a scale of rateable value per assessment, i.e. the average assessment for each ward. These figures only relate to ratepayers but do provide a reasonable comparative guide, and when this scale was compared with the rateable value *per capita* for the 12 township wards there were only minor differences in the rank order. Therefore in the interests of producing a scale for all 12 wards the rateable value per assessment was used, calculated from figures relating to 1836. Table 16

lists the wards of Liverpool in order of wealth and compares this with the
rank order of support for Conservatives as expressed in the share of seats
won between 1835 and 1867. The fact that the safest Conservative ward
was the second richest must be taken in the context of an overall
correlation of only 0·3. Of the five most Liberal wards, four are to be
found at the extremes of wealth: Castle Street and St Peter's among the
first three ranked wards, Vauxhall and Scotland the bottom two.
Equally among the Conservatives, support of two-thirds or over could
be found in the upper quartile, Pitt Street and West Derby, as in the
lower, the Toxteths. Indeed, these results do not in any way undermine
the idea of a party system led by the wealthy but with large support
among men of modest means which emerges from the political narrative
discussed earlier in the book. Above all the table does not unseat the
pre-eminence of a genuine political commitment among the urban
electorate. Castle Street, the safest Liberal ward, was almost identical
in wealth to Pitt Street, the safest Conservative ward; South Toxteth,
which returned 66 per cent Conservative councillors, was almost identical

Table 16. Wealth and municipal voting in Liverpool 1835–67

Ward	*Rateable value per assessment, 1836* (i.e. total value divided by number of assessments), in pounds*	*Rank order of Conservative share of seats*
1 Castle Street	43·37	16
2 Pitt Street	41·56	1
3 St Peter's	33·72	13
4 West Derby	27·25	=6
5 Rodney Street	25·71	=8
6 Exchange	25·14	2
7 Lime Street	24·48	14
8 Great George	21·65	=3
9 Everton	21·63	=8
10 Abercromby	20·64	10
11 St Paul's	19·71	=3
12 St Anne Street	16·94	11
13 North Toxteth	16·32	5
14 South Toxteth	14·98	=6
15 Vauxhall	14·23	12
16 Scotland	12·58	15
Average whole borough	22·14	

* Source: *Rearrangement of Wards* (1879), Borough Treasurer's Report.

with Vauxhall, which returned 60 per cent Liberals. In each case two wards ranked contiguously by economic status behaved dissimilarly in politics. Municipal elections could thus confirm that the urban electorate exercised a consciously political choice.

Such evidence must be related to the data derived from parliamentary elections themselves. These elections were fought under a franchise that severely limited the number of citizens entitled to vote. While it is valid to refer to the size of the urban electorate in order to explain the necessity of organization, it is equally important to take note that between the first two Reform Acts the larger towns were electing M.P.s with no more than between about 10 and 20 per cent of the adult males enfranchised. In a number of places this may have reached 25 per cent in the mid-1860s, but even so small a proportion overstates the position because both within constituencies and in the electorate as a whole electoral registers exaggerate the number of individual voters. Multiple entries in electoral registers were common simply because it was common for men to own a place of business and a residence in the same town. Multiple entries in the burgess roll enabled citizens to vote strategically in municipal elections by choosing to vote in the ward where their support would do most good. In the parliamentary election the ban on multiple voting in the same constituency merely meant that multiple entries overstated the numbers entitled to vote. In Leeds it was estimated that up to 20 per cent should be deducted for deaths, double entries and removals to get an accurate estimate of the true electorate. Consequently all calculations based on raw data from electoral registers overstate the true position and hence turnout figures consequently understate the level of voting. Furthermore the national electorate which is sometimes calculated even more exaggerates the numbers, because in addition to the problem of multiple entries within constituencies there is the question (usually ignored) of the large numbers who voted in more than one constituency. This was obviously most common in towns where £10 householders were also separately qualified as forty-shilling freeholders and so voted in the county also. The Anti-Corn Law League campaign to manufacture votes illustrated how common this was and one supporter told Wilson 'my six borough and county votes will be given for total and immediate and no mistake'.[1] By subsuming this free trader and men like him in six separate constituencies the fact that he was one man with six votes and not six men with one vote is hidden. The number of individuals who were entitled to exercise the franchise was thus considerably less than the number of voters recorded in electoral registers.

With this in mind it will not be surprising to find that within this exclusive and shrunken electorate the opportunities for working-class participation were severely limited. The urban electorate was not then

structured for a resolution of the class war and most scholars who have
worked on mid-century elections have noticed how it acted as the setting
for a conflict for supremacy within the middle class, rather than between
the middle class and the working class.[2] Most electors did not fit easily
into either social category, since the struggle between labour and capital
was not yet the dominant economic let alone political fact of urban life.
Even by the mid-1860s, when increased wealth had enfranchised many
artisans and skilled operatives, the proportion of the electorate which
could be termed working-class was extremely low. Table 17 presents
some of the estimates made by a parliamentary return in 1866.[3]

Table 17. Proportion of electorate deemed to be working class, 1865

Town	%	Town	%
Birmingham	19	Leicester	40
Bristol	26	Liverpool	13
Bolton	21	Manchester	27
Carlisle	24	Newcastle upon Tyne	24
Halifax	10	Nottingham	39
Hull	17	Oldham	14
Ipswich	16	Sunderland	18
Leeds	7		

It is no easy matter to render statistically the wishes of this supra-
working-class electorate mainly because of the problems associated with
the two-member constituency. The modern method cannot be used
because it does not distinguish between electors who cast both their
votes and those who plumped (i.e. cast only one), nor between those
parties which contested both seats and those which contested only one.
Figures which rely upon raw data and compute share of total votes cast
are prone, therefore, to the most fundamental distortions. Less objectionable is the method of aggregating total votes cast for a party and
dividing the total by the number of candidates or the number of votes
each elector had. The main drawback is that it distorts party strength
either by overstating through adding on the votes of 'also ran' candidates
or by understating through aggregating a strong and weak candidate of
the same party, so reducing the optimum total which an individual
candidate received. The most technically competent scholar in this field,
Dr T. J. Nossiter, has devised a standardized method whereby weaker
candidates are eliminated and votes aggregated and divided by the
number of serious candidates.[4] Again the disadvantage is that where
there was a significant discrepancy between two candidates of the same
party (and this often decided who was returned to Westminster) the
result is distorted. Similarly by aggregating independent candidates

(e.g. radicals) who did not wish to fight elections within the orbit of the main parties, this standardized method assumes an electoral alliance between, for instance, Liberal and radical which did not exist. In both cases the wishes of the electorate are not faithfully mirrored in the statistics.

The question facing us is surely this: by what statistically viable method may the genuine will of the electorate be meaningfully quantified over a period of time? No method yet devised is wholly satisfactory because of the complexity of the electoral system but the method preferred here would appear to have less disadvantages than all others. It will be assumed for statistical purposes that the two-member constituency was in fact a one-member seat and the result computed as though the parties were fighting for one seat. Hence the statistical

Table 18. Percentage Conservative share of poll in large two-member constituencies 1832–80*

	1832	1835	1837	1841	1847	1852	1857
Birmingham	NC	34·75	32·78	45·61	44·85	NC	NC
Bolton	43·97	51·75	49·67	44·48	52·27	49·04	52·81
Bradford	38·21	0·00	41·09	53·12	47·85	47·71	NC
Brighton	3·54	33·45	43·06	37·67	44·09	42·65	32·16
Bristol	54·00	59·47	54·44	52·86	36·06	43·69	NC
Hull	46·05	54·45	51·43	51·14	0·00	44·69	49·34
Leeds	44·11	51·84	46·45	50·40	53·67	32·57	48·99
Leicester	43·22	52·33	44·47	NC	46·00	39·97	0·00
Liverpool	46·35	51·96	52·21	56·27	53·34	51·66	47·01
Manchester	34·80	43·04	34·85	45·74	NC	43·09	0·00
Newcastle upon Tyne	44·39	40·49	48·70	NC	43·41	42·61	40·61
Norwich	52·70	54·31	50·30	NC	41·37	42·09	42·13
Nottingham	28·92	NC	40·46	21·40	62·75	48·73	43·42
Oldham	12·98	NC	36·63	NC	0·00	0·00	0·00
Plymouth	NC	48·09	41·40	40·20	47·61	50·78	34·77
Portsmouth	0·00	46·42	44·93	NC	NC	NC	50·43
Preston	50·75	50·86	40·05	43·34	49·22	51·58	48·81
Sheffield	0·00	0·00	0·00	21·39	0·00	36·06	39·15
Stockport	55·38	45·30	50·00	37·73	46·99	43·09	37·81
Stoke	41·47	NC	59·13	41·06	46·14	45·50	60·42
Sunderland	36·00	54·35	52·28	NC	57·79	51·61	49·05
Wolverhampton	41·98	45·89	36·84	NC	NC	NC	NC

* Fraser method assuming leading Liberal against leading Conservative.

result will be the computation of an assumed contest between leading Liberal and leading Conservative. There are a number of advantages to be derived by using this method. Presumably the aim of the exercise is to quantify political strength at given elections and this method accurately pinpoints levels of support by recording the optimum strength of parties at a particular moment. Whether the total came from split votes, cross-party votes or plumpers, the figure computed gives the best the party could achieve through its strongest candidate. This method does take account of discrepancies between the number and performance of candidates and it neither underestimates nor overestimates by aggregating votes in violation of the wishes of the electorate. It is equally at home with the two-member seat up to 1867 or the three-member seat with the minority clause after 1867 and its results are not distorted by

						Nossiter	
1859	*1865*	*1868*	*1874*	*1880*	*Mean*	*mean*	
25·86	NC	36·71	NC	40·65	37·32	37·52	Birmingham
NC	51·07	52·65	50·87	48·30	49·72	50·73	Bolton
54·58	NC	0·00	46·02	38·83	36·74	†	Bradford
36·37	41·05	46·61	56·70	49·95	38·94	40·24	Brighton
48·69	0·00	43·32	49·18	46·74	44·40	43·74	Bristol
48·13	42·58	46·71	46·67	35·92	43·09	42·54	Hull
49·56	51·42	37·19	49·13	35·11	45·81	46·40	Leeds
48·29	45·87	25·88	43·11	28·17	37·94	38·53	Leicester
NC	52·35	52·23	54·74	NC	51·81	51·51	Liverpool
40·81	0·00	52·18	50·81	45·20	35·50	36·55	Manchester
0·00	0·00	27·87	52·72	33·63	34·04	34·99	Newcastle upon Tyne
47·82	44·28	50·07	48·68	44·46	47·11	47·34	Norwich
42·78	49·57	72·24	58·53	39·61	46·22	47·56	Nottingham
NC	44·83	49·90	50·55	45·80	26·74	25·08	Oldham
51·50	46·89	41·93	54·40	50·37	46·18	47·16	Plymouth
51·03	43·66	57·84	56·32	52·53	44·79	45·14	Portsmouth
56·07	NC	55·39	63·82	53·81	51·25	53·86	Preston
NC	43·51	26·28	0·00	49·01	19·58	20·85	Sheffield
43·58	44·95	50·52	48·42	47·79	45·97	47·78	Stockport
46·06	51·59	NC	47·98	29·71	46·90	50·12	Stoke
34·10	42·58	0·00	37·99	35·75	41·05	43·51	Sunderland
NC	2·81	NC	25·94	32·51	30·99	32·50	Wolverhampton

† Dr Nossiter excluded Bradford from his sample.
NC = No contest.

the number of votes an elector cast. It is contended here that this method
reflects more accurately than others the movements of political opinion
among the urban electorate across several decades. Its only disadvantage
is that it counts cross-party votes twice. This is acceptable when so often
the cross-party vote was low and in any case *all other methods share this
same disadvantage.*[5]

That this method's major disadvantage is common to all while it has
unique advantages over its rivals establishes its viability in testing the
state of the urban electorate between 1832 and 1880. Table 18 provides
the data for a number of towns on the assumption of a contest between
leading Liberal and leading Conservative. Dr Nossiter has argued that
this method evades the issue and ignores the problem; with all due respect
one might reply that it faces the issue squarely and solves the problem.
One might add the common phrase 'yer pays yer money and yer takes
yer choice.' Table 18 computes the Conservative share of poll in 22
English provincial two-member constituencies whose population was at
least 50,000 in 1851. The sample contains pre-reform constituencies and
the towns have not been restricted to the North and Midlands. To
facilitate comparison between the two methods the mean of all 12
elections as computed by the Nossiter standardized method is also given.
A number of differences emerge by the use of an alternative method of
computation.

It will be seen that in all but four cases the Nossiter mean records a
higher level of Conservative support, and this is almost certainly the
result of downgrading Liberal support somewhat by aggregating strong
and weak candidates. Liberals would suffer more by this since it was
common in towns for Liberals to put up more candidates than Conservatives. The Nossiter mean brings out the top third of the Conservative
constituencies in a somewhat different order and in the largest discrepancy records Stoke-on-Trent as a marginally Tory borough. The
efficacy of the two methods may be judged by the fact that Stoke
returned 14 Liberals and 10 Tories in the period 1832–80, a situation
more faithfully mirrored by a Liberal mean of 53·1 per cent than a Tory
mean of 50·1 per cent. A small percentage difference on the mean over
12 elections in fact hides larger discrepancies in the share of poll at
individual elections. This is important since Dr Nossiter has perceptively
argued that the true movements of political support over the towns as a
whole may be most accurately measured by working out the number of
towns falling in each decile of Conservative support. The histogram
pattern which demonstrates these movements may look very different
when constructed from data using the present alternative method. That
different conclusions may be drawn from using a different method is
illustrated finally in the calculation of swing in 131 English two-member

constituencies and the consequential computation of the standard
deviation among contested constituencies at each election. Table 19
provides the data as computed by both methods.[6] It appears from this
that Dr Nossiter's suspicion that the present method distorts by ex-
aggerating individual influences is not borne out. In fact the swing
calculated here shows opinion to be moving within a much narrower
range and the standard deviation is generally lower, though telling much
the same story. The strong 'national' movement of opinion in 1841 is
highlighted as well as the tendency towards a *national* political consciousness at the end of the period. The present method hints at the
existence of a somewhat less volatile, more disciplined political consciousness.

Table 19. Swing in English two-member boroughs, 1832–80*

	Mean swing to Conservatives		Standard deviation		No. of cases
	N	F	N	F	
1832–5	11·4	11·3	16·1	14·8	92
1835–7	− 2·2	− 1·4	14·1	14·0	92
1837–41	0·7	1·4	13·0	12·7	78
1841–7	− 4·3	− 4·0	15·5	15·9	72
1847–52	4·0	1·0	12·7	13·5	79
1852–7	− 4·9	− 2·8	16·0	15·1	76
1857–9	4·0	2·8	16·8	15·3	65
1859–65	− 0·7	0·5	15·8	15·6	69
1865–8	3·3	3·2	16·0	14·7	66
1868–74	4·3	4·0	12·2	11·5	77
1874–80	− 4·4	− 3·6	10·1	9·2	82

* F = Fraser method. N = Nossiter standardized method.

Whatever method is used, the Liberalism of the large boroughs shines
through, and only two boroughs had a mean Conservative share of poll
above 50 per cent (four on the Nossiter method). Perhaps equally
significant is the fact that half the boroughs had a Conservative share in
the 40–9 decile and in these towns the Liberals never totally swamped
their rivals. A ratio of roughly 11 : 9 in Liberal favour was not uncommon,
and such a ratio enabled Leeds Tories to win a third of the seats contested
between 1832 and 1880.

To move from such political conclusions to a social analysis of voting
involves the poll books, which can be used in two main ways. Firstly, we
may start with the poll book itself and take a sample therefrom to seek
conclusions about the electorate as a whole. This might involve listing

occupations from the poll book or tracing occupation from local direc-
tories. The great difficulty here is the classifications to be used for the
multifarious titles listed. Secondly, we may establish occupational
homogeneity first, usually from a directory, and trace the occupational
sample through the poll book. Both methods are illustrated below.

Those who have started from the poll book have devised categories for
the grouping of occupations (it would hardly seem worth while merely to
list every occupation without attempting some social classification).[7] By
aggregating the sample into broad social categories one can provide some
indication of the general social breakdown of the electorate's choice.
Table 20 gives a number of examples using this approach. This reveals a
marked tendency towards the Conservatives among the professional
groups and drink interest, and less so among manufacturers. The
tendency among craft and retail groups is towards the Liberals.

Table 20. Percentage Liberal support in designated social groups*

	Upper/ professional	*Manufacturer/ merchant*	*Craft*	*Retail*	*Drink*
Birmingham 1837	41	40	71	61	58
Leeds 1834	38	50	62	53	37
Liverpool 1841	46	38	43	41	31
Manchester 1839	48	42	47	64	36
Leicester 1847	30	64	57	51	52
Nottingham 1852	41	45	32	36	15

* These figures were kindly supplied by Dr Nossiter.

These general tendencies among broad social groups may be refined by
exhaustively analysing the votes of specific occupational groups, selected
as being typical of the general social category. To demonstrate this
method evidence is provided for Leeds from 1832 to 1841, during which
period there were five elections. The occupations include two from the
upper/professional group (doctors and lawyers), three from the manufacturing group (wool merchants, flaxspinners and engineers), and one
each from craft and retail (curriers and hatters). Because this was a
concentrated period of political involvement, with five elections in eight
and a half years, it is potentially fruitful in demonstrating a fairly
consistent relationship between occupation and voting.

Table 21 provides clear indications of Tory support among the
professional classes and Liberal support among the commercial middle
class. Only between 25 and 40 per cent of professional men voted
Liberal while at least double that did so among the leaders of the three
main staples of the Leeds economy. The hatters and curriers also

displayed a marked preference for liberal politics. Yet even in so pronounced a political predeliction the minority could usually muster a
third of the occupational group, sometimes more. Since inevitably these
minorities would produce some prominent activists, the social analysis
of urban political leadership does not produce so marked a connection
between occupation and politics. Indeed, both contemporaries and
historians have noticed that there were men of the same rank and occupation in both parties. Among political leaders there is no clear difference
in the social composition of the respective parties. This was well illustrated in 1840–1 when the Leeds town council was evenly divided between
Liberal and Tory, and a social analysis of council membership produces
the breakdown in table 22. Broadly speaking the parties were similarly
composed, with a greater inclination to the Liberals in group 2 and to
the Conservatives in group 3.

Table 21. Occupation and voting, Leeds, 1832–41

	A. MEDICAL PROFESSION				
Year	*No. in Sample*	% *Liberal*	% *Tory*	% *Split*	% *Abstained*
1832	41	30	61	2	7
1834	42	24	69	0	7
1835	44	25	64	2	9
1837	44	25	61	7	7
1841	40	40	58	2	0

	B. LEGAL PROFESSION				
Year	*No.*	% *Liberal*	% *Tory*	% *Split*	% *Abstained*
1832	47	30	38	0	32
1834	47	28	44	0	28
1835	47	28	49	0	23
1837	45	31	60	0	9
1841	50	32	60	0	8

	C. WOOLSTAPLERS AND WOOL MERCHANTS				
Year	*No.*	% *Liberal*	% *Tory*	% *Split*	% *Abstained*
1832	65	65	29	0	6
1834	67	63	34	0	3
1835	66	56	33	2	9
1837	69	45	25	2	28
1841	60	60	27	5	8

D. FLAX SPINNERS

Year	No. in Sample	% Liberal	% Tory	% Split	% Abstained
1832	23	65	22	4	9
1834	22	64	32	0	4
1835	22	68	32	0	0
1837	30	60	27	0	13
1841	38	73	24	0	3

E. ENGINEERING

Year	No.	% Liberal	% Tory	% Split	% Abstained
1832	26	62	16	11	11
1834	25	56	44	0	0
1835	25	52	40	0	8
1837	15	60	27	0	13
1841	30	77	20	0	3

F. HATTERS

Year	No.	% Liberal	% Tory	% Split	% Abstained
1832	20	55	35	5	5
1834	25	60	36	0	4
1835	25	60	36	4	0
1837	17	65	29	0	6
1841	17	53	47	0	0

G. CURRIERS

Year	No.	% Liberal	% Tory	% Split	% Abstained
1832	20	65	25	0	10
1834	23	57	43	0	0
1835	22	55	36	0	9
1837	24	55	37	4	4
1841	25	64	36	0	0

Table 22. Percentage of each party falling into occupational groups, Leeds council, 1841

	Liberal	Conservative
1 Gentry and professional	34·3	34·3
2 Merchants and manufacturers	56·3	40·7
3 Craft/retail	3·1	18·7
4 Drink/corn interests	6·3	6·3

This reference to council membership takes us back to the data on municipal voting discussed earlier in the chapter. If one is fortunate enough to have ward voting figures for parliamentary elections then the data from the two sorts of elections may be compared. In Leeds this is possible, with certain gaps. The Leeds township wards used up to 1835 cannot be compared with those afterwards and so no data for the 1832, 1834, and 1835 elections can be utilized. However, in the out-township wards comparison is possible and a full run of figures is available from 1832 to 1868. Table 23 computes share of poll in the wards of Leeds using the method of leading Liberal against leading Conservative. 1847 has not been included since the cross-party vote (51 per cent) was so high as to invalidate the calculation. The use of such evidence enables us to pinpoint variations within the constituency at one election and to discover the degree of swing in specific wards between elections. The use of the mean also enables us to establish a rank order of support on the basis of voting over three decades. This can be related to the pattern of municipal voting and the variations in wealth identified above in table 14. Table 24 brings together all three variables.

There is in fact a good correlation between parliamentary and municipal voting. It is immediately obvious at the extremes that the same four wards are the strongest for the Conservatives in both parliamentary and municipal elections, likewise the same three for the Liberals. A Spearman correlation of 0·87 demonstrates the validity of using municipal elections to add an important dimension to urban voting patterns. There is no clear correlation, however, with the wealth variable and at 0·28 the correlation between parliamentary voting and wealth is even less than the 0·4 between municipal voting and wealth. As before, however, we find that the three richest wards are among the first four ranked in order of Conservative share of poll. Yet the relationship of Mill Hill and North East for the Conservatives of Leeds, like that between Castle Street and Scotland wards for Liverpool Liberals, showed that the same party could do as well in rich as in poor areas. Wealth was no predicter of voting preference and by inference neither was social class, or so it appeared to contemporaries. When West Riding politics threatened in 1848 to become a battle between classes the Leeds radical J. G. Marshall told a Whig aristocrat, 'I should be sorry to see the Whigs entirely merged in the Conservatives. I do not like party divisions to run by classes and not by principles: all the aristocracy and landed gentry on one side, the democracy and town people on the other: or all church against all dissent. Our old party organisation was far better.'[8] By his last phrase Marshall confirmed that politics as he knew them had always been based upon differences of opinion rather than upon differences of class. While the urban electorate expressed an opinion through

Table 23. Percentage Conservative share of poll in Leeds wards, 1832–68*

	1832	1834	1835	1837	1841	1852
Mill Hill				52·14	51·82	38·40
West				45·06	50·64	32·29
North West				50·00	50·80	31·03
North				44·37	48·66	28·17
North East				52·07	57·56	30·95
East				32·14	47·57	23·68
Kirkgate				43·38	49·42	36·63
South				31·44	46·46	16·84
Hunslet	30·81	37·57	32·70	32·98	35·65	22·11
Holbeck	39·60	42·77	40·29	36·80	37·85	20·52
Bramley	42·09	50·10	54·24	49·41	51·00	35·34
Headingley	58·70	76·21	77·95	74·70	75·27	52·40

* Fraser method.

Table 24. Rank order correlation between parliamentary voting, municipal voting, and wealth, in Leeds wards

Wards in order of Conservative share of poll, 1832–68	Rank order of Conservative share of municipal seats, 1835–80	Rank order of wealth, 1841
1 Headingley	1	3
2 North East	4	12
3 Mill Hill	3	1
4 Kirkgate	2	2
5 North West	9	7
6 North	5	8
7 Bramley	7	6
8 East	6	11
9 West	8	5
10 Holbeck	12	10
11 South	11	4
12 Hunslet	10	9

the casting of votes, it also participated in a wider expression of political view in the field of political agitation. The election decided which member was returned and it is to the pressures brought to bear upon the member that we must finally turn.

1857(1)	*1857(2)*	*1859*	*1865*	*1868*	*Mean*	
46·13	53·88	52·24	54·19	49·07	49·73	Mill Hill
43·39	45·39	42·55	46·42	41·01	43·35	West
49·31	53·49	52·11	50·37	39·42	47·06	North West
55·34	49·10	52·35	55·50	41·73	46·90	North
60·33	57·06	56·80	56·65	38·23	51·20	North East
55·09	46·31	52·08	58·03	35·14	43·75	East
51·72	53·46	51·37	57·15	51·97	49·38	Kirkgate
39·79	43·53	37·84	41·23	40·31	37·18	South
44·24	44·96	42·55	40·99	37·02	36·59	Hunslet
48·44	44·68	45·93	46·25	29·49	39·32	Holbeck
46·66	42·26	50·92	51·65	41·50	46·83	Bramley
63·04	69·07	61·45	60·93	47·07	65·16	Headingley

Part Four
Political Agitation

10
The free trade movement

'Whatever pressure is to be put upon the House of Commons must come from without.' Richard Cobden to George Wilson, 24 February 1842

Political agitation, or 'pressure from without' as contemporaries called it, was a major component of nineteenth-century British political history and forms the fourth theme in this analysis of urban politics. Perhaps in some ways it represented the first stage of political commitment for a citizen since, as we have already seen, there was a marked tendency towards organization in the city and to join a political movement was often a man's first political act. Participation in a political agitation in turn motivated activities in parish, municipal or electoral politics. Yet, in terms of institutions on which the political activity focused, pressure from without was the highest level of urban politics because its aim was to convert Parliament. Where the parish politician wished to control a vestry, the municipal politician to manage a council or the party agent to return a couple of M.P.s, the political agitator wished to secure a majority in Parliament for his cause. The most striking characteristic of mid-nineteenth century political agitation was its enormous variety. Movements rose and fell for such causes as a free press, an amended Poor Law, municipal reform, temperance, public health, university reform, administrative reform, pacifism, moral reform, the abolition of slavery, co-operation, land reform, and many more. Running through this complex web of agitations were three broad strands which were not only the most prominent movements but were also akin to seed plots from which others sprouted. The three dominant issues were free trade, the suffrage, and the grievances of Dissent.[1] To some extent these three were identified with the larger cities: Manchester with free trade, Birmingham with suffrage, and Leeds with Dissent.

Free trade, which became by the second half of the century the central dogma of British economic policy, represented the economic demands of the city and of the trade and industry which sustained it. Indeed there is a close chronological relationship between the pace of urbanization and the adoption of free trade. The economic policy of the 1860s recorded as surely as the 1861 census that the majority of the British population was urban. Yet that apparently firm equation between the city and free trade which applied in the third quarter of the century was not so obvious in the first half, when it required the support of popular political agitation. In terms of general moves towards free trade policy there was a sequence of executive action (Pitt, Huskisson, Peel, Gladstone) which operated independent of any formal pressure from without. Beyond this lay the issue of the Corn Laws, which was at the heart of both the free trade ideology and the assertion of the primacy of urban interests. The Corn Laws were a symbolic denial that England had become an urban industrial society.

One of the myths created by the Anti-Corn Law League was that it introduced opinion to the evils of the Corn Laws. In fact urban opinion was aroused in 1814 and 1815 when the new Corn Law was under discussion. The anti-Corn Law feeling in these years was part of an awakening political consciousness that began in many cities in 1812. There was a continuity in political activity from the movement against the Orders in Council, through public meetings for peace, to the strong urban opposition to the 1815 Corn Law. Towns were beginning to assert the distinctive urban commercial interests threatened alike by the Orders in Council, the war and the Corn Law.

When the proposed changes were first mooted in 1814 the tone of urban opinion was set by a Leicester Tory who urged that 'every manufacturing and trading town should by petition and the general agitation of the subject' assert urban interests against those of land entrenched in Parliament. A week later the appeal was echoed by a Nottingham radical pleading, 'awake from your lethargy ye men of property in trading towns and resist this deadly blow aimed at you by the landed interest'.[2] This all-party support for urban commercial interests characterized the response of towns in 1814–15. Though there was no formal organized movement there was a remarkable continuity in the views expressed in different towns about the importance of commerce, the privileged position of the land and the need to propound vigorously the requirements of the city. The urban response to the Corn Law of 1815 was an important stage in the emergence of a distinctively urban view of both politics and society.

The war had thrown up the evidence of Britain's dependence upon industry, as the Manchester anti-Corn Law petition indicated: 'the great importance of trade and manufacture in this country has been fully evinced during the period of the late war, by enabling us to call forth resources impracticable in any state that was merely agricultural.'[3] The same idea was expressed at a Birmingham public meeting where one speaker argued that Commerce was 'the main support of the Nation on which our wealth and greatness depend', and another proudly boasted, 'England is the pride of Europe but it is not for her agriculture; her glories arise from her ships colonies and commerce'.[4] There was no party disagreement on this issue and in the light of subsequent developments it is interesting to note the enthusiastic support given by urban Tories to the anti-Corn Law movement. In 1814–15 a matter of commercial policy united all shades of political opinion in a town *versus* country, trade *versus* agriculture battle. Urban petitions were a remarkable tribute to this political unity. The Manchester petition was signed by 54,000, that from Birmingham by 48,000, and that from Nottingham by well over 18,000; and in each case these signatories represented something like half the total population of the towns concerned.[5] With opposition such as this the following contemporary comment on the League was surely apposite: 'It is absurd to say that Manchester was either the birth-place or the cradle of free trade; it can only claim the merit of reviving the demand for the repeal of an impolitic law'.[6]

Within a decade of 1815 the Corn Laws had become a shibboleth of party, and the coalition of forces against the 1815 Corn Law was permanently shattered. In the post-war years the repeal of the Corn Laws became just one demand in a developing radical programme which included parliamentary reform and Catholic emancipation. It was correspondingly more difficult to take a stand on the Corn Law question independent of the other reform issues. Increasingly Tories, even urban ones who had previously favoured free trade, found it necessary to defend the Corn Laws in the act of defending Church and constitution. Moreover on the occasions when the Corn Laws were discussed independently, as in the mid-1820s, the whole tone of anti-Corn Law sentiment had become more offensive to the landed interest. In a subtle yet significant way the battle between impersonal interests had become one between personalized classes. By 1826, when the Corn Laws figured (with the Catholic question) as an important election issue, that anti-aristocratic sentiment which characterized the League agitation was already manifest, as seen in this Nottingham election squib: 'And the Nuns and Nobs and the Tax Eaters and the Tax Gatherers with all those who fatten on the miseries of the people yea they all with one accord cried out "High Rents, Corn Laws, Dear Bread" '.[7] It was long ago contended that all the economic arguments against the Corn Laws were fully explored in the 1820s,[8] and the same was true of the social and political ones.

From the late 1820s reform of Parliament became the most pressing public issue, but the Reform Act did nothing to bring free trade nearer and so from the early 1830s the anti-Corn Law movement began to stir again. From 1833 a suburban anti-Corn Law Association in Nottingham was active and continued to operate right through until 1846.[9] It was, however, the formation of the Anti-Corn Law League which really put the fire back into the Corn Law question and from the late 1830s this issue became an overtly social and political test case. Because of this, some support the contention that the Anti-Corn Law League may have in fact delayed Corn Law repeal. The Corn Laws were not allowed to remain solely a matter of economic policy.

Nevertheless, League propaganda focused initially on the economic arguments in favour of free trade in corn. Cobden never concealed from himself that the agitation originated in what he called 'a pocket argument which pressed more urgently upon the great spinners and manufacturers of Lancashire than any other class'.[10] There is much to the argument that the League was 'profit packaged as high principle' and from 1815 onwards Manchester cotton men looked to repeal to increase exports or reduce wages or both. There was, however, another side to the economic argument that was more than mere window dressing, more than a rationalization of a selfish middle-class interest. Many of the League leaders genuinely believed that all classes would benefit from what has been termed cumulative prosperity. A man like Archibald Prentice with no economic interests of his own to serve sincerely felt that repeal would conduce to the general welfare and so was proud afterwards to have participated in a movement for the benefit of the whole community because of which 'millions who were wretched are now comfortable'.[11] The narrow and broad economic arguments could often be seen in the same man, choosing his tactics to suit the occasion. Thus Samuel Bean, chairman of the Nottingham free traders, admitted that he gave his £100 to the League confident that he would soon 'have the pleasure of regaining the sum by the abolition of the master monopoly'. As critics complained, the League funds were as much a speculative investment as any joint stock bubble. Yet on other occasions Bean adopted a high moral tone, emphasizing the philanthropic aspect and complaining that 'our enemies heap all sorts of abuse on us for our Christian endeavours to feed our fellow man who works for his living'.[12]

The moral argument also centred on the impiety of restricting to a few the bounties God had given to all. However, the real nub of the moral case for free trade lay in the international harmony it would promote. As Cobden explained to Joseph Sturge, himself a Quaker, 'The best effect of all will be that the whole civilized world will become quakers in the practice of peace and mutual forbearance'.[13] Hence it was natural for free traders to move from Corn Law repeal to pacifism and to attempt to reduce expenditure on defence. Indeed, when such a movement was being launched in 1848 Cobden asserted that he viewed 'this struggle against armaments to be the real free trade battle'.[14] Pacifism and disarmament were more than simply moral objectives, because they would weaken the power of the landed aristocracy, who found careers in the army and navy.

In one of Cobden's first public pronouncements, his pamphlet *England Ireland and America* of 1836, he previewed the idea of a naturally pacific middle class and a warlike aristocracy: 'The middle and industrious classes of England can have no interest apart from the preservation of peace. The honours the fame the emoluments of war belong not to them; the battle plain is the harvest field of the aristocracy, watered with blood of the people.'[15] Because the landed classes were so entrenched in the military establishment, the moral case for pacifism, and its corollary disarmament, took on a distinctly political hue. The middle-class moral conscience conveniently served the middle-class political cause, as a free trader explained in 1848:

> I do think the time is coming – and now is – when a fresh movement may start up and give a finishing blow to the political power of the aristocracy – Cut down the army and navy expenses 5 or 6 million and you do much more than save the money! . . . if the free traders will work it out the game is in their own hands and the time not distant when they will be the real rulers of the country.[16]

It was this ambition for bourgeois social and political predominance, underpinning all the economic and moral arguments, which transformed the anti-Corn Law campaign from a clash of opinions into a clash of social interests. At the heart of the Corn Law question lay a middle-class desire to supplant the aristocracy as the natural ruling class, as a Halifax reformer explained to Sir Charles Wood: 'The Cobden and Bright party are striving for power. Their object is to form a middle class administration in contradistinction to the aristocratic element which has hitherto predominated in the country.'[17] What more natural, in the light of this aim, than that Cobden should suggest to Peel in 1846 that he should abandon 'the juggle of parties, the mere representatives of traditions' and govern through the natural ruling class whose status was confirmed by repeal?[18] Peel rejected the idea and Cobden and Bright soon discovered that the landed classes were as powerful as ever in the social and political system.

During the campaign, however, it seemed possible that repeal would both psychologically and practically break the aristocratic hold upon power and much of the League propaganda derived from this belief. The whole anti-Corn Law campaign was, in the words of one League lecturer, no less than a struggle 'between the aristocracy and the nation – between 30,000 landowners and 26,000,000 men'.[19] A Birmingham observer placed this in historical context by arguing that this was merely a new phase of a long-standing conflict between peers and people:

> The struggle between the Oligarchy and the Nation has assumed many phases and has been shifted from one ground to another as the pressure of class legislation varied but never yet had the people a fairer battle-field than on the question of the Corn Laws . . . as they have clustered round the Corn Laws for defence let us join to assail that position for the recovery of our rights.'[20]

The image of the Corn Laws as a fence built around the whole social and political system caught on among both opponents and defenders of protection. That the real object, the attack upon aristocratic rule, lay beyond the Corn Laws was explicit: 'The Corn Law is the outwork of the citadel of corruption and if we can bombard this outwork until we gain admission we shall then plant the banner of rational liberty upon the ruins of the despotism of the aristocracy.'[21] In such circumstances the need to protect the Corn Laws in defending the existing constitution, already clear in the 1820s, became exaggerated in the 1840s. The League became in Tory eyes a giant conspiracy against Church and State and therefore it was commonly held that 'he who is not friendly to the Corn Laws is an enemy to the altar and the throne'.[22] The close identification between Dissent and the League, confirmed by the meeting of ministers of religion in 1841, induced urban Tories to see the free trade movement as 'nothing more than one of the Protean forms which Dissent assumes in its warfare against Church and Throne'. Although there was no urban agitation in favour of the Corn Laws, all towns had a vociferous Tory minority which believed that the League was, in the words of a Birmingham editor, 'a conspiracy banded together for the destruction of British Agriculture, of Property, the rights of the Landed Aristocracy, the Church, the Throne and the Constitution'.[23] It was such a view which induced urban commercial Tories to put the political battle against Liberalism above their own economic interests which might be served by free trade. As Samuel Smiles said of the Leeds manufacturers who supported protection, 'they can only see the corn law question through the medium of party'.[24]

This political division of the urban middle class explains why the League could never speak for the city as a whole, not even in Manchester. Many, even among free traders, did not share the anti-aristocratic sentiment of Cobden and Bright. The mother of a leading Liverpool free trader could clearly see 'the desirability for the nation to put its aristocracy to good use and employ them in the only work they can do', while the Gregs, among the élite manufacturing families of Manchester, asserted quite simply 'our legitimate rulers are the landed "swells".'[25] The tensions within Manchester Liberalism which were to wreck the Manchester School in 1857 (see above, p. 206) were already present during the life of the League and these can be clearly identified in the relationship of the League and the Manchester Chamber of Commerce, which also illustrates how a non-political institution could be politicized by an extra-parliamentary movement.

The Chamber of Commerce provided a politically divided Manchester middle class with a non-partisan forum for the expression of commercial views. The Chamber had in 1830 petitioned in favour of total free trade but during the following years had not been a notable advocate of general principles.[26] In December 1838 J. B. Smith was able to stir up enough enthusiasm among the members to persuade them to adopt Cobden's 'total and immediate' petition in preference to the low-duty petition the Chamber had previously agreed. This was the first stage of an assault upon the Chamber by the free traders, who went a stage further by securing the election of J. B. Smith as president in February 1839. The previous president, G. W. Wood, M.P. for Kendal, had made the free traders something of a laughing stock in Parliament and Parkes strongly advised Cobden to get rid of him or 'he will at such a crisis of the Question, be always emptying his slops over you.'[27] Many resented what was seen as the politicizing of a non-political institution* and beyond the Corn Law question lay the general local political battle in Manchester. The liberal capture of the Chamber of Commerce in 1839 was one aspect of a total victory in which vestry, police commission and council came into Liberal control.

In 1845, a more serious version of this episode occurred which led to the formation of a rival commercial association. The League suffered a great blow by its defeat in the 1844 South Lancashire election which was much commented on elsewhere. A Nottingham observer pointedly asked the League leaders 'what hopes they have of success . . . if their own division . . . cannot return a member in favour of free trade'.[28] That the victorious M.P. was a Manchester Tory, William Entwistle, was bad enough; that the chairman of his committee, Richard Birley, was a director of the Chamber of Commerce once more put the free trade commitment of that body into doubt. J. B. Smith, with Cobden's strong support, organized a purge of the directors and Birley failed to get re-elected at the 1845 annual meeting. As one free trader explained, 'Mr.

* Cf. *Manchester Guardian*, 13 February 1839, on why the Chamber should not become 'anything like a political union' and its pride that 'hitherto there has been a scrupulous desire to keep the chamber clear of party politics'.

Birley appears in talent and deportment every way *but one* well qualified to be a director', and that one flaw was, in Cobden's words, his opposition 'to the immediate practical application of the principles of Free Trade to which the majority of the chamber was pledged'.[29] The relatively unimportant fact that a certain gentleman did not secure re-election as director of Manchester's Chamber of Commerce became a major issue in the town's politics. The easy victory of 1839 was not repeated.

Though constitutionally directors could be elected only at the annual general meeting Birley's supporters rallied to call a special meeting to review the election, and a full scale battle was joined. Many of the elements of political division which we have already noticed in the decade after repeal were visible in 1845. There was the radical-Conservative confrontation, the questionable role of a political machine, the resentment caused by a failure to offer due homage to a natural social leader and the opposition by a Liberal *Guardian* to Manchester Liberals. This last facet was most significant, confirming once again the need for a League journal in the town which would not be, like the *Guardian*, 'always ready at a pinch to throw us over and play into the hands of the Tories'.[30]

If in one sense the 1845 Chamber of Commerce crisis was a preview of the next decade's political developments in Manchester, in another it was a miniature version of the whole anti-Corn Law question with its intermingling of economic and political issues. The politicizing of the Chamber of Commerce meant that it could not state its views solely in economic terms, just as the politicizing of the Corn Law problem meant that it could not be resolved solely by economic policy. The 1845 annual meeting and the supplementary attempt to reverse its decisions polarized political opinion in Manchester so that the protagonists became rivals on economic issues on which there had been a measure of agreement. Few Tory manufacturers were outright protectionists and many of Birley's sympathisers simply did not support the League's full demand for total and immediate repeal. J. B. Smith later referred to the anti-League forces as simply 'half and half free traders'. Yet at the time the challenge to the League on its own doorstep was so profound that it became in Cobden's propaganda a final battle between outright opponents. Cobden advised Smith: 'you ought not to compromise in any the slightest degree with the people who are calling the chamber together. If you yield it will be a voluntary submission to the enemy of free trade – for disguise it as they may it is nothing but a battle between Free Trade and monopoly.'[31] For such a battle the whole League machinery was required and it was only with careful preliminary arrangements that the League carried the second meeting. Even then this was something of a pyrrhic victory for, as the *Guardian* explained, the Chamber as a mere committee of the

League 'would not be a great fact, nor a little fact, nor a fact at all, but a mere sham, a pretext a make believe without a single atom of force influence credit or reality'.[32] The consequent formation of a commercial association as a rival to the Chamber was evidence of the division in the Manchester mercantile community as the League's hour of victory approached.

The limits on the League achievement outside Manchester lay in the difficulties of converting the Manchester question into a national question, as illustrated in the anti-Corn Law movements of Birmingham and Leeds. In Birmingham there were two fundamental obstacles to be surmounted; these were the town's commitment to currency reform, and its association with the suffrage movement. Attwood's currency notions had a firm hold upon Birmingham opinion and motivated his own political actions. The formation of the Birmingham Political Union and its revival, the support for the Reform Bill and later the People's Charter, all derived from a belief that Britain's problems were fundamentally financial and would be solved by a managed paper currency. In the 1830s Birmingham opinion was imbued with an unchallengeable moral certitude on this issue: 'We are decidedly of the opinion that without an alteration in the currency laws it is impossible that anything like permanent prosperity can be restored to England. We are so convinced of this that we look upon such an alteration as the end of all legislative improvement.'[33] Attwood's successor, G. F. Muntz, carried on this almost religious belief in currency reform and his reply to criticisms from the *Anti-Corn Law Circular* appeared as an editorial in the *Birmingham Journal* because 'the answer of the Birmingham men is contained in it'.[34] Muntz published a series of letters to show that Corn Law repeal could not be considered independently of the currency question.[35] To Birmingham, at least until 1841, free trade was something of an irrelevance.

The logic of currency reform took Birmingham Liberals towards Chartism. The leading political agitators in the town, Attwood, R. K. Douglas, T. C. Salt, Benjamin Hadley and P. H. Muntz, were closely identified with the initiation of the Chartist movement through the launching of the National Petition. Temporarily in 1838–9 Birmingham was at the very centre of the suffrage reform movement and resisted the intrusion of repeal. When Joseph Sturge was attempting to launch an anti-Corn Law association in the winter of 1838–9 Birmingham had committed itself to Chartism. A. W. Paulton gave two lectures at the end of November 1838 which were both taken over by Chartists, and at the second the motion to form an association was overwhelmingly defeated. This victory by what Sturge called the 'ultra political party' forced him to form the association in private and, when the first public meeting was called, he reported to Manchester, 'the Chartists still mean to oppose us and I should not be surprised at their outvoting us'.[36] His fears were justified and the usual Chartist amendment to the petition was carried amid fierce condemnation of what Salt called 'a worse than foolish, fraudulent appeal'.[37] A petition was eventually sent and delegations including the veteran of Birmingham radicalism, George Edmonds, attended League meetings, but the Birmingham association was almost still-born, a sickly child unable to compete with the lusty infant of Chartism.

In the two years from the spring of 1839 there was much evidence of apathy on the Corn Law question in Birmingham, symbolized by the election in 1840 of Muntz, the currency reformer, in preference to Sturge the free trader. Interest revived in the spring of 1841 and although the Chartists once more took over a free trade meeting in May this in fact ushered in a period of activity which saw the rebirth of the Anti-Corn Law Association in August 1841.[38] This was the result of the efforts of working men and non-electors, for even Sturge, left to pay off the debts of the original association, only became involved once the new body had been launched. Cobden noticed that the active members were all working men and William Scholefield, Birmingham's first mayor, confirmed that the 'association owes its origin entirely to the exertions and public spirit of the working classes and . . . they are almost exclusively its only members'.[39] For several months great activity and enthusiasm were in evidence and it appeared that the League cause was putting down strong roots. Then Sturge's resignation from the free trade movement and his launching of the Complete Suffrage Union took away the life-blood of the Birmingham Anti-Corn Law Association. Large numbers of free traders followed Sturge in 1842 in his efforts to foster class co-operation. In 1839 Birmingham's connection with suffrage reform took away potential leaders, in 1842 it drew off the rank and file.

When forces were regrouped in 1842–3 and 1843–4 for the League funds and the registration activity, the working-class presence was less prominent and the majority of members were shopkeepers and manufacturers. Birmingham made only a modest contribution to the £50,000 fund and though the next appeal produced a better response, inducing Bright to remark 'Birmingham seems more reasonable than on former occasions',[40] the town could never be counted on for massive contributions. As Charles Geach, a banker and leading free trader, explained, Birmingham's economic structure was not in the hands of 'a few capitalists' and of the £4,600 collected for all three League appeals only seven contributions were over £200. Joshua Scholefield certainly had a point when he said that Birmingham people had been very tardy in coming forward in support of the League.[41]

Leeds was much more active than Birmingham in the early stages, yet here also the League was never totally satisfied. Initially the contrast between Leeds and Birmingham was very marked since the repealers were able to fight off a Chartist challenge at their first meeting in January 1839, despite O'Connor's claim to the contrary.[42] An association was formed with the wealthy flaxspinner J. G. Marshall as president, high-powered delegations attended conferences in London and Manchester, and the services of a paid lecturer were employed. The lecturer, George Greig, a registrar under the Poor Law, carried the torch of the Leeds repealers into the surrounding districts, covering the area from Doncaster to Sunderland. Not everyone liked Greig's approach and one free trader complained 'he speaks too much to the passions of his audience and too little in the way of reasoning'. Yet his commitment could not be doubted and the Leeds free traders felt that his energetic advocacy was just what was required in London. The Leeds association offered, at their own expense, to send Greig to London as a full-time League worker in the belief that 'a pistol discharged in the Metropolis would produce as great an effect as a cannon here'.[43]

Greig's departure in the spring of 1840 marked the end of an encouraging first phase of League activity in Leeds. Thereafter the town fell away badly in the League's opinion. In the summer of 1840 prominent free traders, including the brothers James and Henry Marshall, Hamer Stansfeld, George Goodman and the radical editor Samuel Smiles, launched the so-called 'Leeds new move' aiming at household suffrage, a precursor of Sturge's movement two years later (see below, p. 260). The free trade movement was shattered in Leeds and anti-Corn Law meetings were easy prey for the Chartists in both spring and autumn of 1841, in marked contrast to January and December 1839 when the repealers were demonstrably masters in their own house.[44] When some of the suffrage deserters meekly returned to the free trade fold they looked not to total and immediate repeal but to a generalized free trade movement or even the Whig moderate fixed duty. To both of these Cobden was hostile. He told Baines, 'we have done our duty in eschewing Chartism – Toryism – Household Suffrageism – and now we are determined to resist ministerialism' and warned Smiles that linking corn with other duties 'will be a virtual secession from the League'.[45] The 18 months from the spring of 1840 were a grave disappointment for the League and in October 1841 Cobden could find little to applaud in either Leeds or Birmingham. He told Smiles that Leeds had had greater potential than Manchester at the outset and had made bad use of its advantages and despondently remarked to George Wilson, 'Leeds ran away after a political *ignis* fatuous . . . Birmingham has never had a lucid moment yet.'[46] The protectionist hold on Leeds seemed to be confirmed by the council's refusal to receive a letter from Wilson in April 1841 and the election of the Tory William Beckett in July.

The rehabilitation of Leeds in Manchester eyes began in 1842 and in February the Anti-Corn Law Association held the line against Chartist intervention at a public meeting. The public meetings in December in support of the £50,000 appeal were splendid occasions with the Liberals once more fully united. The only shadow across the proceedings was the disappointing total achieved, £1,350 – little more than the amount recorded at Huddersfield – which caused Cobden to commiserate with Baines, 'we are obliged to you for the energetic appeals in your paper. It is not your fault if the Leeds people do not contribute all that we would wish'.[47] Smiles blamed the poor response on the Toryism of so many Leeds manufacturers. In Birmingham the economic structure depressed the financial contributions; in Leeds it was the political structure. In 1843 the League outlook brightened somewhat in the town. Baines in the *Leeds Mercury* kept up a barrage of propaganda some of which the League circulated, including a quarter of a million copies of his letters to Russell.[48] The Leeds response to the £100,000 appeal was much more encouraging than that of the previous year and nearly £4,000 was subscribed. Moreover, Leeds organized county and delegate meetings early in 1844 and Thomas Plint, the secretary of the association, lectured throughout the West Riding.

When the campaign neared its climax coincidences in both Leeds and Birmingham gave to those towns a prominence in the free trade movement during 1845–6 which their earlier activities hardly merited. In Birmingham there had long been plans to hold a public dinner to C. P. Villiers, M.P. for neighbouring Wolverhampton, which was organized during the summer and booked for November 1845. All the main League leaders attended one of the most splendid public occasions the town had seen and, more important, the dinner coincided with the rumours of potato blight in Ireland. Thus Birmingham by accident found itself at the head of the free trade movement for, as Prentice later claimed, the dinner 'gave a tone to public opinion everywhere' and one of the London papers rejoiced 'to see Birmingham once more taking its old place in the front ranks of the cause of rational and practical reform'.[49]

An even more significant coincidence in the following month placed Leeds in the forefront. The death of Lord Wharncliffe in December 1845, with the consequent elevation to the peerage of one of the West Riding's M.P.s, created a parliamentary vacancy at a crucial time. The League-sponsored registration campaign was already yielding great gains on the register and in November Baines had been the intermediary between the free traders and Lord Morpeth in his conversion to total and immediate repeal. Once Morpeth had come out in full support of the League case there was a widespread desire that he should go straight into Parliament and Mark Philips offered to resign to create a vacancy at Manchester.[50]

It was more appropriate that Morpeth should resume the seat in the West Riding that he had lost in 1841 and, since Baines had skilfully married the League invasion with traditional social leadership in the county, Wharncliffe's death could not have been more timely for the free traders. Cobden commented; 'if we had had the cap of Fortunatus for a moment that is what we would have wished'; and Baines confirmed that 'our meeting and election will tell at this juncture'.[51] The town and county meetings organized by Leeds, together with Morpeth's un-contested return in February 1846, took much of the limelight away from Lancashire. Indeed Morpeth's election, resting as it did on the in-vincibility of a free trade register, was the League's greatest electoral success, a fact partially concealed by Morpeth's uncontested return twice in 1846 and again in 1847.

In those years the free trade achievement was identified with an agitational partnership between Yorkshire and Lancashire. The return of Cobden for the West Riding and Villiers for South Lancashire in 1847 was an association of the two greatest parliamentary free traders with the two greatest industrial counties. This was intended as a stroke of propaganda on behalf of free trade and George Wilson, with John Brooks, the organizer of this twin thrust, wrote before the election, 'Mr Villiers for South Lancashire and Mr Cobden for the West Riding would speak to the empire and to the world as the irreversible verdict of the British people against the delusions and oppression of monopoly'.[52] More than a confirmation of an economic policy, the dual elections were part of the underlying aim of the League to give to the men of Lancashire and Yorkshire their due political weight. Cobden warned in Leeds, 'Sir Robert Peel will govern through Lancashire and Yorkshire or he will not govern at all. . . . We are going to assert the right of the great mass of the middle and industrious population to the influence which they are entitled to in the government of the country.'[53]

Nobody saw more clearly than Cobden in the later 1840s that Corn Law repeal of itself was not enough to give the middle class real political power. The dilemma facing the free traders was by what route they should enter the political kingdom. By 1848 Bright was attempting to revive the League in order to launch a new movement for suffrage reform, about which Cobden had severe reservations. Such doubts were strengthened when Cobden was warned by a former ally that his troops would march behind practical but not organic reform. W. R. Greg's letter is worth quoting since it exposes the real problems facing urban agitators in 1848:

I have had much conversation of late with many who went heart and hand with you in the League struggle and laboured diligently in their

small and humble way for the success of that good cause . . . and I
have found them almost unanimous in condemning the peculiar time
and objects chosen for the new agitation. . . . They think it far wiser to
work with the tools we have than to spend years of contest in obtaining
new tools, when our *real work* would still have to be done . . . a large
portion of the middle classes will oppose you steadily and to the last
on questions involving any radical remodelling of our representative
system . . . you will be able to obtain all the *practical* reforms you
wish for far sooner than the organic reforms which the Chartists say
are necessary preliminaries.[54]

Cobden would certainly have agreed with Greg's suggestion that the real
middle-class benefits were to be found in retrenchment, in taxation
reform and in a pacific foreign policy. These practical reforms were
indeed dear to Cobden's heart.

The problem was that none of these could arouse real public support.
Birmingham launched an association for financial reform, especially to
promote direct taxation, but it did not prosper. Liverpool had a more
successful body, the Financial Reform Association, which, though long
lived, never sparked widespread enthusiasm even in Liverpool. Cobden
addressed his 'National Budget' to the Liverpool group in 1849 which
might have injected some life, but the following year one of its members
reported 'the progress of our association here is but indifferent – there
are only 3 or 4 who take any active part'.[55] Retrenchment, especially in
defence expenditure, served both the free traders' political and moral
objectives. It was still unable to counteract the drowsiness of political
movements in the mid-Victorian years. When opinion was aroused it
was in favour of Palmerstonian chauvinism to which the Manchester
School was hostile. The logic was inescapable: practical reform would
have to be replaced by organic reform.

Immediately after the defeat of 1857 Cobden, perhaps a little gingerly,
committed himself to parliamentary reform, with which he had been in
sympathy for some time. He wrote to Sturge;

Though I am aware that the people require education to make them
the safe depositaries of political power yet I have always felt we have
a greater security when the government is under the control of the
whole people which we never can have when it is at the mercy of the
privileged classes . . . I have therefore always felt inclined to take my
chances with the millions.[56]

Cobden already had ample evidence that many middle-class Liberals
would not take a chance with the millions and he knew that the
Manchester School had to find new homes as well as new causes.

Manchester, he predicted, 'will not in our time become the headquarters of another great movement of any kind'. Birmingham, on the other hand, having rescued Bright would provide him with 'a more suitable political home than the one he has lost'.[57] It appeared to Cobden, the leading urban political agitator of his day, that in the field of pressure from without Manchester and free trade was giving way to Birmingham and the suffrage.

11
Suffrage reform

'What does Parliament ever do of its own accord? Every good measure is carried in the country first and in Parliament afterwards. . . . If the people want to carry a Reform Bill they must not look to Parliament but themselves.'
Ernest Jones, August 1866

In the century and a half following the loss of the American colonies the suffrage question was a key issue in English politics. A broad swathe of history links the days of Wilkes to those of the suffragettes, as England painfully resolved the question of how Parliament should be elected. The process of industrialization sharpened the suffrage issue by creating an imbalance between the social and the political structure. The dominance of landed wealth in early-eighteenth-century society was faithfully mirrored in a political system run by landed gentlemen. A century later the hold of the landed classes upon political power was scarcely less sure, yet urbanization and industrialization were increasingly calling the dominance of land into question. The bourgeois challenge focused, as we saw in the previous chapter, upon free trade, but both before and after 1846 many middle-class reformers recognized that parliamentary reform was an essential ingredient in the battle against the dominance of land. The wider working-class faith in parliamentary reform derived from the belief that only a democratization of the political system could ensure justice to the people. There was always an essential cleavage of aim between middle- and working-class reformers. Middle-class Liberals put much greater faith in the distribution of seats, whereas working-class radicals looked to the direct representation of the population through an extension of the suffrage itself.

The growing political consciousness of towns in the early nineteenth century was much stimulated by popular support for parliamentary reform. Before the end of the war there had been considerable propaganda in favour of reform which emanated from the newly founded Liberal newspapers such as the *Nottingham Review* begun in 1808, the *Leicester Chronicle* in 1810 and the *Midland Chronicle*, founded in Birmingham in 1811. These journals and others took the line that reform was 'the only change from which the people can hope for an alleviation of their miseries'.[1] This view was strengthened when peace brought no relief to suffering, and in the post-war years intermittent reform agitation was the source of a great deal of political activity, including public meetings, petitions, political clubs, and printed propaganda.

The beginning of 1817 saw a peak of political agitation for reform in urban areas of the North and Midlands, and in Birmingham the events of January and February were described by a local chronicler as 'the first act of our great political agitation'.[2] Appropriately enough Birmingham's first great reform demonstration was held on Newhall Hill, the scene of many of Attwood's later triumphs. The excitement was not sustained but in 1819 it reached a new pitch. The earlier hints of radical opinion, tapped by J. Orton Smith in his *Midland Chronicle* (1811–14), and by his brother W. Hawkes Smith in his *Birmingham Inspector* (1817), were exploited to the full by the press and public propaganda of George Edmonds. It was he who conceived the idea in 1819 that Birmingham was entitled to elect an M.P., basing the case for the people of Birmingham upon what they contributed towards public expenditure: 'They are compelled by the House of Commons to give a great proportion of the fruits of their labour to carry on unjust cruel and expensive Wars abroad . . . while at home they are *compelled* to support an establishment of Placemen, Pensioners and Sinecurists; and to pay every year their proportion towards the interest of a debt of many hundred millions of pounds.'[3] The election of Sir Charles Wolseley as 'legislatorial attorney and representative' for Birmingham played a major part in the build-up to Peterloo, for the authorities wished to prevent a similar election in Manchester.

By the 1820s these two towns and Leeds were alive to the necessity of representation of their interests, three great witnesses to the obsolescence of the electoral system. During the milder economic climate, which in the 1820s damped down the reform movement, the possibilities of suffrage reform were limited to piecemeal proposals for the representation of the unenfranchized large towns. The Grampound seats, destined under Russell's proposals for Leeds, were in the event given to Yorkshire for fear of creating a precedent, in 1821. When Penryn dangled invitingly before Manchester in 1827 it promoted an unusual alliance of political opinion in the town. As Prentice remarked, it was bizarre to find H. H. Birley, villain of Peterloo, proposing a petition for a measure of parliamentary reform at a Manchester public meeting.[4] Manchester's seats proved chimerical as did those of East Retford for Birmingham in 1828,

when local Tories, like their northern counterparts, supported reform.
That the town was not yet a full-hearted parliamentary reform stronghold was evidenced by the equanimity with which the reversal of the
town's hopes was greeted:

> so far as the interests of this town are concerned, we consider the
> refusal of the privilege of elective franchise not to be regretted. The
> advantages to be derived from sending representatives to Parliament
> are merely theoretical, and the elections would on the other hand be
> most certainly attended with much disorder and debauchery, which
> would keep the town in a state of uproar, perhaps for weeks and be
> the means of relighting the torch of faction and increasing the spirit
> of party and disunion.[5]

The depression at the end of the 1820s finally convinced Birmingham
opinion that the advantages of representation were practical and that
the potential benefits were worth the risk of divisive elections. The
formation of the Birmingham Political Union provided Birmingham with
a quite novel political machine. The B.P.U. was the very hub of
Birmingham politics in the early 1830s. Its role in the Reform Bill crisis
has been frequently explained; in addition it organized political activity
right across the board in local affairs. Men united by a faith in parliamentary reform operated as a group on many other issues in local politics.
It was the main B.P.U. leaders who were most active on behalf of
Dissenters in the celebrated Birmingham Grammar School case of 1830,
when it was proposed that only Anglicans could become governors.
Attwood, Parkes, Edmonds, Hadley, Salt, Muntz, and Scholefield, the
nucleus of the B.P.U. leadership, were active members of the committee
to oppose the controversial bill proposed by the governors.[6] Two years
later the B.P.U. officially entered Salt as a candidate for the office of
churchwarden and in 1832 and 1833 the organization was closely involved
in the church rates struggle (see above, pp. 43–4). The B.P.U. called
many public meetings on the reform issue and its activities sustained the
parliamentary reform movement both locally and nationally. The
primacy of suffrage reform did not exclude other issues of the day and the
B.P.U. organized meetings on a large number of questions, including
currency reform, Ireland, taxes on knowledge, the high bailiff's expenses,
county elections and Poland.[7] The B.P.U. also organized the registration
and Liberal campaign for the town's first election. In short the
Birmingham Political Union, primarily an organ of parliamentary
reform, operated as a focus of town politics overall.

Part of the B.P.U.'s success in so doing depended on the loose social
structure of the town which made possible a union of middle- and working-
class reformers. Elsewhere middle-class parliamentary reformers were

not able to adopt so all-embracing a role, although similar tendencies can be detected, as witnessed in Leeds. There were interesting differences of approach between reformers in the two towns. The Birmingham Political Union deliberately sought publicity and wished for overt acknowledgement of its leading political role; the Leeds Association, run by Baines senior, shunned publicity despite the obvious outlet in the *Leeds Mercury*. The Leeds Association was formed in December 1830 out of the temporary committee which had secured the election of Brougham in the county.[8] Its aim was to return Liberal members and to promote a variety of Liberal causes, the most prominent of which was parliamentary reform. Like the B.P.U., the Leeds Association promoted many meetings but it did so in private and its role in organizing political activity was never publicized. Town and county reform meetings were never meetings of the Association, which acted only as a private prime mover generating the initial spark of political involvement. When, towards the end of 1831, it became clear that the moderate Baines line could not hold local opinion together, then the Association found it necessary to have a popular organization that would operate publicly. Significantly, the Leeds Association did not adopt this role itself but instead it promoted the formation of the Leeds Political Union led by Joshua Bower, which sought to unite middle- and working-class reformers behind the Reform Bill. Its great rival, the Leeds Radical Political Union, rejected the Reform Bill as a delusion and remained faithful to universal suffrage, the ballot and shorter parliaments.[9]

The Whig-radical cleavage, manifest in the reform organizations, became part of the struggle over the factory question which dominated the first Leeds election. Thereafter it emerged in the full light of day as the limitations of the Reform Act became clear. Within a year of the days of May 1832, Attwood was once more leading the crowds on Newhall Hill in an attempt to make the Whig ministry put the Reform Act into effect.[10] Within a year of the parliamentary reformers' victory in the 1832 election, Leeds radicals were already breaking ranks on the need for further reform. Joshua Bower, an ally of Baines in 1831–2, became his enemy in 1833–4, and the radical forces which had supported Sadler in 1832 fell in behind Bower in 1834.[11] In most towns by the mid-1830s the suffrage reform issue had spread its fissiparous tentacles into the heart of urban liberalism. For over three decades it was to be the shibboleth which divided Liberals most. The divisions, persisting throughout the first half of Victoria's reign, between radical and moderate Liberals centred above all upon suffrage reform.

Early Victorian suffrage reformers saw their most promising opportunity in Chartism. This complex movement emerged from a number of economic, social and political antecedents. Its main economic origins lay in the process of industrialization itself, in the fluctuations of the economy and in the suppression of trade unionism, particularly in the Glasgow cotton spinners' case. Its social inheritance came mainly through the anti-Poor Law movement with its rejection of the values of the new society implicit in the 1834 Act. It was through hostility to the new Poor Law that Chartism gained its first mass army and its major demagogue, O'Connor. Its political heritage derived from the uncluttered political radicalism dating back to the late eighteenth century which had always emphasized the primacy of political democracy. This philosophical political radicalism was most recently sustained by Lovett and the London Working Men's Association. The tributary by which different groups flowed into the mainstream of Chartism determined subsequent attitudes and contributed to the tension within the movement. Its social composition was variegated and, though the first major expression of working-class consciousness, it contained many non-proletarian elements. The People's Charter was all things to all men and so it brought together in one movement a cross-section of society from bankers and solicitors to depressed handloom weavers. In general, Chartism comprised four main social groups; middle-class sympathizers, artisan and shopkeeper radicals, factory operatives and depressed handworkers. The first two groups were primarily motivated by political commitment, the third by economic fluctuation and the last by desperation.[12]

The one thing that most Chartists had in common was that they lacked the vote, separated from the parliamentary constitution by the Reform Act itself. Peel had argued, as soon as Russell revealed his proposals in March 1831, that their major defect was that they severed all connections between Parliament and all those above pauperism but below the arbitrary line of £10. Perhaps speciously, he argued that under the old system this class had been represented through the handful of seats with a wide franchise, but in the new they would be deliberately set beyond the pale of the constitution.[13] In more sophisticated terms Dr Gatrell has similarly commented with reference to Manchester,

> the distinction between electorate and non-electorate was . . . the institutionalised and legally sanctioned expression of every other form of social and economic division within the town. No statute asserted less equivocally the correlation of property with power than the Reform Act; no act . . . purported more categorically to assort men into two distinct groups or to define the areas of political action each could legitimately inhabit.[14]

The Reform Act made the division between Commons and people and on the whole the latter accepted the primacy of the former and attempted to gain access to this political kingdom rather than replace the whole system. It is true that there were tendencies in the 1830s which suggest that an alternative to parliamentary government was contemplated. One of the major criticisms of the political unions was that they were self-constituted political clubs, local parliaments in every town. During its revolutionary phase in the mid-1830s trade unionism flirted with the idea of a rival authority to Parliament and the Grand National Consolidated Trades Union was partly an alternative focus of power constructed upon a non-parliamentary political base. The National Convention was deliberately set up as a parallel Parliament and its M.C.s were overt rivals to the real Parliament's M.P.s. Yet all three, political unions, G.N.C.T.U. and the Convention, were but means of bringing pressure to bear upon Parliament and implicit in all of them was some recognition of the supremacy of parliamentary authority at least in practice.[15] The People's Charter was an unequivocal statement of the essentially constitutional nature of the suffrage reform movement, the National Petition a confirmation of the faith in lawful methods of protest. Perhaps naïvely, Chartists believed that if their petition had enough signatures Parliament would acknowledge the justice of their claims. Even the ulterior measures were tactical ploys in the battle to persuade Parliament to admit wider participation in its constitution. Harsh economic circumstances, especially in 1839, 1842, and 1848, did lead to desperate actions yet many, even among so-called physical force Chartists, among them O'Connor, were merely hoping to stampede Parliament into giving way. Those who wished to overthrow Parliament forcibly and create a new, perhaps republican, system were never more than a fringe minority.

Chartist activities grew out of an acceptance that Parliament had to be persuaded rather than destroyed. The main Chartist tools – public meetings, conventions, delegations, petitions and marches – were intended as evidence of overwhelming support for the Chartist cause. The less boisterous variations, Chartist chapels, teetotal Chartism, Chartist adult education, were intended to convince the 'ins' that the 'outs' were entitled to the vote by their moral respectability. This could also be demonstrated by participation in local politics. It was in towns that Chartists were most active and the urban political structure provided opportunities in a variety of local institutions. In Leeds, perhaps more than elsewhere, there was a real effort to make the Charter live in a local context and Leeds municipal Chartism is worthy of a second look.*

* J. F. C. Harrison, 'Chartism in Leeds', in A. Briggs (ed.), *Chartist Studies* (1962), 65–98, was a valuable pioneering study but is marred by errors and omissions. Professor Harrison appears to have made selective use of the sources. There are errors on the improvement commission; he fails to mention Chartist participation in the Improvement Bills, in the Poor Law and in the board of surveyors of highways; his remarks on the consistency, unity, and parsimony of Chartist councillors are highly misleading.

Leeds Chartists derived much from local political tradition. Finding themselves proscribed citizens they imitated their Liberal Dissenting predecessors by establishing a power base in parochial and township affairs. Their first concerted effort was in January 1840 in the election for improvement commissioners when they were frustrated by a legal decision.* In the following year they shared power with Liberals and in 1842 gained full control, attempting to amend the Improvement Act in the Chartist image (see above, p. 94). In 1842 it was the Chartists who inherited the office of churchwarden, a Liberal monopoly since the 1820s, and for five years they ran parish affairs until defeated by Tories in 1847 (see above, p. 36). Having lost the improvement powers to the council in 1842, the Chartists found in the board of surveyors of highways a new area of local power and minor patronage. From 1843 until well beyond the demise of Chartism, Chartist surveyors were elected and it was this office which gave Robert Meek Carter his first taste of political power (see above, p. 106). When the board of guardians was established in December 1844, right in the middle of the upsurge of municipal Chartism, it was natural for Chartists to become guardians. Three did so in 1844 and 1845 and no less than ten stood in the 1846 election although only one was elected.[16] In Leeds in the 1840s Chartists acted as improvement commissioners, churchwardens, highway surveyors and guardians: here was an all-embracing attempt to make the People's Charter live. The vision of participation by 'the people' became a reality in urban administration and if poor men could run local government surely they should vote.

Of course, Leeds Chartists were not necessarily poor men. To have participated in these township offices they had to be rated at £30 or £40, well above the 1832 parliamentary qualification, and some of those who became Chartist councillors were able to swear that they possessed £1,000 in real property.[17] It was the council which had most local power and for a decade from 1842 Chartists either individually or as a body participated in municipal elections. The notion of using the council to advance the cause of parliamentary reform did not originate with Chartists themselves. As early as 1838 a local radical advised working men to choose their own candidates and 'make the Municipal Council of Leeds in miniature what we want the Commons House of Parliament to be'.[18] In that year John Jackson stood unsuccessfully on such a platform and the case of Jackson exposes the difficulty of the Chartist designation in Leeds municipal politics. Professor Harrison mentions Jackson as a Chartist in 1840 yet omits his candidature in 1842, while including him as a Chartist in 1843. Similarly Thomas White is claimed as a Chartist in

* J. T. Ward, *Chartism* (1973), 175, citing Harrison, understandably but wrongly claims that John Jackson was elected for the Chartists.

1845 but not in 1842.[19] Jackson, White, and others were long-term radicals who temporarily adopted the Chartist label. Many who were not designated Chartist were nevertheless strong supporters of universal suffrage and so the idea of a separate Chartist group on the Leeds town council is misleading. In fact Chartists were usually found to be voting along with advanced Liberals, either middle class with strong radical opinions or from that same shopkeeper/craftsmen class which produced most of the Chartists.

An analysis of the division lists in municipal minutes exposes other deficiencies in the received picture. Chartists were not united and did not vote together, especially not on items of expenditure. John Jackson voted against a rate for drainage and a new sewerage scheme in 1844 but in favour of enlarging the court house and altering the market in 1845–6. George Robson voted with Jackson on the former but not on the latter and William Brook voted against Jackson on both. On the six votes on the building of the town hall between January 1851 and May 1852 the Chartists were split every time.[20] Like other Leeds councillors they did not see eye to eye or vote as a bloc. This disagreement on expenditure weakens Harrison's pronouncement that 'they could always be counted on voting in favour of keeping down expenditure',[21] and it is also countered by more positive evidence. Joshua Hobson urged in 1845 the laying-out of a new street which would comprise 'a new street of shops in first rate style to serve as a model street for the town' and which would include a new town hall.[22] He was a powerful advocate of efficient drainage, as were Robson and Brook who argued that there was greater economy in paying for a drainage scheme than in not. Brook pointed out revealingly that the working class 'dread the doctor's bill more than the rate'.[23] It was this same Chartist who spoke up most strongly in favour of 'a good town hall' in January 1850 before the idea had caught the imagination of local opinion.[24] Similarly in Poor Law affairs it was a Chartist guardian, John Ayrey, who first suggested to the Leeds board of guardians that they should build an industrial school, the only major Poor Law building scheme in the West Riding in the 1840s.[25]

It was not 'economy' which gave consistency to Leeds Chartism but a belief in democratic control. Brook was in favour of municipal expenditure in 1846 or 1850, relatively prosperous years, but advocated economy and delay in 1848–9 when his constituents would be embarrassed by increased rates in a depression. This may be related to other ideas expressed by local Chartists; on the Improvement Act (attempting to ensure popular participation and control); on education (in favour of locally elected boards and rate-aided schools); on highways (strongly against centralization and in favour of locally controlled township boards). Here was that popular involvement and control so beloved of

Isaac Ironside. Leeds municipal Chartism was an exercise in real local democracy.

Leeds Chartist councillors voted with middle-class radicals and the lesson of the wider Chartist movement, as eventually recommended by O'Connor, was the need for a middle-class alliance. Several attempts during the 1840s to form such an alliance in favour of parliamentary reform foundered. After the purging of middle-class sympathizers in 1839, personified by the withdrawal of the Birmingham delegation from the Chartist convention, bourgeois radicals were frightened by the physical force spectre. However, the failures in 1840 to obtain from an ailing Whig administration anything on the Corn Law question convinced some radicals that suffrage reform was a better prospect. Two leading Leeds radicals, Hamer Stansfeld, a cloth merchant, and J. G. Marshall, the flaxspinner, convened a meeting in London to discuss the question in the spring of 1840. Support built up in the summer for a concerted effort to unite reformers of all classes behind a radical programme somewhat short of the Charter. With Samuel Smiles, editor of the *Leeds Times*, as main publicist, the Leeds Parliamentary Reform Association was launched in August 1840. The so-called 'Leeds new move' favoured household suffrage, the ballot, equal constituencies, triennial elections, and the abolition of the property qualification.[26]

Years later Smiles looked back to his efforts and commented that it was 'like flogging a dead horse to make it rise and go. It would neither rise nor go.' At the time he was more optimistic and wrote to Roebuck, 'Do you observe how our Association has already set the Bees a discussing the question of further Reform? This is the extent of the good we will accomplish. We will ripen public opinion and this is certainly no small thing.'[27] In similar vein Stansfeld had written to Smith that the only potential stumbling block was the *bona fides* of the bourgeoisie: 'Chartism is the fruit of increasing suffering and increase of intelligence and the only cure is to do justice to our fellow creatures. Our new political organisation is filling well and the operatives so well satisfied with the terms that they are only afraid the middle classes are not sincere.'[28] The high point of the movement was the splendid festival held in Marshall's new mill in January 1841 with Hume, Roebuck, Perronet Thompson, and Sharman Crawford in attendance. Ominously the Chartists passed a universal suffrage amendment and O'Connor dubbed the gathering the Fox and Goose Club. The *Northern Star* published a crude but biting cartoon showing the working-class audience as geese among the Egyptian pillars of Marshall's mill, and depicting the middle-class leaders as foxes ready to feast upon an easy prey.[29]

The Leeds new move was condemned to a sort of limbo between mainstream working- and middle-class movements. It could count on support from Working Men's Association members, such as David Green and Robert Martin, and on operatives who had always followed middle-class radical leadership, such as John Butterfield, secretary of the Holbeck Operative Reform Association. Such support was more than counter-balanced by the implacable hostility of the main Chartist leaders and the persistent criticism of the *Northern Star*, which railed against 'mere segments of reform and class crotchets'.[30] On the other side, many middle-class reformers retained faith in the Anti-Corn Law League and rejected radical reform. Smiles, Stansfeld, the two Marshalls, and George Goodman were the main middle-class leaders, along with a number of Liberal councillors. The rest followed Edward Baines junior in funda-mental opposition to an extension of the suffrage.[31] It was a unique achievement to have launched a political movement that was simultane-ously attacked by the *Leeds Mercury* and the *Northern Star*, the major organs of Yorkshire middle- and working-class reform opinion.

The Leeds new move gradually withered away and was eventually absorbed in Sturge's Complete Suffrage Union, which gained considerable momentum in 1842. Class co-operation had been the Birmingham message under Attwood and now Sturge was updating the Attwood approach. His movement was a great advance on the Leeds effort because it went so much further in its suffrage programme. Because of this it received the support of Lovett, Collins, and O'Brien among the Chartist leaders.[32] It could not count on O'Connor and those who wanted the Charter 'hog and bristles', and the more Sturge might attempt to placate the out-and-out Chartists the more uneasy his middle-class followers would be. It was not only, as Sturge always said, that the Charter had certain unsavoury connotations, but Chartists were tarred with the physical force brush. Brougham was but one who sedulously warned Sturge of the dangers of extremism:

> I cannot sufficiently impress upon you . . . how necessary it is that you avoid all inflammatory topics and show yourselves determined to repress all violent proceedings and to assist as far as you have the power in preserving peace . . . it is absolutely necessary to show that reformers of all respectable kinds are the determined enemies of illegal proceedings.[33]

Sturge hardly needed the warning and eventually in December 1842 made the People's Charter itself the sticking point in his personal rejection of extremism. This forced Lovett into the O'Connor corner and effectively killed off the C.S.U. as a real popular movement. It struggled on until 1846 but Sturge was relieved to be able to 'withdraw from much uncongenial fellowship'.[34]

John Bright had attended Sturge's initial conference in April 1842 and it was Bright in 1848 who was the strongest middle-class advocate of a revived parliamentary reform movement. Indeed he saw this as a means of destroying the power of the aristocracy who 'continue to frighten the middle classes into acquiescence . . . we must oust the dominant class or they will destroy us'.[35] Cobden was unenthusiastic and there was a marked cooling in the friendship between the two political agitators. Essentially a practical man, Cobden based his opposition to reform in mid-century not upon theoretical objections (he was a stronger believer in democracy than Bright) but upon a realistic assessment of the mid-Victorian political scene.[36] Above all, he was aware that a large proportion of middle-class reformers would not support suffrage reform and of this group the Greg family was a good example. In 1848 W. R. Greg told Cobden that he and others like him could not agree to any 'radical remodelling of our representative system, of which the consequences are quite incalculable.'[37] Four years later he explained his political position to Gladstone:

> I am one of a considerable and daily increasing class who belong to the liberal party by early connections, long and active association and by many surviving opinions also, who are yet decidedly conservative in all that relates to the further infusion of the democratic element into our constitution. We still consider ourselves earnest reformers but thorough anti-democrats.[38]

Others of the Greg connection took a similar position in the mid-Victorian years and one of them thought that even the £10 franchise was too low, promising he would vote for no £6 reformers who would give the vote to 'all the operatives in the great towns'.[39] The Gregs would not acknowledge the legitimacy of working-class claims for the vote, as one of them forcibly explained as late as 1865:

> I don't see why I should bow my head to a cry of today because it may have force some 30 years hence; nor as a voter do I wish to have my vote made a cypher, in order to admit to the franchise fifty of my workmen only five of whom are fit for it . . . we may have a man intelligent in his special handicraft but totally unfit to decide on the relations of church and state, foreign policy, fiscal matters etc., I don't think more than one in ten are fit for a vote.[40]

The two premisses sustaining the Greg family case (and the Gregs were typical of the bourgeois élite in many towns) were first, that an extension of the suffrage even to a £6 franchise would swamp the middle-class vote, and second, that working men were unfit for the vote and hence reform was a potential danger to the State and the social system. In 1840 during the Leeds new move Edward Baines junior wholly supported

such views, but by the 1850s he had decided that the fears were un-
founded.[41] The conversion of Baines and of men like him who gradually
deserted the Greg point of view made possible the reunion of middle-and
working-class reform movements. Such a reunion was a real possibility
from the winter of 1851–2, which marks a turning point in the suffrage
reform movement, although the seeds sown then were to take a long
time to bear fruit. Bright and Wilson organized a conference in
Manchester in December 1851 which attracted the attendance of Baines
and Cobden, each in their own way previously doubtful about further
reform.[42] The conference was a great success in attracting also the
support of former Chartists, and in the early months of 1852 many cities,
including Glasgow, Manchester, Leeds, and Birmingham, experienced a
re-uniting of radical forces often split since 1839. Typical of this development was Leeds where Baines, J. G. Marshall, and Francis Carbutt
joined forces with former Chartists R. M. Carter, William Brook, and
David Green.[43]

The relationship between two of these, Baines and Carter, was of
crucial significance in the coming of reform in the 1860s. Baines wished
to keep control of popular radicalism by leading the campaign for
moderate reform and he was able to join the small group of parliamentary
radicals pressing for reform when he was elected M.P. for Leeds in 1859.
His patronage was sought and given to the Leeds Working Men's
Parliamentary Reform Association launched in 1860 and he continually
tried to ally working-class radicals with the Liberal party. Like Cobden,
he was aware that most middle-class Liberals were hostile to reform but
acted as a vital link between Liberal and radical groups in Leeds politics.[44]
Robert Meek Carter, self-made coal merchant, had been prepared to
compromise on his Chartist principles in the interests of unity and from
1852 had adopted the instalment strategy of gaining middle-class support
for part of the legitimate demands of the working class. By the mid-
1860s he had rejected moderation in favour of outright support for
manhood suffrage. There was much personal animosity between Baines
and Carter, who were also journalistic rivals from 1862 when Carter and
Frederick Spark launched the radical *Leeds Express*, a thorn in the side
of the *Mercury*.

The ambivalence of Baines's position was revealed by his moderate
parliamentary proposals in 1865, which were too extreme for Parliament
yet not radical enough to inspire popular support. Cobden, near the end
of his life, was as percipient as ever:

I have little confidence in the Leeds Liberals or the Yorkshire
politicians generally . . . nothing but registered manhood suffrage
would induce the masses to agitate . . . Baines plan will not excite any

sympathy from the working class and in my opinion nothing will be done until the excluded classes demand in loud tones their rights. *Then* if *they* call for household suffrage the Lords will pass a substantial measure to escape something worse. But nothing will be got by *cooing* and I look upon what is coming from Leeds as little better than child's play.[45]

Carter's conclusions were identical and in 1866 he decided to go for manhood suffrage, to reject expediency in favour of principle.

In January 1866 he announced to Baines that Leeds radicals would accept nothing less than manhood suffrage and in August Carter launched a new reform association, the Manhood Suffrage League. Bainesite leadership was now being thrown over and, though Bright spoke at the great reform demonstration in October 1866, Baines was a conspicuous absentee. Carter threw in his lot with the Reform League in November and became one of its vice-presidents.[46] By early 1867 Baines knew that to persist with moderate reform in the face of imminent radical achievement could only drive him into an adullamite wilderness and so began to swim with the tide with self-conscious reluctance. He spoke at the height of Reform League activity at the great Easter demonstration in April 1867 and in October he joined a League banquet to celebrate the passing of the second Reform Act.[47] In Leeds, Manchester, and many other towns, the Reform League was a political force to be taken seriously in the 1868 election.[48] Liberals everywhere had to take under their wing a radical minority or risk splitting the vote. The defeat of Jones at Manchester and the victory of Carter at Leeds in part were a reflection of the stronger position of the Reform League in the West Riding than in Lancashire, which had always been a Reform Union stronghold. The tensions in urban politics towards the end of the third quarter of the nineteenth century centred above all upon suffrage reform which had been a live urban political issue since the 1790s.

12
Church and education

*'The Christian man is bound to bear his part here that good
shall prevail over evil; he may serve Christ on the polling
booth or on the platform, in Parliament, in the Town
Council or on the Board of Guardians.'* A. W. W. Dale,
The Life of R. W. Dale of Birmingham (1899), 250

The conflict between Church and Dissent was fundamental to the
political arena for most of the nineteenth century. The battle was fought
out at many different levels in political life and political controversies
were continually embittered by tensions that were at heart theological.
Men who disagreed about the very nature and purpose of existence were
natural rivals, though a common economic interest or political belief
might blur the more basic difference of opinion. Many who regretted
that religious disagreements exacerbated social or political relationships,
nevertheless were forced to admit that they lived in an age of inevitable
confrontation between the Established Church and nonconformity. In
this confrontation the Church found itself very much on the defensive,
when even its more positive attempts to justify its existence through
moral reform and social usefulness were based essentially on the
cry 'Church in danger'. Urban society, so dominated by Dissent,
was an obvious setting for these religious conflicts which underlay so
much of the political development of towns in the middle decades of
the nineteenth century. Urban political leaders saw religious grievances as a vitally important motivation for political action and the
redress of those grievances was a long standing popular political
ambition.

In pursuing that ambition, Dissenters used all the available political
channels and were not simply concerned with extra-parliamentary
pressure group activity. Dale's comment, quoted at the head of this
chapter, was an exhortation to utilize the full potential of the political
system. Indeed Dale implicitly supports the interpretation, offered in

this book, of a variegated political structure in which participation was possible in agitational, parliamentary, municipal and parochial politics. Since Dissenters were essentially practical men and since many of their grievances were likewise essentially practical, they sought relief initially in the parochial institutions which put into operation the system which oppressed them. Church rates were removed as a grievance in most towns by vestry activity specifically designed to abolish ecclesiastical financial imposts *de facto* if not *de jure* (see above, chapter 2). The religious aspects of Poor Law administration (such as whether all denominations had equal access to the workhouse pulpit), or the persistent problem of Nonconformist burials, could equally be dealt with by political involvement in parochial affairs. When in the mid-1850s, following the House of Lords decision on the Braintree case, the Liberation Society urged the staging of vestry contests to prevent church rates being levied, they were resorting to a well-tried Dissenting tactic which had been widely implemented two decades earlier.[1]

At about the same time that many urban Dissenters were relieved of paying church rates, they found that their social and political horizons were widened by municipal reform. Exclusion from close corporations was one of the galling reminders of social inferiority which had in practice been unaffected by legislation in 1828. It was of psychological importance in soothing a collective sense of injustice that leading Dissenters should occupy prominent positions in the new corporations. The new benches of aldermen and magistrates were overwhelmingly Nonconformist and an indication of the dominance of Dissent in the new corporate structure was provided by the mayoralty of Leeds in the first dozen years of reform. In that period only one Anglican became mayor, as a Baptist, an Independent, a Catholic, three Wesleyans, and five Unitarians accepted the mayoral chain. Many leaders in the Dissenting movement believed it to be of prime importance for Dissenters to be fulfilling their responsibilities as social leaders in their own areas. It was because Dale and Dawson found their followers wanting in this respect that they developed the idea of a civic gospel in the 1860s. Earlier a Manchester Baptist minister had emphasized the propriety of civic office: 'His was not a theology that would desire Christian men to withold themselves from such offices as the mayor's. Rather would he see every office from these petty monarchies up to the highest in the land filled with persons of undoubted piety.'[2] A large-scale Dissenting presence on councils did allow them to be used in support of the nonconformist cause; James Heywood in Manchester, Baines in Leeds, and Sturge in Birmingham used municipal authority to sustain the Dissenters' case. A minority, however, took the view that civic leadership weakened the zeal of Dissenters and in this vein one observer complained of 'a species of dissenting dandyism' which involved 'hovering about the purlieus of our town hall, playing at magistrates, mayor, aldermen and common council men'.[3]

Dissenters were perhaps slower to realize the full potential of parliamentary elections and the first moves in this direction in 1834 did not fully bear fruit until 1847. However, individual M.P.s, such as Baines, could push dissenting issues in Parliament, and urban elections in the 1830s were often the occasion for the airing of Nonconformist views. The stronger the dissenting viewpoint, the more extreme the Anglican backlash and during the Leeds election of 1837 an Anglican society attacked 'the Infidel, the Sceptic, the Unitarian and the political Dissenter all united with the Papist all engaged in an unhallowed warfare against everything sacred, great or good in our land'.[4] The notion of a conspiracy against the Church was commonplace in the 1830s and underlay the 'Church in danger' slogan: 'all sects are now leagued together as a political society whose chief employment is to conspire like Gebal, Ammon and Amalek against the Israel of God.'[5] In such attitudes 'no Popery' was never far below the surface, as was seen in the Maynooth issue of 1845 and the Ecclesiastical Titles quarrel in 1851.

It was in 1847, as a result of the education issue discussed below, that Dissenters tried to formalize their involvement in parliamentary elections, especially in the selection of candidates. For the first time Dissenters were given positive guidance on voting and were instructed to support 'those ecclesiastical principles which constitute the sole basis of religious freedom and equality'.[6]* During the election one Dissenting journal reported enthusiastically that 'Parliamentary candidates are subjected to a new and to them perplexing test; old political organisations are being broken up: new ones are in the course of formation'.[7] Another took this even further, predicting a new political force: 'The Anti-State Church principle, the principle of religious freedom and equality has in it sufficient vitality energy and aptitude to the times to become the germ of a new party.'[8] We have already noticed this new militancy in operation when Leicester Liberals were seeking a new candidate whose opinions had to be in sympathy with the extreme Dissenters (see above, p. 198). It could also operate in a more subtle way as pressure was brought to bear upon sitting members. Thus James Heywood, launched as M.P. for North Lancashire by Newall's Building, was to be warned about the exercise of his powers as a trustee of Owen's College in Manchester: Wilson was instructed

* In similar vein in 1848 Baptists were advised to vote 'so as to render it impossible for our rulers to carry public measures against the conviction and wishes of the virtuous part of the community'. Minutes of the Lancashire and Cheshire Association of Baptist Churches, 1848, 5.

to say that as there is a great deal of excitement amongst the liberal party on the subject of Religious Instruction at the Owen's College, and he being one of the Trustees, you wish to make him aware of it:– that it was by the exertions of that party he was returned for North Lancashire, and that if he were to counteract their wishes on the present very important occasion to them and to all others in this town, it might have a very damaging effect at the next election.[9]

The message was clear: a Dissenting Liberal M.P. had to advance Liberal Dissenting causes or he would sit no longer.

Heywood was in fact one of the staunchest Dissenting M.P.s and during the 1850s was pressing very hard for university reform, by which time he could count on the support of the Liberation Society, the formal extra-parliamentary pressure group of Dissent.[10] This body, which was originally named the Anti-State Church Association, placed nonconformist pressure from without on a much more organized footing from the mid-1840s. Prior to this the unit of organization tended to be the chapel, which was much more than an ecclesiastical institution. It was often through chapel activity that urban Dissenters first became politically conscious, for chapels and churches were political as well as social organizations in urban life. Political activity through chapels did not, however, produce united action, since there were many tensions within Nonconformity, not least those concerned with legal disputes over chapel property in the later 1830s and early 1840s.[11]

The Anti-State Church Association launched in 1844 imposed some order on Dissenting protest movements but was itself the focus of a new phase of controversy in long-standing dissensions within Nonconformity. There was a running battle through the middle decades of the century between those who wanted the relief of practical grievances and those who wanted total disestablishment. In the 1830s the weight of opinion was for redress in such fields as church rates, civil registration, burials and chapels licensed for marriage. During the 1840s more radical forces led by Edward Miall brought disestablishment to the fore: in the 1850s and 1860s the Liberation Society gradually moved from this radical to a more moderate position. Disagreements on this question were parallel to similar disputes within the suffrage movement, which was equally divided over whether incrementalist reform was preferable to fundamental changes in principle. Much depended on the local context. In the 1830s Birmingham could boast a journal which fully supported total disestablishment yet that paper soon collapsed because, it claimed, local Dissenters did not patronize it. A similar paper launched at almost the same time in Leicester went from strength to strength, while in Nottingham a long-standing paper of radical views supported disestablishment from 1828 onwards.[12] The local variable was not so much the strength of radical Dissent but the role of the Anglican Church in the town. Both Leeds (through Baines) and Leicester (through Miall and J. P. Mursell) were identified as centres of Dissenting opinion yet their situations were very different. In Leeds, church rates had been abolished in practice, the Leeds Burial Act of 1842 seemed to settle the cemetery issue, a High Church vicar had been forced to adopt an enforced voluntaryism in the rebuilding and running of his parish church and had modified his position so much by 1846 that he was prepared to admit that Anglicans were not entitled to privileged treatment. Leicester showed a completely different picture, with a church rates martyr imprisoned for non-payment, annual humiliations in distress warrants for rates levied until 1849, and Anglicans in an entrenched position in one or two important parishes. It was little wonder that Miall and Mursell emphasized disestablishment where Baines fought the practical operation of Anglican supremacy in the field of education.

To an extent, the dispute between the resolution of practical grievances and total disestablishment was a reflection of a conflict between London and the provinces. Miall's leadership was seen partly as an attempt to wrest control from moderate Whig London influences in favour of provincial radicalism. His journal, the radical *Nonconformist*, was a clear rival to Josiah Conder's moderate *Patriot*; the Anti-State Church Association (and later the Liberation Society) rivalled the Protestant Dissenting Deputies. Provincial radicalism did seem to challenge London moderation though the situation was more complex than this. Not only did the Liberation Society have important London connections, but the provinces did not fully identify with it. For instance, its campaigns over church rates in the 1850s had little appeal in the great cities which had long ceased to levy them. The society was strongest in the broad swathe of Dissenting country between Devon and the Wash but relatively weak in the large towns. There was in fact much provincial support for Dr Robert Vaughan's acceptance of the State Church, for even in Leicester it was clear that 'there has always been among Nonconformists a party who are not unfriendly to the existence of a state endowed Church'.[13]

A more fundamental tension within Dissent was the moral objection to political involvement itself. Many towns threw up some highly political pastors such as Dale and Dawson in Birmingham, Miall and Mursell in Leicester, J. E. Giles and Thomas Scales in Leeds. Yet the same towns had many examples of Dissenting ministers who refused to acknowledge a political role at all. As a Lancashire Baptist minister commented, 'I cannot reconcile this warm part in all political matters which is taken and openly defended, with the spirit of Christ's Kingdom, which is not of this

world, nor with the true position of Christians as strangers and pilgrims
on earth.'[14] A fundamental rejection of politics was issued by the
Congregational Magazine on the launching of the Anti-State Church
Association in 1844:

> we object to this Conference as a means for the promotion of political
> ends – for the redress of civil grievances – because we think that in
> such an object Christian ministers have no special concern, and
> Christian Churches and congregations, as such, no proper concern at
> all. . . . Our Christian societies are formed for mutual improvement in
> piety, and for the extension of Christian truth and privileges to all.
> If they are ever made political associations, so far their Christian
> character must be obscured, and their Christian usefulness lessened.[15]

Such views never fully caught on among the general body of Dissent
and were strongly countered by politically conscious Dissenting leaders,
many of whom argued that the true Christian battle had to be fought in
the political arena. This attitude was strongly rooted in Birmingham,
where Dawson proudly proclaimed, 'I was born a politician when I was
born an Englishman' and Dale pronounced, 'those who decline to use
their political power are guilty of treachery to God and to man'.[16] Above
all there was widespread acceptance that the very position of a Dissenter,
legally, psychologically and socially subservient to an Established
Church, politicized him inevitably, as an extreme Dissenting journal
explained: 'as a Dissenter he is a politico-religious radical . . . a radical
of the first water and so far as the Church is concerned a revolutionist,
yea a destructive. . . . He is a radical by Act of Parliament . . . his every
religious action is a political demonstration in favour of the political
downfall and political subversion of this Established Church.'[17]

Even non-political Dissenters could be aroused when Anglicanism
appeared to be taking gross advantage of its privileged position, and an
impressive expression of Nonconformist opinion was provoked by
Graham's 1843 Factory Education Bill. More than 13,000 petitions
were presented, signed by over two million people, as Dissent gave notice
that it would not tolerate Anglican state education. It was through the
1843 agitation that Edward Baines junior achieved national prominence
as a spokesman of voluntaryism. By 1846–7, as even Miall acknowledged,
Baines was the leading exponent of dogmatic voluntaryism and he was
to maintain that position for two decades. This was of decisive importance in the overall dissenting movement, in the continuing controversy
over education and in urban politics itself, especially in the West
Riding.[18]

In each of these areas the influence of Bainesite voluntaryism was
divisive. The political strength of Dissent was weakened, the pace of

educational advance slowed and the fabric of urban Liberalism torn asunder by one man's search for truth. Because Dissenters had always used the full potential of the political system, it was natural that voluntaryism should not allow the head of steam generated by the government's 1847 educational proposals to evaporate in pointless extra-parliamentary pressure. The election was utilized to press the voluntary cause even to the point of Liberal schism and the loss of Liberal seats.[19]* In Leeds, Baines launched Joseph Sturge, whose supporters would not coalesce with the moderate Liberals and so a Liberal-Tory coalition kept the voluntaryist out. A similar alliance at Halifax ensured Miall's defeat. As what was called 'the fire from Leeds'[20] spread through the West Riding, acute tension was created within the Liberal party. In 1848 the process was repeated, when at a by-election in the West Riding the voluntaryists nominated Sir Culling Eardley, whose prospects were acutely summed up by a local Wesleyan:

1. The Tories seem *united* against him, and with them are joined many Whig families belonging to the landed interest . . .
2. The supporters of Sir Culling do not seem to embrace heartily all who call themselves Liberals. . . . Another reason separating some of the Liberals from Sir Culling's ardent supporters is, at least so I fear, the prevalent ungodliness amongst us. . . . For the great mass of Liberals, Sir Culling is too good a man. They may support him because he is a Liberal but they would rather have a man like Roebuck.[21]

Culling Eardley might get Wesleyan support because 'he fears God and hates Popery',[22] but that was not sufficient to compensate for Liberal apathy in the face of a Whig-Tory coalition. The sacrifice by Baines and the voluntaryists of three important seats in the West Riding in 1847–8 was a measure of the impact of education upon opinion in the mid-nineteenth century.

Cobden, himself a member for the West Riding, was highly critical of the narrow sectarian platform of Baines. The rivalry between Cobden and Baines personified the rivalry between Manchester and Leeds, for education caused disagreement both within and between cities. Leeds housed 'the great oracle of voluntaryism'; Manchester was the birthplace of the state education lobby, through the Lancashire Public Schools Association, the Manchester and Salford Education Committee and,

---

* Maynooth marked the first breach between voluntaryism and Liberalism and it was in 1845 that Liberal free traders were warned, 'the Voluntary Friends have hitherto restrained their watchword as a cause of division but they will now be compelled to rally their strength and vote for their own candidates'. J. W. Massie to G. Wilson, 9 April 1845, Wilson Papers.

later, the Manchester Education Aid Society.[23] Manchester was as divided as Leeds, though along very different lines. In Leeds the question was whether the State should intervene at all, while in Manchester it concerned the form that intervention should take. It will be clear that long after the Leeds dilemma was disposed of the Manchester problem would still have to be resolved. Leeds imposed a proscriptive ban upon state education *per se*; Manchester sought to define the proper goals of a state education scheme that was both necessary and desirable.

The Lancashire Public Schools Association, officially begun in February 1848 under the chairmanship of Samuel Lucas, brother-in-law of John Bright, campaigned for rate-aided, locally controlled, secular education. These three principles were central. Schools should be publicly financed, run by elective boards and wholly concerned with secular education. When it changed its name to the National Public Schools Association it spelled out its commitment clearly:

> The National Public Schools Association is formed to promote the establishment by law, in England and Wales, of a system of free schools:– supported by local rates and managed by local committees, specially elected by the ratepayers for that purpose; and which, imparting secular instruction only, shall leave the teaching of doctrinal religion to parents, guardians and religious teachers.[24]

The secular education lobby did not monopolize local opinion in Manchester, which also boasted a strong movement for state aided denominational education. The latter scored a spectacular victory over the L.P.S.A. on its own ground at a meeting in the Free Trade Hall in March 1849.[25] The Association's response to this defeat was to sponsor working-class branches which would 'destroy any doubt as to the issue of any public meeting which the Association might call for in the Free Trade Hall or elsewhere'.[26] By bitter experience the Association came to appreciate the need to pack meetings.

While Baines continued in the 1850s to preach the evils of state education and the virtues of voluntaryism, Manchester tried unsuccessfully to resolve locally the issues the nation was to face in the 1870s. Indeed in 1852 when it appeared that the two Manchester proposals would be definitively judged by Parliament, it was argued that Manchester would set the seal on the whole national issue: 'It is certain that a portion of the population and influence of *Manchester* will settle this great question for the present on the principles of one or other of the two schemes which Manchester has promulgated.'[27] The two schemes were similar only in that they were based on state aid. The denominationalists accepted some form of central control, wanted the endowment out of public funds of denominational establishments, firmly believed in religious education and opposed universal free access to state schools. The secularists vigorously opposed centralization, believed in strictly secular education, rejected the idea of state endowed religious institutions and were committed to universal free schooling on the rates.[28]* Many Dissenters who viewed with horror the idea of banishing religious instruction from the schools were nevertheless equally aghast at state endowment of religion. What was wrong for Maynooth could not be right for Manchester and Salford. In the event neither proposal was adopted and a resolution of these issues was delayed until the late 1860s, by which time the initiative had passed from Manchester to Birmingham.

The National Education League, founded in Birmingham in 1869, was in a sense the heir of the Manchester tradition. Indeed one of its moving spirits, George Dixon, believed that Manchester 'ought to have headed, and was entitled to lead a national movement'.[29] The Birmingham movement brought together prominent radicals, leading Dissenters, and the advocates of the civic gospel.[30] Underlying the pressure for education in the late 1860s lay the reluctant admission by voluntaryism that it had failed. Baines admitted to Kay Shuttleworth in 1867 that voluntaryism 'was allowed too absolute a sway and as a practical man I am compelled to abandon the purely voluntary system'.[31] Baines was as much a barometer as a mentor of Dissenting opinion and as his unbending voluntaryism in 1847 struck a chord in the Nonconformist conscience, so his reluctant acceptance of state aid 20 years later was in tune with contemporary Dissenting attitudes.

The shift in opinion was well illustrated by the changes within the Baptist movement in Lancashire, itself highly dependent upon urban congregations. In 1843 Lancashire Baptists joined their fellow Dissenters in all-out opposition to Graham's proposals and in 1847 they publicly disapproved of the parliamentary vote, and constituent chapels were urged to decline all pecuniary aid under the new scheme.[32] They welcomed the evidence provided by the 1851 census which seemed to confirm 'the self-reliance of the people and the success of the voluntary principle' and opposed government plans in 1853 because they would 'crush all independent voluntary effort for the support of Congregational schools'.[33] All this was a perfect reflection of Bainesite voluntaryism, although a minority of Baptists did support the Manchester secularists partly as a means of relieving Sunday schools of impossible educational burdens.[34] By 1870 the annual conference of Lancashire and Cheshire

* The L.P.S.A. scheme was described later by a prominent education reformer as 'based on the principle that the cost should be thrown on property, that the management should be confided to local representatives, and that the people should be taught to regard education, not as a bone of contention between churches and sects, but as the rights of free citizens'. F. Adams, *History of the Elementary School Contest.* . . . (1882, reprinted 1972), 152.

Baptists was pushing a very different line. Having previously resisted state intervention, Baptists now defined a positive role for the state:

> Let it be the aim of the government to sweep the streets of our large towns, and gather in those neglected dirt begrimed arabs whose dense ignorance is the shame of our civilisation, and prevent them from growing up with minds as dark as the untutored savages. . . . Let it see that no child shall be defrauded of its right to a fair start in life through the criminal neglect or pauperised condition of its parents.[35]

At almost the same time that Dissenting temperance groups admitted that the task of reform could only be accomplished by the state, Dissenting educationists came to the identical conclusion. Drink and ignorance, the two evils which were test cases for voluntaryist moral reform, were admitted to be unresponsive to mere individualism.

Yet the admission of a role for the State was merely a beginning, for opinion was still divided on the nature of that role. Lancashire Baptists arrive in 1870 at that secularism which Manchester had suggested two decades earlier, yet Baines believed the exclusion of religion to be 'a violation of our duty to God and man, and the elimination from the schools of the most precious element of education'.[36] The National Education League was itself uncertain on this issue. It began by supporting what it called 'unsectarian' education (which confused many even among its own members), which would have allowed the use of the Bible without commentary. Later it moved to a rigorously secularist position, driven in that direction by Forster's bill and by Chamberlain's manoeuvres, but with some reservations from George Dixon, one of the originators of the League. The religious question was no longer a simple Church versus Dissent battle but a fundamental schism within Dissent itself. Baines admitted that many Dissenters even by 1867 favoured secular education as

> more impartial, more free from Clerical influences and more effective; whilst the working classes and strong radicals have a prejudice against that which is denominational. Now I fear that the Church schools are too completely under the control of the Clergy; yet I dare not on that account adopt a system which must exclude religion from the schools and sever them from the religious communities.[37]

Such views drove Baines not towards the League or the Central Non-conformist Committee of 1870, which contained so many radical Dissenters, but into the arms of the rival National Educational Union, launched in Manchester as a partnership of traditional Anglican paternalism and residual voluntaryism.

Urban politics in 1870 were characterized by disputes between the

League and the Union as each sought to impress Parliament with the public support for its policies. George Dixon was clear in his own mind that the nature of Forster's bill would depend on his assessment of the strength of the League and he told George Melly, 'We are doing Forster's work for him, testing the power of the opposing forces in the country . . . exactly in proportion to Forster's estimate of the strength of the League will be the liberal colouring of the Bill – he will be afraid of the churches until we convince him that we are stronger.'[38] In the battle for public support passions were inflamed and in March 1870 Manchester Town Hall had to be cleared after fighting between League and Union. The latter made great capital over the alleged desire of the League to run down existing voluntary denominational schools. The League was not always clear on what ought to happen to existing schools but it certainly expected that a comprehensive state scheme would supersede them. In this respect, as in many others, Forster's bill was a victory for the Union, for he declared quite openly that his proposals were intended to supplement existing provision, definitely not to replace it.[39]

Forster became public enemy number one as far as the League was concerned, bitterly criticized for his compromises which seemed so reasonable to later generations. The continued endowment of denominational schools was the fundamental issue for dissenters and, for instance, Lancashire Baptists pronounced that unless amendments 'definitely secure the unsectarian character of the schools supported or aided by School Boards' the bill was unacceptable since it was not 'in harmony with religious liberty and progress'.[40] The militant pastor Dale gave notice in Birmingham that

> not even at the bidding of a Liberal minister will we consent to any proposal which under cover of an educational measure empowers one religious denomination to levy a rate for teaching its creed and maintaining its worship . . . we are determined that England shall not again be cursed with the bitterness and strife from which we hoped we had for ever escaped with the abolition of the Church Rate.[41]

Unable to secure satisfactory amendments, the League eventually opposed the passing of Forster's bill, warning that Dixon would introduce amending legislation the following session. In the incredibly complex division of parties Forster's bill, with its explosive clause 25, passed into law while the League fumed in the wings, never more than a minority even in the Liberal party, though a powerful voice from urban England.

The battleground switched from Parliament, not as expected to the town councils, but to the directly elected school boards.[42] The League's strategy was to use the political power of the school boards to implement their principles in practice for, as George Dixon argued, while it was claimed that League principles had been defeated, in fact 'we have secured in the Education Act of 1870 a lever, by the wise use of which their adoption has become merely a question of time'.[43] School boards were politicized by issues of educational policy and beyond education lay a more general commitment to popular participation and control. The League was very much aware of this aspect and added to one of its resolutions, 'in urging the universal establishment of school boards, we are supporting the principles of popular government and local control'.[44] That school boards were overtly political institutions was admitted privately by a Conservative minister, anxious in 1874 that pernicious urban influences should not spread to the countryside:

> School Boards . . . in the smaller country towns and in villages . . . will produce very serious political results. They will become the favourite platforms of the Dissenting preacher and local agitator, and will provide for our rural populations, by means of their triennial elections and Board meetings, exactly the training in political agitation and the opportunity for political organisation which the politicians of the Birmingham League desire, and which will be mischievous to the State.[45]

School boards thus came to symbolize the political difference between urban and rural society.

The Birmingham school board was not in the event amenable to immediate League influence, for the cumulative voting system, which allowed 15 votes to be cast for one candidate, secured an Anglican/Conservative victory. School board elections were always a mixture of politics and religion in which normal party alliances were confused. Thus a Liberal Anglican became the first chairman in both Birmingham and Leeds (Sargent and Fairbairn), towns each with a non-Liberal majority. School board politics in Birmingham in the early 1870s largely concerned Liberal attempts to reverse through municipal authority the defeat suffered in the first school board election. Chamberlain and his allies held over the board first the threat to refuse to collect the rate and, when this was deemed illegal, the threat to refuse the payment of rates. By one or other the board was prevented from fully implementing either clause 25 or its bye-law on compulsory attendance. The Liberals were engaged in a holding operation until the 1873 election allowed them to gain control and enforce the even more secularist programme they had adopted in 1872. The key to a Liberal victory lay in the repetition of the methods used in the parliamentary election of 1868, when three Liberals had been returned. The Birmingham Liberal machine had to find a way round the cumulative vote as it had done round the minority clause. Wards were organized so that all voters cast five votes for each of three specified candidates. Voters had to resist the temptation of plumping for Chamberlain in 1873, just as they had to resist the desire to plump for Bright in 1868. The Liberals nominated only eight candidates but got them all returned and with Chamberlain as chairman a programme of secular schools was begun.[46]

Elsewhere the League's cause did not generally prosper. Manchester elected a clerical board in both 1870 and 1873 and in the twin towns of Manchester and Salford an Anglican/Catholic alliance maintained control for many years. In Sheffield there was one of the fiercest popular resistance movements utilizing a refusal to pay rates, yet Dissenters were cheated out of an expected victory in 1873 by an electoral mishap which left the 1870 denominational board in office. Prior to the 1873 election there had been an agreement between the Reform Association, the Trades Council and the League to support the 'undenominational eight' and with the support of the Liberal Association the undenominationalists secured a narrow majority in 1876. Liberal control was never secure and Liberal victories in 1876 and 1882 were reversed by Anglican/Conservative victories in 1879 and 1885.[47]

In Leeds the initial decision of the official Liberals and Liberal denominationalists to stand separately allowed an Anglican/Catholic victory in 1870. Politically the board was composed of eight Liberals and seven Conservatives but the message of the election was taken to be that the ratepayers favoured religious education, to which most Liberals were opposed.[48] Local Liberals recognized that the party had to be 'as capable of organising its forces as is the Liberal Party in Birmingham'[49] and though ward adoption was not used the combined Liberal/unsectarian list was returned in 1873, to give an 8–7 majority over the Anglican/Catholic members. The parties agreed to avoid a contest in 1876 but by then municipal economists led by the fruit merchant Archie Scarr were in full flow and wished to stage an election 'as a protest against the extravagant expenditure of the board'.[50] The religious difficulty reappeared in 1879 when the board was fragmented over the secularist issue and Anglicans, Catholics and Wesleyans joined forces to protect denominational schools. Baines was forced to acknowledge that 'the elements of disunion and disintegration have reappeared among us', as the Liberals won only three of the 15 seats in 1879.[51] The Conservative-dominated board severely limited the development of unsectarian board schools in the interests of denominational schools. This policy was reversed in 1882 when Liberals regained control when the voters 'condemned the policy carried out by the sectarian majority'.[52]

In 1882 Baines regretted that unnecessary heat had been injected into a school board struggle which had been fought on lines 'partly political, partly sectarian and unsectarian'.[53] Then in his 80s, he must have been struck by how similar this all was to the politico-religious battles he fought half a century earlier. The politicizing of school boards in the 1870s had much in common with the politicizing of vestries in the 1820s. They were both characterized by a mixture of religious, financial and political issues and they were both an expression of the Nonconformist search for real religious equality. Institutionally too there were important similarities. The school board was not precisely among the parochial or township institutions with which this book began but neither was it a municipal institution, from which it had been deliberately separated. Indeed in its role of providing education for the underprivileged urban mass, it had close links with the Poor Law guardians to whom the controversial clause 25 was remitted in 1876. Having begun with vestry institutions, the wheel of urban politics comes full circle back to the bodies most analogous to them. That this upward guide through the levels of urban political activity should reach the summit in the field of political agitation only to be redirected to the minor offices of urban life is but a reminder of the totality of the urban political experience. He who would understand the nature of politics in Victorian cities must define the components of the urban political structure and explain the relationship between them.

Conclusion:
Urban politics in modern England

'THE HASLINGDEN LIBERAL ASSOCIATION respectfully urges all Liberals to vote for each and every Candidate nominated by the Association. . . . This election is important. DON'T SPLIT YOUR VOTES.' Handbill for Haslingden local board election, 1890 (Lancashire Record Office DDX 118/15)

The structure of politics in English provincial metropolises in the mid-nineteenth century was the product of the interaction between the institutional and social structure of Victorian urban communities. The pattern and boundaries of politics in Victorian cities were determined by a struggle for control between social groups, a conflict over the exercise of power in urban society. Such political battles were fought across a wide range of battlefields which it has been the object of this study to identify and characterize. The analysis has rested upon the discovery and exploration of four levels of political activity within the urban community. The foundations of the Victorian urban political system were to be found in the minor parochial and township institutions of city life. Growing out of the pre-industrial vestry, the churchwardens, boards of guardians, improvement commissions and highway surveyors struggled with the problems of the new urban milieu. These posts carried intrinsic authority and were further politicized by becoming either focal points in a wider struggle for power or agents for implementing a wider political (often reform) objective. Many political activists who served their apprenticeship in these minor offices looked to town councils as the next level in the urban hierarchy and it was widely believed that councils were natural political institutions. Municipal government was enmeshed in the urban political scene partly because, as the local 'House of Commons', councils were politically contested, and partly because, in embarking on a programme of social reform, councils provoked contention about the nature and exercise of urban authority. Frequently the same political organization which maintained municipal control also fought parliamentary elections. Always the focus of great local interest, parliamentary elections provided the opportunity for a symbolic group identification and were taken as a barometer of local political feeling. Parliamentary elections affected and were affected by the other seams in the urban political structure. They were part of an all-embracing local political system and deserve to be studied as such. The element of politics which went furthest beyond the local community was the political agitation which sought to persuade the nation and change Parliament's will. It was often commitment to a fundamental political cause which gave rationality to the diverse political involvement which characterized Victorian cities. Yet the wider political cause always returned near to home and so political forces ran in a circle, launched from the minor institutions, transmitted through municipal government, expressed in a parliamentary election, forced into Parliament's view and bounced back again to the minor institution.

It is hoped that this study has established the case for this mode of historical methodology, but this is not just a model of historical analysis. It reflects a real contemporary political structure. To conceive of a variegated and layered political system is to perceive the urban reality of Victorian England. Contemporaries well understood this reality, an awareness illustrated by three brief comments, quoted earlier and re-quoted here. When Manchester Tories won a churchwarden's poll in 1840 their victory was invested with imperial significance. The local Tory journal claimed that the result demonstrated the 'abhorrence of Whiggery and of Whig devices such as Whig Corporations, Whig Poor Laws and Whig police' and by virtue of this parochial election Manchester citizens were deemed to have 'no confidence in the present ministers'.[1] In such ways the minor offices of urban administration registered great political issues. Moreover, contemporaries recognized the possibility of political participation within a complex political system and this was well indicated by Dale's injunction to his followers to do God's work at all levels of the urban political structure: 'he may serve Christ on the polling booth or on the platform, in Parliament, in the Town Council or on the Board of Guardians.'[2] Underlying all was a political context and content which ran like blood coursing through the veins of the body politic. The very first words of this book sum up the unity of a political process characterized by elections at all levels: 'politics are the vital element of *all* elections – parliamentary, municipal, parochial or philanthropic'.[3]

Some may query whether a political system so characterized was distinctively urban. In one sense it may be argued that the politics of great cities were merely a mirror image of the shires in which the monopolists of wealth controlled the local destiny. The deliberate attempt to create spheres of urban influence in which the bourgeoisie could lord it over the citizenry would support such an interpretation. Against this, it may be argued that it is already clear that the urban political structure was intrinsically more diffuse, variegated and competitive than that prevailing in the countryside. The fear of urban political influences permeating the counties indicates the existence of political forces and customs which were alien to rural England. The relatively simplified vertical social structure of rural society produced the politics of deference whereas the complicated horizontal social structure of the cities produced the politics of election, persuasion, opinion and participation. The variegated urban institutional structure which allowed the layered political system to develop in the cities had no equivalent in the counties. Significantly enough the institutions created in the mid-nineteenth century (the boards of guardians, new town councils, school boards etc.) reflected the political culture of the new urban society rather than that of the traditional rural society. The paternalism of the eighteenth century produced close corporations and self-elected commissions; the individualism of the nineteenth century produced open institutions freely elected. Perhaps the belief in election *per se* was the political equivalent of a social and economic philosophy based upon free competition.

It was with the politics of the caucus in the 1870s that our fourfold model received its most formal expression. In that decade politics conducted in the Birmingham image began very firmly in the minor institutions. The caucus contested power in the boards of guardians and school boards, recognizing the intrinsic power of these institutions and their role in establishing strong political foundations at the grassroots level. The caucus ran the councils, basing its strength on ward organization. The same organization enabled parliamentary elections to be fought with a discipline which in Birmingham made all three seats safe for the Liberals, despite the 1867 minority clause. All three levels were used to advance the cause of reform in the field of political agitation. Many have seen such a political system as a new departure in British politics, but the evidence cited in this book suggests rather that the 1870s witnessed the formalization, systematization and perhaps exaggeration of a political structure which had existed in English towns for half a century. The structure of urban politics at the end of the third quarter of the nineteenth century was a recognizable likeness of that prevailing at the beginning of the second quarter of the century.

Though politics in the 1870s were but an augmented echo of those of the 1830s, the half-century beyond 1880 witnessed a fundamental change in the political process. From the vantage point of 1880 a retrospective view encompassed familiar terrain, a prospective view opened up a new world. The characteristic urban political structure of the mid-nineteenth century did not, of course, dissolve overnight. The minor institutions continued to have a political role and, as the head-piece to this chapter indicates, the politicizing of local boards at the end of the century extended the party conflict from the greater to the lesser urban communities. The pioneers of the Labour party, like their Chartist and Dissenting forebears, looked to the minor institutions to provide a launching pad for the new political force. The school boards were a means of enforcing a programme of educational development in late Victorian England which was frequently politically oriented and sustained. 'Poplarism', a feature of the 1890s and the 1920s, evidenced the con-tinuance of the traditional battle between central and local agencies on the issue of poor relief. Similarly in the early 1930s, unemployment, rather like Dissenters' grievances a century earlier, was a crucial issue at many levels. It was a tense social question for local public assistance committees operating a family means test; its treatment became a make or break issue for the Labour government; and its removal was advocated in the great extra-parliamentary pressures of hunger marches. Town councils have continued (not begun) to be politically contested and from time to time the issue of the exercise of power has caused great political dispute. Social questions such as education, and moral issues like birth control, have enlivened twentieth-century municipal politics.

These flashes on the political screen, reviving images of the Victorian political culture, do not destroy the impression that the political process in the cities of England has fundamentally changed. Perhaps four main elements of change may indicate the extent of the transformation. First, the very organization of politics in late-Victorian England in-evitably weakened the hold of an urban élite which had for half a century dominated town politics. The extension of the suffrage, itself a prime reason for the development of caucus politics, created a mass electorate, protected by the ballot, which undermined oligarchic control of city affairs. The individual political judgement, so important in the mid-century, became less significant than the political expression of great social forces. Moreover, the redistribution of 1885, fragmenting urban political organizations and enfeebling the sense of political community, made the suburban constituency rather than town the political unit. Federal ward structures, attempting to maintain city unity, could not compensate for a constituency system in which at last numbers, *per se*, had begun to count.

While these changes altered the political structure from within, there were, secondly, wider political forces operating from outside. During the half-century from about 1870 British politics became fully nationalized. Essentially in the mid-nineteenth century politics were regionally oriented. Only occasionally, as in 1831, did a national issue uniformly dominate urban politics. Rather, the political process was a means of resolving local disputes. In 1847 Birmingham questioned its own political identity on the issues of currency and suffrage reform, while in the same year Leeds and the West Riding were split on education. Similarly the 1857 Manchester election, though couched in Palmerstonian terms, was fundamentally about political and social control in that city. Though national trends were often apparent, regional influences were always crucial. Subject as the country now is to national means of diffusing political information, England expresses its contemporary viewpoint with a considerable degree of uniformity. A general election is frequently won and lost within a narrow range of political swing and the 1975 referendum was a remarkable indication of the consistency of political attitudes throughout contemporary England. Furthermore the town councils are now prey to national forces which makes them the most sensitive indicator of changing political opinions. In recent decades it has been public attitudes towards the government of the day rather than towards the achievements of local councillors which has determined municipal election results. Yet in the mid-nineteenth century a crucial local election might not only go against the national trend but also reverse a parliamentary election result in the same town. Always part of an overall political system, municipal politics possessed an independent existence which is now largely lost.

Above all the most crucial national factor was the social structure itself. *Pace* Edward Thompson, 1832 did not mark the emergence of the English working class and this is just the reason why proletarian issues formed relatively so minor a role in urban politics in Victorian England. A political system which sharply delineated the boundaries of social participation and one in which the key factor was a struggle within the middle class was certainly not one which was dominated by the Marxian conflict between capital and labour. However, between *c.* 1880 and *c.* 1920 England came nearest to a rigorously class-structured society in which a coherent working class emerged. It is surely no coincidence that the period which witnessed the growth of a relatively uniform proletariat should have given birth to a parallel political proletarian movement in the creation of the Labour Party. By the 1920s the rise of the Labour Party, the product of a more sharply defined proletarian social and political consciousness, had fundamentally altered the nature of British politics. Just as the political imperative flowing from bourgeois dominance in the mid-nineteenth century decreed that the natural location of politics should be the city itself, so the corollary of proletarian consciousness in the 1880–1920 period determined that politics should be fought on a national scale. City politics, where proletarian numbers eventually delivered power into Labour hands, then became a cog in a national political process, where in mid-Victorian England national affairs only occasionally deflected the flow of dominant city issues. In the mid-nineteenth century the city was an independent political unit with its own internal consistency and primary political drives; by the early twentieth century it was clearly no longer a discrete focus of politics.

The third change we may identify lay in the nature of local government. By 1930 the minor institutions had completely disappeared and as far as cities were concerned this strand in the political system simply did not exist. Even within the 1830–80 period we noticed the gradual decline of political institutions at the lowest level. By about 1850 most urban churchwardens had been divested of political authority and interest. By 1870 most boards of highway surveyors and improvement commissioners had been absorbed into town councils. The creation of school boards did restore one powerful body to the minor level, but school boards went the way of the others in 1902 when councils assumed responsibility for education. Finally in 1929 the boards of guardians too were absorbed by the municipal leviathan. By then town councils not only performed all the functions previously exercised by a whole range of institutions (surveyors, commissions, guardians, etc.), they also had powers and provided services earlier deemed inappropriate for the public sector. Yet it is a paradox which political scientists have neither fully explored nor explained that as municipal government has extended its powers and functions, so public interest in municipal politics has declined. The initial extensions of municipal authority in the middle decades of the nineteenth century generated much fierce heat, but the ever-increasing increments of municipal power have on the whole failed to ignite comparable public interest. Public apathy for local government and low turnout at municipal elections have to be explained in the paradoxical context of immense local power and widespread municipal involvement in the citizen's everyday life. In another sense local government changes have blurred the distinctiveness of the urban political system. From the last decade of the nineteenth century county areas were municipalized and the growth of county councils has clearly lessened the differences between the urban and rural institutional structure which were so marked in the Victorian years. It is a symbolic indication of the unity of urban and rural government that the four great provincial cities which dominate this book and which sustained the urban consciousness of Victorian England, have now been designated as metropolitan counties.

Finally, the role of political agitation, in many ways a unifying force in mid-nineteenth-century urban politics, has fundamentally changed.

It has been argued that extra-parliamentary pressure groups were a characteristic feature of the period between the first two Reform Acts, largely displaced by the growth of national parties in late-Victorian England.[4] The National Liberal Federation was seen partly as a means of channelling radical demands directly into the political system through radical control of the Liberal party. Similarly a number of leagues and organizations were loosely associated with the Conservative party. Later the Labour party through its annual conference and constituent organizations provided a link between society and politics. In these ways national parties were able to provide the means of expressing popular political demands, a function previously performed through political agitation. Yet pressure groups and lobby politics by no means died with Victoria and the Campaign for Nuclear Disarmament raised many echoes of an earlier age. Nevertheless pressure from without now operates much more in private, through lobbying by business, professional or sectional interests. Despite the march of democracy there is much less opportunity for popular participation in great political movements than existed in the provincial cities of Victorian England.

One man who would have regretted the lack of political involvement in modern Britain was Archibald Prentice. His political life was indeed conditioned by the fourfold political structure here exposed. He was a prominent advocate in Manchester vestry politics in the 1820s and 1830s. He was a staunch supporter of the charter of incorporation and sat as a councillor for New Cross ward from 1838 to 1842 and from 1843 to 1846. Prentice also played a prominent role in Manchester parliamentary elections and frequently spoke on behalf of Liberal candidates. Above all, he was an able lieutenant in the great campaign for the repeal of the Corn Laws and was the League's first historian. In all these spheres of politics his contribution was enhanced by his close involvement with the radical press. When his paper died and he was found a minor post with Manchester corporation (the only spoils he ever received from a lifetime of politics) his modest £150 per year left him far from bitter. Five years before he died he pronounced himself happier than any merchant prince:

> It is something now to have taken part in that League agitation. Millions who were wretched are now comfortable. I would not exchange the satisfaction this gives for ten thousand a year. Knight, Baronet, M.P.? Dross! dirt! To have been one of the humblest instruments in this great change is beyond all rank and all wealth.[5]

Politics gave to Prentice's life both meaning and dignity, as they had done to countless other citizens in this 'age of great cities'.

Notes

Note. The location of manuscript sources is given in the first reference to it in each chapter; newspapers cited are available at the appropriate local library or at the British Museum newspaper collection at Colindale.

Introduction

1. J. Foster, *Class Struggle and the Industrial Revolution* (1974), 51–64.
2. *Manchester Guardian*, 22 April 1840.
3. *Porcupine*, 11 June 1864, 83.
4. E. Stephens to G. Wilson, 4 March 1844, Wilson Papers (Manchester Reference Library).
5. A. W. W. Dale, *The Life of R. W. Dale* (1894), 250.
6. *Sheffield Independent*, 24 January 1852.
7. *Birmingham Advertiser*, 9 April 1840.
8. *Leeds Intelligencer*, 1 December 1838.
9. W. Barton to J. Bunting, 6 December 1848, Bunting Papers (transcripts supplied by Professor W. R. Ward).
10. *Porcupine*, 11 October 1862, 220.
11. *Ibid.*, 5 November 1864, 252.
12. C. E. Rawlins jun. to G. Wilson, 31 December 1846, Wilson Papers.
13. *Leeds Mercury*, 1 November 1877.
14. *Manchester Guardian*, 29 October 1842.
15. Cf. 'political life in the boroughs between election times was comparatively quiet': W. L. Guttsman, 'The General Election of 1859 in the Cities of Yorkshire', *International Review of Social History*, ii (1957), 233.
16. *Christian Witness* 1848, 294–5, 572, quoted by H. R. Martin, 'The Politics of the Congregationalists' (Ph. D. thesis, University of Durham, 1971), 13–14.
17. Circular letter, Lancashire and Cheshire Association of Baptist Churches, 1850, 8.
18. Address to Joseph Sturge from property owners in Edgbaston, 3 April 1855, B.M. Add. MS. 43845, f. 48.
19. *Porcupine*, 25 October 1862, 233.
20. W. Brumfitt to G. Melly, 27 July 1865, Melly Papers 2384 (Liverpool Record Office).
21. E. Ambler to G. Melly, 13 April 1863, Melly Papers 1614.
22. *Leeds Mercury*, 26 November 1836.
23. Circular letters, Lancashire and Cheshire Association of Baptist Churches, 1867, 7; cf. below, Chapter 8 n. 26.
24. *Ibid.*
25. E. Ambler to G. Melly, 27 May 1863, Melly Papers 1628.
26. G. Hadfield to G. Wilson, 12 September 1851, Wilson Papers.
27. J. Whyatt to G. Wilson, 25 November 1842, Wilson Papers.
28. H. C. Bright to G. Melly, 24 February 1864, Melly Papers 1909.
29. C. P. Villiers to G. Wilson, 22 August 1846, Wilson Papers.
30. C. P. Melly to G. Melly, 25 May 1868, Melly Papers 3203.
31. L. Greg to G. Melly, 4 December 1869, Melly Papers 3607.
32. E. Baines to C. Baines, 5 March 1837, Baines Papers (Leeds City Archives).

33. J. G. Marshall to H. C. Marshall, 11 March 1853, quoted by W. G. Rimmer, *Marshalls of Leeds Flaxspinners* (1960), 269.
34. M. Philips to G. Wilson, March 1847, Wilson Papers.
35. Mary Wilson to G. Wilson, 1 March 1843, Wilson Papers.
36. W. Brown to G. Wilson, 10 January 1854, Wilson Papers.
37. J. Rushton to W. Brown 21 January 1848, Wilson Papers; cf. J. Shipley to J. Brown, 15 January 1848.
38. W. Brown to G. Wilson, 22 January 1848, Wilson Papers.
39. *Sheffield Times*, 20 November 1852.
40. J. F. Prange to G. Melly, 16 September 1872, Melly Papers 4519.
41. T. Goodair to G. Melly, 1 May 1863, Melly Papers 1679.
42. R. Cobden to G. Wilson, 14 February 1845, Wilson Papers.
43. *Porcupine*, 8 November 1862, 252.
44. *Incorporate Your Borough*, 2.

Chapter 1

1. Letter of Boroughreeve, 10 July 1833, Letter Book of the Boroughreeve 1826–36, Manchester Reference Library M9/61/1/2.
2. J. Toulmin Smith, *Local Self-Government and Centralization* (1851), 222.
3. J. Redlich and F. W. Hirst, *The History of Local Government in England* (1970 edn), 168.
4. J. Aston, *Metrical Records of Manchester* (1822), 65.
5. *Appendix to First Report Commission on the Poor Law*, xxxvi (1834), 782.
6. *Liverpool Burgesses and Ratepayers Magazine*, no. 1 (2 June 1851).
7. *First Half Yearly Report of the Salford Ley-Payers Association*, 24 January 1833, Lancashire Record Office 1309.
8. Toulmin Smith, *op. cit.*, 200.
9. A. Prentice, *Historical Sketches and Personal Recollections of Manchester* (1851), 317.
10. *Report of the Commissioners . . . Municipal Corporations*, xx (1835), Leeds Report, 6.
11. S. and B. Webb, *Statutory Authorities For Special Purposes* (1963 edn) 448.
12. A. T. Patterson, *Radical Leicester* (1954), 189.
13. *First Report . . . Commission on the Poor Law* (1834), 107.
14. T. Gair to G. Melly, 23 June 1868, Melly Papers 3171 (Liverpool Record, Office).
15. Address of the Committee of the Salford Ley-payers Association, 17 January 1833, Lancashire Record Office 1309.
16. Extempore letter, MS. 16 February 1833, *ibid.*

Chapter 2

1. *Leeds Mercury*, 17 April, 1 May 1819, 19 January 1822.
2. Vestry minutes 1813–28, 29 March 1826, 9 April 1828 (Leeds parish church).
3. *Leeds Mercury*, 13 April 1833.
4. *Ibid.*; vestry minutes 1828–44, 68.
5. *Leeds Mercury*, 10 August 1833; vestry minutes 1828–44, 73.
6. *Leeds Intelligencer*, 5 April 1834.
7. *Leeds Mercury*, *Leeds Times*, 5 April 1834; vestry minutes, 84.

8. *Leeds Intelligencer*, 7 February 1835; cf. Mandamus on the Choice of Churchwardens, King and Churchwardens of Leeds, Baines Papers (Leeds City Archives).

9. *Leeds Intelligencer, Leeds Mercury*, 14, 21, 28 February 1835.

10. *Leeds Intelligencer*, 21 February 1835, *Leeds Mercury*, 28 February 1835

11. E. Baines to E. Baines jun., 15 March 1834, Baines Papers.

12. Vestry minutes 1828–44, 113–14.

13. *Ibid.*, 123; *Leeds Intelligencer, Leeds Times, Leeds Mercury*, 5 December 1835.

14. Vestry minutes, 1828–44, 157–60; *Leeds Mercury, Leeds Intelligencer, Leeds Times*, 1 April 1837.

15. W. R. W. Stephens, *The Life and Letters of Walter Farquhar Hook* (1878), i, 377.

16. Vestry minutes, 166; *Leeds Mercury, Leeds Times*, 12, 19 August 1837.

17. *Leeds Intelligencer, Leeds Mercury*, 14, 21 April 1838.

18. *Leeds Mercury*, 26 March 1842.

19. *Ibid.*, 30 January 1841.

20. *Leeds Times*, 27 November, 4 December 1841.

21. *Leeds Mercury*, 24 December 1841.

22. *Ibid.*, 1, 8, 15, 22 January 1842.

23. Report Book Municipal, vol. 1 86 (Leeds Civic Hall).

24. Stephens, *op. cit.*, 2, 118; *Leeds Times*, 2 April 1842.

25. Stephens, *op. cit.*, 2 (175).

26. W. F. Hook, *A Letter to the Lord Bishop of St Davids* (1846), 38.

27. *Leeds Intelligencer* 10 April 1847, 29 April 1848, 14 April 1849, 6 April 1850.

28. See D. Fraser, 'The Leeds Churchwardens', *Publications of the Thoresby Society*, LIII (1970), 20–1.

29. S. Simon, *A Century of City Government* (1938), 51.

30. The Personal Narrative of George Hadfield M.P., 69 (Manchester Reference Library).

31. *Wheeler's Manchester Chronicle*, 2 July 1825.

32. *Manchester Guardian*, 2 July 1825.

33. *Manchester Courier*, 2 July 1825.

34. Churchwardens' poll, Manchester City Archives M3/3/11.

35. Hadfield, *op. cit.*, 70.

36. *Ibid.; Manchester Guardian*.

37. *Manchester Times*, 29 March 1834.

38. *Ibid.*, 5 April 1834.

39. *Ibid.*, 23 August 1834.

40. *Ibid.*, 13 September 1834; Hadfield, *op. cit.*, 71.

41. *Manchester Times*, 6 September 1834.

42. *Ibid.*, 20 September 1834.

43. *Ibid.*, 11 July 1835; Hadfield, *op. cit.*, 72.

44. *Manchester Guardian*, 9 April 1836.

45. *Ibid.*, 16 April 1836.

46. *Ibid.*, 29 March 1837, 31 March 1838.

47. *Manchester Chronicle*, 6 April 1839.

48. *Manchester Guardian*, 6 April 1839.

49. *Ibid.*, 27, 31 July, 10 August 1839, 19 February 1840.

50. *Manchester Chronicle*, 18 April 1840.

51. *Manchester Guardian*, 22 April 1840.

52. *Ibid.*

53. *Manchester Chronicle*, 25 April 1840.
54. *Manchester Guardian*, 29 April 1840.
55. *Ibid.*, 30 March 1842.
56. W. R. Ward, *Religion and Society in England 1790–1850* (1972), 221–31
57. *Aris's Birmingham Gazette*, 22 November, 6 December 1830.
58. *Philanthropist*, 4 August 1836; J. A. Langford, *Modern Birmingham and Its Institutions* (1873) i, 20.
59. J. A. Jaffray, Hints for a History of Birmingham (1851), Chapter 39 (Birmingham Reference Library).
60. *Aris's Birmingham Gazette*, 30 April 1832.
61. *Ibid.*, 13 August, 10, 24 September 1832.
62. *Birmingham Journal*, 6 October 1832.
63. *Aris's Birmingham Gazette*, 8 October 1832.
64. *Ibid.*, 15 April 1833, 7 April 1834.
65. *Ibid.*, 8 December 1834.
66. *Birmingham Advertiser*, 11 December 1834.
67. *Aris's Birmingham Gazette*, 15 December 1834.
68. *Birmingham Advertiser*, 18, 25 December 1834.
69. J. A. Langford, *A Century of Birmingham Life* (1867), 2, 566.
70. *Aris's Birmingham Gazette*, 11, 18, 25 April 1836; *Birmingham Advertiser*, 21 April 1836; *Birmingham Journal*, 23 April 1836.
71. *Philanthropist*, 29 September 1836.
72. *Birmingham Advertiser*, 23 February 1837; *Philanthropist*, 16 February 1837.
73. *Birmingham Journal*, 1 April 1837.
74. *Aris's Birmingham Gazette*, 29 April 1838; *Birmingham Advertiser*, 5 April 1838.
75. *Aris's Birmingham Gazette*, 19 November 1838, 27 January 1840.
76. *Ibid.*, 23 April 1838.
77. *Birmingham Journal*, 21 December 1839.
78. *Birmingham Advertiser*, 23 April 1840, *Aris's Birmingham Gazette*, 27 April 1840.
79. *Aris's Birmingham Gazette*, 23 April 1841.
80. J. A. Langford, *Modern Birmingham* i, 11–13.
81. *Aris's Birmingham Gazette*, 25 October 1841, *Birmingham Advertiser*, 28 October 1841.
82. *Aris's Birmingham Gazette*, 22 November 1841.
83. *Ibid.*, 28 February 1842; *Birmingham Journal*, 5 March 1842.
84. *Aris's Birmingham Gazette*, 4 April 1842.
85. *Nottingham Review*, 23 August, 27 September 1833, 13 November 1835; *Nottingham Journal*, 20 September 1833, 29 August 1834.
86. *Nottingham Review*, 3 January 1834.
87. *Ibid.*, 10 January 1834.
88. *Ibid.*, 4 April 1834.
89. *Ibid.*, 6 June 1834.
90. *Ibid.*, 3 February 1837; *Nottingham and Newark Mercury*, 4 February 1837; *Nottingham Journal*, 27 January, 5 February 1837.
91. *Nottingham Journal*, 17 March 1837; cf. *ibid.*, 20, 24 February, 10 March 1837.
92. *Ibid.*, 31 March 1837.
93. *Ibid.*, 7 April 1837; *Nottingham Review*, 3 March, 7 April 1837.
94. *Nottingham Journal*, 14 April 1837.

95. *Nottingham and Newark Mercury*, 8 April 1837.
96. *Nottingham Review*, 27 July 1838.
97. *Ibid.*, 13 January 1843.
98. *Ibid.*, 20 January 1843; *Nottingham and Newark Mercury*, 20 January 1843.
99. *Nottingham Journal, Nottingham Review*, 10 February 1843; *Nottingham and Newark Mercury*, 17 February 1843.
100. *Nottingham Journal*, 10 March 1843.
101. *Ibid.*, 24, 31 May 1844.
102. *Leicester Herald*, 30 July 1834.
103. A. Miall, *Life of Edward Miall* (1884), 38.
104. *Leicestershire Mercury*, 20 February 1847; A. T. Patterson, *Radical Leicester* (1954), 247.
105. *Leicester Chronicle*, 4 June 1836.
106. *Leicester Journal*, 29 April 1836; *Leicester Corporation and Parochial Reformer*, 19 May 1836.
107. *Leicester Herald*, 29 October 1836.
108. *Leicestershire Mercury*, 17 September 1836.
109. *Leicester Herald*, 31 December 1836.
110. *Leicester Chronicle*, 7 January 1837; *Leicestershire Mercury*, 7 July 1838; *Leicester Journal*, 25 January 1838.
111. *Leicestershire Mercury, Leicester Herald, Leicester Chronicle*, 6 May 1837.
112. *Leicestershire Mercury*, 22 April 1838.
113. *Leicester Journal*, 3 May 1839; *Leicester Herald*, 4 May 1839.
114. *Leicester Conservative Standard*, June 1836.
115. *Leicester Journal*, 8 December 1837.
116. *Leicestershire Mercury*, 13 June 1840.
117. *Sermon Preached at the Great Meeting by Rev. C. C. Coe* (1871) (Leicester Reference Library Pamphlets 03 ii).
118. *Leicester Chronicle*, 23 November 1839.
119. *Ibid.*, 24 December 1836; *Leeds Journal*, 22 January 1841.
120. *Remarks on the Persecuting Spirit of the Church of England by a Dissenting Minister* (Leicester, 1840), 34.
121. *Leicestershire Mercury* 10 April 1841.
122. *Ibid.*, 2 July 1842.
123. *Ibid.*, 12 March 1842.
124. *Ibid.*, 25 August 1849.
125. *Electors of the Borough of Leeds*, Handbill 9, December 1833.
126. *Leeds Mercury*, 24 December 1841.

Chapter 3

1. Vestry minutes, 1828–44, 124 (Leeds parish church).
2. Robert Baker to Poor Law Commission (hereafter P.L.C.), 18 March 1836, Public Record Office (hereafter P.R.O.), MH12/15224.
3. *Leeds Intelligencer*, 26 December 1835.
4. M. Johnson to P.L.C., 23 April 1836, P.R.O. MH12/15224.
5. *Leeds Mercury*, 28 October, 4 November 1837; J. Beckwith to P.L.C., 20 November 1837, 19 May, 8 June, 4 August 1838; M. Johnson to P.L.C., 11 June 1838, P.R.O. MH12/15224.
6. *Leeds Intelligencer*, 7 January 1837.
7. E. Baines to J. A. Ikin, 30 January 1837, Baines Papers (Leeds City Archives).

8. A. Power to P.L.C., 13 January 1837, P.R.O. MH12/15224.
9. *Ibid.*, 18 November 1836, 6; J. D. Luccock to P.L.C., 15 June 1840, 21 June 1841, MH12/15225; C. Clements Report to P.L.C., 20 January 1843, MH12/15226.
10. J. Beckwith to P.L.C., 22 May 1845, P.R.O. MH12/15227.
11. R. Bissington to M. T. Baines, 16 January 1851, P.R.O. MH12/15230.
12. M. Johnson to P.L.B., 13 January 1848, P.R.O. MH12/15229.
13. *Leeds Intelligencer*, 24 July 1852.
14. Report of H. B. Farnall, 6 August 1852, P.R.O. MH12/15230.
15. *Leeds Times*, 3 July 1852.
16. *Leeds Mercury*, 21 April 1860.
17. Enquiry of H. Longley and D. B. Fry, October 1870, 421, P.R.O. MH12/15243.
18. *Ibid.*, 385.
19. *Ibid.*, 558.
20. *Ibid.*, 508.
21. *Leeds Mercury*, 18 April 1872.
22. *Ibid.*, 23 April 1874.
23. *Ibid.*
24. S. Kelly, 'The Select Vestry of Liverpool and the Administration of the Poor Law 1821–71' (M. A. thesis, University of Liverpool, 1972), 32–5.
25. E. C. Midwinter, *Social Administration in Lancashire 1830–1860* (1969), 13.
26. Resolution of churchwardens, 8 June 1837, Boroughreeve's Letter Book vol. 3, Manchester Reference Library M9/61/1/3.
27. *Manchester Guardian*, 26 December 1840.
28. *Report of the Retiring Board of Guardians of the Manchester Union* (1841), 16.
29. D. A. Farnie, 'The Establishment of the New Poor Law in Salford 1838–1850' (B. A. thesis, University of Manchester, 1951), 9.
30. *1st Half Yearly Report of the Salford Ley-Payers Association* (1833), Lancashire Record Office 1309.
31. *Manchester Times*, 4 April 1835.
32. *Ibid.*, 29 March 1834.
33. R. L. Greenall, 'The Development of Local Government in Salford 1830–1853' (M.A. thesis, University of Leicester 1970), 24.
34. *Manchester Times*, 4 April 1835; W. Paul, *A History of the . . . Operative Conservative Societies* (1838), 27.
35. Garnett Papers, Lancashire Record Office 1514.
36. *Manchester Times*, 4 April 1835.
37. *Manchester Guardian*, 2 April 1836.
38. *Ibid.*, 25 January 1837.
39. *Ibid.*, 29 March 1837.
40. *Report of the Salford Operative Conservative Association* (1837), 17, Lancashire Record Office DDQ 1837.
41. *A Plain Statements of Facts* (Manchester, 1837), 19.
42. *Manchester Guardian*, 31 March 1838.
43. *Ibid.*, 4 April 1838.
44. *Ibid.*, 14 July 1838.
45. *Ibid.*, 21 July 1838.
46. *Ibid.*, 11 July 1838.
47. *Manchester Chronicle*, 14 July 1838.

48. Charles Mott to P.L.C., 18 May 1841, P.R.O. MH12/6220.
49. *Ibid.*, 4 June 1842.
50. *Manchester Guardian*, 1 April 1840.
51. S. P. Robinson to P.L.C., 11 February 1841, P.R.O. MH12/6220.
52. F. Wrigley to P.L.C., 12 December 1840, *ibid.*
53. C. Mott to G. L. Lewis, 23 January 1841, *ibid.*
54. P.L.C. to John Hope, 26 April 1841, *ibid.*
55. C. Mott to P.L.C., 18 May 1841; P.L.C. to J. Hope, 27 May 1841; P.L.C. to J. P. Bunting, 4 June 1841, *ibid.*
56. J. Hope to P.L.C., 27 May 1842; C. Mott to P.L.C. 4 June 1842, *ibid.*
57. C. Clements to P.L.C., 27 November 1842, *ibid.*
58. J. Hope to C. Mott, 28 May 1842, *ibid.*
59. Thomas Allen to P.L.C., 21 June 1844, P.L.C. Contract 12 June 1844, P.R.O. MH12/6221.
60. A. Austin to P.L.C., 6 July 1847; R. Attkins, 14 July 1847, *ibid.*
61. C. Mott to P.L.C., 31 July 1847, *loc. cit.*
62. Midwinter, *op. cit.*, 47.
63. N. McCord, 'The Government of Tyneside 1800–1850', *Bulletin of the Institute of Historical Research*, xx (1970), 20; cf. *idem.*, 'Gateshead Politics in the Age of Reform', *Northern History*, iv (1969), 167–83.
64. T. J. Nossiter, 'Shopkeeper Radicalism in the Nineteenth Century', in Nossiter *et al.* (eds.), *Imagination and Precision in the Social Sciences* (1972), 407–38.
65. F. W. Rogers, 'Local Politics and Administration in the Borough of Gateshead c. 1835–c. 1856', (Ph.D. thesis, University of London, 1971), 214–60.
66. *Ibid.*, 178, 402.
67. Nossiter *et al.*, *op. cit.*, 432.
68. F. W. Rogers, 'Gateshead and the Public Health Act of 1848', *Archaeologia Aeliana*, xlix (1971), 158.
69. *Idem.*, 'Mayoral Elections and the Status of Mayoralty in Early Victorian Gateshead', *Gateshead District Local History Society Bulletin* (1968), 31.
70. Rogers, *op. cit.*, (thesis), 447.
71. *Ibid.*, 225–6.
72. C. Mott to P.L.C., 4 June 1842, P.R.O. MH12/6220.
73. Rogers, *op. cit.*, 248.
74. P. J. Dunkley, 'The New Poor Law and County Durham' (M.A. thesis, University of Durham, 1971), 130.
75. Midwinter, *op. cit.*, 35.
76. Manchester Poor Law Guardians Books, Manchester Reference Library M4/2/1.
77. R. Boyson, 'The History of the Poor Law in North East Lancashire 1834–1871' (M.A. thesis, University of Manchester, 1960), *passim.*
78. Rev. John Hand *et al.* to P.L.C., 16 February 1856, P.R.O. MH12/15474.
79. Farnie, *op. cit.*, 74.
80. Boyson, *op. cit.*, 14.
81. *Bradford Observer*, 2 April 1840.
82. *Birmingham Journal*, 25 March 1837, 4 April 1840.
83. *Birmingham Advertiser*, 9 April 1840.
84. *Leicester Chronicle*, 18 May 1839; A. T. Patterson, *Radical Leicester* (1954), 227.
85. *Nottingham Review*, 17 April 1846; *Leeds Mercury*, 17 April 1869.

86. See N. C. Edsall, *The Anti-Poor Law Movement 1837–1844* (1972); M. E. Rose, 'The Anti-Poor Law Movement in the North of England', *Northern History*, I (1966); C. Driver, *Tory Radical The Life of Richard Oastler* (1946); J. T. Ward, *The Factory Movement* (1962).
87. *Leicester Journal*, 16 February 1838.
88. *Leicester Herald*, 26 November 1836.
89. *Leicester Journal*, 23 February 1838.
90. *Manchester Guardian*, 27 October 1852.
91. *Nottingham and Newark Mercury*, 26 June 1840; *Nottingham Review*, *Nottingham Journal*, 17 July 1840.
92. *Nottingham Review*, *Nottingham Journal*, *Nottingham and Newark Mercury*, 28 August 1840.
93. *Nottingham Review*, 28 August 1840.
94. *Ibid.*, 11, 18, 25 September 1840.
95. *Ibid.*, 6 November 1840.
96. *Nottingham and Newark Mercury*, 6 November 1840.
97. *Nottingham Journal*, 6 November 1840.
98. *Ibid.*, 9 April 1841; cf. R. A. Church, *Economic and Social Change in a Midland Town, Victorian Nottingham* (1966), 120.
99. *Ibid.*, 16 April 1841.
100. J. Sutton, *Date Book. . .* (1852) 446; *Nottingham Review*, 30 April 1841.
101. *Sheffield Times*, 15 March 1851, 10 December 1853.
102. *Sheffield Free Press*, 3 November 1855.
103. *Sheffield Daily Telegraph*, 1, 8, 9, 13, 15, 16, 22 November, 14, 25, 29 December 1855.
104. *Sheffield Free Press*, 24 November 1855.
105. *Ibid.*, 8, 22, 29 March 1856; *Sheffield Daily Telegraph*, 12 April 1856.
106. *Sheffield and Rotherham Independent*, 29 March 1856.
107. *Sheffield Daily Telegraph*, 28 May 1857, 21 January 1858.
108. J. Mainwaring to P.L.B., 26 May, 21, 28 June, 1, 8, 13 August 1857; W. W. Beever to P.L.B., 18 September 1857; P.L.B. to J. Spencer, 30 September 1857, P.R.O. MH12/15474.
109. *Sheffield Daily Telegraph*, 21, 28 January 1858; *Sheffield Times*, 4 August, 18 September 1858; *Address Delivered by Mr George L. Sanders* (1859).
110. *Sheffield and Rotherham Independent*, 10 November 1855.
111. *Sheffield Free Press*, 5 April 1856; *Sheffield Daily Telegraph*, 30 April 1857.
112. *Sheffield Times*, 22 March 1856; Farnall to P.L.B., 17 March 1856, P.R.O. MH12/15474.
113. J. Mainwaring to P.L.B., 21 June 1857, P.R.O. MH12/15475.
114. *Sheffield Daily Telegraph*, 15 December 1855, 27 March 1856.
115. *Ibid.*, 15 December 1856; (cf. *Sheffield Free Press*, 15, 29 December 1855, 29 March 1856).
116. *Ibid.*, 9 November 1855.
117. *Sheffield Times*, 10 November 1855; cf. 1, 8 November 1855.
118. R. Younge to P.L.B., 23 February 1856, P.R.O. MH12/15474.
119. *Sheffield Free Press*, 22 March 1856.
120. *Sheffield and Rotherham Independent*, 29 March 1856.
121. *To The Ratepayers of Sheffield* (April 1856), P.R.O. MH12/15474; see also *Sheffield Times*, 10 November 1855.
122. *Sheffield and Rotherham Independent*, 17 November 1855.
123. *Sheffield Daily Telegraph*, 15 December 1855; *Sheffield Free Press*, 22 March, 5 April 1856.

124. *Sheffield Iris*, 13 November 1855; *Sheffield Daily Telegraph*, 18 November 1855.
125. *Sheffield Iris*, 13 November 1855.
126. *Sheffield Free Press*, 22 March 1856.
127. *Sheffield Iris*, 16 April 1856.
128. *Sheffield Free Press*, 15 December 1855.
129. *Sheffield Iris*, 15 April 1856.
130. *Sheffield Free Press*, 19 July 1856.
131. J. Mainwaring note, 21 April 1857, P.R.O. MH12/15475.
132. Resolutions 7 October 1857, *ibid.*
133. *Sheffield Iris*, 13 November 1855.
134. *Sheffield Times*, 18 September 1858.
135. Cf. D. Fraser, 'Poor Law Politics in Leeds 1833–1855', *Publications of the Thoresby Society*, LIII (1970), 23–49.
136. *Leeds Mercury*, 13 April 1844.
137. *Leeds Intelligencer*, 8 April 1843.
138. *Leeds Mercury*, 8 April 1868.
139. Memo to P.L.B. 15 August 1859, Ramsden Papers LCA Box 47 B2 (Leeds City Archives).
140. *Liverpool Mercury*, 21 March 1845.
141. *Ibid.*, 4 April 1845.
142. *Ibid.*, 13 March, 17 April 1846.
143. *Ibid.*, 31 October 1848.
144. C. Mott to G. L. Lewis, 23 January 1841, P.R.O. MH12/6220.
145. P.L.C. to J. Hope, 26 April 1841, *ibid.*
146. *Ibid.*
147. J. Hope to C. Mott, 28 May 1842, *ibid.*
148. Farnie, *op. cit.*, 75.
149. See H. A. Taylor, 'Politics in Famine Stricken Preston'.
150. E. Ambler to G. Melly, 10 April 1863, Melly Papers 1613 (Liverpool Record Office).
151. E. Ambler to G. Melly, 8 March 1864; Melly to Ambler, 12 March 1864, Melly Papers 1987/8.
152. E. Ambler to G. Melly, 13 August 1863, *ibid.*, 1638.
153. Report . . . Leeds 1870, 409, P.R.O. MH12/15243.
154. E. Ambler to G. Melly, 25 July 1863, Melly Papers 1637.
155. *Ibid.*, 21 June 1864, Melly Papers 2005.
156. *Ibid.*, 8 April 1863, Melly Papers 1612.

Chapter 4

1. *First Report of the Royal Commission on Municipal Corporations in England and Wales*, 1835, XXIII, Leeds Report, 8.
2. *Ibid.*, 6.
3. *Leeds Mercury*, 7 January 1837, 6 January 1838, 5 January 1839.
4. *Ibid.*, 11 January 1840.
5. *Leeds Intelligencer*, 4 January 1840.
6. *Ibid.*, 9 January 1841.
7. *Leeds Mercury*, 4, 11 January, 1, 8 February 1840; vestry minutes 1828–1844, 203. J. F. C. Harrison, 'Chartism in Leeds' in A. Briggs (ed.), *Chartist Studies* (1959), 86, erroneously claims that the Tories were defeated.
8. *Leeds Times*, 9, 16 January 1841, 1, 8 January 1842; Proceedings of the Commissioners, 7 January 1841, 6 January 1842 (Leeds Civic Hall).

9. Vestry minutes, 245–60.
10. Cf. Robert Perring in his new ephemeral venture *Leeds Conservative Journal*, 4, 18, 25 June 1842.
11. Vestry minutes, 261; *Leeds Intelligencer*, 30 April 1842.
12. S. and B. Webb, *Statutory Authorities For Special Purposes* (1963 edn), 246.
13. A. Prentice, *Historical Sketches and Personal Recollections of Manchester* (1851), 313.
14. A. Redford, *The History of Local Government in Manchester* (1939), i, 305.
15. Prentice, *op. cit.*, 317–18.
16. F. Vigier, *Change and Apathy* (1970), 148–9.
17. Redford, *op. cit.*, i, 319–25.
18. Manchester Police Commissioners Minutes, vol. 8, 50 (Manchester Reference Library).
19. *Ibid.*, vol. 9, 267.
20. *Ibid.*, 367, 432–4.
21. For membership of the Commission see by way of example *ibid.*, vol. 8, 5; vol. 9, 59.
22. *Manchester Times*, 25 January, 1834.
23. Police Commissioners Minutes, vol. 9, 168.
24. *Ibid.*, vol. 8, 50.
25. *Ibid.*, vol. 9, 354.
26. *Ibid.*, 359.
27. *Ibid.*, vol. 8, 116–19, 133.
28. *Ibid.*, 309–17, 329–30.
29. *Manchester Guardian*, 5 January 1839.
30. *Ibid.*, 30 October 1839.
31. Police Commissioners Minutes, vol. 8, 417.
32. *Ibid.*, vol. 9, 161.
33. Report of the General Purposes Committee, 18 June 1843, Wilson Papers (Manchester Reference Library).
34. R. L. Greenall, 'The Development of Local Government in Salford 1830–1853' (M.A. thesis, University of Leicester, 1970), 40.
35. *Manchester Guardian*, 27 July 1839.
36. *Manchester Times*, 27 January 1844.
37. *Manchester Guardian*, 13 April 1844.
38. *Manchester Times*, 27 April 1844.
39. C. Gill, 'Birmingham Under the Street Commissioners', *University of Birmingham Historical Journal*, i (1947–8), 255–87.
40. *Birmingham Journal*, 23 February 1839.
41. E. P. Hennock, *Fit and Proper Persons* (1973), 25.
42. *Birmingham Journal*, 21 October 1837.
43. *Ibid.*, 18 November 1843.
44. *Ibid.*, 11 May 1844 *et seq.*; cf. J. T. Bunce, *History of the Corporation of Birmingham*, i (1878), 296.
45. *Birmingham Journal*, 28 July 1849.
46. *Ibid.*, 30 March 1850.

Chapter 5
1. *Bradford Observer*, 30 March 1843.
2. *Second Report of the Commissioners for Enquiring into the State of Large Towns and Populous Districts* (1845) ii, 184.

3. *Bradford Observer*, 28 March 1844.
4. *Manchester Guardian*, 4 April 1838.
5. *Bradford Observer*, 12, 19 June 1845.
6. *Ibid.*, 27 March 1845.
7. *Ibid.*, 2 April 1846.
8. *Leeds Conservative Journal*, 25 June 1852.
9. For the elections see vestry minutes 1828–44, 264–6, 270–1; *Leeds Mercury* 6, 13 April 1844, 28 March 1846, 1 April 1848, 31 March 1849, 30 March 1850, 29 March 1851.
10. *Leeds Intelligencer*, 3 April 1852.
11. *Leeds Mercury*, 3, 10 April 1852.
12. *Ibid.*, 31 March 1855.
13. *Ibid.*, 1 April 1854.
14. *Ibid.*, 27, 31 March, 17 April 1860.
15. *Ibid.*, 26, 28 March 1861.
16. *Ibid.*, 1 April 1854.
17. For Ironside see J. Salt, 'Experiments in Anarchism 1850–1854', *Transactions of the Hunter Archaeological Society* (1972), 37–53.
18. J. Toulmin Smith, *Local Self Government and Centralisation* (1851), 36.
19. *Second Report. . . . Large Towns . . . 1845*, ii, 188.
20. *Sheffield Times*, 29 March 1851.
21. *Sheffield Free Press*, 27 March 1852.
22. *Sheffield Times*, 25 September 1852.
23. *Sheffield and Rotherham Independent*, 25 September 1852.
24. *Sheffield Free Press*, 25 September 1852.
25. *Ibid.*, 9 October 1852.
26. *Sheffield Times*, 9 October 1852.
27. *Ibid.*; 22 October 1853, 25 March, 1 July 1854 *Sheffield and Rotherham Independent*, 9 October 1852, 17 June 1854.
28. Salt, *op. cit.*, 49.
29. *Sheffield Times*, 2 April 1853.
30. *Sheffield Free Press*, 2 April 1853.
31. *Sheffield and Rotherham Independent*, 9 April 1853.
32. *Ibid.*, 1 April 1854.

Chapter 6

1. R. W. Greaves, *The Corporation of Leicester* (1939), 86.
2. Report of J. R. Drinkwater and R. J. Saunders, 26 January 1833, P.R.O. H052/23.
3. *First Report of the Municipal Corporations Commission*, iv (1835), 2706; cf., for a contrary interpretation, F. Vigier, *Change and Apathy* (1970), *passim*.
4. *Leeds Mercury*, 28 December 1833; *Municipal Corporations. . . . Leeds Report*, 6.
5. *Liverpool A Few Years Since* (1852), 103.
6. *Liverpool Mercury*, 25 October 1833.
7. *Leicester Chronicle*, 5 February 1831.
8. *Leicester Corporation and Parochial Reformer*, 18 September 1835.
9. *Nottingham Journal*, 27 September 1833.
10. E. P. Hennock, *Fit and Proper Persons* (1973), 185.
11. *Leicester Herald*, 19 December 1835.

12. W. E. A. Axon, *Cobden as a Citizen* (1907), 69.
13. Proceedings of Public Meetings in Manchester . . ., 326–7, 9 February 1837 (Manchester Reference Library).
14. *Ibid.*, 410, 9 February 1838.
15. Axon, *op. cit.*, 70.
16. *Incorporate Your Borough by a Radical Reformer* (1837), 4.
17. *Manchester Guardian*, 10 February 1838.
18. *Ibid.*
19. *Sheffield Iris*, 9 January 1838, quoted by N. C. Edsall, 'Varieties of Radicalism . . .', *Historical Journal*, XVI (1973), 99; Axon, *op. cit.*, 88.
20. *Manchester Guardian*, 10 February 1838.
21. *Incorporate Your Borough*, 9–12.
22. J. Morley, *The Life of Richard Cobden* (1903), 124.
23. Quoted by S. D. Simon, *A Century of City Government* (1938), 98.
24. *Manchester Guardian*, 11 February 1837.
25. *Ibid.*, 10 January 1846.
26. Cobden to Wilson, 5 May 1838, Wilson Papers (Manchester Reference Library).
27. Morley, *op. cit.*, 124.
28. *Incorporate Your Borough*, 12.
29. *Liverpool Mercury*, 28 October 1836.
30. *Bradford Observer*, 19 August 1847.
31. *Leeds Intelligencer*, 2 March 1838.
32. *Leeds Mercury*, 30 March 1866.
33. Cf. D. Fraser, papers in *Publications of the Thoresby Society*, LIII (1970). 1–70.
34. *Leeds Mercury*, 15 October 1836.
35. *Leeds Intelligencer*, 16 January, 17 September 1836.
36. *Ibid.*, 17 November, 1 December 1838.
37. *Leeds Mercury*, 11 November 1862.
38. *Ibid.*, 10 November 1864.
39. *Leeds Times*, 30 January 1836.
40. For a full review of the dispute see *Leeds Mercury*, 19 September 1840; for the legal decision see *English Reports*, vol. XLI, *Chancery* XXI, 389–400; see also Council Minutes, vol. 5, 392–409 (Leeds Civic Hall).
41. *Leeds Intelligencer*, 20 June 1846.
42. C. Scarborough, *To the Chairman . . . in the East Ward* (1837); *Leeds Intelligencer*, 18 April 1838.
43. *Leeds Mercury*, 2 February 1839.
44. *Leeds Intelligencer*, 14 October 1848; *Leeds Mercury*, 21 October 1848.
45. *Leeds Intelligencer*, 16 March 1844.
46. *Leeds Mercury*, 3 November 1859.
47. Bribery and Corruption Committee Minutes 1866–7; Report Book Municipal, vol. 5, 299–300 (Leeds Civic Hall).
48. Cf. J. Redlich and F. W. Hirst, *The History of Local Government in England* (1970 edn), 181.
49. J. S. Curtis, *The Story of the Marsden Mayoralty* (1875), 1.
50. *Leeds Mercury*, 1 November 1877.
51. *Ibid.*, 1 November 1873, 1 November 1879.
52. *Ibid.*, November 1874, *passim*; Curtis, *op. cit.*, 65–85.
53. Hennock, *op. cit.*, 253–63.
54. *Liverpool Mercury*, 20 November 1835.

55. Cf. C. D. Watkinson, 'The Liberal Party on Merseyside in the Nineteenth Century' (Ph.D. thesis, University of Liverpool, 1967).
56. H. M. Walmsley, *The Life of Joshua Walmsley* (1879), 91.
57. S. G. Checkland, *The Gladstones A Family Biography* (1972), 336.
58. *Liverpool Mercury*, 6 November 1840.
59. James Mellor to J. B. Smith, 10 December 1841, J. B. Smith's Corn Law Papers (Manchester Reference Library).
60. *Liverpool Mercury*, 13 January 1837.
61. C. E. Rawlins jun. to G. Wilson, 31 December 1846, Wilson Papers.
62. *Liverpool Mercury*, 17 February 1858.
63. M. Williams to G. Melly 22 October 1861, Melly Papers 638 (Liverpool Record Office); cf. L. Greg to G. Melly, 4 December 1869, Melly Papers 3607.
64. *Porcupine*, 11 October 1862, 220.
65. *Liverpool Journal*, 26 October 1878, 8 November 1879.
66. B. D. White, *A History of the Corporation of Liverpool* (1951), 101; cf. *ibid.*, 196.
67. *Liverpool Mercury*, 6 February 1857.
68. S. B. Jackson to G. Melly, 24 October 1862, Melly Papers 984.
69. *Porcupine*, 11, 18 October, 1, 8, 15 November 1862; H. H. Gandy to G. Melly 24 October 1862, Melly Papers 983; see also Melly Papers 980, 987, 988, 989.
70. R. Gladstone to G. Melly, 28 October 1862, Melly Papers 1556.
71. *Porcupine*, 28 October 1865, 260.
72. *Liverpool Mercury*, 16 November 1838, 6 February 1857; E. F. Rathbone, *William Rathbone A Memoir* (1908), 145.
73. R. Gladstone to G. Melly, 12 November 1862; W. Brumfitt to G. Melly, 8 November 1862, Melly Papers, 982, 991.
74. *Porcupine*, 5 November 1864, 252.
75. *Liverpool Mercury*, 23 December 1858.
76. *Porcupine*, 12 November 1864.
77. *Ibid.*, 1 July 1865, 108, 28 October 1865, 260, 30 October 1869, 296, 6 November 1869, 301.
78. *Ibid.*, 18 October 1862, 225.
79. W. Rathbone to G. Melly, 3 October 1863, Melly Papers 1446; cf. *Porcupine*, 24 October 1863, 235–7.
80. P. Holt to G. Melly, 29 October 1865, Melly Papers 2263; see also *ibid.*, 1894.
81. M. Williams to G. Melly, 22 October 1861, Melly Papers 638.
82. S. B. Jackson to G. Melly, 24 October 1862, Melly Papers 984.
83. L. Greg to G. Melly, 4 December 1869, Melly Papers 3607.
84. *Porcupine*, 17 June 1865.
85. L. Greg to G. Melly, 4 December 1869, Melly Papers 3607.
86. J. T. Bunce, *History of the Corporation of Birmingham*, I (1878), 287.
87. *Birmingham Advertiser*, 14 April 1840.
88. *Nottingham Review*, 1, 8, 15 November 1844; cf. R. A. Church, *Economic and Social Change in a Midland Town, Victorian Nottingham* (1966), 176–181.
89. *Manchester Guardian*, 18 August 1838.
90. *Manchester Courier*, 20 October 1838.
91. *Leicester Journal*, 26 October 1838.
92. *Birmingham Advertiser*, 7 November 1844, 5 November 1846.

93. *Bradford Observer*, 18 April 1847.
94. *Manchester Examiner and Times*, 4 November 1848.
95. *Ibid.*, 2 November 1853.
96. *Manchester Guardian*, 3 November 1857.
97. Simon, *op. cit.*, 398; T. Woolley to G. Wilson, 25 February 1843, Wilson Papers (Manchester Reference Library); *Manchester Guardian*, 15 October 1851.
98. *Birmingham Journal*, 10 November 1838.
99. Proceedings of Public Meetings . . ., 410; J. Parkes to R. Cobden, 15 August 1838, Wilson Papers.
100. Quoted by G. B. A. M. Finlayson in *Bulletin of the Institute of Historical Research*, xxvi (1963), 51.
101. *Leeds Intelligencer*, 2 January 1836.
102. *Birmingham Advertiser* 28 December 1837.
103. *Bradford Observer*, 24 October 1850.
104. *Leeds Mercury*, 16 January 1836.
105. S. G. Rathbone to G. Melly, n.d. (1865), Melly Papers 2264.
106. *Liverpool Mercury*, 6 November 1838, 10 November 1864; Walmsley, *op. cit.*, 100–29; *Porcupine*, 12 November 1864.
107. E. Gaskell, *Letters* (ed. J. A. V. Chapple and A. Pollard, 1966), my italics.
108. *Incorporate Your Borough*, 3.
109. R. Hall and A. Titley to Lord John Russell, 29, 31 January 1836, P.R.O. H052/31; Bunce, *op. cit.*, i, 171.
110. *Ibid.*, ii, 267.
111. W. Brown to G. Wilson, 28 December 1852, Wilson Papers.
112. J. Robinson to G. Melly, 21 November 1863, Melly Papers 1556; J. Platt to G. Wilson 7 June 1852, Wilson Papers.
113. *Porcupine*, 16 April 1864 (p. 17).
114. *Manchester Guardian*, 4 November 1843; 10, 31 October, 4 November 1846; *Manchester Examiner and Times*, 2 November 1847.
115. *Manchester Examiner and Times*, 4 November 1848.

Chapter 7

1. *Northern Star*, 7 November 1840; *The Factory System* (1831), 12, Oastler White Slavery Collection (University of London).
2. *Leeds Mercury*, 27 January 1838.
3. *Manchester Guardian*, 10 January 1846.
4. For a fuller survey see D. Fraser, 'The Politics of Leeds Water', *Publications of the Thoresby Society*, liii (1970), 70–90.
5. Statement of the Case in Support of the Bill, Lane Fox MSS. 101–4 (Leeds City Archives).
6. *Leeds Intelligencer*, 15 November 1834.
7. J. Chiesman, *A Brief Review of the Plans of the Several Engineers* . . . (1834), 6–12.
8. H. Abraham, *Leeds Water Works*, handbill, 24 September 1835.
9. *Leeds Intelligencer*, 19, 26 September 1835.
10. *Proposed New Waterworks*, 29 August 1836, Thoresby Society Library 22 B10.
11. *Ibid.*, anonymous MS. note.
12. Leeds Water Works, Proposal to Establish Joint Stock Company, Harewood MSS. (Leeds City Archives).
13. *Leeds Times*, 10 December 1836.

14. *Ibid.*, 7 January 1837.
15. *Leeds Mercury*, 28 January, 4, 11 February 1837.
16. *Ibid.*, 31 March 1838.
17. *Leeds New Waterworks*, 31 January, 14 February 1838; J. W. Leather, *Statement of Facts* (1838) and *Reply to . . . Henry R. Abraham . . .* (1838).
18. *Leeds Mercury*, 31 March 1838.
19. F. H. Fawkes to C. Wood, 16 June 1852, Hickleton MSS. A4/150 (Garrowby; a microfilm set is available in Leeds University Library).
20. *Leeds Intelligencer, Leeds Times*, 6 September 1851.
21. Report Book Leeds Improvement Act, vol. 2, 1–24; Report Book Municipal, vol. 3, 23–39; Council Minutes vol. 8, 396–8 (Leeds Civic Hall).
22. *Leeds Mercury*, 14 August, 20 November 1852.
23. J. Toft, 'Public Health in Leeds in the Nineteenth Century' (M.A. thesis, University of Manchester, 1966), 286.
24. *Leeds Mercury*, 9 April 1867.
25. *Ibid.*, 2 November 1867.
26. *Ibid.*, 9 April 1868.
27. The best account is to be found in N. Thompson Parry, 'The Administration and Politics of Liverpool 1835–50' (B.A. thesis, University of Liverpool, 1939), 149–63; E. Midwinter, *Old Liverpool* (1971), 100–6, is marred by inaccuracies.
28. J. Grantham, *On the Supply of Water to Liverpool* (1848), 14.
29. S. Holme, *Want of Water* (1845), 59.
30. H. Banner, *Water, A Pamphlet* (1845), 18.
31. Holme, *op. cit.*, 53–4. See also R. Gossage, *To the Mayor . . . of Liverpool* (1846).
32. *Report of the Special Committee . . . on Water Supply* (1849), 5–9.
33. *Ibid.*, 6.
34. T. Spencer, *The Supply of Water to Liverpool* (1848), 48.
35. *Ibid.*, 41.
36. Grantham, *op. cit.*, 8.
37. Spencer, *op. cit.*, 43–52.
38. *George Holt a Brief Memoir* (1860), 99.
39. *Liverpool Mercury*, 15, 19 September, 20, 27, 31 October, 3, 10 November 1848.
40. J. Simpson and J. Newlands, *Liverpool Water Supply* (1849).
41. *George Holt*, 100.
42. *Liverpool Mercury*, 16 February 1849.
43. *Ibid.*, 25 September 1849.
44. Grantham, *op. cit.*, 17.
45. *Report of the Special Committee . . .* (1849), 12–17.
46. *Liverpool Mercury*, 9, 30 October, 2 November 1849.
47. R. Stephenson, *The Supply of Water to the Town of Liverpool* (1850), 47–8.
48. A. T. Patterson, *Radical Leicester* (1954), 335–9.
49. *Leicester Chronicle*, 21 September 1844; cf. *ibid.*, 21 January, 19 August, 2 September, 18 November, 16 December 1843.
50. *Leicestershire Mercury*, 24 May, 16 August, 6 September, 8, 15 November 1845.
51. *Leicester Chronicle*, 13 December 1845.
52. *Ibid.*, 21 September 1844.
53. *Leicestershire Mercury*, 20, 27 December 1845, 3 January 1846.

54. *Leicester Chronicle*, 27 December 1845.
55. *Ibid.*, 13 December 1845.
56. *Ibid.*, 17 October 1846; *Leicestershire Mercury*, 31 October, 7 November 1846.
57. *Payne's Leicester Advertiser*, 12 July 1845.
58. *Leicester Journal*, 27 March 1846.
59. *Leicester Chronicle* 17 October 1846.
60. *Payne's Leicester Advertiser*, 13 June 1846.
61. *Leicester Chronicle*, 3 November 1849.
62. *Manchester Guardian*, 13 July 1844.
63. *A Letter to William Lockett . . . on the new Salford Improvement Act* (1844).
64. *Manchester Guardian*, 21 January 1843.
65. Cuttings, 24 November 1847 in Jenkinson Papers, Lancashire Record Office 1309.
66. *Ibid.*, 15 December 1847.
67. R. L. Greenall, 'The Making of the Borough of Salford 1830–1853', in S. P. Bell (ed.), *Victorian Lancashire* (1974), 53–8.
68. R. Rawlinson, *Report to the General Board of Health . . . Pendleton* (1851), 48.
69. *Birmingham Journal*, 11 May 1844, 3 May 1845.
70. *Ibid.*, 29 March 1845.
71. *Birmingham Advertiser*, 27 March 1845.
72. *Birmingham Journal*, 1 March 1845.
73. *Pilot*, 3 May 1845.
74. *Ibid.*, 16 November 1844.
75. *Birmingham Journal*, 3 May 1845.
76. *Midland Counties Herald*, 8 October 1846.
77. *Birmingham Journal*, 3 April, 9 July 1847, 12 February 1848; *Midland Counties Herald*, 16 November 1848; *Birmingham Advertiser*, 3 June 1847; *Aris's Birmingham Gazette*, 13 March 1848.
78. *Birmingham Mercury*, 3 February 1849; *Birmingham Journal*, 4 August 1849.
79. *Midland Counties Herald*, 16 November 1848.
80. Quoted by C. Gill, *History of Birmingham* (1951), I, 358.
81. J. T. Bunce, *A History of the Corporation of Birmingham*, I (1878), II (1885); C. Gill and A. Briggs, *History of Birmingham* (1951) I and II; E. P. Hennock, *Fit and Proper Persons* (1973), I.
82. Quoted by Hennock, *op. cit.*, 171.

Chapter 8

1. S. Greg to G. Melly, 6 January 1858, Melly Papers 293 (Liverpool Record Office).
2. E. Baines to Charlotte Baines, 5 March 1837, Baines Papers (Leeds City Archives): cf. J. Bright to G. Wilson, 12 June 1847, Wilson Papers (Manchester Record Office).
3. S. R. Rathbone to G. Melly, n.d. [1867?], Melly Papers 2818.
4. *Aris's Birmingham Gazette*, 7 June 1847; *Address of . . . Oastler*, Oastler and The Factory Movement No. 541 (2); *Leeds Intelligencer*, 31 March 1838.
5. J. Brotherton to G. Wilson, 25 May 1840, Wilson Papers; cf. R. Cobden to G. Wilson, 14 June 1840, Wilson Papers, and R. Cobden to J. B. Smith, 28 June 1840, Manchester Reference Library MS. 923.2.5345.

6. J. Bright to G. Wilson, 26 November 1846, Wilson Papers.
7. E. Baines to Lord John Russell 29, 31 January 1836, P.R.O. H052 /31.
8. *Porcupine*, 17 June 1865.
9. G. Smith jun. to G. Melly, 28 November 1864, Melly Papers 2155; Melly had earlier attempted to get a magistracy for Smith: see J. Vincent, *The Formation of the Liberal Party 1857–1868* (1966), 135.
10. A. Henry to G. Wilson, 5 January 1848, Wilson Papers.
11. W. Brown to G. Wilson, 28 December 1852, Wilson Papers.
12. C. H. Jones to R. Cobden, 3 January 1848, Wilson Papers.
13. J. Stansfield sen. to C. Wood, 13 October and 15 October 1849, Hickleton MSS. A4/50 (Garrowby; a microfilm set is available in Leeds University Library).
14. *Ibid.*, 9 April 1845.
15. S. Smiles to J. A. Roebuck, 23 December 1840, Smiles Papers (Leeds City Archives).
16. *Aris's Birmingham Gazette*, 15 July 1844; *Birmingham Journal*, 26 June, 31 July 1847.
17. R. Cobden to G. Wilson, 14 June 1840, Wilson Papers.
18. R. H. Greg to G. Melly, 2 March 1867, Melly Papers 2848.
19. D. C. Moore, 'The Other Face of Reform', *Victorian Studies*, v (1961–2), and 'Social Structure . . . etc.' in R. Robson (ed.), *Ideas and Institutions of Victorian Britain* (1967); J. R. Vincent, *Poll Books* (1967); T. J. Nossiter, 'Elections and Political Behaviour in County Durham and Newcastle' (D.Phil. thesis, University of Oxford, 1969), and *Influence, Opinion, and Political Idioms in Reformed England* (1975).
20. Moore, 'Other Face of Reform', n. 6.
21. Vincent, *Poll Books*, 4.
22. Quoted by *Leeds Mercury*, 7 February 1846.
23. *Ibid.*, 27 January 1838.
24. *Ibid.*, 2 June 1849.
25. *Ibid.*, 12 December 1840.
26. Circular letters, North Western Association of Baptist Churches (1867), 5.
27. G. Melly to W. Grenfell, 2 October 1867, Melly Papers 2829.
28. J. Bright to G. Wilson, 23 June 1848, 1, 10, 15 July 1850, Wilson Papers.
29. *Leeds Mercury*, 26 November 1836.
30. Wortley MS. Notebook, Thoresby Society Library (Leeds) 37A.
31. For fuller details see D. Fraser, 'The Fruits of Reform: Leeds Politics in the 1830s', *Northern History*, vii (1972), 90–5.
32. *Report of the Committee of the Leeds Association . . .* (1832), 3.
33. C. D. Watkinson, 'The Liberal Party on Merseyside in the Nineteenth Century' (Ph.D. thesis, University of Liverpool, 1967). 132–54.
34. *Liverpool Mercury*, 21 October 1836.
35. *Ibid.*, 13 February 1869, quoted by Watkinson, *op. cit.*, 349.
36. J. Butterworth to G. Wilson, 7 September 1839, Wilson Papers.
37. *Manchester Guardian*, 25 March 1857.
38. J. Ashton to G. Melly, 13 May 1859, Melly Papers 338.
39. P. Whitaker, 'The Growth of Liberal Organisation in Manchester From the Eighteen Sixties to 1903' (Ph.D. thesis, University of Manchester 1956), 48–70.

40. The best account is to be found in A. Briggs, *History of Birmingham* (1950), II, Chapter VI; cf. Hennock, *Fit and Proper Persons*, 131–8.
41. H. W. Crosskey (1877), quoted by Briggs, *op. cit.*, 166.
42. G. Melly to W. E. Gladstone, 10 August 1867, quoted by Watkinson, *op. cit.*, 329.
43. Cf. D. Fraser, 'Politics in Leeds 1830–1852' (Ph.D. thesis, University of Leeds, 1969), 213–21.
44. Watkinson, *op. cit.*, 267.
45. *Liverpool Mercury*, 6 February 1857.
46. E. W. Cox and S. G. Grady, *The New Law and Practice of Registration and Elections*, quoted by H. J. Hanham, Introduction to C. R. Dod, *Electoral Facts* (1853, new edn 1972), XLVII.
47. Quoted by Briggs, *op. cit.*, 172.
48. Vincent, *Poll Books*, 10–11.
49. B. Harrison, *Drink and the Victorians* (1970).
50. *Northern Star*, 21 April 1838.
51. Cf. W. Paul, *A History of the Origins and Progress of Operative Conservative Societies* (1838).
52. W. J. Lampen to G. Melly, 14 November 1870, Melly Papers 3968.
53. *A Plain Statement of Facts* . . . (1837); cf. . . . *Second Anniversary Dinner of the Salford Operative Conservative Association* (1837), 13–19.
54. *The Public and Parliamentary Speeches of Sir William Molesworth* (1837).
55. S. Smiles to J. A. Roebuck, 23 December 1840, Smiles Papers (Leeds City Archives).
56. W. Biggs to G. Wilson, 28 February 1847, Wilson Papers.
57. J. Bright to G. Wilson, 13 June 1844, T. Woolley to G. Wilson, 13 July 1844, Wilson Papers.
58. *Birmingham Advertiser*, 1 July 1847.
59. *Birmingham Journal*, 23 October 1847.
60. *Aris's Birmingham Gazette*, 2 August 1847.
61. R. Cobden to G. Wilson, 7 August 1852, Wilson Papers.
62. J. Lockwood to G. Melly, 10 April 1862, Melly Papers 1296.
63. A. Briggs, 'The Parliamentary Reform Movement in Three English Cities', *Cambridge Historical Journal* (1952), and *Chartist Studies* (1959).
64. Quoted by D. E. Fletcher, 'Aspects of Liberalism in Sheffield 1849–1886' (Ph.D. thesis, University of Sheffield, 1972), 1.
65. R. Cobden to J. B. Smith, 12 August 1857, Manchester Reference Library MS. 932,2,5345.
66. J. O. Foster, *Class Struggle and the Industrial Revolution; Early Industrial Capitalism in Three English Towns* (1974).
67. F. Schwann to R. Cobden, 13 April 1852, Wilson Papers.
68. R. Cobden to G. Wilson, 3 August 1846, Wilson Papers.
69. T. Potter to Jacob Bright, 26 July, 1 August 1843; J. Bright to G. Wilson, 5 November 1846, Wilson Papers.
70. J. Bright to G. Wilson, 26 November 1846, Wilson Papers.
71. W. Neild to G. Wilson, 8 June 1847, Wilson Papers.
72. R. Cobden to H. Ashworth, 13 December 1849, B.M. Add. MS. 43653, f. 152.
73. *Manchester Examiner and Times*, 30 October, 2, 13 November 1850.
74. *Ibid.*, 4 November 1848.
75. W. Brown to G. Wilson, 30 March 1851, Wilson Papers.

76. J. A. Williams, 'Manchester and the Manchester School 1830–1857' (M.A. thesis, University of Leeds, 1966), 177.
77. J. Bright to G. Wilson, 10 December 1854, Wilson Papers.
78. R. Cobden to G. Wilson, 10 December 1854, Wilson Papers.
79. Williams, *op. cit.*, 227, 235.
80. J. B. Smith to R. Cobden, 20 May 1857, B.M. Add. MS. 43669, f. 138.
81. *Manchester Guardian*, 4 July 1846.
82. *Ibid.*, 14 March 1857.
83. *Manchester Courier*, 4 April 1857; *Manchester Guardian*, 20 March 1857.
84. J. Vaughan to G. Wilson, 1 April 1857, Wilson Papers.
85. J. Bright to R. Cobden, 22 March 1857, Wilson Papers.
86. *Manchester Examiner and Times*, 18 March 1857.
87. V. A. C. Gatrell, 'The Commercial Middle Class in Manchester c.1820–1857' (Ph.D. thesis, University of Cambridge, 1971), 382–466.
88. J. Bright to J. Brooks, 26 October 1846, Correspondence of John Brooks (7), Lancashire Record Office, DDX 821/2/1.
89. R. Cobden to F. Cobden, n.d. 1857, Cobden Papers, Manchester Reference Library, M87/4/2.
90. *Manchester Examiner and Times*, 30 March 1857.
91. J. Parkes to A. Watkin, 20 August 1857, Wilson Papers.
92. J. Bright to G. Wilson, 31 March 1857, Wilson Papers.
93. *Ibid.*, 19 April 1857.
94. R. Cobden to G. Wilson, 30 May 1857, Wilson Papers.
95. *Birmingham Commercial Herald*, 5, 12, 19 October 1812; *Aris's Birmingham Gazette*, 9, 16, 23, 30 October 1820.
96. N. Gash, 'Brougham and the Yorkshire Election of 1830', *Procs. Leeds Phil. and Lit. Soc.* (1956), 19–35.
97. A. Henry to G. Wilson, 20 March 1852, Wilson Papers.
98. *Birmingham Journal*, 4 October 1845.
99. Earl Fitzwilliam to Sir C. Wood, 22 July 1844, Hickleton MSS. A4/36.
100. D. Fraser, 'Edward Baines' in P. Hollis (ed.), *Pressure From Without In Early Victorian England* (1974), 183–209.
101. R. Cobden to J. Parkes, 16 February 1846 (?), B.M. Add. MS. 46664, f. 5.
102. J. Fielding to G. Wilson, 25 June 1847, Wilson Papers.
103. C. P. Villiers to J. Brooks, 6 August 1847, Correspondence of John Brooks (9).
104. F. M. C. Thompson, 'Whigs and Liberals . . .', *English Historical Review*, LXXIV (1959), 239.
105. Hatherton Diary, 22 December 1853, quoted by V. I. Tunsiri, 'Party Politics of the Black Country and Neighbourhood 1832–1867' (M.A. thesis, University of Birmingham, 1964), 103.
106. J. Parkes to G. Wilson, 12 June 1852, Wilson Papers.
107. *Ibid.*, 7 June 1852.
108. E. Ashworth to G. Wilson, 13 February 1857, Wilson Papers.

Chapter 9

1. A. McCall to G. Wilson, 12 February 1846, Wilson Papers.
2. Cf. T. J. Nossiter, *Influence, Opinion and Political Idioms in Reformed England* (1975), 174; V. A. C. Gatrell, 'The Commercial Middle Class in Manchester' (Ph.D. thesis, University of Cambridge, 1971), 125–6; J. R. Vincent, *Poll Books* (1967), 26–32.
3. Borough Electors (Working Classes) Return, *P.P.* 1866, LVIII, 47ff.

4. Nossiter, *op. cit.*, 181–4; for the use of other methods cf. T. J. Nossiter, 'Aspects of Electoral Behaviour in English Constituencies, 1832–68', in E. Allardt and S. Rokkan (eds.), *Mass Parties* (New York, 1970); J. P. D. Dunbabin, 'Parliamentary Elections in Great Britain 1868–1900: A Psephological Note', *English Historical Review* LXXXI (1966), 82–99.

5. A 'tolerable' level of cross-party vote must be a matter of individual choice, but it should be noticed that in large towns it was often very low, e.g. less than 2 per cent in Liverpool in 1837 and 1841, a little above 2 per cent in Leeds in 1837, 1841 and 1852. On the other hand Sunderland consistently had a high cross-party vote of well over one-third. The average was perhaps of the order of 10 to 25 per cent, i.e. the overwhelming majority of electors voted on normal party lines.

6. Cf. Nossiter, *op. cit.*, 183.

7. See Nossiter, *op. cit.*, appendix E, and Vincent, *op. cit.*; for suggested classifications see E. A. Wrigley (ed.), *Nineteenth Century Society* (1972), 198–310.

8. J. G. Marshall to Earl Fitzwilliam, 29 November 1848, Wentworth Woodhouse MSS. G7 (d), Sheffield Public Library.

Chapter 10

1. Quite independently Dr P. Hollis came to the same conclusion; cf. her *Pressure From Without* (1974), 7: 'three groups of reformers appear and reappear: the parliamentary reformers, the Manchester free traders, and dissent.'

2. *Leicester Journal*, 27 May 1814; *Nottingham Review*, 3 June 1814.

3. A. Prentice, *Historical Sketches and Personal Recollections of Manchester* (1851), 70.

4. W. H. Smith, *The Corn Laws* (1815), 2–5; *Birmingham Commercial Herald*, 13 March 1815.

5. D. Read, *The English Provinces* (1964), 79; R. K. Dent, *Old and New Birmingham* (1880), 351; *Nottingham Review*, 10 March 1815.

6. W. C. Taylor, *Life and Times of Sir Robert Peel*, quoted by Prentice, 75.

7. *The Blues in a Sweat* (1826), Nottingham Reference Library L.34.4.

8. D. G. Barnes, *The History of the English Corn Laws* (1930), 186.

9. Cf. D. Fraser, 'Nottingham and the Corn Laws', *Transactions of the Thoroton Society*, LXX (1966).

10. R. Cobden to J. Vaughan, 23 May 1857, B.M. Add. MS. 43668, f. 147.

11. A. Prentice to J. B. Smith, 5 January 1852, Smith Papers (Manchester Reference Library); Prentice, *op. cit.*, 76.

12. *Nottingham and Newark Mercury*, 16 December 1842; *Anti-Corn Law Circular*, 2 April 1840.

13. R. Cobden to J. Sturge, 26 March 1846, B.M. Add. MS. 43656, f. 13.

14. R. Cobden to G. Wilson, 17 January 1848, Wilson Papers.

15. *England Ireland and America by a Manchester Manufacturer* (1836), 11, Manchester Reference Library M87/4/1.

16. T. Woolley to G. Wilson, 7 February 1848, Wilson Papers.

17. E. Akroyd to Sir Charles Wood, 1 March 1852, Hickleton MSS. A4/135 (Garrowby; a microfilm set is available in Leeds University Library).

18. J. Morley, *The Life of Richard Cobden* (1903 edn), 390–7.

19. *Leeds Mercury*, 22 December 1838.

20. *Birmingham Journal*, 13 July 1844.

21. *Nottingham Review*, 28 February 1840.
22. *Ibid.*, 10 January 1840.
23. *Nottingham Journal*, 19 May 1843, *Birmingham Advertiser*, 18 January 1844.
24. *Leeds Times*, 10 December 1842.
25. E. Melly to G. Melly, n.d. (1865); E. H. Greg to G. Melly, 28 April [1859?], Melly Papers 2253, 336.
26. Petition 20 January 1830 in Cobden Papers, Manchester Reference Library M87/4/1: J. B. Smith's Chamber of Commerce Papers, Manchester Reference Library MS. 923.2.5338.
27. J. Parkes to R. Cobden, 8 February 1839, quoted by N. McCord, *The Anti-Corn Law League* (1968), 46; cf. Morley, *op. cit.*, 145.
28. *Nottingham Review*, 31 May 1844.
29. O. H. Rissinson (?) to J. B. Smith, 16 February 1845, Smith Chamber of Commerce Papers (Manchester Reference Library); R. Cobden to G. Wilson, 28 February 1845, Wilson Papers.
30. R. Cobden to J. B. Smith, 15 February 1845, Smith Chamber of Commerce Papers.
31. *Ibid.*, 20 February 1845; J. B. Smith, notes to Dr John Watts, 22 February 1866, Smith Chamber of Commerce Papers.
32. *Manchester Guardian*, 5 March 1845.
33. *Birmingham Journal*, 7 October 1837.
34. *Ibid.*, 17 October 1840.
35. G. F. Muntz, *Letters Upon Corn and Currency* (1841).
36. *Birmingham Journal*, 1 December 1838; J. Sturge to Lord Brougham, 33 November 1838, Brougham Papers (University College London), 30,022; J. Sturge to J. B. Smith, 16 January 1838 (1839), J. B. Smith's Corn Law Papers (Manchester Reference Library).
37. *Birmingham Journal*, 2 February 1839.
38. *Ibid.*, 15, 22 May, 21 August 1841; cf. *ibid.*, 10 September 1842.
39. *Ibid.*, 6 November 1841; R. Cobden to G. Wilson, 16 October 1841, Wilson Papers.
40. J. Bright to J. Sturge, 15 June 1844, B.M. Add. MS. 43723.
41. *Birmingham Journal*, 3 December 1842, 6 January 1844, 4 April 1846; for fuller details see D. Fraser, 'Birmingham and the Corn Laws', *Transactions of the Birmingham Archaeological Society*, LXXXII (1967), 1–20.
42. *Leeds Mercury, Leeds Times, Northern Star*, 19 January 1839.
43. G. Wise to Hamer Stansfeld [n.d.], attached to H. Stansfeld to J. B. Smith, 11 December 1839, Anti-Corn Law League Letter Book; H. Stansfeld to J. B. Smith, 20 February 1840, J. B. Smith's Corn Law Papers.
44. *Leeds Mercury, Leeds Times*, 4 January 1840, 27 March, 3 April, 2 October 1841.
45. R. Cobden to E. Baines, 4 January 1841, Correspondence of Sir Edward Baines no. 25 (Leeds City Archives); T. Mackay (ed.), *The Autobiography of Samuel Smiles* (1905), 99.
46. R. Cobden to S. Smiles, 21 October 1841, quoted in Mackay, *op. cit.*, 112; R. Cobden to G. Wilson, 9 October 1841, Wilson Papers.
47. R. Cobden to E. Baines, 17 December 1842, B.M. Add. MS. 43664, f. 136; the final total was £1,743.
48. E. Baines to G. Wilson, 10 March 1843, Wilson Papers; G. Wilson to E. Baines, 11 March 1843, Correspondence of Sir E. Baines, no. 80.

49. *Birmingham Journal*, 15 November 1845; A. Prentice, *History of the Anti-Corn Law League* (1853), II, 403; *Morning Chronicle*, 14 November 1845.

50. Lord Morpeth to E. Baines, 24 November 1845, Correspondence of Sir E. Baines no. 15; E. Baines to G. Wilson, 26, 27 November 1845, M. Philips to G. Wilson, 28 November 1845, Wilson Papers.

51. R. Cobden to E. Baines, 22 December 1845, B.M. Add. MS. 43664, f. 195; E. Baines to G. Wilson, 24 December 1845.

52. *Address to the Free Trade Electors of the West Riding* . . . (1847), Manchester Reference Library M87/4/2.

53. *Leeds Mercury*, 17 January 1846.

54. W. R. Greg to R. Cobden, 11 May 1848, Cobden Papers (Manchester Reference Library).

55. R. Mather to G. Wilson, 27 January 1850, W. E. Timmins to R. Cobden, 6 June 1848, Wilson Papers; cf. W. N. Calkins, 'A Victorian Free Trade Lobby', *Economic History Review*, XIII (1960–1), 90–104.

56. R. Cobden to J. Sturge, 23 April 1857, B.M. Add. MS. 43722, f. 231.

57. R. Cobden to J. Vaughan, 23 May 1857, B.M. Add. MS. 43668 f. 148; R. Cobden to J. B. Smith, 12 August 1857, Smith Papers.

Chapter 11

1. *Midland Chronicle*, 6 February 1813.

2. J. A. Langford, *A Century of Birmingham Life* (1867), II, 420.

3. *Edmonds Weekly Recorder*, 10 July 1819.

4. A. Prentice, *Historical Sketches and Personal Recollections of Manchester* (1851), 306.

5. *Birmingham Journal*, 29 March 1828.

6. *Aris's Birmingham Gazette*, 24 May, 7, 14, 28 June 1830.

7. *Birmingham Journal*, 29 March, 30 April, 3 September 1831, 2 June 1832; *Midland Representative*, 3 September 1831, 4 February 1832.

8. *Report of the Committee of the Leeds Association* . . . (1832), 3; *Leeds Mercury*, 18 December 1830.

9. *Leeds Mercury*, 19, 26 November, 3, 17, 24, 31 December 1831.

10. *Birmingham Journal*, 25 May 1833.

11. Cf. D. Fraser, 'The Fruits of Reform', *Northern History*, VII (1972), 98.

12. Cf. A. Briggs (ed.), *Chartist Studies* (1960), J. T. Ward, *Chartism* (1974).

13. *Hansard*, 3 March 1831.

14. V. A. C. Gatrell, 'The Commercial Middle Class in Manchester c.1820–1857', (Ph.D. thesis, University of Cambridge, 1971), 126.

15. See for other examples T. M. Parsinnen, 'Association, convention and anti-parliament in British Radical Politics, 1771–1848', *English Historical Review*, LXXXVIII (1973), 504–33.

16. *Leeds Mercury*, 28 December 1844, *Leeds Intelligencer*, 29 March 1845, 18 April, 7 November 1846.

17. Leeds Corporation Declaration Books (Leeds Civic Hall), *passim*.

18. *Leeds Times*, 13 October 1838.

19. J. F. C. Harrison, 'Chartism in Leeds', in Briggs (ed.), *op. cit.*, 88–91.

20. Cf. for analysis of division lists, D. Fraser, 'Politics in Leeds 1830–1852' (Ph.D. thesis, University of Leeds, 1969), 413–15, 465.

21. Harrison, *loc. cit.*, 92.

22. Council Minutes Improvement Act, ɪ, 348; *Leeds Mercury*, 16 August 1845.

23. *Leeds Intelligencer*, 20 June 1846; cf. *Leeds Mercury*, 13 January 1844, *Leeds Times*, 15 May 1847.

24. *Leeds Mercury*, 5 January 1850.

25. Poor Law Guardians Minute Book, ɪ, 241 (Leeds City Archives); prior to the formation of the board an industrial school had been mooted, cf. *Leeds Intelligencer*, 5 October 1844.

26. *Leeds Times*, 2 May, 11, 18 July, 1 August, 5 September 1840.

27. S. Smiles to J. A. Roebuck, 23 December 1840, Smiles Papers (Leeds City Archives). T. Mackay (ed.), *The Autobiography of Samuel Smiles* (1905), 96.

28. H. Stansfeld to J. B. Smith, 20 August 1840, Smith Papers (Manchester Reference Library).

29. *Leeds Times*, 16, 23 January 1841; *Northern Star*, 23 January 1841.

30. *Northern Star*, 23 October 1841.

31. See particularly a series of critical letters from Baines to Stansfeld, *Leeds Mercury*, 21 November, 5, 12, 19, 26 December 1840, 2, 9 January 1841.

32. The most recent account of the C.S.U. is A. Wilson, 'The Suffrage Movement', in P. Hollis (ed.), *Pressure From Without* (1974), 84–93.

33. Lord Brougham to J. Sturge, 17 October 1842, B.M. Add. MS. 43845, fos. 7–8.

34. H. Richard, *Memoirs of Joseph Sturge* (1864), 318.

35. J. Bright to G. Wilson, 18 April 1848, Wilson Papers (Manchester Reference Library).

36. D. Read, *Cobden and Bright* (1967).

37. W. R. Greg to R. Cobden, 11 May 1848, Cobden Papers (Manchester Reference Library).

38. W. R. Greg to W. E. Gladstone, 4 April 1852, quoted by Gatrell, *op. cit.*, 186; Dr Gatrell places these political views in the context of Greg's prolific defence of political economy, *loc. cit.*, 180–6.

39. R. H. Greg to G. Melly, 28 April (1859?), Melly Papers, 336 (Liverpool Record Office).

40. H. R. Greg to G. Melly 30 January 1865, Melly Papers, 2283.

41. He calculated that a moderate reform need not necessarily swamp the middle class and deduced from their respectability, diligence, thrift, and sobriety that working men were not unfit for the franchise; see D. Fraser, 'Edward Baines', in Hollis (ed.), *op. cit.*, 204–5.

42. *Manchester Examiner and Times*, 6 December 1851; J. Bright to G. Wilson, 26, 28 September, 15 November 1851; Conference Resolutions, 3 December 1851, Wilson Papers.

43. *Leeds Mercury*, 10, 24 January 1852.

44. Hollis, *op. cit.*, 206.

45. R. Cobden to J. Bright, 4 February 1865, B.M. Add. MS. 43652 fos. 218–220.

46. *Leeds Mercury*, 24 January, 22 August, 9 October 1866; cf. M. R. Dunsmore, 'The Working Classes, The Reform League and the Reform Movement in Lancashire and Yorkshire' (M.A. thesis, University of Sheffield, 1961), 165–78.

47. *Leeds Mercury*, 24 April, 16 October 1867.

48. R. Harrison, *Before the Socialists* (1965), 137–209.

Chapter 12

1. H. R. Martin, 'The Politics of the Congregationalists 1830–1856' (Ph.D. thesis, University of Durham, 1971), 502–3.
2. *Manchester Examiner and Times*, 22 November 1851.
3. *Nonconformist*, 30 October 1844, quoted by Martin, *op. cit.*, 319.
4. *Address of the Leeds Protestant Association* . . . (1837), Hailstone Collection (York Minster); cf. other similar propaganda in the same collection.
5. *Nottingham Journal*, 6 November 1835.
6. *Nonconformist Elector*, 23 July 1847.
7. *Eclectic Review*, xxii (1847), 108.
8. *Nonconformist*, 9 June 1847.
9. A. Henry to G. Wilson, 10 April 1850, Wilson Papers (Manchester Reference Library).
10. Cf. D. M. Thompson, 'The Liberation Society, 1844–1868', in P. Hollis (ed.), *Pressure From Without* . . . (1974), 210–38.
11. W. R. Ward, *Religion and Society in England 1790–1850* (1972), 203–5.
12. The papers were the *Philanthropist* (Birmingham), *Leicestershire Mercury* and *Nottingham Review*.
13. *Leicester Chronicle*, 1 January 1848.
14. *Baptist Magazine*, 1849, 7, quoted by J. Lea, 'Baptists in Lancashire 1837–87' (Ph.D. thesis, University of Liverpool 1970), 313.
15. Quoted in D. M. Thompson (ed.), *Nonconformity in the Nineteenth Century* (1972), 127.
16. Quoted by A. F. Taylor, 'Birmingham and the Movement for National Education 1867–77' (Ph.D. thesis, University of Leicester, 1960), 13–16.
17. *Leicestershire Mercury*, 19 January 1839.
18. D. Fraser, 'Edward Baines', in Hollis (ed.), *op. cit.*, pp. 195–9.
19. For a full discussion of this issue see D. Fraser, 'Voluntaryism and West Riding Politics in the mid-Nineteenth Century', *Northern History*, xiii (1977).
20. Phrase coined by J. Parker, M.P. for Sheffield; cf. J. Parker to Sir C. Wood, 31 July 1847, Hickleton MS. A4/52 (Garrowby; a microfilm set is available in Leeds University Library).
21. W. Barton to J. Bunting, 6 December 1848, Bunting Papers (transcripts kindly supplied by Professor W. R. Ward).
22. *Ibid.*, 24 November 1848.
23. For Manchester's role see S. E. Maltby, *Manchester and the Movement for National Elementary Education* (1918), and F. Adams, *History of the Elementary School Contest* . . . (1882, reprinted 1972), 147–70.
24. Minutes of the Lancashire Public Schools Association, Report of the Sub Committee . . . 22 November 1850 (Manchester Reference Library).
25. Cf. J. A. Williams, 'Manchester and the Manchester School 1830–1857' (M.A. thesis, University of Leeds, 1966), 197–214.
26. Minutes of the Lancashire Public Schools Association, 18 May 1849.
27. *Ibid.*, 7 January 1852.
28. *Ibid.*, Report on Local Bill, 3 November 1852.
29. Adams, *op. cit.*, 195.
30. The best account of the League is to be found in A. F. Taylor, 'Birmingham and the Movement for National Education 1867–77' (Ph.D. thesis, University of Leicester, 1960).

31. E. Baines to Kay-Shuttleworth, 19 October 1867, Baines Papers, 23/11 (Leeds City Archives).

32. Circular Letter of the Lancashire and Cheshire Association of Baptist Churches, 1843, 5; Minutes of the Lancashire and Cheshire Association of Baptist Churches, 1847, 21.

33. Circular letter of the Lancashire and Cheshire Association of Baptist Churches, 1853, 23.

34. Lea, *op. cit.*, 422–7.

35. Circular letter of the Lancashire and Cheshire Association of Baptist Churches, 1870, 8.

36. E. Baines to W. Arthur, 6 March 1874, Baines Papers, 16/19.

37. E. Baines to Kay-Shuttleworth, 19 October 1867, Baines Papers, 23/11.

38. G. Dixon to G. Melly, 30 October 1869, Melly Papers 3702 (Liverpool Record Office).

39. A. Briggs, Introduction to Adams, *op. cit.*, xxi.

40. Minutes of the Lancashire and Cheshire Association of Baptist Churches, 1870, 19; Circular Letter of the North Western Association of Baptist Churches, 1870, 13.

41. *Birmingham Daily Post*, 8 March 1870, quoted by Taylor, *op. cit.*, 123.

42. Cf. N. J. Richards, 'Religious Controversy and the School Boards', *British Journal of Educational Studies*, xviii (1970), 180–96.

43. Quoted by Briggs, *op. cit.*, xvii.

44. Taylor, *op. cit.*, 157.

45. Lord Sandon, Memorandum, November 1874, quoted by P. Smith, *Disraelian Conservatism and Social Reform* (1967), 246.

46. Taylor, *op. cit.*, 151–205.

47. D. E. Fletcher, 'Aspects of Liberalism in Sheffield 1849–1886' (Ph.D. thesis, University of Sheffield 1972), 198–9.

48. *Leeds Mercury*, 22–30 November 1870.

49. *Ibid.*, 22 November 1873.

50. *Ibid.*, 11 November 1876.

51. *Ibid.*, 22 November 1879.

52. *Ibid.*, 21 November 1882.

53. *Ibid.*, 20 November 1882.

Conclusion: urban politics in modern England

1. *Manchester Chronicle*, 25 April 1840.

2. A. W. W. Dale, *The Life of R. W. Dale of Birmingham* (1899), 250.

3. *Porcupine*, 8 November 1862.

4. Cf. P. Hollis (ed.), *Pressure from Without* (1974), Introduction.

5. A. Prentice to J. B. Smith, 5 January 1852, Smith Papers (Manchester Reference Library.

Select time chart 1812–80

Lord Liverpool P.M.	1812	Movement against Orders in Council
	1814	Urban activity against new Corn Law, esp. Birmingham, Nottingham Manchester, Leeds
End of Napoleonic Wars	1815	
Corn Law		
Six Acts	1819	Birmingham: election of 'legislatorial attorney'; Peterloo, Manchester
Sturges Bourne's Act		
General election	1820	Manchester: church rate defeated
accession of George IV		
	1821	Liverpool: select vestry
	1825	Manchester: vestry dispute Thomas Potter
General election	1826	Manchester: gas dispute began; J. Marshall elected M.P. for Yorkshire
Wellington P.M.	1828	Leeds: Liberals won control of churchwardens J. A. Buttrey, senior warden
Catholic emancipation	1829	Manchester: Police Act dispute · victory for anti-radical forces; plans for Birmingham Political Union
General election	1830	Birmingham Grammar School dispute; Brougham elected M.P. for Yorkshire; Leeds Association formed
accession of William IV		
Grey P.M.		
General election	1831	Leeds Political Union and Leeds Radical Political Union formed; last church rate, Birmingham parish
Reform Act	1832	Birmingham Political Union active in vestry; T. C. Salt churchwarden
General election		
Althorp's Factory Act	1833	Salford: bell-ringing dispute; radical select vestry – J. B. Smith; Manchester: churchwardens' poll – A. Prentice; Manchester: church rate defeated but levied; Leeds: vestry election
Poor Law Amendment Act	1834	Leeds: vestry election – R. Perring (Tory); Manchester: vestry election – J. Wroe (radical); Manchester church rate defeated – G. Hadfield (Lib.); Birmingham: town poll on church rate; Salford: William Lockett (Lib.) overseer; Nottingham: Liberal churchwardens at St Mary's
Melbourne P.M.		

Municipal Corporation Reform Act General election Peel P.M. Melbourne P.M.	1835	Leeds: churchwardens' poll; Manchester abandoned church rates; Leeds: overseers sole control of Poor Law; Salford Operative Conservative Association formed; Liberal victory in municipal elections: Liverpool, Leeds, Nottingham, Leicester
	1836	Leeds: new Liberal churchwardens; Manchester: Liberal nominations for churchwarden defeated; Birmingham: churchwarden's contest; *Leicestershire Mercury* launched (radical) Dissenting); Liverpool Tradesmen's Conservative Association
General election accession of Victoria	1837	Leeds: Poor Law – 'Heaps job'; abortive elections; Tories capture Leeds Improvement Commission; Sir W. Molesworth (radical) elected M.P. for Leeds; Salford; P.L. controversy – R. J. Richardson (radical); Salford election: Poor Law main issue – Tory candidate William Garnett (as in 1832 and 1841); R. Cobden, *Incorporate Your Borough*; Liverpool Tradesmen's Reform Association – J. Walmsley; Leeds: Waterworks Act
People's Charter	1838	Manchester: G. Clarke (Tory) senior churchwarden; first municipal elections, Manchester and Birmingham: both Liberal/radical victories; church rate refused, St Mary's, Nottingham; Liberal control of St Margaret's vestry Leicester, by poll; Salford: Tory select vestry; Tory board of Guardians
National Convention Anti-Corn Law League	1839	Churchwardens' dispute with Manchester Corporation; Tory control, Manchester Police Commission; Birmingham: Chartists reject the League; R. H. Greg elected M.P. for Manchester
	1840	Manchester: Liberal challenge in vestry; Cobden (Lib.) opposed by Wroe and Dixon (radical); Tory victory in churchwardens' poll; Tory victory in Birmingham churchwardens' poll; Leicester: William Baines imprisoned over

		church rates; Nottingham: work-house dispute; Salford: Wrigley case; Leeds: 'new move'; G. F. Muntz elected M.P. for Birmingham
General election Peel P.M.	1841	Liverpool: Tory control of council Walmsley (Lib). defeated in general election; E. Miall left Leicester to edit *Nonconformist*; Nottingham: by-election fought on Poor Law; Leeds: burial grounds dispute – J. Hume (radical) defeated in general election; T. Milner Gibson elected M.P. for Manchester
Second Chartist convention Plug riots Peel's first budget	1842	Leeds Improvement Act; Leeds Burial Grounds Act; Leeds: Chartists win control of Improve-ment Commission and church-wardens; Liverpool: select vestry revived; Salford: Poor Law mani-pulated by W. Lockett (Lib.)
Graham's Factory Bill withdrawn	1843	Manchester Police Commission vested in corporation; Salford: incorporation and improvement dispute; Bradford: elected Liberal board of highway surveyors; Nottingham: church rate defeated, St Mary's
	1844	Salford Improvement Act; Salford charter; Anti-Corn Law League defeated in South Lancs. election; J. A. Jaffray editor of *Birmingham Journal*; Leeds Poor Law union formed – Tory victory.
Maynooth	1845	Liverpool: select vestry political elections; S. Holme, *Want of Water*; Leicester: improvement and economy dispute; Manchester: Chamber of Commerce dispute; Bradford: Tory board of highway surveyors; Yorkshire: Lord Morpeth supports the League
Repeal of the Corn Laws Russell P.M.	1846	Liverpool: Sanitary Act; Leeds: W. F. Hook (vicar) accepts volun-taryism; W. Brown (Lib.) elected as M.P. for S. Lancs.; Lord Morpeth (Whig) elected as M.P. for West Riding; Manchester: municipal elections on economy; Leicester: municipal elections on improvement

General election Education Minutes approved	1847	Leeds: Tories regain church-wardens; voluntaryism dispute in Halifax and Leeds elections; Liverpool: Waterworks Act; Bradford charter – Liberal victory at first election; W. Brown and C. P. Villiers elected M.P.s for S. Lancs.; Lord Morpeth and R. Cobden elected M.P.s for West Riding; J. Bright elected M.P. for Manchester; Salford: boundary dispute
Third Chartist petition Kennington Common fiasco Public Health Act	1848	Liverpool: Rivington Pike dispute; Tory victory in West Riding election; merger of *Manchester Examiner* and *Manchester Times*
	1849	Church rates ended, Leicester, St Martin's; Gateshead: parochial dispute – W. H. Brockett (Lib.); Liverpool: town meetings and municipal elections on Rivington Pike
	1850	Leeds: last contested church-wardens' election; Gateshead: 'clean sweep' anti-Brockett, Poor Law election
Great Exhibition	1851	Birmingham: Improvement Act; Manchester: conference on suffrage
Derby P.M. General election Aberdeen coalition	1852	Enquiry into Leeds Poor Law elections; reunion of middle- and working-class radicals; Liverpool: Reform Association – W. Brumfitt secretary; Manchester: state education proposals; Sheffield: I. Ironside control of highway surveyors
	1853	Liberal victory, Leeds Poor Law elections; Sheffield: gas question; Salford: boundaries extended
Crimean War	1854	
Palmerston P.M.	1855	Sheffield: workhouse dispute – R. Younge; Leeds: Tories regain control of Poor Law, Liverpool: Liberals win one seat at by-election
End of Crimean War	1856	Sheffield: workhouse guardians defeated; Liverpool: J. R. Jeffery (radical) enters council
General election	1857	Sheffield: board of guardians in anti-centralization dispute; Manchester School defeated in elections – Bright and Gibson (Manchester), Cobden (Stockport), Armitage (Salford); Leeds: Conser-

		vatives win one seat at general election, retained at by-election; Bright elected M.P. for Birmingham (by-election)
General election Palmerston P.M.	1859	Manchester Reform Association; Manchester Reformers Union; E. Baines elected M.P. for Leeds; Abel Heywood (radical) defeated at Manchester election; W. E. Forster (Lib.) defeated at Leeds election; Whig-Liberal victory at West Riding election
	1860	Leeds: Working Men's Parliamentary Reform Association
	1862	G. Melly (Lib.) candidate at Preston; Liberal attack on Liverpool council; A. Heywood (radical) Mayor of Manchester; *Leeds Express* (radical), proprietor F. Spark
	1863	Preston: E. Ambler Liberal agent; registration tricks; Liverpool: 'cellar' formed for municipal politics – C. Mozley (Lib.) mayor
	1864	Defeat of Liverpool 'cellar' in municipal elections
Death of Palmerston General election Russell P.M.	1865	Privy Council criticizes Leeds Corporation's public health policies; Liverpool Liberal Association; Birmingham Liberal Association; J. C. Ewart (Lib.) defeated at Liverpool election; A. Heywood (radical) defeated at Manchester election; Conservatives hold one seat at Leeds election
Derby P.M.	1866	Leeds Improvement Act: amalgamation; Manchester: United Liberal party
Second Reform Act	1867	Leeds: Waterworks Act; Baines and Miall renounce voluntaryism; Jacob Bright (Lib.) elected at Manchester by-election
General election	1868	Birmingham: caucus uses ward adoption to win all three seats in election; R. M. Carter (radical) elected at Leeds; E. Jones (radical) defeated at Manchester; Liverpool: Liberals win one seat only
	1869	National Education League founded in Birmingham
Forster's Education Act	1870	Second enquiry into Leeds Poor Law elections; dispute between

		National Education League and Union; school board elections: Liberals defeated, Leeds and Birmingham
Secret ballot	1872	
	1873	Chamberlain's Liberal organization captures Birmingham school board; Liberal victory, Leeds school board
General election Disraeli P.M.	1874	W. Middleton (Tory) defeated after 20 years on Leeds board of guardians; Leeds: Tories' chance to win municipal control; E. Baines defeated at Leeds election; no contest at Birmingham election: three Liberals; Conservatives win two seats at Leeds, Manchester and Liverpool
	1876	Liberal victory in Leeds Poor Law elections; J. Chamberlain (Lib.) elected M.P. for Birmingham
	1879	Liberal defeat at Leeds school board
General election	1880	W. E. Gladstone elected at Leeds (sat for Edinburghshire); Liberals win two seats at Leeds and Manchester

Index